Trey Hudson – Author of *The Meadow Project: Ex* *walker Ranch* and Director of the Oxford Paranc Anomalous Studies and Observation Group (ASOG):

> Matt Vaughn is a name you will be hearing more and more of as he helps us peel back the veneer of these perplexing events and make us all better for the experience. If you are a student of the strange and uncanny, do yourself a favor and add this book to your library, you won't be disappointed.

–•–

Bob Dobbs – Para-media ecologist, author of *Phatic Communion with Bob Dobbs, Magus of the Paramodern Age,* ionandbob.com, dobbstown.com:

Buy this book immediately!

–•–

Jacob W. Glazier, Ph.D. – Author of *Arts of Subjectivity: A New Animism for the Post-Media Era,* Assistant Professor of Psychology & Head of Psychology B.S. Undergraduate Studies Program, University of West Georgia

> Spanning a multitude of perspectives, *My Cosmic Trigger* interrogates the paranormal with a unique analysis of high strangeness offering the reader an accessible, yet highly integrative approach that produces new insights on the seemingly logic-defying interconnections between exceptional experiences of all kinds.

–•–

Stanley Krippner, Ph.D. – Affiliated Distinguished Professor, California Institute of Integral Studies, Coauthor of *Personal Mythology: Using Ritual, Dreams, and Imagination to Discover your Inner Story*

> Fascinating! – experiences of a flesh and blood young man trying to navigate little-charted territory. An enjoyable read and thought provoking.

–•–

Tobin Hart, PhD – Professor in the University of West Georgia's Humanistic, Transpersonal and Critical psychology program, co-founder and chair of the Board of Directors of ChildSpirit Institute. Author of *The Four Virtues: Presence, Heart, Wisdom, Creation*

> We have always tried to make sense of how this world works–from explanations involving the whims of the gods.... This book opens fresh possibility for seeing; it is crazy, fun, smart, startling and ultimately invites us into the mysterious, the unknown. Surely there will be dead ends in the pursuit of high strangeness, but more importantly this work radically opens to a world still full of mystery, one in which our tidy default explanations and dismissive reactions turn out to be way too small and stubbornly naïve. Buckle up.

HIGH STRANGENESS IN THEORY & PRACTICE

MATT VAUGHN

Published by:
Trine Day LLC
PO Box 577
Walterville, OR 97489
1-800-556-2012
www.TrineDay.com
TrineDay@icloud.com

Library of Congress Control Number: 2024938426

Vaughn, Matt.
–1st ed.
p. cm.

Epub (ISBN-13) 978-1-63424-453-4
Trade Paperback (ISBN-13) 978-1-63424-452-7
1. Parapsychology. 2. Supernatural. 3. Body, Mind & Spirit: Unexplained Phenomena. 4. Wilson, Robert Anton, 1932-2007. 5. Leys. 6. Cryptozoology. 7. Consciousness. 8. Occultism. I. Vaughn, Matt. Title

First Edition
10 9 8 7 6 5 4 3 2 1

Printed in the USA
Distribution to the Trade by:
Independent Publishers Group (IPG)
814 North Franklin Street
Chicago, Illinois 60610
312.337.0747
www.ipgbook.com

Publisher's Foreword

... Bringing the fishermen home:
'Twas all so pretty a sail, it seemed
As if it could not be;
And some folk thought 'twas a dream they'd dreamed...
– Eugene Field 1889

Bluto: Hey! What's all this laying around shit?

Stork: What the hell are we supposed to do, ya moron?

D-Day: [*to Bluto*] War's over, man. Wormer dropped the big one.

Bluto: What? Over? Did you say "over"? Nothing is over until we decide it is! Was it over when the Germans bombed Pearl Harbor? Hell no!

Otter: [*to Boon*] Germans?

Boon: Forget it, he's rolling.

Bluto: And it ain't over now. 'Cause when the goin' gets tough...

[*thinks hard of something to say*]

Bluto: The tough get goin'! Who's with me? Let's go!

[*Bluto runs out, alone; then returns*]

Bluto: What the fuck happened to the Delta I used to know? Where's the spirit? Where's the guts, huh? This could be the greatest night of our lives, but you're gonna let it be the worst. "Ooh, we're afraid to go with you Bluto, we might get in trouble." Well just kiss my ass from now on! Not me! I'm not gonna take this. Wormer, he's a dead man! Marmalard, dead! Niedermeyer...

Otter: Dead! Bluto's right. Psychotic ... but absolutely right. We gotta take these bastards. Now we could do it with conventional weapons, but that could take years and cost millions of lives. No, I think we have to go all out. I think that this situation absolutely requires a really futile and stupid gesture be done on somebody's part!

Bluto: We're just the guys to do it.

D-Day: [*stands up*]

Boon: [*stands up*] Let's do it.

Bluto: [*shouting*] "Let's do it"!

–*National Lampoon's Animal House,* (1978)

There are times when you want to howl snarling at the world and all its trappings. Wishing for earlier, simpler times? Denying the frustrations and dreads of the future? Looking for a way out?

Why are we here? To do what? Are the dreams of humanity for justice, peace, the pursuit of happiness and liberty … simply fantasy? Is "God" good? Is the "Devil" evil? Is there more to this world than meets the eye? What are we doing? What "makes things go bump in the night?" Is there a way to walk? Will our actions be correct? Does it matter?

Matt Vaughn's *My Cosmic Trigger, Vol. 1: High Strangeness in Theory and Practice* looks into some of these questions and more. A trained psychotherapist, practicing occultist and aficionado of Robert Anton Wilson, Matt began peering into dark corners and weird spaces as a child. This book's title is a paean to Wilson's *Cosmic Trigger Trilogy.* Wilson penned over twenty books, and became a darling of the counter-culture, earning the sobriquet RAW, co-authoring a book with Timothy Leary.

Wilson, also a psychologist, had become an editor for *Playboy* in the mid-sixties, emerging to critical acclaim with *The Illuminatus! Trilogy* in 1975 with co-writer, Robert Shea. I found those books especially keen as my father and a professor from Vanderbilt just five years earlier had spoken to me about secret societal involvement in world affairs, which my father had come across during his work for the CIA. I was still on the trail, Wilson's and Shea's historical fiction made for heady reading.

Silly me, it would take another thirteen years to figure out my father was speaking of The Order of Skull and Bones. What did I know? I was living my life and having fun, while being labeled a "conspiracy theorist," if I spoke about my "research," but that led to TrineDay whereby, I get the honor and privilege to publish this book.

Matt has done his diligence, dove in and produced an exhaustive look into the paranormal world as it exists in our hyper-connected world of today. *My Cosmic Trigger, Vol. 1: High Strangeness in Theory and Practice* will stand the test of time…

I didn't know the full dimensions of forever,
but I knew it was longer than waiting for Christmas to come.

–Richard Brautigan (2011).
"So The Wind Won't Blow It All Away"

Onward to the Utmost of Futures,
Peace,
R.A. "Kris" Millegan
Publisher
TrineDay
May 11, 2024

With his own bolt; the strong-based promontory
Have I made shake, and by the spurs plucked up
The pine and cedar; graves at my command

Have waked their sleepers, oped, and let 'em forth
By my so potent art. But this rough magic
I here abjure, and when I have required
Some heavenly music, which even now I do,
To work mine end upon their senses that

This airy charm is for, I'll break my staff,
Bury it certain fathoms in the earth,
And deeper than did ever plummet sound
I'll drown my book.

–Prospero, *The Tempest*, William Shakespeare

ACKNOWLEDGMENTS

I view psychotherapy as a mutual process between psychotherapist and client, approaching the relationship from one of "equality before the gods, the archetypes." When the relationship is one of "mutual growth," then "both participants [are] changed," making it "truly alchemical." Furthermore, this mutual process is important "in the history of the development of consciousness." (J. Marvin Spiegelman, Ph.D., *Psychotherapy as a Mutual Process,* 1996, p. 41-48). With that being said: I sincerely thank the clients I've had the privilege of working with for the last 20 years; I have grown in my endeavor to help you grow.

In regards to acknowledging specific colleagues, friends, and family-I'm hamstrung. While I do have specific people to thank, I am unsure how this book will be received; considering that, these days, the group-mind's psychic pressure cooker is set on high. So, to protect the innocent, I will only thank myself.

Self, says I: in the face of ridicule you have persisted for over 30 years in an arduous cosmic quest. In your devotion to uncover the secret of life, the universe, and everything: you have shown tremendous courage and valor. Whether the reception of this book is good, bad, or ugly: take with you the bliss that springs from the consciousness of an obligation carried out diligently, earnestly, and with devotion to a higher cause. May providence bestow upon you: blessings of health, wealth, abundance, fun, laughter, joy, protection, true wisdom, and perfect happiness.

Contents

CONTENTS

Foreword

A Grimoire of High Strangeness

– Jacob W. Glazier, PhD.

This book is heretical. Those who read the text contained herein should be warned. In my view, this is very much to its benefit as it challenges the *status quo* and upends orthodoxy. Yet, the warning signals how heresy is oftentimes dangerous. As a psychologist, I know astutely the fragility of the notions we call "identity" and "reality." Glances into the "abyss," noted by the free-spirited philosopher Friedrich Nietzsche (2002, p. 69), or the "void," echoed by the thinker of immanence, Gilles Deleuze (1995, p. 113), leave one forever altered – sometimes transforming through a renewed relationship with the self and others while, in the worst cases, plunging into the darkness itself: the delusions and hallucinations of psychosis, come to mind, or even more nefarious unfolding events. Glances should not turn into stares, in other words, less the risk becomes a folly.

A quick gaze can shake things up, get us out of our normal way of viewing the world, and help us see how limited our current vantage point may have been. In *My Cosmic Trigger*, Vaughn presents a new perspective on this *impossible* task. I use the term impossible in a similar way that Jeffrey Kripal (2010), the religious studies scholar, pens the term – denoting the struggle to cage phenomena and anecdotes that wildly and savagely buck easy categorical sense. The provocation of this impossible task, as we will see, is precisely glancing into the darkness and reporting the experience – a heresy of exposure to the negative.

I titled this foreword, with allusion to the pages in this book, "A Grimoire of High Strangeness," to point directly to this very challenge. A grimoire popularly refers to a book of spells, incantations, charms, and divinations read by a practitioner of magic (Karlsson, 2009). The word's etymology or linguistic history stems from the old French word for grammar, *grammaire,* which in the Middle Ages was used to designate vulgar grammar, scrawl, and scribble (Grimoire, n.d.). Indeed, the kind of grammar and scribble contained on these pages does not provide recipes for incantations or summonings but, rather, maps of unfamiliar territories populated by strange and exotic entities and stories. These eccentricities marked by Vaughn within these alien lands duly invoke a feeling of uncanniness, of not being at home with ourselves, foreigners in our own skin. Yet, the summoning of this self-strangeness pales, in many ways, to what they clue us into about reality: their inexplicable interconnection should really cause us to take note.

This is what the astronomer and UAP researcher J. Allen Hynek (1979) termed *high strangeness.* High strangeness occurs when there seems to be some linkage between relatively co-occurring anomalous experiences that, more often than not, include psi phenomena (Hunter, 2021). Vaughn captures this exceedingly well when, to name just a few examples, blending the psychological theory of archetypes with cryptids and detailing their relationship to synchronicities, exploring cultural currents like the New Age movement with esotericism and secret societies, and tracing the interconnection of advanced technologies among UAPs and aliens, all while interjecting personal anecdotes and lessons that help this high strangeness feel more possible and palatable.

The content of this book, its high strange character, echoes that found in traditional grimoires. Over and above the material covered, the structure is a bricolage of prose put together in a way that mirrors the idiosyncratic grammar and scrawling found in other such magical books. Indeed, one gets the sense when reading Vaughn's musings and accounts that there is a *trickster* factor at play. Trickster theory in parapsychology was initially elaborated on by George P. Hansen (2001) to indicate the way that paranormal experiences destructure normative frameworks and contain an agential quality that lies beyond the control of the researcher or experiencer. Part of the benefit of Vaughn's contribution is the openness to name the trickster in the room and, further, to cobble together fragments from media, parapsychology, parapolitics, and "you name it" with trickster-esque fervor in order to tussle with the high strangeness.

In a similar spirit, critical approaches to the paranormal (Glazier, 2023) take seriously this power of language in molding and shaping our accounts – indeed, *impossible accounts* – of exceptional experiences. Perhaps the trickster shows up precisely because of the limits of language. That is, the overabundance and overflow of meaning intrinsic to high strangeness indicate its failure to adequately capture, relegate, categorize, and tame the wily nature of these interconnections. Language may be "the house of being" (Heidegger, 1998, p. 239), but some of us would rather venture beyond this comfort and develop a new grammar to scribble what has yet to be given form. Vaughn embarks on such an adventure, scouting these heretical vistas and flagging the dangers along the way.

Given the instances of high strangeness in this book, the question to the reader remains: Are we willing to jeopardize our safe and homelike models for something much weirder? If so, we stand at a precarious precipice of transformation. Ultimately, though, we may not have a choice in the matter – the trickster may have the last laugh.

Sources:

Deleuze, G. (1995). *Negotiations: 1972-1990* (M. Joughin, Trans.). Columbia University Press.

Glazier, J. W. (Ed.). (2023). *Paranormal ruptures: Critical approaches to exceptional experiences.* Beyond the Fray Publishing.

Grimoire. (n.d.). *Le Grand Robert.* https://grandrobert.lerobert.com/robert.asp

Hansen, G. P. (2001). *The trickster and the paranormal.* Xlibris.

Heidegger, M. (1998). Letter on "humanism" (F. A. Capuzzi, Trans.). In W. McNeill (Ed.), *Pathmarks* (pp. 239-276). Cambridge University Press.

Hunter, J. (2021). Parapsychology and the varieties of high strangeness experience. *Mindfield: The bulletin of the parapsychological association, 13*(3), 7-11.

Hynek, J. A. (1979). *The UFO experience: A scientific inquiry.* Corgi Books.

Karlsson, T. (2009). *Qabalah, qliphoth and goetic magic.* Ajna.

Kripal, Jeffrey J. (2010). *Authors of the impossible: The paranormal and the sacred.* The University of Chicago Press.

Nietzsche, F. (2002). *Beyond good and evil* (J. Norman, Trans.). Cambridge University Press.

NONFIC

45218-5-$3.95 · POCKET 

HAVE WE ALWAYS SHARED THIS PLANET WITH BEINGS THAT REMAIN INVISIBLE TO US?

BESTSELLING CO-AUTHOR OF THE ILLUMINATUS TRILOGY

ROBERT ANTON WILSON

COSMIC TRIGGER

THE FINAL SECRET OF THE ILLUMINATI

Introduction

Out of the Cosmic Closet

(Includes crucial warnings and context. Do NOT proceed without reading)

No one in their seven-eleven senses can miss my cosmic drift,
even though it's incendiary.
In this volume – every letter is a copy of the sibyl's,
and the holy words I show, are of that celestial kingdom.

This old world is getting pretty strange. Like many people, myself included, you may be wondering just what the heck is going on. This book seeks to provide as much clarity for today's confusing reality as is humanly possible. And if clarity cannot be found, then we will settle for a fertile bewilderment to the illusory certainty.

Contrary to what you may initially expect, I believe the answers we seek may be found in a thorough analysis of what seems odd, bizarre, silly, preposterous, made-up, disturbing or just untrue. Said plainly, the answers we need most are going to be found in the patterns, caverns and nuances of the weirdest stuff imaginable – Bigfoot, UFOs, ghosts, gnomes, and portals to other dimensions – and *not* in a heady analysis of political power provided by some ivory tower intellectual, a talking head on screen, or anything even remotely conventional. This is not to say the conventional approach to societal problem-solving is useless, but it is to say that now is the time for the correction of our western worldview by adding to the big picture with an unconventional approach of cosmic proportions.

Diving in, this *weirdest stuff imaginable* is "high strangeness," a subset of the overall paranormal field.[A] It is where two or more paranormal subjects intersect. An example: looking at connections between UFOs and Bigfoot sightings in the same area. High strangeness supports explanations of reality so unlikely they might be described by an onlooker as science fiction. These unusual happenings are so uncanny they are deemed "utterly absurd," highlighting an eerie undergirding of reality itself which makes a simple UFO sighting seem tame by comparison.

A My use of the paranormal field here refers to the individual study of such subjects as: UFOs, cryptids, ghosts, psychic abilities, & the occult.

The consensus reality we are presented on the nightly news is highly strange – from global pandemics to a nuclear Armageddon. More and more, what the daily news reports look like something out of the Book of Revelation. And never mind the increasingly bizarre paranormal phenomena trickling out from our mainstream media, such as the Congressional UFO hearings of July 2023 and one of the richest men alive admitting he has "spent years warning that his friends in Silicon Valley ... may inadvertently be 'summoning the demon' ... an invisible evil A.I. that would wipe out humanity." Musk goes on to say that in five years or less society is "headed toward a situation where" artificial intelligence is "vastly smarter than humans," which means in less than five years "things" are going to get "weird."[1] Great, as if *things* weren't already *weird* enough.

I think it's reasonable to assume, at this point, that we have gone through the looking glass. However, this fact raises important questions: how *might* one explain all this craziness? And why is it important to name life on the other side of Alice's mirror?

Consider the fairytale of Rumpelstiltskin. As the story goes, a fair maiden is forced by a king (due to the lies and bumbling of her miller father) to stay up all night trying to achieve the impossible: spinning ordinary straw into pure gold. A magical imp appears and completes the task for the weary maiden in exchange for a piece of her jewelry. The greedy king, thrilled to have more gold, locks her away for the next two nights and the imp appears offering the same deal. When the young woman runs out of things to give the magical little man, he asks her to promise her firstborn child to him in exchange for him providing the gold. She's caught between a rock and a hard place: a greedy king *demanding gold* and an evil, supernatural being *demanding life*. Her only hope of escaping the predicament is to guess the imp's name.

With luck, or perhaps synchronicity,[B] the maiden discovers Rumpelstiltskin's name, and the wicked deal is broken. Will we be so lucky?

Author and spiritual practitioner Paul Levy says, "naming is a magical act, typically done when something new is born into life," and conversely we can also say that naming facilitates something new being born into life. That naming is a powerful psycho-spiritual act and is, of course, the metaphor behind the above fable, showing us "the way humanity has overcome the negative aspects" of reality "is by naming it."[2] Carl Jung also echoes these sentiments when he points out that "for mankind it was always like a deliverance from a nightmare when the new name was found."[3]

B See chapter 7 on the Cosmic, Synchromystic, Galactic, Gnostic, Gonzo, Group, Quantum Questing (Quad G, Dub Q) approach to researching and investigating high strangeness.

In this book, I attempt to *name* our highly strange reality while suggesting a way to spin the straw of confusion into cosmic consciousness gold. While this is certainly no easy feat, I believe I am up to the monumental task. In addition to decades of intense study of high strangeness, my astrological birth chart indicates I have "the ability to see transcendent realms and translate them for the rest of humanity." So in advance: you're welcome! And I would add this is well worth the price of the book. If this was a text message I would write "LOL" after the previous sentence, but since this is a book, I will just hope you pick up on my use of humor. I advise the reader to always keep in mind that I often write with my tongue squarely in my cheek, but make no mistake – I am also deadly serious at-most-all-times. Perhaps more accurately I could say, "I'm neither joking nor serious but another secret third thing."[4]

I have been working on this cosmic naming for a lifetime. The book you are now reading is over two decades in the making and I would be remiss if I didn't invoke Joseph Campbell's hero's journey to explain how difficult a path I have traveled to bring you this material. Dark nights of the soul, paranoia, madness *and* failure; I'll spare you the details ... for now. At any rate, I sincerely hope you take this journey with me and if you do, I hope reading my book helps make your road less bumpy than it was for me.

This book started out life as Robert Anton Wilson (hereafter referred to as RAW) fan non-fiction. I began work on an original manuscript after I experienced similar phenomena to those described by RAW in his 1977 counterculture classic, *Cosmic Trigger Volume 1: Final Secret of the Illuminati*. Said experiences began around 1997 and involved consciousness expansion, encounters with synchronicities, ultraterrestrials, cryptids, and/or archetypes revealing the fluidity of reality. I finished an original manuscript, entitled *My Cosmic Trigger Finger is Broken*, in 1999. For reference, I graduated from my undergrad in 2000 from East Carolina University. I am 45 at the time of this writing, around the same age RAW was when he wrote his influential book on high strangeness.

With all of this talk of cosmic triggers, I will explain the term before we move any further. RAW's title comes from Robert Temple's 1976 book, *The Sirius Mystery: New Scientific Evidence of Alien Contact 5,000 Years Ago* where the author proposes there might be "an extraterrestrial civilization based at Sirius" that is "monitoring our development to see when we will *ready ourselves* for their contacting us." Temples speculates if his book is a signal to Sirius that we are ready for contact and asks: if so, "then am I pulling a cosmic trigger?" RAW answers, saying: "if the McKenna scenario[C] is right [then] we are pulling a cosmic trigger."[5]

The phrase "cosmic trigger" has evolved to encompass experiences that trigger a substantial shift in one's perception, resulting in a more open-minded comprehension of the world, extending beyond just the influence of Sirius on the human lifewave. In this understanding of the term, pulling one's cosmic trigger causes a mental awakening which allows individuals to question their preconceived beliefs, opening them up to new realities and possibilities.

When I published my original manuscript online, the Internet was in its early days, but surprisingly it garnered a lot of interest. I received many positive responses via email and lots of people were keen to share with me their own personal encounters with paranormal phenomena. I ended up taking the manuscript offline due to paranoia, self-doubt, and my inability to handle being the sudden repository of so many weird tales. I was smack dab in the middle of the anomalous and often negative psychological state which RAW referred to as Chapel Perilous, which is a state where an individual becomes deeply immersed in exploring alternative beliefs and mystical experiences. With such an immersion one becomes uncertain about what is true or false because reality seems to undergo a strange metamorphosis. This mindset is dangerous because the lines between insight and delusion become blurred, making it difficult to discern what is, was, or will be, really real reality.

Ten years after taking the original manuscript offline I had finished grad school, gotten married, become a psychotherapist working with children at a highly regarded psychiatric treatment center, and had long since successfully resolved the Chapel Perilous initiation; I found someone who wanted to help me edit the manuscript and self-publish it. However, the perilous chapel quickly seized my editor, throwing him into a psychotic episode (very common when you swim in these highly strange cosmic waters) and the project was abandoned just as quickly as it began.

The $64,000 question is whether or not Chapel Perilous is merely psychosis or a genuine shamanic initiation. Or are they two sides of the same coin? The connection between psychosis and spiritual awakening is explored in the transpersonal psychology literature, in research about what is now called a spiritual emergency.[D]

C See the conclusion for McKenna's scenario.

D This topic will be more fully explored in Volume 2 of this series, *My Cosmic Trigger: Perilous Chapels & High Strangeness Magick*. Also see, *Spiritual Emergency: When Personal Transformation Becomes a Crisis* by S. Groff and C. Groff, 1989.

Before my editor was lost in the great pooka's rabbit hole, I corresponded with a noted occultist about providing a blurb for the book. Nema, who is most known for her 1995 book *Maat Magick,* had her work brought to the larger occult world by Kenneth Grant in his book *Outside the Circles of Time* (1980). Grant was the last living student of Aleister Crowley and, some claim, his true spiritual successor. If you are unaware of who Crowley was or immediately think: *he's a Satan worshiper,* then this may not be the book for you until you familiarize yourself with his writings a little more.[E]

The core principle of Maat magick involves establishing a connection with humans living thousands of years in the future, where they have attained perfection and are thriving in a civilization of complete harmony. By tapping into this harmonious future energy in our present, we can keep ourselves on the most positive timeline (from which they come) and prevent the risk of species annihilation through events like nuclear war.

The gist of this approach is found in the 1989 movie, *Bill and Ted's Excellent Adventure.* In the story, the two main characters meet Rufus, a guide from the future who informs them their band's music will one day inspire world peace; but to ensure this happens, Bill and Ted must pass their final class assignment: an oral history report. Rufus provides the two spaced out, slacker high school students with a time machine and hilarity ensues as the two kidnap historical figures which they bring back to speak in their presentation. Thanks to their *excellent adventure* through time, they not only pass their history class, but also ensure a harmonious future for all of humanity.[F]

I know, I know ... we're already talking about time-traveling humans from the future and the book has just begun. To make it through and enjoy the text, you may want to suspend disbelief as you would a work of science fiction. After all, it could be said this book is of the "psycho-mythology" genre, which is a genre that presents a "union of fact and imagination," if you will, "a marriage of psychological knowledge" with fantasy that exists on the "archetypal, mythological level."[G,6]

E See my essay, "Thelema and Humanistic Psychology," in my book of essays, *The Red Planet Arrives* to understand what his philosophy was all about and how it was obviously the opposite of "evil." Scribd.com/document/ 205582634/ Tanranin-Uhcheek-Gozaknee-The-Red-Planet-Arrives.

F While writing this I found a tweet by Dr. Michael P. Masters (@MorpoTime, Aug. 9, 23), where he provides an excerpt from a book that quotes Commander George W. Hoover, saying "The entities were 'not so much interplanetary as much as they were literally also time travelers.' They are 'from the future' and may even be 'us' from a future earth." Masters wrote *Revelation: The Future Human Past,* a satirical sci-fi novel about an "anthropologist" joining a "team of time-traveling scientists ... as they venture back through the distant past, seeking to enact a change that will bring peace to his time and avert the Great War" all while "society teeters on the brink of nuclear" Armageddon (Publisher's summary).

G This book could be said to be psycho-mythology. I mean, it could be said to be a cheeseburger. To chill out the normies, just say it's all myth and archetypes – then they can handle the weirdness. Also the norms don't typically bother to read footnotes.

In the book, I'm not going take time to apologize and skeptically deconstruct every bit of information I present. You can find many other books which take this approach; so if that is what you are looking for, you will definitely not find that here. After all, it would take an entire book to provide *evidence* to the skeptical mind about one aspect of the paranormal, let alone a book like this which deals with just about *every aspect* of the paranormal.

For example, I am not going to explain the theory of Maat magick by using qualifiers such as: "it is *reported* that humans from the future beam back energy to keep us on the most positive timeline, but this can not be *scientifically confirmed*" or "the author *claims* to have channeled ultra-advanced humans from the future, but this is *merely her perception* which can not be *definitively scientifically confirmed* by mainstream scientists." Also, just because I will report such outrageous ideas without these annoying qualifiers, doesn't necessarily mean I believe them, so don't get your knickers in a twist; I will explain what I believe by the end of the book.

Back to the future-inspired Maat magician. In my correspondence with Nema regarding her providing a blurb for the original manuscript we were to self-publish, she prophetically told me: "I can hear RAW whirling in his grave, chuckling."[7] Just what he might be laughing *at* is a matter of debate. Perhaps he was laughing at the fact that ten years later, when I was writing this chapter, I would receive a message on Instagram stating:

> *"The Universe has chosen you to be a part of the world's biggest conglomerate and reach the peak of your career as we begin this year's recruitment programme. Do you agree to be a member of the Illuminati New World Order? Send a Direct Message immediately or message the Grandmaster on WhatsApp."*[8]

Or perhaps he is chuckling at the fact that one of the hardest things about writing this book was figuring out what to include. The manifestations of high strangeness phenomena have only increased in the world since 1999 when I first published *My Cosmic Trigger Finger Is Broken* online. On top of that, my own paranormal personal experiences have also increased and evolved since then. Whatever the case may be, I can only hope that RAW was laughing *with* me and not *at* me.

Looking back, the paranormal experiences I encountered in college – the occasions which led me to write the original manuscript – were junior varsity compared to what would happen later in my life. For example, circa 2010, a head of a plump matronly woman materialized in my room while I was completely sober after I had a session with a channeled entity named Ion. Said trans-dimensional entity is the "creation" of Bob Dobbs, meaning Bob found the person to be the vessel of Ion. Bob also claims to be the real-life inspiration of JR "Bob" Dobbs of the Church of the SubGenius[H] fame and noted media theorist, Don Theall Ph.D., claimed Bob is "the new [Marshall] McLuhan." I've personally studied with Bob since 2008 and do "believe"[I] he is the real-life Bob Dobbs. You would think that too, if you had faces popping out of thin air in your bedroom after talking with his channeled entity!

When I presented the first outline of this book to my wife,[J] she said, "You have ten books here." This volume of the book series was born out of that feedback: the foolish hope to stuff everything I had to say about high strangeness into one book. Thus, this book is an introduction to a series of books: *My Cosmic Trigger, Vol. 2: Perilous Chapels and High Strangeness Magick* and *My Cosmic Trigger, Vol. 3: Gurus, Ancestors, and Friends in Highly Strange Places* are already in the works. Prior to this, my ancestors had communicated to me (via a professional medium) that the book would be "well-read" and would be the first in a series of books. At the time I was envisioning *My Cosmic Trigger* as simply one book, seemingly, the universal reality had other plans.

Motivation for Writing this Book

> "It's long been known [in] the supernatural world [that researching] the ghosties, and extraterrestrials and the ... bigfoots [representing] the whole cacophony of the paranormal [that] If you are not grounded, it can easily send you into ... mental health turmoil-delusional thinking [including] projections onto things that have nothing to do with reality."[9]

I have led a double life that I use to my advantage. In addition to being a high strangeness researcher, I'm also a practicing psychotherapist (really ... it's my day job and one I'm pretty good at, in fact). This puts me in a unique position to offer advice on how to maintain one's mental balance during the journey down the high strangeness rabbit hole.[K]

H This claim has caused a fair amount of controversy; see: SubGenius.com/bigfist/classic/classics/GRAY-AREAS-SubGInt.html

I I put scare quotes around believe to feature RAW's famous quote: "Belief is the death of intelligence" which highlights the idea that when people hold rigid beliefs they can become closed off to new perspectives. He encouraged a more open-minded and flexible approach to beliefs and encouraged people to examine their beliefs regularly.

J She insisted I mention that I'm married in the introduction, claiming it would help people not think I was crazy. Never no mind the fact y'all just might think we're both crazy.

K I believe the high strangeness rabbit hole is Harvey's (the pookah) rabbit hole and the only

Also, in quoting a message from a New Age channel at the beginning of this section, I'm engaging in two taboo acts. One, I'm taking mental health advice from aliens! and two, I'm bringing New Age literature into the study of high strangeness. The taboo in the first act needs no explanation; for the second I point out that high strangeness researchers in general are not open to so-called New Age material. The third bonus taboo is that New Age practitioners and high strangeness researchers are both against psychotherapy, which is to their detriment and readily apparent when you chance upon an interaction with a member from either of these two groups.

My intention is that the *My Cosmic Trigger* project will not only provide mental stability during your journey down the rabbit hole but also play a role in facilitating a more enriching life, finding yourself a better person on the other side of the looking glass. Most high strangeness content introduces more psycho-spiritual challenges than solutions and while said material may expose you to a different reality; it seldom equips you with the necessary tools to navigate that newness, let alone harness it for personal growth.

Discovering yourself in the Chapel Perilous marks a crucial juncture in one's exploration of consciousness. Once inside the chapel, individuals face a choice of either being trapped in a cycle of bewilderment or emerging with a more expansive understanding of reality. Frequently, immersing oneself in cosmic content of the weird will inadvertently deepen one's entanglement within Chapel Perilous, offering no clear path to exit. The *My Cosmic Trigger* project endeavors to provide a road map of escape.

This volume in the book series provides a thorough analysis of the phenomenon which often sends people into psychological disequilibrium; my hope is this exhaustive study will make the unintelligible code on the computer screen understandable and by the end of the book, like the character in *The Matrix,* all you will see is blonde, brunette, redhead.

My Personal History

I've been researching high strangeness topics since the mid-80s when I was in elementary school. I started with Greek myths, the Loch Ness monster, the Son of Sam serial killer, and the satanic panic.[L] My elementary school li-

psychic message I got from RAW on this book was to include a lot of footnotes. RAW details his synchronicity with Harvey in *Cosmic Trigger Vol. 2: Down to Earth*, saying "when High Weirdness occurred, I would just file … it as a six-foot-tall white rabbit from County Kerry, playing games with me" (2019, E-book: p. 114).

L Perhaps at an early age I was picking up on the high strangeness of the serial killer phenomenon that Hoffman explores in *Twilight Language*, where he says their sub rosa is about keeping "the American Group Mind pressure cooker on 'high'" (p. 259). See also, David McGowan's *Programmed to Kill: The Politics of Serial Murder* (2004) & *Weird Scenes Inside the Canyon: Laurel Canyon, Covert Ops, and the Dark Heart of the Hippie Dream*, (2014).

brarian called my parents to rat me out for researching the latter two subjects but a friend of mine who also shared the same interests snuck me a copy of a book about the Son of Sam which included excerpts of his diary.

By the end of middle school, I added UFOs, *Twin Peaks*[M] and the ghost hunting duo Ed and Lorraine Warren to my list of research interests. Interestingly enough, many years later in 2015, my wife and I stayed with our friends in Connecticut who lived virtually next door to Lorraine,[N] where I saw her driving down the street. I also will never forget taping *Twin Peaks* on VHS and later trying to explain the plot to my best friend[O] while frequently pausing the tape to explain the impossibly arcane plot.

In my high school years I became well versed in theories regarding ancient aliens and the power of entheogenic plants after reading *UFO and the Bible* (1956) by M. Jessup and *Plants of the Gods: Their Sacred, Healing, and Hallucinogenic Powers* (1979) co-authored by the person who discovered LSD, Albert Hoffmann. I utilized interlibrary loan to obtain these rare books.

The other information I obtained by utilizing the precursor to the Internet, the BBS. Bulletin Board Services were accessed via modems and you were essentially visiting one website at a time, one modem to one modem. Visiting a BBS that specialized in high strangeness research, I learned that JFK's true assassin was most likely not Oswald and that a scientist named Bob Lazar claimed Area 51 existed. The secret base was an unsubstantiated rumor at the time and is now a tourist attraction, while Lazar has recently appeared on arguably the most famous podcast of our time.[P]

During high school (class of 1996), I had a chip on my shoulder about *The X-Files* which was popular at the time and never watched a single episode. This was because I had been studying the topics explored in the show for years and felt I didn't need a popular mainstream show to educate me on these topics. I viewed the show as simply entertainment for the normies who didn't really understand the true import of high strangeness subjects.[Q] Leaving the BBS behind (circa 1995), I became an early adopter of the Internet. After reading S. Godin's *E-Mail Addresses of the Rich & Famous*

M See, *High Strangeness Factor – Twin Peaks and the Paranormal*, Paranormal, UK Radio Network, 2020.

N She had an occult museum in her home, see: "Inside the Warrens' Occult Museum in CT where Annabelle 'lives,'" (CTinsider.com, Sept. 2022) however I was unable to arrange a time to visit when I was staying with my friends and by 2015, Ed had already passed.

O This same friend's father was named Stephen Greer and growing up their family would receive calls for the "UFO guy" because Dr. Steven Greer was an ER doctor at our county's only hospital at that time.

P See, "Bob Lazar & Jeremy Corbell," *Joe Rogan Experience* #1315, June 2019.

Q While writing this book I have started to make my way through the series, specifically the mythology episodes. I very much enjoy the show and believe it holds up, as they say. See: wiki/Mythology_of_The_X-Files

(1994) I entered into a brief email exchange with Wayne Knight (who played Newman in *Seinfeld* and one of Jim Garrison's attorneys in Oliver Stone's *JFK*). This was one of my early synchromystic[R] connections, bringing me into contact with the JFK assassination mystery in both a humorous and roundabout way.

My wife encouraged me to also point out that while I was conducting my highly strange research, oddly enough I was living the life of a normal American teenager. The double-life aspect was present in my trajectory since the beginning. As hard as it may be to believe for those who know me now, I was a three-sport letterman and was the captain of my wrestling and American football teams my senior year.

The sport I was best at was American football, starting at wide receiver, place kicker, and long snapper. I was above average but slightly below the star status; however, my flair for making spectacular plays helped my team win several games, one of which was featured on regional television.[S] My high school girlfriend was one of the most beautiful girls in the school and was the prom queen. I point these facts out to demonstrate that I was not the stereotypical asocial weirdo in the basement feverishly studying weird subjects. In fact, I was a fairly social weirdo born with good hand-to-eye coordination and a decent facial structure. Actually, the weird has always been fundamental but existing in the background of my life. This book is about to change that I suspect.

Looking back at the writing of the original manuscript, *My Cosmic Trigger Finger Is Broken,* I now understand I was also trying to figure out the paranormal experiences I went through at a young age. This included the metallic AI female voice I would hear in a hypnagogic state at the age of four (similar to the voice described by Phillip K. Dick in his *Exegesis*[T]), encounters with gnomes on a field trip in the fifth grade (possibly the mythological Cherokee little people and definitely verified by others), and the mysterious green light (or orb) experience of my junior year of high school. Maybe

R Synchromysticism is the study of meaningful coincidences between seemingly unrelated events, often suggesting a deeper, interconnected order to the universe. I will explore this subject in depth in this text.

S See the recap of my West Caldwell Warriors vs South Caldwell Spartans, 1994, Charlotte's WBTV, *Football Friday Night*. I was most probably playing against country superstar, Eric Church (youtu.be/-Qgxdvgog9o).

T "The faint, tiny AI voice inside my head at night is greater than the entire universe" (p. 643), "The lovely AI Voice" (p. 349), "The AI voice I hear is [VALIS'] voice. I am in symbiosis with it. This is to my benefit because it can crossbond me into it and hence make me immortal. It is a higher species using us for its purposes" (p. 659), "I am very happy to think of the woman (Sibyl, AI Voice) as part of myself. (Recognize it as a hallucination from my unconscious: my anima, and not emanating adventitiously.)" (p. 812), *The Exegesis of Philip K. Dick*, 2011.

I was drawn to the material because I grew up on a North American ley line that extends from the center of the Bermuda Triangle.[10]

Like any true fan of RAW's *Cosmic Trigger,* I went crazy when I read the book. Or maybe the book brought me out of madness. It's impossible to tell. Be that what it may, I like to say: "If you didn't go crazy after reading *Cosmic Trigger*, did you really get the point?" Though the notion of people going batty after venturing down the rabbit hole is now a well-worn trope, the psychological distress which accompanies this phenomenon has profound repercussions in an individual's life.

To be clear, I point out that I am uniquely situated to offer guidance through one's encounter with destabilizing otherworldly strangeness, being that I have been a paranormal researcher since 1986, a mental health professional since 2001, and a practicing psychotherapist since 2007. Being a psychotherapist who is off in the weeds of the weird puts me in good company (or bad, depending on who you ask): Jung and Reich's life stories make mine appear mild. Regarding high strangeness and mental health, I like to say: "It's not crazy if it's true."[U] That said, in the words of Philip K. Dick, "Sometimes the appropriate response to reality is to go insane."[11]

This book offers a way around the path of insanity so common in this domain of research. For RAW, there are only two ways to resolve one's descent into Chapel Perilous: coming out the other side agnostic or insanely paranoid. No offense to RAW (laughing merrily from beyond the grave), but both options appear less than ideal. I offer a third approach: genuine psycho-spiritual growth, existential cosmic reorientation, or, as the New Age crowd says, spiritual ascension. This third way allows people to pull their own individual cosmic trigger – the *raison d'être* of the overall *My Cosmic Trigger* hypersigil.

Find the Others: Solidify a Community

My Cosmic Trigger has evolved into so much more than a mere book. Indeed, the phenomenon can't adequately be considered, studied, or understood through print alone. As an outgrowth of this book, I also have a podcast where specific chapters and subjects are discussed in greater detail. I encourage readers to send their personal encounters with high strangeness to MyCosmicTrigger.com so we can explore this phenomenon together and help others going through similar experiences to make connections, too.

U This is not exactly true, as a mental health diagnosis of being "crazy" has more to do with holding beliefs that go against the consensus reality and not if those beliefs are true per se. I will explore this in the conclusion.

I also run a psycho-spiritual group, the Çhaplains öf Peril, designed to help people better process their encounters with high strangeness and, quite simply, avoid going loony as they plunge down the cosmic rabbit hole in particular and in general deal with the craziness that is life post 2020.[V] One might even call Ç.Ö.P. ("Ç" is pronounced "ch" and the acronym means trash in Turkish) an apocalyptic eschatological support group. Think of it as a "Hi, my name is Matt and I believe in portals to other dimensions" type of thing. Readers are encouraged to contact this writer if they resonate with the material in this text and are interested in joining the Ç.Ö.P and/or are seeking individual psycho-spiritual instruction and support from this writer.

That said, this book hopes to remind the high strangeness researcher that we are not looking for evidence to convince the incredulous masses. The skeptical mind is continually moving the evidence goal posts and, as such, it's a futile pursuit to try and convince the skeptic. Instead, we are looking for information to take us deeper into our own shamanic initiation process.

This book also aims to be a way in to the high strangeness phenomenon for people in its outer orbit: those who haven't jumped in the cosmic deep end, for want of knowing a good place to start; and people who are high strangeness curious (perhaps a friend or family member of a researcher) and are vaguely familiar and interested in the paranormal. And lastly, this book aims to provide clarity, hope, humor, inspiration and a guidance to a new generation of people who have been sucked into the high strangeness vortex in general and the cosmic trigger vortex in particular.

What the Reader Can Expect to Gain

I will explain the theory and practice behind high strangeness. Again, casting no aspersions on the late, great RAW, I don't think he did a great job explaining the theory behind the high strangeness phenomena he experienced. In my estimation, he focused more on providing an entertaining personal account of his paranormal encounters. This volume's focus on the theory and practice of high strangeness is designed to give people the grounding for their own encounters with the phenomenon: as it is said, knowing is half the battle.

I also lay out the beginnings of a magick of high strangeness. I believe to have a sound magical practice in this regard, we need to first go through the ins and outs of high strangeness phenomena. This is because understanding this phenomenon in depth is a first step in staying sane as you go down the

V Similar to Charles Eisenstein's Sanity Project which is a "program and forum to hold and grow sanity in turbulent times" (charleseisenstein.org/courses/sanity project/).

rabbit hole. Otherwise, it all will just appear a bunch of swirling colors of cosmic madness.

It is also my hope that readers will use this text as a guidebook to help them pull their own individual "cosmic trigger" and in turn help the community pull the collective "cosmic trigger." As I said earlier, this personal and collective pulling is what the *My Cosmic Trigger* hypersigil is all about. My fervent hope is that this process will help facilitate the return of the Golden Age of peace and lift us out of the Kali Yuga (or dark age). Can I get an amen!?

Who This Book Is for

This book is written for people who have gone through or are currently going through a *high strangeness initiation*, which is a powerful subjective encounter with these weird phenomena. I would also not be surprised if you have encountered this book after a series of synchronicities, as such, this book is meant for just the right people at just the right time.

More concretely, this book is for people intimately familiar with high strangeness phenomena in general and the subjects explored in RAW's *Cosmic Trigger* in particular. Other groups (mentioned above) may find this book useful, but the book is designed for people already well versed in the subject. Still, bold but relative newcomers are welcome because, as we speed head long into the weird apocalyptic future, we need all hands on deck and as many eyes on this phenomenon as possible. If we don't figure out the name of this goblin, then we are all screwed.

How This Book Is Written

In a manner of speaking, I'm envisioning this book as an apocalyptic book report. To that end, I encourage the reader to look at each author referenced and book quoted as jumping off points for your own individual research. This book is full of rabbit holes, I can't go down all of them in this book, but I can point out as many of them as possible. I'm utilizing as many sources as possible in an effort to demonstrate that I'm not the only person saying these highly strange things. As such, I have attempted to exhaustively reference everything I talk about, perhaps obsessively so and if you find a theory that I have not properly cited then please let me know, as one of my goals is to have every theory of high strangeness properly cataloged in one place.

Given the fact that in this introduction I reference the Christian Bible and Buzzfeed, it should be clear that I pride myself on pulling material from high and low culture. This is because when you have gone through the cosmic looking glass you no longer see much of a distinction in the artifacts of human culture.

Who This Book Is Not For

Decidedly, this book is *not* for people brand new to the paranormal in general; and, specifically, this book is not for skeptics. As I have said (and will continue to say) this book is not a book that is meant to convince. Don't get me wrong, books written to convince the skeptical are all well and good and have their place; but this is just not one of those books. The best book I know of in that genre is *Real Magic: Ancient Wisdom, Modern Science, and a Guide to the Secret Power of the Universe* by Dean Radin, Ph.D. I have seen this book change the mind of a skeptic, but it takes courage and intellectual honesty to change one's mind: two things that are in short supply these days. And as I like to say, I am skeptical of skeptics.

Not only do I say this book is not for the uninitiated, I also implore the normie (yes, that is what we call y'all) to *not* read this book. You may be a family member or friend that has bought this book because you hold me or my family in high esteem; if this is the case, I sincerely thank you. Please leave a 5-star review on Amazon, but don't read the book. This is because, if you are brand new to this material, I don't think you reading the book will lead to a positive outcome for me or you. In order to make sense of this material, you are going to need to grapple with it for many years: high strangeness is not something that comes easy. The high strangeness genre is a niche of the overall paranormal field. It is the weirdest of the weird and as such not the best place to begin one's learning journey.

If you are a normie and read this book then two things will most probably happen. One, you will be thrown down the rabbit hole too quickly and will experience a serious mental health disturbance. Or two, you will come to believe I am stark raving mad.[W]

If you experience number one, then so be it: it is your karma. I sincerely wish you the best, and please leave a positive review. However, if you land in number two, then you may become fixated on me personally and actively work against this book. Curiously enough, I have run into this dynamic over the years when sharing my non-mainstream thoughts online. I have had to defriend people on social media who not only disagreed with me but seemingly became obsessed with me, so much so that it felt like it was creeping into harassment.

W I don't want to alarm the normies who might reach this conclusion, but I am quite sane these days. In fact, in a world that has become increasingly chaotic, I would argue that not having faith in at least one unconventional idea is more indicative of mental instability than the opposite. Also, my job is to decide who is and is not sane. In fact, people pay me (not the judgmental skeptic) good money for that determination.

This is not just particular to myself; it is a dynamic that happens in the paranormal field. Take, for example, the fact that sociologist Marcello Truzzi (1935–2003) "resigned from the professional skeptics organization he cofounded, Committee for the Scientific Investigation of Claims of the Paranormal (CSICOP)...about a year after its 1976 launch." This was because "Truzzi protested the group's dominance by 'pseudo-skeptics' more interested in injurious behavior toward claimants of the paranormal versus actual skeptical inquiry."[12] I don't think you have to be Freud to see the skeptic's tendency to engage in "injurious behavior" toward paranormal believers has a "The lady doth protest too much" type of energy.

I have been told I am a polarizing figure, which is odd because that is truly not my conscious intention. On a personal level I'm a fairly mild mannered kinda guy- think a Matthew McConaughey character (not quite that nicely built) from the southern region of the United States. However, the truth has a way of being inherently polarizing. In this regard I am reminded of the following wisdom from Jesus, when he said: "Think not that I am come to send peace on earth: I came not to send peace, but a sword. For I am come to set a man at variance against his father, and the daughter against her mother.... And a man's foes shall be they of his own household."[13]

I love my best friend dearly, but he is normal as the day is long. He even jokingly said that he may read this book and it might be so weird that he could no longer be my friend. Of course he was *just kidding*, but, as the saying goes there is no such thing as a joke.[X] As a practitioner of New Age mysticism, this type of comment invokes a reaction named after Neo's antagonist in *The Matrix*. In our highly strange reality "there is a form of psychic attack that could be called the 'Agent Smith' effect. This form of attack comes through the energy fields of someone you have a strong connection to that has not been unplugged from the ascending 3D world."[14] We could colloquially describe this dynamic as the "cosmic player hater effect".

While writing this manuscript I have warned my friends and family that previously I had actually been attempting to appear normal. This is shocking for my beloved normies because I have always appeared quite strange to them, *as is*. Over the years, I have heard family members lament *why can't you just be normal?* Such a thing is hard to hear, considering you were attempting to be as normal as your poor little legs would take you. So, if you are a normal friend or family member and happen to be reading this, full disclosure: I have been holding back my strangeness a considerable amount

X See Freud's 1905 book, *Jokes and Their Relation to the Unconscious* where he "claims that 'our enjoyment of the joke' indicates what is being repressed in more serious talk" (wiki/Jokes_and_Their_Relation_to_the_Unconscious).

up until this point. But, it is now 2024 and the world has gotten so strange that I am now just saying "The hell with it! This is me. I am weirdo – hear me roar!" I have been inspired in this regard by Hunter S. Thompson who said "When the going gets weird, the weird turn pro."

In the spirit of full disclosure, another reason I decided to come out of the cosmic closet is because I have been an aspiring screenwriter for the last twenty years and failed to obtain any notable success in this area.[Y] A little known fact of this creative endeavor is that writing a script is the easy part: the hard part is to get somebody in the industry to read it. So, I came to the conclusion that I would rather reveal my highly strange side if it meant somebody might actually read what I have written. Facing the potential of *injurious behavior* from skeptics is better than your creative labor just going to the spam folder of some Hollywood producer, where it is never read. An unread book has honor; an unread screenplay is just sad.

What This Book Is About

As I said, this book is about high strangeness which is a subset of the paranormal domain, involving the intersection of multiple paranormal phenomena, such as Bigfoot and UFO sightings occurring in the same geographic location. This highly strange coalescence demonstrates that reality is more bizarre than we can imagine and that the tapestry of paranormal weirdness makes a simple UFO or bigfoot sighting tame by comparison.

I believe there are two ways to look at the truth about high strangeness. One would be in line with Phillip K. Dick's view that reality is "that which, when you stop believing in it, doesn't go away,"[15] meaning there is one definite truth to figure out. The second would be more in accordance with RAW's view of the plurality of reality, meaning there is no such thing as one true reality, but rather multiple realities exist.

RAW reported that he and the co-author (Robert Shea) of their famous sci-fi novel, *The Illuminatus! Trilogy* would argue with one another about the nature of reality. RAW says Shea maintained reality denoted "something concrete and external to any observer." While he, on the other hand thought "'reality,' like 'illusion' … designates a judgment … by the observer and has no meaning apart from the observed transaction."[16]

Y I did sell a reality TV show concept to a guy who (it could be argued) is responsible for a certain president getting elected, had George Clinton (master of intergalactic funk & member of the Rock n' Roll Hall of Fame) attached to a script for a time, and had a show idea that is the same as an A-lister's hit show on HBO (a sad coincidental case of parallel thinking or because the friend I co-created the show idea with is a friend and colleague of this particular A-list celebrity).

Another Wilson pertinent to the *My Cosmic Trigger* project is Colin Wilson, who rose to international fame in 1956 with his philosophical text, *The Outsider.* The book "was a study of the self-destructive path of many confused artistic types who had sought an outlet for their inner dynamism in a society that could not adequately accommodate them." He said that great artists like Van Gogh and Nietzsche "were all examples of intense talents that imploded. Their urge to super-consciousness came up against consensus pessimism, a major symptom of the sleepwalking trance of humanity that Gurdjieff had explained." Wilson is a great example of a high strangeness researcher because he started out writing about existential themes in literature and philosophy, but his research and intellectual honesty led him to cover such topics as the "occult and paranormal, serial killers, UFOlogy, ancient civilisations, literature and sexuality."[17] He developed an understanding of human consciousness that was able to hold these seemingly disparate aspects. He is absolutely worth reading further.

I happened to meet Wilson at an Alfred North Whitehead[Z] conference during my time at the University of West Georgia (UWG) psychology graduate program, due to my wife being an avid student of his books and being invited to an exclusive lecture at Emory University – all facilitated by synchronicity. Whitehead is important to mention as we begin our journey because he "argued that reality consists of processes rather than material objects ... thus rejecting the [underlying assumption] that reality is fundamentally constructed by bits of matter that exist" more or less distinct from "one another."[18] He was one among many philosophers who believed the way we have conceptualized reality, focusing on distinct objects or units, was not up to the task of understanding it.[AA] While philosophy is not my thing, rejecting commonly held perceptions of reality is what *My Cosmic Trigger* is all about.

I attended UWG's graduate program from 2000 to 2003. The department was started on orders of Abraham Maslow himself, who, along with Carl Rogers, was one of the co-founders of the Humanistic Psychology movement in the 1960s. Maslow popularized the terms self-actualization and the hierarchy of needs (concepts that are too often misunderstood). This psychology department at UWG in Carrollton, Georgia is one of the only humanistic and transpersonal oriented departments in the United

Z Whitehead was a mathematician and philosopher. His school of thought is called process philosophy or ontology of becoming. Michael Bertiaux claims he is "the best example" in "secular philosophy" of Transyuggothian physics and power. (*Voudon Gnostic Workbook*, p. 301)

AA Another such contemporary philosopher is Eugene Gendlin (see: wiki/Eugene_Gendlin). My wife's doctoral dissertation is on his work, see: *Magic in the Circle: A Process Oriented Inquiry into Restorative Circles*, (N.B. Vaughn, 2015). I was able to meet Gendlin at his home shortly before he passed, accompanying my wife when she went to study with him.

States and will be further discussed in chapter 10. The department was my personal Hogwarts where I unleashed my inner Harry Potter and met my very own Hermione (yes, I know he ended up with Ginny Weasley; but I'm a weirdo, not a nerd). The significance of encountering Colin Wilson via my association with the department highlights a key part of my own cosmic journey.

Furthermore, there also happened to be a body of the Ordo Templi Orientis (OTO) in Carrollton at the time I attended graduate school there. The OTO's most famous (or infamous) members are Aleister Crowley and Jack Parsons, who founded Jet Propulsion Laboratories and invented rocket science in America.[AB] My de facto mentor at the time, Allen Greenfield, was a high-ranking member of the OTO and put me in contact with the people who ran the camp, leading to my eventual initiation in the order. I had previously met Greenfield online, while I was still in undergrad. Greenfield's 1994 book *The Secret Cipher of the UFOnauts* inspired much of the popular TV show *Hellier* which examines high strangeness and, in some ways, continues the work of John Keel's *The Mothman Prophecies* published in 1975. Greenfield's book explores the connection between extraterrestrials (or ultraterrestrials as he refers to them) and ritual magick.

Maslow and Colin Wilson began corresponding in 1963. This relationship led Wilson to write "one of his most important" books called *New Pathways in Psychology*, which was on Maslow and the Post-Freudian Revolution and "Where Wilson diverged from Maslow was in his belief that we don't have to wait for the peak experiences. We have many ways to cultivate them as part of intentional self-actualisation" which constituted "a kind of new existentialism."[17] Wilson's theories around new existentialism is a component of my magick of high strangeness.

That Wilson was diving deep down the rabbit hole is clear, when, for example, he wrote introductions for books such as F. Holiday's *The Goblin Universe* (1986). In his introduction to the book, he brings up the two prevailing viewpoints on high strangeness, first arguing that cryptozoological monsters and UFOs "may be symbols- or … 'signals'" from the collective unconscious and "their purpose may be to 'remind' human beings that reality is altogether strange and more complex than they think." Elaborating on this point, by saying Jung "advances the theory that unidentified flying objects are not objectively real, but are 'projections' of the human mind" which were "in effect, 'monsters from the unconscious' which had somehow managed to clamber out into the real world." Jung speculated that "man

AB See *Sex and Rockets: The Occult World of Jack Parsons* by John Carter, 2005.

has an appetite for religious meaning which is exactly like his body's needs for vitamins. If he lives a life without real purpose, this function becomes starved." And when humans are starved in this manner "we may begin to see certain 'archetypal' religious symbols floating around in the sky" which would be the "soul's attempt to remind him that something is missing."[19]

The above sums up one viewpoint of high strangeness phenomena, which is that the occurrences are an outgrowth of a function of human consciousness not yet discovered. However, looking at the second theory, and to confuse matters, Wilson points out that "towards the end of his life Jung apparently abandoned" his belief that UFOs were projections from the human unconscious because he "came to admit" that they "may be as 'objectively real' as meteors."[19] This back and forth sums up the mutability of high strangeness in general: just when you think you've got it pegged, someone contradicts everything they've previously said on the matter.

One: are these phenomena all coming from our collective unconscious to remind us of our true cosmic spiritual natures? And, if we don't come to terms with this nature, will we cease to exist as a species? Or two: are there *really* monsters and extraterrestrials (good and bad) and we must contact the good ones while avoiding the bad ones to avoid destruction? At a certain level, I think it makes little difference about which of these is true. Whatever the case, it is clear something highly strange is going on and it is important we try and name it.

And I am not the only one of this opinion. The US military sure thinks it's important to name it; the Defense Intelligence Agency spent millions of dollars researching the epicenter of high strangeness, Skinwalker Ranch, detailed in the 2021 book *Skinwalkers at the Pentagon: An Insider's Account of the Secret Government UFO Program*. The 500 acre ranch in Utah "has long been an alleged epicenter of strange happenings, dating back to tales from the Native American Ute tribe ... who believe in malevolent witches called skinwalkers who can transform into animal-like creatures."[20] *Skinwalkers at the Pentagon* highlights the fact that those researching at the Ranch often "led to the 'attachment' of strange phenomena to military personnel who visited the Ranch and brought 'something' home to their families, resulting in frightening eruptions of paranormal events in their households that terrorized and sometimes injured their children."[21]

You might be asking, "OK, what is the answer? Is this stuff from our collective consciousness, or should I be worried about real, honest-to-goodness monsters?" Even if I could, I'm not sure why I would answer this question in the introduction: then there would be no hope of you reading the rest of the book! But, for now, let's just consider that Wilson says the author of *The Goblin Universe* "leaves the question open; he is far more concerned to remind his readers of 'the flying saucer vision' the vision of man as a part of a far wider universe."[19]

An interesting synchronicity occurred while I was writing this introduction. My wife and I are currently watching *Star Trek* together, starting with the series *Deep Space 9*. Episode 16 of season 1, "If Wishes Were Horses," perfectly encapsulates the questions around the high strangeness phenomenon. In the episode, the crew is beset by mischievous creatures appearing out of thin air. The creatures are led by none other than Rumpelstiltskin, who I bet you didn't think I'd be able to bring back to round off this introduction. The fact that synchronicity helped me tie up the loose ends of this introduction illuminates the important role it plays in the theory and practice of high strangeness.

Just like us high strangeness researchers, the space station crew must figure out whether Rumpelstiltskin and Co. are actual fairy creatures, hyper-externalized projections of their imaginations, or extraterrestrial beings. The crew believes the beings, whatever they may be, are originating from an anomalous rift in space-time near their station. This is analogous to what are referred to as window areas in this area of research. Window areas, which are discussed in this book in great detail, are a major explanation of how and why high strangeness phenomena manifests.

And just like those of us seeking to name the highly strange times of today, the crew face destruction if they don't solve the mystery of what these beings are and where they come from. With the help of Rumpelstiltskin, the crew learn the beings are coming from their imagination and the crisis is averted. However, they later learn of an even more complex reality. The beings are, in fact, higher dimensional creatures who communicate through the human psyche, just as humans use writing and language to communicate.

And so there you have it. The introduction of *My Cosmic Trigger* is complete and finally I will say that "I'm burned out ... so I'm just going to lay this all upon you and trust that you're a visionary reader, because the grand design, such as it is, is going to be hard for you to see."[22]

Matt Oliver Vaughn
ß, Türkiye
Gamewell, North Carolina, USA
Spring 2022-Fall 2023

References:

1. Maureen Dowd, "Interview with Elon Musk," *New York Times,* July 25, 2020.

2. Paul Levy, *Dispelling Wetiko: Breaking the Curse of Evil,* 2013. pp. 262-67.

3. Carl Jung, *Civilization in Transition,* Collected Works 10, para 14.

4.. Jen Shiori Adams, "People On Twitter Are Joking About a 'Secret Third Thing,' and It's More Entertaining Than It Should Be," BuzzFeed.com, Sept. 8, 2022.

5. Robert Anton Wilson, *Cosmic Trigger Volume 1: Final Secret of the Illuminati,* also quoting Temple, 1976; 2016, E-book: pp. 349-50.

6. J. Marvin Spiegelman, Ph.D, *The Knight,* 1982, pp. 21-25.

7. Nema, Personal Communication, Fall 2009.

8. Instagram page, Personal Communication, Austrian number redacted, Spring 2022.

9. Barbara Marciniak channeling the Pleiadians, *Spellbound: Part 1,* Bold Connections Unlimited, Sellfy.com, Feb. 20, 2022, Time: 15:00.

10. "Bermuda Triangle, Mount Shasta and Buffalo Lake Ley Line Map," Vortex-Hunters.com.

11. Philip K. Dick, *VALIS,* 1981.

12. Mitch Horowitz, "The Crisis of Professional Skepticism," Medium.com, Feb. 28, 2023.

13. Matthew, 10, Verses 34 to 39, King James Version.

14. Steve Ahnael Nobel, "Neutralising 'Agent Smith' Psychic Attack Transmission," InsightTimmer.com.

15. Scollurio, "5 Profound Philip K. Dick Quotes," scollurio.medium.com, Jan. 5, 2023.

16. Robert Anton Wilson, *Cosmic Trigger Vol 3: My Life After Death,* 1995; 2019 E-book: pp. 58-59.

17. Paul Weston Glastonbury, "Peak Experiences and New Existentialism: Maslow & Colin Wilson," PaulWestonGlastonbury.com.

18. C. Robert Mesle, *Process-Relational Philosophy: An Introduction to Alfred North Whitehead,* 2008, quoted in wiki/Alfred_North_Whitehead.

19. Colin Wilson's introduction to Ted Holiday's *The Goblin Universe,* 1986.

20. Travis Tretton, "How Believers in the Paranormal Birthed the Pentagon's New Hunt for UFOs," *Military News,* Military.com, March 7, 2022.

21. *Skinwalkers at the Pentagon: An Insider's Account of the Secret Government UFO Program,* 2021, Publisher's summary.

22. Rian Malan, *My Traitor's Heart,* 1991, opening line.

Section One: Utterly Absurd Trash

Space shamans, shape shifting past Pluto –
onto the mind and scrubbing our thought-souls
clear and free with Butter-Scotch Cosmic Candy.

Dr. J. Allen Hynek (left) and Dr. Jacques Vallée (right)

Chapter 1

Introduction to High Strangeness

Divine sparks of Heaven's lamp hide us.
Every fire-turtle, with a trick of the trade, sprouts a legend –
while telling purple tales of Crowley: who pops out of his liar-lair, asking:
what is wrong with this place?

The High Strangeness Factor

In researching UFO sightings, Dr. J. Allen Hynek (an astronomer and advisor on the US Air Force's famous study of the UFO phenomenon, Project Blue Book (1952-1969))[1] thought the presence of *high strangeness* (i.e.- bizarre and utterly absurd phenomena) in a particular case meant it was actually *more* credible, meaning the details of the case were "so unique and unbelievable that it somehow registers as believable." For Hynek, and many others, the presence of high strangeness in a case can be considered "an indicator of [the] plausibility" of the phenomenon.[2] This is akin to the you *couldn't make that up* factor or the notion that *truth is stranger than fiction*. The high strangeness phenomenon speaks "to the multifaceted inter-connections between various psi phenomena" and "the greater frequency of these inter-connections" seems to suggest a "greater trust in their paranormal efficacy" – pointing "to a truer reality that is much weirder and unusual than our current models can comprehend."[3]

This *high strangeness factor* comes from Hynek's Strangeness Rating for UFO encounters which is a "classification system that accounted for how credible the source was."[4] This system is explored by anthropologist Jack Hunter,[A] who explains that "the strangeness rating is a measure of 'the number of information bits the report contains, each of which is difficult to explain in common sense terms.'"[5] Hynek explains this system by pointing out that when a mysterious "light [is] seen in the night sky [it] would ... have a low Strangeness Rating because there is only one strange thing about the report to explain: its motion." By contrast a "report of a weird craft that descended within 100 feet of a car on a lonely road, caused the

A "Dr. Jack Hunter is an anthropologist exploring the borderlands of consciousness, religion, ecology and the paranormal. ... He is a tutor with the Sophia Centre for the Study of Cosmology in Culture, University of Wales Trinity Saint David, and teaches on the MA in Ecology and Spirituality and the MA in Cultural Astronomy and Astrology. He is also a tutor with the Alef Trust on their MSc in Consciousness, Spirituality and Transpersonal Psychology." (Jack-Hunter.yourwebsitespace.com).

car's engine to die … left marks on the nearby ground" while also appearing "to be under intelligent control receives a high Strangeness Rating because it contains a number of separate very strange items, each of which outrages common sense."[6]

This is a novel way of looking at the study of the paranormal to say the least. To researchers who are not yet initiated into high strangeness, the presence of "bizarre and utterly absurd phenomena" would be a good reason to disregard the case out of hand, not embrace it as more valid. A famous example of a high Strangeness Rating in a case of a reported extraterrestrial encounter occurred on April 18, 1961, when Joe Simonton was at his rural home in Wisconsin. Simonton reported a craft landed in his yard and opened the hatch to reveal "one of the aliens was cooking pancakes on a flameless cooking appliance. The creatures gave Joe the pancakes, saluted him, and flew away." Simonton took pictures of the cosmic pancake and even tasted some of it, saying it tasted like cardboard.[7]

In the world of high strangeness research, such a *bizarre and utterly absurd* detail of an alien encounter is seen as more trustworthy than the reports from abductees who claim to have received vague messages of universal peace or dire warnings of nuclear Armageddon. Essentially we are stating that the more complicated the paranormal encounter is and "the more interwoven details" it contains, the more it is a sign to "trust the event as legitimate."[8] Finally, it is maintained that the underlying nature of reality itself is highly strange, so naturally the stranger the report, the closer it is to the truth.

Definition and Origin of the Term

As established by now, this book deals with weird phenomena referred to as *high strangeness,* which is now commonly defined as: "A quality of being peculiar, bizarre, utterly absurd."[9] The term was coined by the earlier mentioned Dr. Hynek.[B] Originally a skeptic, Hynek's intimate study of the UFO phenomenon transformed him into a believer. His change of heart from skeptic to believer, led to the famous statement: "Ridicule is not part of the scientific method, and people should not be taught that it is."[10] Hynek's words urge us not to immediately jump to the base impulse of ridicule in the face of the high strangeness phenomenon. This sentiment is ideal for the opening chapter of the book and I encourage you to hold onto this idea as we delve further into the text.

B This esteemed high strangeness researcher is perhaps best known for his classification system for extraterrestrial encounters. The Spielberg film, *Close Encounters of the Third Kind* is about the third level of an encounter, which is when a person makes physical contact with an alien.

The overall high strangeness phenomenon is now sometimes simply referred to as *the phenomenon*.[C] Jacques Vallée popularized this term, saying his body of work was on what he called "'the phenomenon,' the range of surreal experiences that include UFO encounters."[11] The term used in this context is seen in John Keel's writing when he says: "The phenomenon has driven many people mad; but it has also produced miraculous" effects; as a result it appears a "cosmic system of checks and balances seems to be an actual fact."[12]

High Strangeness Now

The definition of the term has expanded since Dr. Hynek initially coined it. Nowadays it has come to refer to apparently separate but interrelated paranormal phenomena, such as there being a connection between Bigfoot and UFO sightings. Reddit, whose onetime tagline was "the front page of the Internet," has a high strangeness message board (called a subreddit) which deals with "explorations of the paranormal, ufos, ancient cultures, cryptozoology, consciousness, futurism, fringe science, anomalies, [and] animal mutilations."[13] Generally speaking, high strangeness subjects are so weird they can be described as bearing a resemblance to low budget science fiction.

In addition to the above, high strangeness research also deals with para-political theories and the occult. Parapolitics[D] has to do with political "practices and arrangements that are unacknowledged and that intend to misinform or obfuscate a hidden agenda."[14] The word occult has its origins in Latin, coming from the Latin word *occultus*, which means "hidden" or "secret."[15] The term was used in Latin to describe things that were mysterious or not easily understood. Over time, the term came to be associated with various mystical practices and beliefs that involve esoteric knowledge, including subjects such as magick, mysticism, esotericism, secret societies and New Age practices such as channeling entities and spiritual ascension (think a planetary spiritual enlightenment on the individual and collective level).

According to author and noted synchromystic Chris Knowles,[E] the presence of para-political theories in this field of research attempt to explain the

C Or phenomena, for example, in the podcast, *Penny Royal*, the host asks "What is the phenomena? Are magic and enchantment part of the phenomena?" (Nathan Isaac, *Penny Royal*, Causeways, Season 2, Episode 10).

D Also referred to as *deep politics*, which studies covert power structures, networks, and institutions that influence government policies. The term was made famous by Peter Dale Scott (1929), a Canadian poet, academic, and former diplomat. See his books, *The Iran-Contra Connection: Secret Teams and Covert Operations in the Reagan Era* (1987); *Cocaine Politics: Drugs, Armies, and the CIA in Central America*, (1998); *Drugs, Oil, and War: The United States in Afghanistan, Colombia, and Indochina* (2003).

E Chris Knowles is an important individual to introduce early in this book as he is one of the foremost researchers of high strangeness. His Patreon, The Secret Sun Institute of Advanced Synchromysticism, deals with "Creating Renegade Symbology and Pop Culture Scrying." Knowles is also the

"weird interaction" between high strangeness phenomena and "the military and intelligence agencies and other people in the government."[16] Legendary author and occultist Peter Levenda writes about this weird interaction when he points out that "the involvement of intelligence agents in the field of Egyptian archaeology, the UFO phenomenon, and other odd pursuits" are so ubiquitous that the connections "not only make for strange bedfellows" but are, in fact, "positively an orgy."[17]

This weird interaction has become so intertwined he even says "it has become increasingly difficult to separate an intelligence operation from the operation of another [occult] force in the world." Levenda maintains that the secret intelligence operations and occult forces are "linked by a common thread of ... synchronicity." He goes on to ask how we should cope with the effects of this other occult force by asking "how do we exorcize the hungry ghosts of America?"[F] Levenda says these questions seem "frivolous" to a "traditional historian" but actually go to "the heart of what we have come to call 'reality.'"[18,G] Notice the presence of the high strangeness principle at play here: what is considered absurd and frivolous to the normie is actually probing the very fabric of reality itself.

I believe these para-political topics explored in high strangeness can be said to be non-political because they are so *far out* they transcend the squabbling between the left and right in American politics. To the high strangeness researcher such mundane political concerns appear similar to the Lilliputians in *Gulliver's Travels,* arguing about which end an egg should be broken. How could it not appear so trivial when we consider para-political topics which include mind control research, dimensional portals, and the use of remote viewing for militaristic purposes? Examples of this type of research are explored in the 2017 Netflix documentary *Wormwood* (CIA mind control research), the 2021 book *Skinwalkers at the Pentagon* (DIA research at Skinwalker Ranch, said to be the location of a dimensional portal), and the 2019 documentary *Third Eye Spies* (CIA and US military use of remote viewing during the Cold War).

---

award-winning author of the book *Our Gods Wear Spandex: The Secret History of Comic Book Heroes,* 2007, (Simonandschuster.com/authors/Chris-Knowles).

F My magick of high strangeness is concerned with developing a praxis to expel these hungry ghosts. Also see S.K. Bain's *The Most Dangerous Book in the World* (2013) which looks at how this "other force" manifests in the parapolitics of our time.

G He also says the murders of JFK, MLK, RFK, and the Manson murders "are the result of the demonic possession of the American psyche ... it is said that demonic possession is ... a way of testing us.... The fact that so many American men and women in positions of power ... have been specifically involved with occult practices is something that not even I had anticipated before I began research of this work." (P. Levenda, *The Manson Secret,* 2006, E-book; p. 677).

The Higherside Chats

The podcast *The Higherside Chats* features interviews with leading figures in high strangeness research. The podcast illustrates the inclusion of occult subjects underneath the umbrella term of high strangeness with episodes such as "Political Sorcery, Will & Weaponized Magic" with noted magician and writer John Michael Greer; "Tarot Archetypes, Banking Alchemy, & Marketing Magic" featuring writer, film-maker and esotericist Robert Bonomo; and "The Science of Channeling, Consciousness, & the Beings Beyond" with Dr. Helane Wahbeh.[H]

I can't recommend *The Higherside Chats* enough, as it features some of the most important researchers in the field and the host, Greg Carlwood, approaches the subject matter in a humorous, non-egotistical, and down to earth manner – something of a rare combination in this field of study. He also does his best to feature guests who offer positive solutions in these strange, tumultuous times, another of the many reasons why I would recommend his podcast. I believe Carlwood's approach toward offering solutions helps us avoid a psychological trap common in consuming this type of information.

This psychological trap is when learning becomes merely "an act of enthrallment, not liberation." This means that sometimes when people learn about high strangeness they are merely seeking a "thrilling shock of recognition concerning" the negative realities of the phenomenon. This is a dangerous dynamic to get caught in because such shocks "will eventually dissipate and require yet another unprecedented jolt." Researchers caught in this negative cycle "suffer the effects of the mental contagion they imagine they are decoding."[19] My magick of high strangeness is about breaking out of this cycle.

A Crash Course in the History of High Strangeness

The following is a brief rundown of high strangeness in the last hundred and fifty years or so. This section serves as an introduction to complete beginners, a brief refresher course for those who've been around awhile, and a further reading list for anyone who's really hungry for more on the subject. It can also be a reference you return to as you continue reading the book. Please be advised: this is in no way an exhaustive history, as the title says; it is a crash course.

Charles Hoy Fort (1874-1932)

The veritable godfather of high strangeness is Charles Fort, an American writer and researcher who "worked for 27 years at the British Mu-

H The Director of Research at the Institute of Noetic Sciences and an adjunct assistant professor in the Department of Neurology at Oregon Health & Science University.

seum and the New York Public Library gathering material on phenomena from the borderlands between science and fantasy," largely from newspapers and scientific journals. The topics he wrote about were "flying saucers seen ... before the invention of aircraft ... strange noises in the sky ... falls of frogs ... sightings on Mars and the moon ... inexplicable footprints in snowfields ... poltergeist phenomena ... the Jersey devil ... spontaneous combustion; and similar weird effects." Because of this it is said "his work remains the great predecessor to all extraterrestrial speculations."[20]

Charles Fort's influence on pop culture is evidenced in his coining the term teleportation in his 1931 book, *Lo!* The use of teleportation technology is ubiquitous throughout the *Star Trek* franchise. The frog fall phenomena he first brought to the public imagination made a dramatic appearance in the final scene of the motion picture *Magnolia* (1999). It has been said that frogs falling from the sky was the "perfect ending" to this movie because "if there's one thing Paul Thomas Anderson's *Magnolia* wants you to know, it's that there are no coincidences in life."[21] The symbolism of this *bizarre and utterly absurd* ending to a major motion picture illustrating "there are no coincidences in life" is a wonderful introduction to the world of high strangeness as well as an example that the impact of its subjects can be seen everywhere. Because of the success of Anderson's movie, the frog fall phenomenon is arguably the most famous aspect of Fort's work.

However, there was much more to Fort's work than cataloging weird occurrences, and this fact is seen in some of his most famous quotes. His following words set the stage for the importance of synchronicity in high strangeness research: "My liveliest interest is not so much in things, as in relations of things. I have spent much time thinking about the alleged pseudo-relations that are called coincidences. What if some of them should not be coincidences?"[22] When psychology was in its infancy he called into question the intellectual honesty of skeptics, saying "People with a psychological need to believe in marvels are no more prejudiced and gullible than people with a psychological need not to believe in marvels." And well before the explosion of New Age literature, invoked the possibility of a war in heaven when he famously said: "The Earth is a farm. We are someone's property,"[23] likening our human condition to being movable pieces on a "cosmic chess board."[24]

Forteans

The term Fortean phenomena is something of a synonym for high strangeness phenomena. Many researchers of high strangeness simply consider themselves Forteans. For example, noted high strangeness author

John Keel introduced himself as a Fortean in his 1980 appearance on David Letterman's show.[25] Colin Wilson was interviewed for *Fortean Times* (issue 188, November 2004), and RAW's 1977 article on the 23 phenomenon was also included in issue 23.[26]

Another notable individual that one might consider a Fortean was renowned futurist Buckminster Fuller (1895-1983). From 1948 to 1949 Fuller taught at Black Mountain College in North Carolina,[I] "which was one of the centers that gave birth to the Beats[J] in the 1950s." He is perhaps best known for the invention of the geodesic dome, which "was seen as a symbol [of] the future and was adopted in a number of large-scale buildings," most notably Epcot Center's iconic attraction, Spaceship Earth (a phrase coined by Fuller[K]). In general, his work focused on the belief that "technology could create a better future for humans," and the dome at Epcot was the outward manifestation of this belief. Fuller's official status as a Fortean is a matter of debate, but the facts remain. Fuller himself reports being made an honorary life member of the Fortean society in 1938, and the "clearest ... expression of Fuller's Forteanism" is found in the fact he wrote the introduction to the biography, *Charles Fort: Prophet of the Unexplained*. The simple fact he agreed to write this introduction "indicates his affection for Fort."[27]

Fortean Phenomena

The *Journal of the Fortean Research Center* declares its statement of purpose is to "investigate all aspects of unexplained phenomena, including UFOs, cryptozoological mystery, out-of-place animal sightings, geological and archeological anomalies, psychic phenomena, and all other areas of study which may provide data useful to the resolution of these perplexing mysteries."[28] This is essentially the same as the general definition of high strangeness research. As such, there could be objections to my endeavor to help solidify high strangeness as a distinct branch within the larger paranormal field, with some arguing it merely falls under the umbrella of Fortean research. Nevertheless, the precise definition of the term Fortean

I A fact highly relevant to the My Cosmic Trigger project is that I used to live in the county where the college was located.

J The Beat Movement was a cultural and literary movement emerging in the 50s and characterized by a rejection of societal norms, a quest for personal freedom, and a focus on spontaneous expression. It produced influential figures like Jack Kerouac, Allen Ginsberg, Gerd Stern, William S. Burroughs, & Neal Cassady.

K He "was fond of making up phrases when he felt that ordinary words did not express what he meant to say. He coined the phrase 'Spaceship Earth' to describe our planet. He felt that all human beings were passengers on Spaceship Earth, and, like the crew of a large ship, people had to work together in order to keep the planet functioning properly." (Exhibits.stanford.edu/ bucky/feature/ what-is-spaceship-earth)

is challenging to get a consensus on. From my perspective, it appears that Forteans may engage less with the para-political, occult, and synchromystic aspects of the phenomenon, whereas researchers in high strangeness do.

Jacques Fabrice Vallée (1939-)

Encounter Classification System

The legendary Internet pioneer, computer scientist, author, and astronomer, Jacques Vallée Ph.D. is most known to laymen for consulting on the production of Steven Spielberg's 1977 film *Close Encounters of the Third Kind* and serving "as the real-life model for" the Lacombe character.[29] The film is about the third level of an encounter, which is when a person makes physical contact with an alien. For reference, a close encounter of the first kind is when someone "simply observes a UFO" and the second is when a UFO "leaves a physical trace" such as landing craft tracks.[30] Vallée built off the close encounters scale of his mentor, Hynek, by suggesting an encounter of the fourth kind (CE4). He said this type would describe "cases when witnesses experienced a transformation of their sense of reality" from an encounter.[31] This shift in one's perception of reality is said to often occur after an abduction.[L]

By contrast, a close encounter of the 5th kind (CE5) is one initiated by humans, which makes it different from the first four, all initiated by aliens. This term was coined by Dr. Steven Greer and his 2020 documentary, *Close Encounters of the Fifth Kind,* explores his work in this regard. His CE5 Contact app utilizes technological means (specific sounds) as well as parapsychological means (remote viewing) to initiate contact.[M]

Vallée and the Interdimensional Hypothesis

Another reason Vallée is an essential figure in the history of high strangeness research is because he was one of the first researchers to challenge the commonly held extraterrestrial hypothesis (ETH) of the UFO phenomenon (i.e., UFOs are simply spaceships piloted by little green men from other planets). It was actually both Vallée and Hynek who first discussed the interdimensional hypothesis and explored the theory in *The Edge of Reality: A Progress Report on Unidentified Flying Objects* (1975). Vallée championed the interdimensional hypothesis over the ETH because he "found the popular extraterrestrial hypothesis untenable" and instead considered the "awesome alternative- that ufos are similar to psychic manifestations

---

L See *Close Encounters of the Fourth Kind: Alien Abduction, Ufos & the Conference at M.I.T* by C.D.B. Bryan (1995).

M I have utilized this technique and found it effective.

and are produced by complex distortions of space, time and even reality itself."[32] Notice how the very nature of reality keeps getting challenged in high strangeness research.

UFOs and the Fairy Folk

In perhaps his most famous book in high strangeness literature, *Passport to Magonia: From Folklore to Flying Saucers* (1969), Vallée puts forth his theory that the UFO phenomenon of today is in the same classification as mythological entities from the past. He drew a "parallel between religious apparitions" and "the fairy-faith" with the modern UFO phenomenon. Furthermore, he maintained the same human psychological mechanisms which gave rise to the belief in religion and fairies are "identical" to the mechanisms that give rise to UFO encounters.

He said this mechanism's "effect on humans [is] constant" and it led him to the conclusion that "this very deep mechanism is a crucial one" for sociological and psychological reasons. He clarified that this question "has little to do with the problem of knowing whether UFOs are physical objects or not" and asserted that by looking at the past and understanding how this mechanism impacted human consciousness we discover one of "the facts we have missed" in history. This is so important because without this missing fact "we [will] never piece the UFO jigsaw together."[33]

This crucial element of history has been missed because mainstream scholars have ignored "books about the legends ... concerning these beings" and considering them would help us solve "the deeper problem of their impact on our imagination and culture." However, the idea that myths have (and had) a profound impact on culture and the individual is a theme which has been explored by other notable scholars. For example, both Joseph Campbell and Carl Jung discussed the role and power of myths in shaping the human psyche.[N]

A New Mythology

Vallée also maintained that a "new mythology was needed" to be a "bridge" to a new consciousness, a new future.[33] I maintain that a thorough investigation of the high strangeness phenomenon, followed by a practice of high strangeness magick, will help us invent a new mytholo-

N Cultural anthropologist Clifford Geertz explored the cultural significance of stories and narratives by advocating for an approach that delved into the symbolic meanings embedded within cultural texts. He believed that understanding the symbols and interpretations of stories in their cultural context was essential to comprehending a society's values and beliefs. See also Jason Throop's "Interpretation and the Limits of Interpretability On Rethinking Clifford Geertz's Semiotics of Religious Experience," *The Journal of North African Studies*:14:3, 2009.

gy and bridge the gap between our "meaningless present" and our cosmic future. This new mythology is important because "the idea of contact with higher intelligence is a social time bomb" and "when the establishment is rational, absurdity is dynamite."[34] It appears he is saying the *utterly absurd* of high strangeness is powerful enough to dismantle the old system, the matrix if you will, and then be a bridge to a new and bright future.

John Keel (1930-2009)

John Keel was "recognized as one of the world's leading experts on occult, parapsychological and extraterrestrial phenomena" and his research "revolutionized the way in which people have come to think about these subjects."[35] One reason is because he "was among the first to lump together all manner of weirdness including UFOs, cryptid creatures [and] ghosts – all of which pretty much can be labeled what we today call 'Fortean Phenomena,'" or high strangeness. Because his work covered so many aspects of the paranormal, he "didn't like to be called a UFOlogist."[24]

His Road to Magonia

Keel made his living in New York "as a mainstream writer and journalist with his own syndicated newspaper column" and he "also worked in Hollywood, wrote scripts and jokes for television shows and produced a string of comic novels." The subjects he wrote about changed in 1966 when there "was a prolonged period of public interest in UFOs," which led him "to pitch an idea for 'the definitive article' on the subject to *Playboy* magazine" and from "this point he became a full-time investigator of the phenomenon."[36]

The Mothman and Men in Black

Keel was one of the people who first popularized the Mothman phenomenon in his book *The Mothman Prophecies* (1975) which focuses on the cryptozoological sightings of a winged creature in the small town of Point Pleasant, West Virginia. In the book, Keel shares his theories on UFOs and other paranormal phenomena, while looking at how they intersect with the Mothman sightings in the area. The 2002 motion picture, *The Mothman Prophecies,* starring Richard Gere, was based on the book. The yearly Mothman Festival in Point Pleasant "has become a cherished tradition" and is viewed as "a positive development for the local community" because it "brings greater representation to the town and the broader Appalachia region."[37,O]

O The photo used in this West Virginia news article about the festival is by Chad Vaughn. See the section in Chapter 5 on the synchromysticism of my Vaughn surname.

While he "did not invent the legend of the sinister Men in Black he coined the acronym MIB and was responsible for elevating" the "obscure ... legend to the pop culture status it currently enjoys."[36] As such, without Keel's writings on the subject, there wouldn't have been four *MIB* films (1997-2019); and, as of 2020, the *MIB* movies were Hollywood's 37th top-grossing film franchise of all time, raking in $1.94 billion in worldwide gross revenue.[P, 38] A considerable amount more than I plan to make on the *My Cosmic Trigger* book series.

Abandoning Little Green Men (ETH) & Embracing Ultraterrestrials

Keel "thought the ET hypothesis was meritless,"[24] abandoning it "when his field investigations 'disclosed an astonishing overlap between psychic phenomena and UFOs.'"[36] He explains that while "investigating psychic manifestations all over the world for years" he started recognizing a pattern, seeing that some "UFOs were directly related to the human consciousness, just as ghostly apparitions are often the product" of an individual's mind. This led him to see there "are deeply rooted psychic and psychological factors in the UFO phenomenon." For example, he saw that the "sudden appearance of a light in the sky triggers ... human energy" which then "stimulates seemingly supernatural events."[39] This investigative experience led to him to develop the "key concept, 'ultra-terrestrials,'" which was inspired by "the writings of a Californian occultist, N. Meade Layne, who believed the occupants of flying saucers were shape-shifting spiritual entities from 'the etheric realm.'"[36]

Why is the distinction between an extraterrestrial and ultraterrestrial such an important distinction? Occultist and UFOlogist Allen Greenfield answers, saying that when thinking about the "contending alien presences" of good and evil, which have been "interpenetrating our civilizations since remote antiquity"- to suggest they are merely "'from outer space' is simply too narrow." Because the ETH is too narrow of a point of view for the phenomenon, Greenfield says he prefers "my old friend John Keel's term," ultraterrestrials.[Q, 40]

The Phenomenon's link to the Fairy Folk & Religions

Like Vallée, Keel also believed the phenomenon was linked to beings from folklore such as the fae and supernatural beings such as ghosts and demons; and was not just confined to the idea of little green men from

P For reference, the top three were: the Marvel Cinematic Universe, Star Wars, and Harry Potter.

Q Greenfield claims the Enochian language of John Dee was an "Ultraterrestrial Cipher" that was "utilized ... to receive and use an Alien technology, so advanced as to be indistinguishable from magick." He goes on to refer to occultists such as Madame Blavatsky as one of the "human allies" of the Ultraterrestrials (*Secret Rituals of the Men in Black*, p. 87).

outer space (the ETH). Keel explained how he arrived at this idea, saying his inquiries revealed that "a large part of the UFO lore is subjective and many alleged UFO events are actually the products of a complex hallucinatory process, particularly in the contactee." This "same process stimulated religious beliefs, fairy lore, and occult systems of belief in other centuries."[36]

Keel's Unifying Theory of High Strangeness:

The Superspectrum

Keel speculated there may be "a single intelligent force behind" all high strangeness phenomena, while pointing out that "strange manifestations," such as "Beams of light, voices from the heavens, the 'little people,' gods and devils, ghosts and monsters, and UFOs," have been a part of human history and myth since remote antiquity.[R,41]

This single intelligent force is (or comes from) the superspectrum, "the source of all paranormal manifestations, from extrasensory perceptions (ESP), to flying saucers, little green men, and … hairy monsters." It is a "hypothetical spectrum of energies that are known to exist but that cannot be accurately measured with present day instruments" and as such "is hard to pin down scientifically because it is extradimensional, meaning that it exists outside our own space-time continuum yet influences everything in our reality."[24] Keel speculated it existed in the "upper frequencies of the electro-magnetic spectrum" and paranormal phenomena "only became visible when they descended to the very narrow range of light that is visible to the human eye."[36]

Importance of Interdimensional Hypothesis

Shape Shifting Over Time

Keel said the phenomenon "is constantly reaching down to us" in "frames of reference which we can understand and accept." For example, the "angels so frequently reported in the past were replaced by transmogrifications which appeared to match man's own technological achievements." That is, until the mid 1850s "the religious frame of reference was constantly used by the phenomenon. But as man's technology improved and many of our old beliefs were discarded, the phenomenon was obliged to update its manifestations and establish new frames of reference." Keel said this is seen in the UFO flap of 1896-97 where contactees throughout the United States claimed to interact with a "mystery inventor" of a Zeppelin-esque air ship.

R Further, Keel's *The Eight Tower: On Ultraterrestrials & the Superspectrum* "explores [high strangeness] phenomena, and in doing so reveals the shocking truth about our present position and future destiny in the cosmic scheme of things." And this leads him to ask the provocative question, "Are we pawns in a celestial game?" (Publisher's Summary).

He says that "when you really dig into the early literature, it becomes clear that the ultraterrestrials *deliberately conveyed"* the impression of the phenomenon being from a religious "frame of reference." This means the phenomenon manifests in a frame of reference that is acceptable to the humans at the time; first it was religious, then it was mysterious airship inventors, and now it is UFOs. This is an important fact because the "first step to understanding" high strangeness "is to discard all frames of reference and try to view the phenomenon as a whole." Keel calls this shape shifting nature of ultraterrestrials "Operation Trojan Horse"[12] – their cultivation of beliefs in "various frames of references, and then ... deliberately" creating "new manifestations which support those beliefs."[36] Keel views this Trojan Horse process through a negative lens, whereas people like "Layne believed [the ultraterrestrials] were benign." For Keel they were "like Shaver's deros" and "sought to control and manipulate humans."[36]

Importance of the Interdimensional Hypothesis Today

The mainstream's renewed interest in UFOs (sometimes now referred to as Unidentified Aerial Phenomena, or UAP)[S] started due to the reported "Tic Tac" UFO sightings by Navy pilots.[42] The interdimensional hypothesis in regards to UFOs is important to remember, as we see the phenomenon being discussed in the pop-culture narrative. As the talking heads descend to explain to us the lights in the sky we must never lose sight over the fact that "we are dealing with a multidimensional paraphysical phenomenon."[43] As the normies just get started in this debate, I encourage high strangeness researchers to remember we have bigger fish to fry when we study these phenomena beyond the nuts and bolts of a possible alien spacecraft.[T]

And, finally, I want to impress upon newer readers of this material, that nobody in high strangeness is hanging their hat on little green men. If it were only that simple. The complex multi-dimensional, highly strange, nature of this phenomenon has been an integral topic of debate since the beginning of the field, which brings me to the next section.

S Some have speculated the use of UAP is a recent invention, however, while researching this book I have determined this is not true. I saw Timothy Green Beckley use the term in an old UFO journal from the 60s or 70s. However, I cannot be certain of the date, but the fact remains: UAP was in the running for what flying saucers should be called from the early days of UFOlogy.

T On Uri Geller's Insta page (theUriGeller, Oct. 6, 2023) he provides a clip of Jeremey Corbell on *Steve O's Wild Ride* podcast (#81, Oct. 6, 2023) saying the "most common report I get from a military person that doesn't want to be known" is that the "skin of the craft seemed intelligent" or "alive." In the comments Geller claims when he held UFO material given to him by Werner Von Braun in the 70s, "it felt like it was breathing ... as if it was ALIVE ... UFOs/UAPs are not just nuts and bolt craft."

The OGs[U] and Beyond of High Strangeness

With respect to historical accuracy, I'd like to point out that Keel and Vallée were not the first to explore these subjects although they became the most famous (or infamous) in the field. This is evidenced by (and perhaps because of) their aforementioned, respective influence on popular culture: John Keel's appearance on David Letterman's show and the immortalization of Jacques Vallée in Spielberg's *Close Encounters of the Third Kind*. Vallée even recounts trying to get the director to include a more ultraterrestrial aspect of UFOs, saying he "argued with him that the subject was even more interesting if it wasn't extraterrestrials.... So he said, 'You're probably right, but ... this is Hollywood ... I want to give people something that's close to what they expect.'"[44] Giving people what they expect may be the order of the day in LaLa Land, but it certainly isn't what high strangeness is all about!

OG occultist and UFOlogist, Allen Greenfield points out that Keel and Vallée were "newcomers on the scene" when they emerged in the 1960s. Some of the lesser known (but no less important) pioneers in the field of high strangeness research are James Mosley and Gray Barker, who Greenfield refers to as "first gen" researchers.[45] Even though Greenfield is referring to these two as first generation UFOlogists – not necessarily high strangeness researchers – I would argue their research goes beyond UFOs and branches out into other areas of the paranormal. And as I will show, the origins of UFOlogy were more fused with high strangeness than they are today.

James "Jim" W. Moseley (1931-2012)

The Nazca Lines were discovered in the Peruvian desert in 1927 and it was "Moseley who first wrote about" them as "an intriguing Fortean phenomena ... in October 1955." He was "suggesting a mysterious origin" of the lines "long before they interested alternative writers such as Erich von Däniken" in his 1968 *Chariots of the Gods*. Moseley founded the newsletter *Saucer News* in 1954 and sold it to Gray Barker in 1968. In 1970 he started the publication that came to be known as *Saucer Smear* which dealt with less serious content, highlighting Mosley as a "ufology humorist." His use of humor was so prevalent, that in his 2002 memoir, *Shockingly Close to the Truth: Confessions of a Grave-Robbing Ufologist*, "few were able to decipher which of his 'facts' were jokes and which were reality."[46,V]

U "short for 'original gangster'...is a slang term for someone who's incredibly ... authentic or 'old-school'...was originally used in gang culture, but it is now used as a general term to praise someone who is an expert at something" (dictionary.com/e/slang/og/)

V These quotes are from Loren Coleman's blog. His 2004 book, *The Copycat Effect: How the Media*

Moseley approached the UFO phenomenon with "satire, humor … and a light hearted but positive" outlook.[47] This is an approach that is sometimes lacking in the present day study of UFOs in general and high strangeness in particular. I believe taking a light-hearted but positive approach to study of high strangeness can help with staying grounded as one goes down the rabbit hole. Also, an overly serious and holier than thou attitude is simply off-putting.

Gray Barker (1925-1984)

The Men in Black phenomenon popularized by Keel was first introduced by Gray Barker in his 1956 book, *They Knew Too Much About Flying Saucers*. He also was the first to write about the Mothman mysteries in his 1970 book, *The Silver Bridge*, suggesting the deadly collapse of Point Pleasant's Silver Bridge was somehow related to the sightings of the winged creature. Barker also published *MIB: The Secret Terror Among Us* in 1984, shortly before his death.[48] *Shades of Gray*, the documentary about his life, "Peels the layers off" of an individual that was "Part Fox Mulder … part Mark Twain" and who "almost single-handedly created much of the gospel of UFOs" that we know today.[49]

Timothy Green Beckley (1947-2021)

Allen Greenfield refers to himself and his friend Timothy Green Beckley as "second gen" researchers.[50] Beckley was "a pioneer in his field of UFOlogy, the paranormal, and all things bizarre." He was a publisher and author "with Inner Light Publications … and film reviewer for *Hustler* magazine. He ran the NY School of Occult Arts and Sciences and worked promotions for the School of Rock and Roll."[51] He was also "described as the 'Hunter S. Thompson of UFOlogy'" and was "a popular guest on Coast to Coast AM." He also appeared on "William Shatner's *Weird or What?*" He had his own podcast, *Unraveling the Secrets*, and ran a YouTube channel named *Mr UFO's Secret Files*. Beckley reports he was "one of the few Americans ever to be invited to speak before closed door meetings on UFOs presided over by the late Earl of Clancarty at the House of Lords in England." And before his death in 2021 he probably knew "more about the history of the UFO movement since the early 1950s than anyone."[52]

His company, Inner Light Publications, published over two-hundred books covering all aspects of high strangeness phenomena, including *The*

---

and Popular Culture Trigger the Mayhem in Tomorrow's Headlines, "explores how the media's over-saturated coverage of murders, suicides, and deadly tragedies makes an impact on our society" and creates "the phenomenon through which violent events spawn violence of the same type" (publisher's summary).

Miracle of Nikola Tesla's Purple Energy Plates; Secret Exploits Of Admiral Richard E. Byrd: The Hollow Earth, Nazi Occultism, Secret Societies, and the JFK Assassination; Screwed by the Aliens: True Sexual Encounters With ETs; Evil Empire of the ETs and the Ultra-Terrestrials; UFOs, Time Slips, Other Realms and the Science of Fairies.

Beckley held a similar view to Keel and Vallée in regards to the inter-dimensional hypothesis, saying, "We are not dealing solely with physical craft from outer space occupied by off-world astronauts coming to warn us that we might possibly annihilate ourselves." The nuts and bolts of possible alien craft was not where our focus should be, he thought, maintaining that "more emphasis needs to be placed on the spiritual and occult paranormal nature of the phenomena seen in our skies and invading our homes."[53] In this regard, he also claimed the phenomena experienced during a seance is similar to those involved in UFO encounters.[54]

Beckley's work also includes topics that would be considered New Age and thus taboo in today's high strangeness community. For example, his company published *Inner Light Magazine: The Voice of the New Age* and the 1990, issue no. 17 of this publication has the following on the cover: "Brad Steiger asks: is America the reincarnation of *Atlantis?*"[W] I point this out to highlight the fact that Beckley infused New Age subjects in his study of the phenomenon, something that is sorely missing today.

To highlight his willingness to include New Age subjects, I point out that he also published books featuring channeled messages from the Ashtar Command,[X] including such books as *A New Book of Revelations: A Harvesting of Souls at Earth's Final Moment*; *Ashtar: Revealing the Secret Identity of the Forces of Light and Their Spiritual Program for Earth*; and *Project World Evacuation: UFOs to Assist in the "Great Exodus" of Human Souls Off This Planet.*[Y]

Robert Anton Wilson (RAW) (1932-2007)

RAW, a major counter-cultural figure arising out of the zeitgeist of 1960s America, has had his influence compared to legendary psychonauts

W This issue also featured an article about "Info on New Age Star People Connection" and the 1991 issue, no. 20 featured the article: "Introducing the Woman from Telos, the City Beneath Mount Shasta: Sharula."

X Ashtar is "a higher alien being … who is the head commander of a group of … overseers called the Ashtar Command. They are peaceful … aliens from the higher dimensions" devoting "part of their long lives to helping … planets such as Earth, ascend to a higher" dimension. "They belong to a huge organization called the Galactic Federation of Planets" which works "for good in the Universe" and is "similar to the Federation of Planets [in] Star Trek." A major objective of these groups "is to assist spiritually unevolved planets" and they achieve this "by assisting Starseeds and Lightworkers" (*NOT YET! Earth and the Ashtar Command*, by The Abbotts, 2014).

Y Other New Age books he published were *The American Indian UFO Starseed Connection* (2012) and *Angels of the Lord: Calling Upon Your Guardian Angel for Guidance and Protection* (2012).

Timothy Leary and Terence McKenna and has also been called "a giant of American counterculture."[55] I believe his most important philosophical work centered around *reality tunnels*. Timothy Leary first coined the term and RAW expanded on this concept throughout his life. Some claim the philosophy behind reality tunnels "is the single best tool for understanding the chaos of the 'post truth' postmodern world."[56] The concept refers to the idea "we each live in a selective view of perception determined by our setting, genetics, imprints, condition, and learning."[57]

Embracing the philosophy behind reality tunnels helps us to have less fixed beliefs, which RAW advocates, by playfully saying: "convictions create convicts."[Z] He also said the idea that "one's current model of the world contains the whole universe and will never need to be revised appears so primitive ... and absurd to me that I am ... astonished that people still manage to live with such a medieval attitude."[58] He thought it was important "to break down conditioned associations" so people could then "look at the world in a new way" because they were then "able to consider many different reality tunnels with none 'elevated to the truth.'"[55] Embracing the subjective nature of our reality gives us "access to a tremendous power" because when we "can control the filters we use" to construct our reality "we can 'tune into different realities at will.'"[56] The philosophy behind reality tunnels is an essential tool in high strangeness research because it gives us a psychological method to grapple with the *bizarre and utterly absurd* nature of the phenomena involved.

One reason *Cosmic Trigger* is a cult classic is because of the profound influence it has on people's lives. This profound influence is due to the book becoming a catalyst for the reader to experience, on a personal level, the high strangeness phenomena RAW is writing about. This is because one doesn't "just read this book, you go along on [RAW's] intellectual, spiritual and physical adventure with him." The subjects he writes about in the book "start happening in his life." And, just as they did for the author, the reader also starts to experience "strange things [and] unexplained events ... linked by underlying synchronicity."[59]

RAW summarized his book saying it featured a "cosmic Fun House" of subjects, such as: "UFOs, possible presidential assassination plots ... messages from Sirius, pancakes from god knows where ... Aleister Crowley ... Uri Geller ... futurists ... and the latest paradoxes of quantum mechanics."[58] To describe this phenomenon, he used the term "high weirdness," as opposed to my chosen term. RAW used this term when he had his famous synchronicity involving a pooka,[AA] saying, "From then on when High

Z The quote is originally credited to Kerry Thornley, founder of the parody religion, Discordianism.
AA "Nagualism implies rapport between a human and an embodied animal spirit. A disembod-

Weirdness occurred" I would just conceptualize it as "a six foot tall white rabbit ... playing games with me."[60]

Weird is also used in favor of strange in the seminal book, *High Weirdness: Drugs, Esoterica, and Visionary Experience in the Seventies* by Erik Davis. The book is an "exploration of the emergence of a new psychedelic spirituality in the work of Philip K. Dick, Terence McKenna, and Robert Anton Wilson." The author is described as "America's leading scholar of high strangeness," which I point out to show the terms, high strangeness and high weirdness are used interchangeably.[61,AB]

The New Strange

The popular Netflix TV show *Stranger Things* is a perfect example[AC] of a contemporary sci-fi drama with high strangeness phenomena driving the action. The show features secret government use of psionic powers, MK Ultra-esque mind control, secret portals to other dimensions and cryptozoological monsters. The show was originally named *Montauk*, a reference to a rumored governmental project that went awry, much in the same way as it did in the series. In their 2022 Masterclass on how to develop an original TV series, the Duffer brothers speak in detail about their interest in high strangeness subjects in general and how that interest in particular inspired their show.

The Montauk Project is rumored to have involved secret government experiments with captured alien technology, time travel, psi research, and escaped trans-dimensional monsters.[62] To increase the high strangeness quotient, some claim the project is linked to the magick of Aleister Crowley. It is speculated that "it was the Sirians who provided the Montauk chair used for the time experiments" and a Mr. X obtained this cosmic chair; then it was this same Mr. X who was the first to suggest that the project was due to the "resulting effects of Crowley's magick"[63] from his 1918 visit to Montauk. Due to these synchromystic connections the project is "inextricably linked to ... Aleister Crowley."[64]

Edward Alexander "Aleister" Crowley (1875-1947)

I need to take a moment to briefly explain Crowley since he comes up quite a bit in high strangeness in general and this book in particular. First,

ied animal spirit is called a pooka and such an animal spirit is depicted in the imaginary six-foot tall rabbit spirit named Harvey. Any possible rapport with such a disembodied animal spirit can be considered Nagualism, too. " (*Stalking the Great Whore: The Lost Writings of James Shelby Downard*, p. 297).

AB See also the book edited by Jack Hunter, Ph.D, *Deep Weird: The Varieties of High Strangeness Experience*, 2023..

AC Other examples are *Twin Peaks* and *The X-Files*. I'm only using *Stranger Things* for my example because it is the most recent.

"Contrary to common belief, he was never known to participate in satanic ritual," but he was very open about challenging and mocking the hypocrisy of Christian morals in society of his day.[AD] His influence on world culture is just now being properly assessed. For example, "He was one of the first Westerners to seriously study Buddhism and Yoga" and "was prominent in the movement to bring Eastern philosophies into Christian England and America."[65]

He was also an early "proselytiser for the drug" mescaline (the psychoactive chemical in peyote) as evidenced by the fact that "Between 1913 and 1917" Crowley hosted parties "in London and New York in which he gave peyote to many figures from occult and literary circles." Notice: this is well before Huxley's 1954 book, *The Doors of Perception,* where he wrote in detail about his experience with mescaline. Crowley did meet with Huxley in Berlin in 1930, but it is a matter of debate if this is where Huxley first learned of the psychoactive properties of peyote.[66]

No, he didn't work for Hitler as one rumor suggests; quite the opposite actually. In his book, *Secret Agent 666: Aleister Crowley, British Intelligence and the Occult,* Richard Spence makes a compelling case that Crowley worked with British Intelligence during WW2. However, definitive proof of this intriguing possibility is lacking because the "destruction of Crowley's MI5 files took place in the early 1950s, part of a mass culling of 'records no longer worth keeping'" according to what officials told Spence.[67]

Partly, the rumors of Crowley being an evil sorcerer come from a misinterpretation of his philosophy of Thelema, summed up in the phrase *Do what thou wilt shall be the whole of the Law.* I find this misunderstanding curious because he said "it should be clear that" the phrase "does not mean 'Do what you like,'" but means finding one's true purpose in life "then do nothing else" besides this "holy task." And not only that but if "every man and every woman did his and her ... true will – there would be no clashing," meaning if one's will interferes with another's path then it is evidence it is not one's true will. Finally, the confusion over, *Do what thou wilt* is especially annoying because the second half of the philosophy is *Love is the law, love under will,* which he said meant "while Will is the Law, the nature of that Will is Love."[68]

All of the above sounds like the exact opposite of a human who is said to be the most evil person to ever walk the planet. However, this is not to say you will "find Crowley a likable figure" but if you do a little research you

AD However, it can be argued he was not against the true spirit of Christ's teachings. See *Christ and the Master Therion,* which is a "shocking attempt to reconcile the visions of enlightenment from one age into another, including a previously little-known essay by Frater Achad ... that the Son of Righteousness shall shine in the Mythos of the Aeon of the Crowned and Conquering Childe" (Allen Greenfield, 2012).

will find he was "a flamboyant man who challenged all forms of religious, sexual, and social oppression and hence became a revered visionary and a reviled demon."[65]

Hellier

The first season of the high strangeness documentary TV show *Hellier*[AE] originally aired in early 2019 on YouTube. Season 2 was released later that year on Amazon Prime before also becoming available on YouTube. Various paranormal subjects are explored in the show, including the work of John Keel, secret underground bases, ghosts, cryptozoology (the Mothman and goblins), Crowleyean magick, the ancient god Pan, psi research, alien abduction, UFOs, window areas, angelic channeling, synchronicity, and some topics I dare not mention.[AF] The show has developed a cult following among fans due to the powerful subjective impact the show has on viewers. Many report the show being the catalyst for them being drawn into high strangeness phenomena, much in the same way as readers of *Cosmic Trigger* report.[AG] The official *Hellier* subreddit had 7,735 members as of August 2023.

The show has drawn remarkably mixed reviews and viewers seem to either love it or hate it. In fact, the creators even sell *Hellier* merchandise featuring the phrase "no goblins" and an image of a one-star-out-of-five rating, a reference to the most common negative review of the show. Greg Newkirk addressed this all or nothing response saying, "If you take a glance at the Amazon reviews ... you'll see that it has a nice solid, middle of the road, three-star rating, which is fine.... But what's really interesting" is that if you look closely "at it, 40% of those reviews are five-star reviews of people saying, 'This is what I wish other shows were doing.... This is real.' And then the other people are saying, 'You didn't find any goblins. No stars!'"[69] I will discuss possible reasons behind such intense negative reactions to *Hellier* in particular and high strangeness researchers in general in the next chapter.

Conversely, an intensely positive reception is evidenced by the unofficial *Hellier* subreddit called "Hellier Disciples" which currently has 627 members. The group is for fans of the show and "those who have had their own related experiences to share ideas and realizations." Members discuss their individual synchronicities and paranormal experience around the

AE The podcast *Penny Royal* is a great companion to the *Hellier* docuseries and features a deeper dive into the same subjects discussed in *Hellier*.

AF The theories associated with Amy's story in season 2 have become such a third rail in high strangeness that I'm not going to mention them in this volume.

AG This assertion is based on my observation of the *Cosmic Trigger* community for over twenty years and being involved in the *Hellier* community since the show first aired.

show's content, discuss such topics as Thelema, Enochian magick, and the psycho-spiritual impact of initiation-things which were rarely discussed in the mainstream paranormal community before *Hellier* aired.

High Strangeness Initiation

An extremely important component of the *Hellier* series is that it documents what a high strangeness initiation looks like. While RAW did a great job of documenting this in written form in his *Cosmic Trigger* trilogy, *Hellier* has given us, for the first time, film footage of the experience. RAW said his book "deals with a process of deliberately induced brain change. This process is called 'initiation' or 'vision quest' in many traditional societies."[58] If you haven't gone through a high strangeness initiation yourself, it is important that you pay attention to this section. An initiation is a "ceremony, ritual, test, or period of instruction with which a new member is admitted to an organization or … to knowledge"[70] and a spiritual initiation occurs "when we become conscious of the Divine within us, and thereby contact the Divine without us."[71]

One of the reasons I think *Hellier* received so much backlash is due to criticisms of the show from people who have not been through the powerful subjective experience of a high strangeness initiation and don't understand the significance of what the cast are experiencing on a personal level. It really is a case of *if you know, you know*. The show perhaps appears silly to the uninitiated because they have no personal frame of reference to understand what the *Hellier* team are going through on a subjective level. The ceremonies, rituals and instruction during an initiation are designed to evoke internal changes in the participant and those changes are hard to see objectively.

An initiation is, simply put, going from one state to another. Greg Newkirk says "underneath it all" the show is "about non-magicians becoming magicians and sharing that journey with the viewers – many of whom are becoming magicians themselves in the process." This learning process featured in the show attracted criticism from the occult world, seen in a post on the Hellier subreddit titled *The terrible research into the occult.* Newkirk responds saying "you're seeing the progression of people who know next to nothing about ritual magick slowly wading into the waters, making mistakes, talking to the right people and the wrong people, learning gematria, reading lots and lots of books...and trying to distill those things into something somewhat watchable for people.… We're monster hunters, not ritual magicians, so I get how it might be frustrating for someone who is steeped in Thelema to watch us learn."[72] To say the occult community in general and the Thelemic community in particular is a tough crowd would be a cosmic understatement. Newkirk was being very generous in his response to this critique and I point out that the *Hellier* team's occult research was certainly not terrible.

Of particular note and a fact extremely relevant to the My Cosmic Trigger project is that the *Hellier* team became magicians in response to their experiencing high strangeness on a deep, subjective level, undergoing a high strangeness initiation. I maintain this is the best course of action for researchers of these phenomena because I believe embracing a systematic psycho-spiritual practice is essential to navigating these waters and making sure the encounter with the phenomenon impacts one's life in a positive manner. My preferred psycho-spiritual approach is a magick of high strangeness, which I have begun elucidating in this text. Everyone is of course free to embrace the approach and tradition of their choice.

I think the concept of a high strangeness initiation is helpful because it shows the danger element involved in researching the phenomenon. The initiation process is life altering and anything life altering is dangerous. A person "who is ripe for development will unfold the higher consciousness rapidly" during an initiation but "the person who is not ready may find these influences profoundly disturbing."[73]A way to make sure one is ready is by embracing a psycho-spiritual practice. When someone finds these experiences "profoundly disturbing" they experience mental instability and find themselves in Chapel Perilous.

It is crucial to understand that the phenomena you encounter in this weird research is an initiation process.[AH] Keeping this fact squarely in your mind will help keep you sane and grow in a positive way from the experience. That being said, as we continue our journey through this text, remember the encounter with high strangeness "is much like that of the vision-quest of ancient American peoples: the person has a traumatic feeling of dissolution" and then "is often given some secret knowledge." This new secret knowledge often causes "a tremendous change of vocation" in the individual "often to shaman" who then "returns to help his people deal with the spirit ... world." However, "the problem" with an encounter of the phenomenon "is that most of us" are "unfamiliar with ancient techniques of initiation" and as a result "misinterpret the experiences with our own frame of reference ... and end up being unable to cope with them."[74] This book aims

AH I will explain what I think high strangeness researchers are being initiated into and why in the last chapter. Also, embracing the initiatory aspect of the phenomenon is a big part of my magick of high strangeness.

to provide the necessary theoretical and historical information regarding high strangeness to help the reader properly cope.

Personal Connection

The negative criticism against *Hellier* has been so intense that some people have urged me to simply not mention the show in this book. I feel so strongly about the importance of the show that I simply cannot follow that recommendation, regardless of the fallout. If you hate the show, then this book may not be for you. One reason I feel the show is so important is because of my personal connection to Allen Greenfield. His book *Secret Cipher of the UFOnauts* is a guiding principle of the show; there would be no *Hellier* without Greenfield's book. I started a daily correspondence via email with Greenfield circa 1999, my senior year of undergrad and it lasted until 2001. I sought his counsel about occult, UFO, and personal matters multiple times a day for almost three years straight; and for this reason I considered him my mentor.

When I first read *Secret Cipher* in 2000, I would have bet my life that the book would never find its way into the paranormal mainstream. Yet, here we are. Seeing Greenfield's work featured in *Hellier* was a major inspiration to write this book. I had kept the highly strange side of myself hidden, but seeing the *Hellier* show gain "mainstream" acclaim made me realize the world had finally gotten so strange it was ready to hear my story. I must confess, the other reasons the show inspired me to write this book were far less noble. Before writing this book I had been attempting to "make it" as a screenwriter for over twenty years and seeing *Hellier* Season 2 end up on Amazon Prime helped me see I may have more success as a writer if I fully embraced my weird side. And two, seeing the *Hellier* team go on about their highly strange encounters with Greenfield's work brought up my competitive side. I thought, "Oh, y'all think that is weird? Your Season 1 is just a normal weekend for me. I'll write my book to show these youngsters what high strangeness is really all about."

Conclusion

The exploration of high strangeness phenomena was an integral to the study of the paranormal at its inception, as evidenced by the work of Charles Fort. The early days of UFOlogy also embraced high strangeness, as evidenced in the pioneering work highlighted in this chapter. It is my belief that in recent times, paranormal disciplines have become overly specialized, with researchers narrowly focusing on specific aspects of the phenomenon such as UFOs or Bigfoot.

One of the primary objectives of this book is to facilitate the reunification of all paranormal subjects under the umbrella of high strangeness, allowing us to gain deeper insights into the enigmatic reality we inhabit. Furthermore, another objective is to foster a willingness among researchers of the phenomenon to delve into and embrace New Age literature, mirroring the approach taken by Timothy Green Beckley.

References

1. Mark O'Connell, *The Close Encounters Man: How One Man Made the World Believe in UFOs*, 2017.

2. Zak Ciotti, "The Quality of 'High Strangeness,'" Zak Ciotti: YouTube, Aug. 7, 2020.

3. J. Glazier, R. Evrard, N. Koumartzis, "Celebrating and Critiquing the Human Element of Exceptional Experiences," *Mindfield: the Bulletin of the Parapsychological Association,* vol. 13, Issue 3: *Exceptional Experiences Going Beyond the Human*, ParaPsych.org.

4. Chantel Tattoli, "Jacques Vallée Still Doesn't Know What UFOs Are," Wired.com, Feb. 18, 2022.

5. Jack Hunter, "Parapsychology and the Varieties of High Strangeness Experience," *Mindfield: The Bulletin of the Parapsychological Association*, vol. 13, Issue 3: *Exceptional Experiences Going Beyond the Human*, ParaPsych.org.

6. J. Allen Hynek, *The UFO Experience: A Scientific Inquiry*, 1979, p. 42.

7. J. Nathan Couch, "Joe Simonton and the UFO Pancakes: That Time Aliens Served Breakfast in Rural Wisconsin," CultofWeird.com.

8. Mike Cleland, *The Messengers: Owls, Synchronicity and the UFO Abductee*, 2015, p.44.

9. Wiktionary.org.

10. J. Allen Hynek, *The UFO Experience: A Scientific Inquiry,* 1972, p.217. The quote is from 1953 according to Hynek.

11. Chantel Tattoli, "Jacques Vallée Still Doesn't Know What UFOs Are," Wired.com, Feb. 22, 2022.

12. John Keel, *Operation Trojan Horse,* 1976 version, p.39, 156, first published 1970.

13. r/HighStrangeness, Reddit.com.

14. "Parapolitics," Wiktionary.org.

15. "Occult," Vocabulary.com.

16. Chris Knowles, "He Will Live Up in the Sky, The Tangled Web, and the Woke Virus," *The Higher Side Chats,* Feb. 5, 2020.

17. Peter Levenda, *Sinister Forces: A Grimoire of American Political Witchcraft, Volume 1: The Nine,* 2005, E-book: p. 264.

18. Peter Levenda, *Sinister Forces, A Grimoire of American Political Witchcraft, Book Three: The Manson Secret,* 2006, E-book: p. 676.

19. Michael Hoffman, *Twilight Language,* 2021, p. 25.

20. Charles Fort, *The Complete Books of Charles Fort: The Book of the Damned / Lo! / Wild Talents / New Lands,* publisher's summary, Feb. 1975.

21. Aurora Amidon, "The Sacred Frog Storm in *Magnolia,*" FilmSchoolRegects.com, Jan. 22, 2020.

22. Charles Fort, *The Book of the Damned: The Collected Works of Charles Fort,* 2008, E-book: p. 846.

23. AZquotes.com/author/5026-Charles_Fort

24. *The Matrix Control System of Philip K. Dick and the Paranormal Synchronicities of Timothy Green Beckley,* 2017, Amazon Kindle sample- 42%, 42%, 42%, 46%

25. John Keel Interview, *Late Night with David Letterman,* (1980) TheMothman. Fandom.com.

26. web.archive.org/web/20080928122012/http://forteantimes.com/features/commentary/396/the_23_phenomenon.html

27. Joshua Blu Buhs, "R. Buckminster Fuller as a Fortean," *From an Oblique Angle,* JoshuaBluBuhs.com. Buhs is also author of *Bigfoot: The Life and Times of a Legend.*

28. Fortean Research Center, *Journal of the Fortean Research Center,* Vol. 1, No. 1, April 1986.

29. Jacques Vallée, *Dimensions: A Casebook of Alien Contact,* 1988, p. 292.

30. Suzie Dundas, "Are UFOs Real? Close Encounters of the First, Second and Third Kinds," HowStuffWorks.com, Sep 30, 2021.

31. Greg M. Schwartz, "Close Encounters of the 4th Kind with the Sun Ra Arkestra in San Francisco," PopMatters.com, Aug. 21, 2017. In the article he claims the show was "akin to a CE4." I've been to a Sun Ra Arkestra show and I can confirm.

32. John Keel, *The Eighth Tower: On Ultraterrestrials and the Superspectrum,* 1975, p. 160.

33. Jacques Vallée, *Passport to Magonia: From Folklore to Flying Saucers,* 1969, pp. 149-150, 49.

34. Jacques Vallée, *Messengers of Deception: UFO Contacts and Cults,* 1979, p. 69.

35. *High Times* Greats: John Keel: The Astute Chronicler of the Bizarre, HighTimes.com, 2021.

36. David Clarke, "A New Demonology: John Keel and The Mothman Prophecies," in *Damned Facts: Fortean Essays on Religion, Folklore and the Paranormal,* edited by Jack Hunter, 2016.

37. "The Mothman Festival: A Legendary Celebration Draws Crowds in West Virginia," WVnews.com, Sept. 18, 2023.

38. Joal Ryan, "Biggest Movie Franchises: Marvel, Star Wars, Harry Potter and More Ranked by Box Office," CBSNews.com, Jan. 24, 2020.

39. John Keel, "UFOs, Mothman and Me," *High Times,* #57, May 1980.

40. Allen Greenfield, *Secret Rituals of the Men in Black,* 2005, p. 87.

41. John Keel, *The Eighth Tower: On Ultraterrestrials and the Superspectrum,* 1975. Anomalist Books' summary.

42. Pavithra George, "'Normalizing' UFOs: Retired U.S. Navy Pilot Recalls Tic Tac Encounter," Reuters, June 2021.

43. Brad Steiger, *Blue Book Files,* Canadian UFO Report, Vol. 4, 1977.

44. Mack White, "Heretic Among Heretics," Jan. 1997, recovered through WayBackMachine, BibliotecaPleyades.net/ciencia/ciencia_vallee08.htm.

45. Nathan Isaac, "As Above," *Penny Royal,* Season 2: Episode 7, 2022, 2:16.

46. Loren Coleman, "Saucer Smear's James W. Moseley Dies," CopyCatEffect.blogspot.com, 2012.

47. *Saucer Smear Magazine.* Amazon Kindle edition description, 2009.

48. "Gray Barker," Wikipedia.org.

49. Bob Wilkinson, *Shades of Gray,* Internet Movie Database, 2009.

50. Nathan Isaac, "As Above," *Penny Royal,* Season 2: Episode 7, 2022, 2:30.

51. Obituary of Timothy Green Beckley, /boylanfh.com/tribute/details/977/Timothy-Beckley/obituary.html.

52. Timothy Green Beckely, Amazon Author page.

53. Timothy Green Beckely, *The Dark Side of UFOlogy,* no. 33, see also, "UFOs: Wicked This Way Comes: The Dark Side of the Ultra-Terrestrials," September 2, 2013.

54. Paul and Ben Eno, "Strange Synchronicities with Timothy Green Buckley," *Behind the Paranormal*: #548, Aug 18, 2014.

55. Jordan Bates, "Reality Tunnels and E-Prime: A Taste of Robert Anton Wilson," JordanBates.com, July 2014.

56. Mykola Bilokonsky, "Introduction to Reality Tunnels: A Tool for Understanding the Postmodern World," Medium.com/Reality-Tunnels, Jan. 2017.

57. Pamela Holmes, "Reality Tunnels," ImaginalResonance.com, Aug. 2019.

58. Robert Anton Wilson, *Cosmic Trigger, (vol.1): Final Secret of the Illuminati,* 1977, E-book, pp. 21, 40, preface.

59. A.K. Wilks, "Pulling the Cosmic Trigger: The Contact Experiences of Philip K Dick & Robert Anton Wilson," ParanoiaMagazine.com, September 29, 2017.

60. Robert Anton Wilson, *Cosmic Trigger, Vol. 2: Down To Earth,* 1991, E-book: p. 114.

61. Erik Davis, *High Weirdness: Drugs, Esoterica, and Visionary Experience in the Seventies,* MIT Press summary, MITPress.MIT.edu., 2019.

62. David Opie, "*Stranger Things'* True Story Is Based on a Mind-Blowing CIA Experiment," DigitalSpy.com, Dec. 2021.

63. "Aleister Crowley and the 'Sirians,'" BibliotecaPleyades.net/ cienciareal/ cienciareal28.htm

64. Peter Moon, Preston Nichols, *Pyramids of Montauk: Explorations in Consciousness,*1995, pp. 15-16.

65. L. Sutin's *Do What Thou Wilt: A Life of Aleister Crowley,* 2000. Editorial reviews on the book's Amazon page.

66. Richard McNeff, "Crowley and Huxley: A Trip in Berlin?" *Fortean Times,* 409, Aug. 2021

67. Richard Spence, *Secret Agent 666: Aleister Crowley, British Intelligence and the Occult,* 2008, p. 289.

68. Aleister Crowley, *Liber II: The Message of The Master Therion,* first appeared in *The Equinox III(1),* 1919.

69. Patrick Cavanagh, "*Hellier* Producer Greg Newkirk Talks the Terror, Intrigue, and Goblins of Season 2," ComicBook.com, Nov. 2019.

70. Freedictionary.com.

71. Dion Fortune, *The Training and Work of the Initiate,* 1962, E-book: p. 35.

72. Reddit: u/GregNewkirk, r/Hellier, May 2021.

73. Dion Fortune, *Psychic Self-Defense,* 1930, E-book: p. 169.

74. Steve Mizrach, "UFOs Reconsidered as a Fortean Phenomenon." Also see Steven Mizrach, CyberFortean Anomaly Informationalist, anomalyarchives.org/ collections/ file/mizrach-steven/

Trey Hudson is the current Director of the Oxford Paranormal Society (OPS) and the Anomalous Studies and Observation Group (ASOG).

He entered college at the University of West Georgia and decided to major in psychology. UWG is home to a world-renowned psychology department and one of the few universities offering degrees with a humanistic and transpersonal focus. At the UWG psychology program Trey had a chance to study with such luminaries as William Roll, Mike Arons, Don Rice, Chris Anstoos and others.

Chapter 2

How High Strangeness Researchers are Viewed by Other Paranormal Fields and Why

Farming the figments of imagination in the symbolic order -
brings the truly-true truth to light,
as quickly as a star chart will uncover the nakedness of all mankind.
They fouled the root of that sound-sense,
found in the immensity – the spiritualist now holds.

High Strangeness Researchers Have No Table in the Cafeteria

Individuals conducting research into high strangeness phenomena often find themselves marginalized within conventional paranormal circles. To grasp the status of high strangeness investigators in comparison to their peers in the paranormal community, let's consider the imaginary scenario of lunchtime at an allegorical Paranormal High School.

If the study of the paranormal were a high school lunchroom, various research groups could be described thusly: the parapsychologists, who study psi-phenomena, would be the band nerds; the Bigfoot researchers would be the rednecks; the New Agers would be the Christian kids; the mind control researchers would be the potheads sitting on the wall outside; the JFK researchers would be the computer nerds; the UFO disclosure advocates would be the cool kids; and the occultists would be the goth table. The high strangeness researcher, the student who believes *all* paranormal phenomena intersect and are related to each other, would be shunned by each group in turn as they sheepishly tried to find a place to sit ... eventually winding up having to eat by themselves in a bathroom stall, quietly weeping in between bites of their sandwich, while reading an obscure book by John Keel.

This chapter will consider various explanations regarding the intensity and the focus of these responses. Please note that these reactions are present in *all* discussions on high strangeness; my following focus on *Hellier* is because it offers an excellent pop-culture case study.

Negative Reactions

The backlash mentioned in the first chapter experienced by the *Hellier* creators is, unfortunately, part and parcel of high strangeness research. Negative reactions towards anything high strangeness adjacent is very common and, sadly, the majority of this ill-feeling seems to come from inside the paranormal community, as opposed to the larger mainstream culture. Greg Newkirk speaks to this when he points out "the greater ghost / ufo / cryptozoology / etc. communities don't exactly find a lot of common ground with us" and are, in fact, "bothered by us."[1]

New community

As our earlier depiction illustrates, no established groups interested in the paranormal respect the high strangeness researcher. In addition, there is no high strangeness table in the cafeteria because there are so few of us. One of my goals with this book is to help solidify our small community, not just to help us find a seat at the other tables but to create our own table, as it were. G. Newkirk echoes similar thoughts, saying "At the end of the day, *Hellier* won't resonate with most people, but that's ok" because it "calls who it's meant to. In a lot of ways, it's a recruitment effort for a new community." He declares that their team isn't attempting to join the "wider paranormal community" because said community "won't accept us as peers anyway." I agree with him completely. Again, the key here is to solidify the high strangeness community, while also coming up with "new rituals" for high strangeness magick.[1]

But I also want to offer another approach, one that might help with acceptance from the other communities. I encourage people to embrace the Ferris Bueller archetype, happily bouncing from table to table. In the 1986 movie by John Hughes, *Ferris Bueller's Day Off,* Ferris was well liked by all communities of the school because of his affable personality. This is, of course, a difficult attitude to embrace given the years of exclusion and condescension. Mainly, I'm encouraging people to not fight fire with fire or to respond to ridicule with more ridicule. I'd like to encourage the students of high strangeness to take the high road, which I admit I'm not perfect at myself. Of course, I know full acceptance is a long walk. I doubt it will happen anytime soon but hope springs eternal. And embracing the Ferris Bueller archetype could prove to be a winning approach.

Jack of All Trades, Master of None

The simple fact is that high strangeness researchers have to investigate *everything* paranormal and it is *impossible* to be thoroughly knowledgeable in all areas, especially since one can't know what will emerge from the phenomenon. Recall the incident I mentioned in the previous chapter, where a ritual magician criticized the *Hellier* team for not being experts in magick. High strangeness researchers look at *everything* paranormal because we believe all of its subject areas are interrelated. This is in stark contrast to the other paranormal fields; as Keel observed: "Unfortunately, those interested in flying saucers had no interest at all in psychic phenomena, and vice versa. Those who were busy trying to trap a Bigfoot frowned upon all other forms of the weird and supernatural." I agree with him when he calls this unfortunate because "Abominable snow persons, poltergeist, frog rain-falls and UFOs are all interrelated" and as such you "can't possibly investigate one without some knowledge of the others."[2]

Desire for Acceptance in the Mainstream

I believe the reason high strangeness researchers are shunned from all tables is in part rooted in the desire to be accepted by the mainstream. Staying with our high school analogy, we can say the redneck table of Bigfoot researchers want to be seen by the school administration as a legitimate table; allowing the high strangeness freak to sit with them could get them in trouble with the principal, not to mention attract ridicule from fellow students. In fact, Bigfoot researchers are often very critical of anyone who suggests a theory of Bigfoot outside their traditionally accepted theory: that the creature is simply a previously unidentified, nocturnal North American great ape. To support this traditional point of view, they highlight that the mountain gorilla was seen as a myth up until 1902.[3]

They also proudly explain that the world's most famous primate researcher, Jane Goodall, is open to the possibility that there exists an undiscovered North American primate. She is, in fact, so open to this possibility that she agreed to give the keynote speech at the 2003 International Bigfoot Symposium and in 2023 told late night talk show host, Jimmy Kimmel, that she believed they may exist.[4]

Conventional Bigfoot researchers appear to desperately want acceptance from the mainstream scientific community. After all, what could be more mainstream in primate research than approval from Jane Goodall? Suggesting a paranormal aspect[A] to Bigfoot pushes this group further

A An example of a book discussing theories shunned by traditional bigfoot researchers can be found in *Where the Footprints End: High Strangeness and the Bigfoot Phenomenon* (Joshua Cutchin, Timothy Renner, 2020). The book considers intersections between bigfoot and other paranormal phenomena.

from their goal of acceptance because it makes them appear less substantial to the primate establishment (Big Monkey, one might say).

High strangeness researcher and author, Trey Hudson details the less-than-welcome response he has personally received from the mainstream Bigfoot research community. Hudson "claims to have witnessed some truly bizarre things" in his Bigfoot research and he has had experiences that have "made him consider that Bigfoot could be more than 'flesh and blood' and have special powers."[5] In his book *The Meadow Project: Explorations Into the South's Skinwalker Ranch,* Hudson talks about his experience of going to a Bigfoot conference, wearing a t-shirt bearing the name of his research group, "Oxford Paranormal Group." He reports receiving unpleasant, suspicious looks throughout the conference because he openly identified himself as someone interested in the paranormal. Hudson claims that during breaks in the conference, researchers sympathetic to the paranormal aspect of Bigfoot would secretly come up to him to share their personal experiences that they couldn't disclose openly.

Hudson's research into high strangeness (and my personal overlap with his research) will be explored in chapter 10. Briefly, I will point out that he attended the university I attended for graduate school where he majored in psychology. The University of West Georgia is "home to a world renowned psychology department and one of the few universities offering degrees with a humanistic and transpersonal focus." I also point out that he was "commissioned as a second lieutenant in the US Army and branched as Military Intelligence."[6] Again, notice the overlap with high strangeness research and Intelligence.

Podcast host Lauren Smith also talks about the derision high strangeness theories concerning Bigfoot receive in the mainstream community.[B] For example, according to Smith scorn is "prevalent in the community," if one shares any paranormal stories involving the creatures, such as those suggesting Bigfoot possesses psi abilities.[7] This same dynamic of derision is seen in the mainstream occult community, a dynamic I have personally witnessed first hand. I have been a member of the Ordo Templi Orientis (OTO) since 2001 and I acquired several of my books on high strangeness from a Dove and Serpent Oasis (the OTO body in Atlanta, Georgia) yard sale in 2011. For example, my copy of Timothy Green Beckley's *Sub-*

B L. Smith said this in her interview with high strangeness journalist, Mary Joyce. I highly recommend Joyce's research at skyshipsovercashiers.com and her books: *BIGFOOT – Beyond the footprints, Underground Military Bases Hidden in North Carolina Mountains, Cherokee Little People Were Real,* and *Tangible evidence of Jesus left behind for us to find.*

terranean Worlds Inside Earth bears a sticker that reads "This book belongs to: Dove & Serpent Oasis."

Some years before the yard sale, a previous body master who had been sympathetic to high strangeness subjects, apparently donated his Keel, Vallée, and Timothy Green Beckley books to the body's library before passing the mastership to another person. To the new leadership, apparently even having these books in the body's library was a bridge too far, as evidenced by selling them in a public yard sale. A "mainstream" occultist wouldn't be caught dead with high strangeness literature in their book collection. After all, in their opinion, practicing magick, is something respectable and academically rigorous. In my opinion, they desire to gain acceptance from the mainstream establishment, hoping to be seen as a more academic discipline – the way Buddhism is seen as a respectable area of study and practice in the academy.

Allen Greenfield's high strangeness research (looking at the intersection of UFOs and magick) was initially shunned by the mainstream occult world. For example, Greenfield maintains that "because of pressure from the Frater Superior" of a noted occult order he was part of, he did not publish the follow up to his 1994 book *Secret Cipher of the UFOnauts–Secret Rituals of the Men in Black*, which was not published until 2005. Greenfield reports that he was told the future of the occult belonged to academics and apparently not UFO researchers such as himself.[8] I do find it ironic that the *Hellier* docuseries did a lot more to popularize Thelemic magick, than a thousand fancy academic essays ever could.

These two books by Greenfield are in no way widely accepted within mainstream Crowley and magick circles. Because of the popular success of *Hellier* I think there might be a tendency for high strangeness researchers to mistakenly assume there is acceptance of Greenfield's assertions about a link between UFOlogy and magick, in mainstream occult circles. His pronouncements, such as: "the entire literature of magical invocation and evocation" can be seen as "a disguised transmission" of "Ultraterrestrial technology" and that "All serious magical rituals are hidden advanced technology" of Ultraterrestrials which have been our "puppet masters" "since ancient times" are viewed as utterly absurd by mainstream occultists.[9]

The Giggle Factor

Essentially, this is the desire for mainstream cultural acceptance by people who are trying to avoid affiliation to any topic that evokes laughter. This occurs when an idea or theory "appears too ridiculous to be seriously considered" resulting in it having a "high giggle factor."[10] Physicist Michio Kaku talks about how the giggle factor keeps scientists from studying the UFO phenomenon.[11] Plain and simple, no one wants to be laughed at.

Simple closed-mindedness

As established, a newcomer's impression that a paranormal enthusiast would be someone who, for example, believes in UFOs *and also* believes in Bigfoot is just a common misconception. This is based on the understandable notion that anyone who believes in one paranormal subject believes in all paranormal subjects. This couldn't be further from the truth.

I think *this* is due to *another* common misconception: people who are involved in the study of paranormal subjects must be open minded in general. To illustrate, I quote Joe Rogan when he said "the bigfoot world is pretty open minded" in the context of a joke he made with comedian Nate Bargatze. The premise of the joke rested on the misguided notion that the Bigfoot community was so open minded that if *they* thought somebody was full of crap then it *must* be true. Full disclosure, I do not know to whom they were referring to in the clip, but the fact remains – the fallacy of open-mindedness is so widespread it is not even questioned by people who don't research high strangeness in particular and the paranormal in general.[12]

On a personal level, during my 35 years of research of the paranormal I have not, generally, found the various paranormal disciplines to be open minded at all. Perhaps we could say they are open minded enough to embrace one field of paranormal research but once they embrace that subject the gates of open-mindedness close. A possible explanation is that most people only have the intellectual room (or emotional space) to be open-minded about one paranormal subject. To embrace one paranormal subject, for example that humans have latent psi powers, doesn't change one's overall world view too radically. To embrace the high strangeness world view that all paranormal phenomena intersect and are interrelated is a radical challenge to one's *paradigmatic* world view. Believing one weird thing, such as there is an undiscovered North American nocturnal primate, does not alter one's paradigm of reality too drastically. It is easier to keep believing the world is not that different than we're told, except for this one shiny detail.

High strangeness phenomena are so bizarre they challenge our understanding of reality itself, often creating cognitive dissonance in the process; which is the inner discomfort that arises when an individual encounters information that conflicts with their pre-existing beliefs. To resolve this tension people may reevaluate their belief systems or go into a psychological state of denial.

Boggle Threshold

The tendency to psychologically resist new information may be triggered by something called the boggle threshold. This term was coined "by the psychical researcher Renee Haynes, to describe the point at which even the most open-minded ufologist or parapsychologists cries 'enough is enough.'"[13] This subjective restraining tendency has steered mainstream parapsychological research away from studying the high strangeness phenomenon because it has a tendency to "place limits on the kinds of experiences that a study will take into consideration." However, "the sense of 'high strangeness' might well be a core underlying feature of extraordinary experience" and "instead of being neglected" by mainstream parapsychological researchers, "the 'deep weird' should be granted greater and renewed scholarly attention." Therefore, one may conclude this tendency towards restraint actually stops us from being able to see deeper and wider into things.

Another interesting outcome of staying under the boggle threshold, is that "the more outlandish elements of paranormal experience are often ignored" by parapsychologists and as a result "the responsibility to investigate them has often fallen to journalists and other popular writers."[14] I want to remind readers that John Keel was a journalist. He even pointed out the limited position this put him in, saying "I am not a scientist, theologian, or philosopher. I am only a reporter. My business is asking questions, not answering them."[15] Imagine how many more questions could be answered if other professions and academic disciplines got over their boggle threshold and started seriously studying high strangeness…

Trans-territorial

Given the hard territorial boundaries that exist in the different paranormal fields of research it is easy to see why high strangeness researchers (who maintain they are all connected) are not recognized or even acknowledged. People simply don't want their intellectual territory invaded by an outsider. This reaction is also seen in non-paranormal academia. The father of media studies, Marshall McLuhan (1911-1980), had his picture taken in every department at the University of Toronto (i.e.: anthropology, psychology, sociology, etc) to show that his school of media studies had implications for all departments. His overall work in general and such an act in particular, symbolized "his point that traditional modes of learning were dead" and such pedagogical approaches to highlight this fact, "served only further to madden his detractors" in the late 1960s.

According to McLuhan's son, Eric, "'there were at least two concerted efforts...to have his tenure revoked'" and "Such efforts would seem to put the lie to the shopworn contention ... that the rationale for the institution of tenure is the protection of freedom of thought." In actuality, the reaction to McLuhan demonstrated the sad reality that there is no group more "devoted to thought control than the self-perpetuating survival of the medieval guild known as the academic tenure committee." The university is "an institution whose foundations reach back to the Middle Ages"[16] and it is not shocking that quite often academics are not open to studying anything outside the box; especially given how the system is structured to reward specialization and the commodification of academic publications.[C]

Getting back to an academic study of the paranormal, Jack Hunter maintains there was an "historical shift from field-based psychical research to laboratory based parapsychology" that "resulted in a disconnect between psi research and the actual lived experience of the paranormal." High strangeness is found in the lived experience, not the laboratory – a statement that holds true for any meaningful human experience. High strangeness transcends "the neat categories of experiences that have been compiled by researchers" because the experiences of the phenomenon "merge and overlap with one another in the flux of real-life experiences."[17] High strangeness phenomena fall by the wayside in paranormal research simply because they are too hard to classify using the traditional classification system.

Tough crowd

Another factor that leads to the omission of high strangeness by other paranormal fields may be due to the fact people into the paranormal are simply a tough crowd. This phrase is often used in stand-up comedy and means a crowd that is difficult to make laugh. Of course, this begs the question as to why they are a tough crowd, for insight we turn to Keel, who says when he was first tasked with writing an article on the UFO phenomenon by *Playboy* in 1966, he found "people who called themselves experts" but were "all wallowing in egocentric delusions of self-importance"

C See, *Publish AND perish: how the commodification of scientific publishing is undermining both science and the public good*, transformativelearning.education, April, 2018.

and were "all feuding with their fellow experts."[2] In my opinion this is an apt description of the worst of the occult community and is based on my personal experience for over the last twenty years. Egocentric delusions, seldom make a receptive audience.

This is also a good time to point out that the field of high strangeness is not one big happy family. For example, some people in the high strangeness field are very against the *Hellier* project. There are some in high strangeness that believe anything having to do with the occult is evil, and the *Hellier* team did embrace magick and Crowley in the show. There are some Christian based high strangeness researchers who believe anyone who isn't overtly a Christian in the traditional sense is a tool for the devil. Also, the hyper polarized political climate of the United States has not escaped the high strangeness community so there are camps forming along those lines which adds to the tensions. In short, there is little consensus and group spirit. If a highly strange table was given to us at Paranormal Highschool we would probably end up in a food fight with each other.

However, I'm *a uniter not a divider*[D] and I advocate for a big tent approach to the field of high strangeness. The notion of a big tent is most often used in politics and calls for "a widely inclusive composition" of a group which then "allows people of differing backgrounds, opinions, and interests to be members of a group."[18] This is not to say I'm against a good spirited debate but I am advocating we all find some common ground, and collaborate through our differences as us folks into high strangeness have enough enemies in the world right now. I also point out that, to the outside world, we all look pretty much the same anyway. So, from that point of view, fighting over how many angels can dance on the head of a pin looks somewhat silly.

Different findings

Let's now explore the final significant factor contributing to the strong negative response toward research on high strangeness, with *Hellier* serving as an illustrative example. This specific aspect also sheds light on potential sources of intensely positive reactions in similar contexts. Researchers exploring high strangeness are proposing novel theories that challenge historically accepted conclusions in traditional paranormal fields.

D Yes, I know Bush Jr. said this and as such I am using it in a tongue and check manner. A good book on his father's presidency is: *Dark Alliance: The CIA, the Contras, and the Crack Cocaine Explosion* (Gary Webb, 1996). As of Jan. 2024 this book is rated #31 in Writing & Publishing and #34 in Law Enforcement Politics, on Amazon.com.

The traditional Bigfoot establishment have already made up their minds regarding what the elusive creature is and "If you are not extremely scientific based, flesh and blood, data collection, evidence, you are not a real researcher" in their eyes and as a result "are scoffed at." This mindset is frustrating to highly strange bigfoot researchers because there are "so many that have had alternate experiences," such as having telepathic encounters and "gifting" experiences with Bigfoot. The fact that the mainstream Bigfoot community pushes people away who have had such weird encounters is a shame because "we need to study all the facets of this topic in order to learn what this is."[7]

Greg Newkirk ponders why *Hellier* was "met with so much aggression" from members of various mainstream paranormal communities, "the old guard." He concludes that despite whatever reason they give, it is because the findings of their show, "scares them because so much of it is uncharted territory through the forests they feel like they've already sufficiently explored."[1] In other words, the old guard believes they have already discovered the truth of their respective paranormal field and anybody who offers an alternative explanation is viewed with suspicion at best and derision at worst.

Furthermore, G. Newkirk also points out that "It's not easy to make a project" such as *Hellier* because "people who want literal goblins get super angry when we don't give them what TV has trained them to expect: blurry thermal footage" of a "'goblin.'" The first season of the series starts with the researchers searching for Kentucky cave goblins and ends with them finding ... wait for it ... a *tin can.*

Yes, you read that correctly. The climax of the show's first season is centered around an old, discarded tin can. The researchers of the show started out their paranormal research careers as traditional ghost hunters of the type seen on cable TV shows. Many *Hellier* viewers, therefore, tuned in expecting to see typical evidence of paranormal activity presented in those types of shows: EVPs (electronic voice phenomena) and anomalies caught on film. They were not expecting to be drawn into a tale of high strangeness where the climax was, simply, trash.[19]

Intense – But Positive – Reactions To High Strangeness Research

High strangeness projects like *Hellier* turn some viewers off for the very reasons some people, such as myself, have extremely positive reactions to the material. Viewers watching *Hellier* who were already fans of high strangeness research were beyond pleasantly surprised when the series turned out to be so much more than a regular, run-of-the-mill ghost hunting TV show. We got a genuine tale of high strangeness, a continuation of the Mothman mystery and, for people like me and mine, there is nothing more interesting.

The season 1 finale, wherein the team find their tin can (a long story that is best explained by watching *Hellier*), and the focus on discarded mylar balloons in the second season appear the most absurd thing possible to normal, mainstream paranormal investigators hoping to see footage of something spooky. To initiates of high strangeness, the seeming triviality of mylar balloons and a tin can are specifically what *made* the show; there is already a precedent regarding the cosmic significance of cans in particular and trash in general in the work of a godfather of high strangeness: Philip K. Dick (1928-1982).

At the time of writing this book, Philip K. Dick barely needs an introduction. Following his death in 1982, his book *Do Androids Dream of Electric Sheep* was adapted into the film *Blade Runner* and "since then, no fewer than 10 other motion pictures have been based on his work, including 'Total Recall' and 'Minority Report.'" There is also a TV series on Amazon Prime based on his book *The Man in the High Castle* about an alternate timeline where the Nazis won WW2. Dick is "widely regarded as one of the most conceptually innovative writers in the 20th century."[20]

VALIS and Cosmic Trash

Philip K. Dick

The psychedelic, Gnostic-Christian space opera of a sci-fi novel – *VALIS* – was reportedly based on real life experiences. Dick claimed to have been beamed information directly into his brain by V.A.L.I.S (Vast Active Living Intelligence System), a benevolent, sentient, Gnostic-Cyber-Quantum space-god … or *something* like that.

The experience in question occurred in 1974: while recovering from dental surgery, medications were delivered to him by a woman wearing a necklace with a fish pendant that was "a symbol of early Christianity" and after seeing the symbol he was triggered to see "a mysterious flash of pink light and collapsed onto his bed." Dick speculated that "the pink light was a spiritual force activated by the fish pendant" and while he lay "in bed, visions of abstract paintings appeared, followed by philosophical ideas and engineering blueprints." These visions continued over the next few months and during them he "caught glimpses of a strange, humanoid being," deciding that "it was a benign deity that could 'enter anything, animate or inanimate' and 'take volitional control of causal processes.'" Dick also saw "three-eyed extraterrestrials who warned there was a cosmic" plot at play in the assassinations of the Kennedys and Martin Luther King, Jr. He was told the "ancient Roman Empire, stealthily hidden over the centuries but still active, was responsible." On top of that "Nixon was a modern Caesar" and now Dick "felt guided by helpful spirits" one of which "he believed to be an ancient Christian revolutionary." I must say, that was one hell of a delivery woman![21,E]

To provide further, highly strange context for this prophecy, I quote RAW, when he pointed out that "MLK had introduced Gandhi's nonviolent tactics" when he "finally ... took a public stand against the Vietnam War" and then "Senator Robert Kennedy called for a halt in the bombing." As a result of these individuals "public sentiment was turning against the war ... but King and Kennedy would both be assassinated within a year – by two of the 'deranged lone assassins' who were becoming as common in America then as crushed beer cans on a beach."[22]

The notion that a secret Roman Empire was still active in perpetuating evil in the world was seen in Dick's often repeated phrase: The Empire never ended. RAW also speaks to this idea when he conveys a notion communicated to him by legendary Zen philosopher Alan Watts. RAW reports that Watts told him the "'greatest error of historians' ... 'is the idea that the Roman Empire fell. It never fell. It still runs the Western world, through the Vatican and the Mafia.'" RAW said this idea was so utterly absurd when he first heard it that "I didn't believe ... it; I thought it was one of [Watt's] jokes. Now I wonder."[22] Thinking something is an utterly absurd joke and then realizing it may be a reality is a hallmark of high strangeness research. The theory that the Roman empire never ended, is echoed in the following by a co-founder of the psychoanalytic movement, Otto Rank[F] (1884-1939), when he said: "Although a disintegrating Roman Empire was finished off by the Barbarian invasion from the North it survived spiritually in and through Christianity."[23]

E Kyle Arnold is a psychologist at Coney Island Hospital and Clinical Assistant Professor of Psychiatry at SUNY Downstate Medical Center in Brooklyn, New York. He is the author of *The Divine Madness of Philip K. Dick*. There is the question of whether Dick was simply "crazy" but I will not explore that in this text, for more info, see Arnold's book.

F Carl "Rogers was transformed by" lectures given by rank in 1936 "and always credited Rank with having profoundly shaped 'client-centered' therapy and the entire profession of counseling" (wiki/Otto Rank), Also see, *Acts of Will: the life and work of Otto Rank* by E. James Licherman, M.D.

At any rate, after this mystical experience, Dick became "obsessed with his close encounter with the pink light" and in "Trying to make sense of it, he wrote an 8,000 page commentary he called his Exegesis."[24,G] The author's estate was even against publishing the *Exegesis,* fearing it would attract "unwelcome attention and threatened to undermine their father's growing academic and literary reputation with its disreputable aura of high weirdness."[20] Again, notice the negative light that high strangeness is viewed by the mainstream establishment of whatever discipline in question.

Cosmic Trash

In his seminal novel, *VALIS,* Dick claimed "the symbols of the divine initially show up at the trash stratum."[H,25] The concept of cosmic mysteries being revealed in trash is an important motif for Dick and explored in Gabriel McKee's *Pink Beams of Light from the God in the Gutter: The Science-Fictional Religion of Philip K. Dick* (2003). To better understand what Dick was getting at vis-á-vis divine symbols showing up in the "trash stratum" we will turn to his writing on the subject in his non-fiction, *Exegesis*.

First, let's look at exactly what was showing up in the trash. Dick referred to it by several names: VALIS, Zebra, "ubik, the logos … or the plasmate." He described this multi-named entity as an "info-firing … quasi-energy … non-humanoid life form" that was from "millions of years in the future."[26] For clarity we will refer to this entity as VALIS,[I] which he claims "is a Creator God" that is "building a (new) earth *out of* … the old". Coming through as the "'debris discarded'" is how this entity "enters our world:" – "camouflaged" as the "trash stratum" where it is "becoming steadily stronger."[26] It can become stronger in the trash stratum because there it is, unmolested by the *black iron prison.* VALIS has decided this is the best way to manifest itself in our reality because it "may have fore-

G "In it, he proposed that the source of the pink light may have been God, the KGB, a satellite, aliens, a 1st century Christian named Thomas with whom he was in telepathic communication, the CIA, a version of himself from a different dimension, or possibly his deceased twin sister contacting him from the spirit world. Each new theory seemed to telescope outward into further possible theories, ad infinitum." Endnote: 24.

H In the VALIS opera by Tod Machover, it is sung that VALIS was once seen as a "beer can run over by a taxi." (song: Pt. 2: Valis), media.mit.edu/events/valis-an-opera-by-tod-machover/

I I am aware that in *Secret Cipher of the UFOnauts* Greenfield refers to VALIS as being evil, saying Dick "wrestled through his literary career and secret life as a Christian Gnostic philosopher with whether VALIS was a benevolent, if machine-like deity … or an insane extraterrestrial super computer." I respectfully disagree with Greenfield saying "The Black Lodge may be defined as the organized institution guided by VALIS for the purpose of holding back human evolution" (p. 81, 82). I also believe that Dick's *Exegesis* clears up the question as to if Dick thought VALIS was "benevolent" or evil; Dick refers to VALIS, over and over, in a positive manner.

seen" our current world predicament, where *the empire never ended* and the black iron prison (or the Matrix) reigns supreme. Seeing our future predicament, it "put into action the salvific[J] response: to penetrate the lowest" level of physical reality.[26]

This level Dick called "the trash stratum ... is debased" and he said that VALIS manifesting in this utterly absurd way, was designed to "reverse" the current, fallen state of the world. Saying, "In essence what I have done ... is locate a sacerdotal[K] power buried in the trash layer"[26] and it is in the trash layer that we find the redeeming power for "this world." Sifting through the trash layer for this divine redeeming power is a major aspect of high strangeness magick.

As I pointed out, VALIS must camouflage itself in the trash stratum because: "it has an opponent" which is, "the Black Iron Prison" or "the Empire" which is now "back and stronger than ever."[26] Dicks says that, "In a startling response to the crisis" of a re-emerged, evil empire, VALIS "takes on the likeness [of] cans in gutters ... trash discarded," where it waits, "lurking."[26] Also, responding to this crisis is an "underground Christian resistance" that is "dedicated" to fighting the evil empire.[26] This battle is "the dialectical struggle of two historical constants:" good and evil and this heavenly battle, "gives rise to Valis the Cosmic Christ."[26] Long story short, Dick is something like Neo in *The Matrix* and you, the one reading this book, are tasked with toppling the Matrix. No pressure.

Unfortunately, high strangeness mysticism is rarely warm and fuzzy, meaning VALIS is "The remedy" to this dire situation but it is also "the malady" for people who subjectively encounter it. This is because VALIS "literally ambushes reality and us as well" and in "very truth attacks and injures us, in his role as antidote," finally pointing out that "it is a scary experience to encounter this."[26] I believe Dick is explaining an aspect of, what I'm terming, a high strangeness initiation.

Note the disease and cure function of VALIS, which I mentioned in the introduction of this text, in regards to reading *Cosmic Trigger* for the first time. RAW's book can push someone into Chapel Perilous but also help them get out at the same time, making it hard to determine if the book was the disease or the cure. I will explore these topics at length in volume two of this series: *My Cosmic Trigger: perilous chapels and highly strange magick*. However, through the trash stratum, VALIS will "'con-

J Meaning, "having the intent or power to save or redeem". (Merriam-Webster)

K "The IRS has indicated that the term 'sacerdotal functions' generally includes performing baptisms, communion, marriages, and funerals." (nonprofitcpa.com). I thought it was funny that the IRS defines what is sacred in our culture. If the IRS says it, then it must be true.

spire' to signal people information" and this information is meant to "aid us." It aids us because VALIS' message is a "Pansophiaistic' message": a message of universal knowledge.[26] Keeping the Pansophiaistic message of VALIS in mind during a high strangeness initiation will help the person successfully navigate Chapel Perilous.

Lest we forget – the message of VALIS is one of hope, reminding us that in our modern times "things are inside out (but will at the 'Apocalypse' assume their real shape)." And because "things are inside out" at present, the "right place to look for the" divine is in "the trash in the alley" and to look "for Satan: in vast cathedrals." This topsy-turvy reality of the divine being relegated to the trash and evil given the place of prestige is a message of hope because: "Through enantiodromia they will 'on that day' assume their rightful shapes:" meaning, evil will go to the gutter and the divine will return to the cathedrals. Dick refers to this process as "the great reversal."[26] Carl Jung described enantiodromia as "the most marvellous [sic] of all psychological laws," because it is "the regulative function of opposites … running contrariwise" which means "that sooner or later everything runs into its opposite."[27]

Pivoting back to *Hellier*'s cosmic can and balloons, Dick reminds viewers that VALIS shows us that "the trash of the alley [is] a major event, and not to be ignored or forgotten" because it represents a "transformation of the landscape" into a "vision of the next world." Meaning, we can go from "this world … to the Spiritual Universe" because it is "immediately at hand, if we could but see it."[26] Highly strange trash shows us this reality. The finale of *Hellier* was not mere trash, but was a small glimpse of a vision of the next world, a spiritual universe of peace.

The above detour helps explain why there was such a positive response to the *Hellier* season one finale of utterly absurd trash. Keep in mind that the team didn't learn of the importance of cosmic trash vis-á-vis Dick's *VALIS* until a year later when the host of the *Talking Weird* podcast brought it up to them.[19] While I'm not claiming that every viewer of the show knew of Dick's writing on the importance of divine trash, I am saying that a viewer initiated into high strangeness intuitively grokked[L] the importance of the tin can and discarded balloons. This is because evidence of a case being valid, according to high strangeness research protocol, is the presence of the *utterly absurd*. What is more absurd than concluding the climax of your paranormal case (and docuseries) with a discarded tin can that symbolizes the triumph of good over evil?

L Grok: to understand profoundly and intuitively (Merriam-Webster).

Both positive and negative responses to the tin can and mylar balloons in *Hellier* highlight a hallmark of high strangeness research: the phenomenon is a case of – if you know, you know. In this regard, Carolyn Lovewell[M] says, "it's a funny curse that stories about synchronicities are rarely impressive when they are told second hand – they're very impressive when you experience the lived reality of their unfolding."[28] Terence McKenna is another guide in this regard, explaining "much of my thinking is not rationally ... defendable" because "it comes basically from a strong intuition or a kind of visionary expostulation."[29]

Personal connection

Cosmic Trash

In the original version of this book project, *My Cosmic Trigger Finger is Broken* (1999), I wrote about one of the strange experiences that occurred during my first initiation into high strangeness. This experience involved ultraterrestrials signaling information in the *trash stratum*. The following excerpt is from my original manuscript:

> The next incident that happened at my painting job involved an image of an alien in the dirt. One day we had to clean up a bunch of paint drops that we had accidentally dropped all over the stairwell floors one day while painting. Our boss (once nicknamed *the quaalude kid*) made us clean them up with paint thinner and rags, all nine floors. After we were done one of the workers opened up his rag and pointed out the dirt on his rag. Sure enough the paint on the rag looked like an alien with his hand raised and what appeared to be the silhouette of a human face in the corner. I asked if I could have the rag and he let me have it ... The guy with the rag was also into weird stuff. I had discussed various New age type philosophies with him and he had shared some of his out of body experiences with me ... I [later] showed the rag to everybody. Some thought it was simply dirt but others actually were freaked out by it and agreed that it looked like an alien. One person who saw it ... even said he thought it was some sort of a sign.[30]

Around that same time a close friend, who was into high strangeness subjects, believe it or not, also encountered a similar message in the trash

M Carolyn Elliot (now Lovewell) is one of the most creative and culturally relevant magicians today. Her DARE course on liminal magick, "the magick behind high strangeness," helped inspire this book (Carolyngraceelliott.com/dare) Also, see her book, *Existential Kink: Unmask Your Shadow and Embrace Your Power (A method for getting what you want by getting off on what you don't).*

stratum. After I told him about the "alien rag" he shared a similar story that had recently happened to him, while working in a factory as a supervisor, his summer job. He reported that workers came to him because they had encountered an image of what appeared to be an alien fetus in the dust on the factory floor. If I'm not mistaken these workers were mostly Latinos, so they may have been freaked out from a religious perspective (a la the phenomenon of seeing Jesus' image pop-up in unusual places). He claimed one even suggested they use tape to preserve the image. My friend said his response was to quickly wipe the dust away and tell them to get back to work, even though he confirmed it appeared to be an alien fetus in remarkable detail.

These are two examples of utterly absurd, high strangeness type encounters with "extraterrestrials." Looking back at the original manuscript, I find it interesting that right before I spoke of my "Alien Rag" experience, I wrote the following about another person on the college paint crew who had a nuts and bolts encounter with aliens:

> He also thought aliens had played a big role in the past of humanity and also thought they were the gods and angels of the Bible. We frequently talked about the subject and over our lunch break one day while we were discussing Nostradamus, he told me that he felt like he had 'something big to do'...In 'something big to do' I took it to mean in regards to the future of humanity. I laughed and told him I had been thinking the same thing about myself. After the summer was over we lost touch. I would see him on campus sometimes, he mentioned … that he thought he and his girlfriend had been abducted and he thought they had some sort of implant in them … By the way this guy was not all that weird of a guy. He had short hair, was an R.A. of a dorm at one time, I believe played the guitar, and had never smoked pot. He looked and acted like a typical American college student.[30]

I think these two types of encounters sum up the difference between a normal extraterrestrial encounter and a highly strange one. One involves something utterly absurd (messages in the trash) and the other involves nuts and bolts alien technology (implants). If I were to have to choose, I'd rather receive a dirty rag as opposed to an implant. And looking back on that summer painting dorm rooms, I'm amazed regarding how much high strangeness was occurring with this ordinary college student paint crew, even taking into account all the fumes we inhaled.

In the original manuscript I also featured a friend's reply to the above alien rag story. I had met this friend in an online group that centered around synchronicities with the number 22, called the *22 Numerotropic Group*. I can not stress enough how rare the repeating number phenomenon was in the late 90s, so it was quite amazing to find this group. My friend was in his 70s, which felt ancient to a college student in his 20s and he was writing a sci-fi book based around the idea of Jesus being an extraterrestrial.

The online group we belonged to was started by an individual named Terry Alden[N] who wrote the essay, *The 22 Enigma,* first published on the Internet in 1995. The essay detailed "personal experiences of intensive synchronicity ... involving the number 22" and "compares his experiences ... with the exactly parallel experiences of" RAW and his encounters with 23. Alden said he also "discovered that a number of other persons share the experience of synchronicity with the number, 22. [Who] sent in email messages to the author telling their own stories"[31] and as it so happened me and my friend were some of those people. My older friend had this to say after reading my "Alien Rag" story:

> About 20 years ago, a friend of mine visited Israel. She gave me a small stone she had randomly picked up in a river bank, something for me to have from the Holy Land. It wasn't 'till after the movie *Close Encounters* that I noticed an image on this stone strikingly similar to an alien! Now think about it. Of all the millions of stones in that river, not to mention all of Israel, what made her choose that one?[30,O]

Green Light

Like Dick and Keel[P] I also had a mysterious encounter with an anomalous light. Dick and Keel's light was pink but mine was a green light, which I wrote about in my early manuscript:

N "Alden's thought-provoking discussion covers reality and magic, astronomy, nuclear fission, and the significance of the tarot. Simultaneously, Alden weaves in examples of 22 appearing throughout his life. He refers to the experience as a possible 'obsession' and admits the difficulty in proving it to anyone without similar experiences. Alden believes that by sharing his experience others will not feel as alone and uncomfortable as he did before being able to put the 'phenomenon into some kind of context.'" *Number Synchronicity: A Beacon of Light for the Soul's Journey* by Skot Jonz, 2004.

O Of course, one can easily dismiss these experiences as pareidolia (the brain's tendency to see faces in things). What adds to the weirdness, in my opinion, is both me and my friend having alien dirt encounters in the same Summer. What are the odds? You are free to make up your own story, but I do not have the space, time or interest in discussing alternative explanations as I said in the introduction. I will explore the line between psychosis and high strangeness initiation in Vol. 2 of this series. I also remind the skeptic that an East Carolina – Summer dorm-room paint crew – in the 90s, is such an intense experience that their feeble minds can't comprehend it.

P "When he was 18, he had a strange (but classic) illumination experience in his furnished room on times Square. He remembered the room 'filled with an indescribable light, a pinkish glow'; and his mind 'flooded with a torrent of information.'" *John Keel's Anomaly Newsletter 1969-1976*, Dr. Raymond W Boeche.

> When I was 17 years old junior in high school … I had what I call the green light experience. I had just turned out the light to go to bed. About 2 minutes after I had turned out the light I saw out of the corner of my eye a green light. I turned to face it and it started getting bigger and closer until all I could see was the green light in my vision. The whole incident lasted around 10 seconds … After the light went away I immediately ran into my parent's bedroom to tell them what had just happened … What do I think the green light experience means? … I pondered the question one time while under the influence [of an entheogen], which I took with the sole purpose to write in my journal and see if I gained any insight into some of the things I had been experiencing and researching. On 3/18/1998, I wrote: "The green light I think was the initial implantation of the Aliens to start me on my mission. But I really can't say for sure what I think it means because I just don't know. I mean, I think it means something but I'm not certain."

In my original manuscript I also included the following, from the director of an obscure (but respected) occult order. After reading about my encounter with the green light, he said:

> I had a rather odd dream about five years ago that involved being followed by a ball of green fire/light. It was in the midst of what Lilly would call Cosmic Control Central experiences, and I regarded it as a form of Contact from a sentient praeterhuman entity.[30]

Pink

The color pink featured in a channeling I witnessed and recorded in graduate school, which I called *The Channeled Messages From the Carrollton Vortex*[Q] (see chapter 3 and 10). The reason I call this a channeling is because the person I was with (who was quite naive to most subjects on the paranormal) appeared to have their consciousness taken over by an outside force and started giving me messages from a representative of the "light command." This representative implored me to "keep up with the life wave." The life wave is a complex concept important to Theosophy and has to do with "The evolutionary force … which is sent out by the LOGOS [and] Speaking generally, this Life-Wave descends through the spheres of matter, causing ever-increasing differentiation, and then returns, causing reintegration into unity."[31.1] The channel enigmatically kept saying the word "pink" and then "pink sea shells." The channel had no awareness

Q See my, collection of essays, *The Red Planet Arrives*, by Tanranin Uhcheek Gozaknee, Scribd.com/document/205582634/Tanranin-Uhcheek-Gozaknee-The-Red-Planet-Arrives

of, or previous exposure to any use of the term life wave or significance of pink in Dick's work. At the time I had heard of Dick's pink light experience but had never heard of the Theosophical concept of a life wave.

Hagia Sophia

The term Sophia / Hagia Sophia is explored extensively in Dick's fiction and non-fiction writing. In his novel *VALIS,* the characters meet "the divine child Sophia (a gnostic Wisdom figure who, like VALIS, is also a sentient AI)" and her message to them is a "humanist revision of Jesus' beautiful Sermon on the Mount." In the novel there are two characters based on Dick: Horselover Fat and Phil Dick, a literary device showing two sides of his personality – the skeptic and believer. At the end of *VALIS,* Horselover Fat flies overseas to visit Hagia Sophia (among other locations), to look "for the Messiah [while] Dick is left alone in front of his TV, looking for secret messages from VALIS."[32] Notice that this covers two sides of high strangeness research: looking for the divine in the trash stratum (i.e. pop culture) and visiting sacred sites.

Hagia Sophia was built in 537 AD in modern day Istanbul, then Constantinople. The name translates from Greek to mean "Holy Wisdom" and is highly symbolic, reflecting the spiritual significance of the structure. It was an Orthodox cathedral until the Ottoman conquest of Constantinople in 1453 when it was turned into a mosque. It was a mosque until 1935, when it was turned into a museum by the founder of the modern Turkish Republic, Ataturk. And then in 2020 it was turned back into a mosque by the current president of Turkey.

In his non-fiction writing, Dick wrote about the spiritual concept of Hagia Sophia, saying: "A human can evolve into Christ if … Christ, as Hagia Sophia, can ignite himself in a man" and when this occurs "the man rises" remembering "all and knows himself by means of Christ as inner light."[26] He also speculates that "Hagia Sophia herself" not his "mere subconscious" was the "cosmic divine mind … which generates" his writing and was the reality he "inhabited in 3-74,"[26] the date of his mystical experience.

Noted author, Peter Mark Adams wrote a seminal book on the spiritual significance of the physical Hagia Sophia which echo the above ideas presented by Dick. Adams' book "is a study of the esoteric doctrines … encoded within the Hagia Sophia, as manifested in its structural and decorative design." And that the building "encodes its spiritual agenda, in stone, resonance and light." He claims the building is an outgrowth of the

Eleusian mysteries, which "For almost a thousand years … had been the greatest sanctuary within the ancient world, and its rites the most revered and archaic mysteries of the gods."[R]

In the book Adams asserts that the Eleusinian sanctuary was "destroyed by monks" in 392 and then "the holders of the thousand year old initiatory lineage embarked upon a mission to preserve the essential core of its spiritual message." In this preservation effort, the building was then "Designed by initiates of the school of Alexandria" who encapsulated into its design "the metaphysics of spiritual union as taught within the Eleusinian tradition." This inspired creation of the building was "in defiance of Imperial religious … oppression" and was done "to preserve a true, faithful and timeless narrative of spirituality." Adams says that presenting this secret history of the building in his book is "ultimately, about the recovery of a shared spiritual legacy of which the esoteric communities of today are direct spiritual descendants."[33]

I've met Adams personally in Istanbul and he gave me some helpful feedback on my book. Regularly on my walks in the mystical city I go to where I can view Hagia Sophia and do my meditations, while contemplating Dick and Adams' writings on Hagia Sophia and the New Age concept: Krystal Star Spires.[S]

Conclusion

I find the following statement a wonderfully pithy summary of high strangeness: "Robert Anton Wilson, Kerry Thornley, John Keel, Terence McKenna and many many more have tried to communicate to others the nature of their interaction with the phenomena. And they have given it various names … But in many ways it's ineffable." We can say this because the synchronicities one encounters in this research are "often such a personal experience" in that they "possess so much meaning for one person" and "bring so many elements together into a significant moment for a particular individual" but, they "don't translate when describ-

R I was told by a Turkish colleague that it is common knowledge that Hagia Sophia was built on top an earlier "pagan" temple like many other ancient churches.

S As outside forces are "running corrected frequencies and life force patterns into the planetary grid network, there is a systematic process of rehabilitation happening in their coordinate locations on the planetary grid. These Krystal Star Spires (Kisses Network) are able to run living energy fields back into the earth.… This strengthens the planetary body and is acting as a buffer field that is building to protect the entire planetary body and all of her inhabitants. This field is building new Ascension" and is "a literal 'cutting off' of the power plant and from other timelines being used [by] the Fallen Angelic network. The cutting off of the actual power source … being used this way rendered the NAA [Negative Alien Agenda] system in the Middle East inactive." (Krystal Star Spires, AscensionGlossary.com)

ing that experience to another person." One reason for this is because "The phenomena and the associated magic are responsive in a personally reflexive way."[34]

The balloons and tin can findings of *Hellier* help a high strangeness researcher attune themselves toward the *ineffable evidence* we are looking for. We are not looking for evidence that can be presented on CNN, FOX News, or at a fancy academic conference. Our evidence is extremely personal, highly subjective, utterly absurd, and is sometimes found in the literal trash. This book does not seek to prove the validity of the high strangeness phenomenon to mainstream paranormal researchers (or god help me, skeptics), this book is about helping high strangeness initiates better understand their interactions with the phenomenon. Full stop.

I also argue the high strangeness phenomenon cannot be proven in the traditional way and perhaps we can say it doesn't *want* to be proven in this way. The way it manifests may actually be an occluding function, designed to mask its detection from foul cosmic forces, that have "the purpose of holding back human evolution."[35] Greenfield's theories of how the cipher of ultraterrestrials may be used, is similar to Dick's idea on how VALIS uses the trash stratum to send messages. Meaning, these aren't explicit messages but are occluded messages. He points out that the secret cipher consists of "strange spellings of conventional names" that are in actuality "coded messages" which speak "of Aeons-old communication between human and ultraterrestrial forces warring for control of earth."

He explains why it would be useful in such a situation, saying "The cipher employs no telepathy, no 'high tech devices' and relies on several subtle but essentially primitive techniques, no more sophisticated than hand carried messages." According to Greenfield "There are good reasons for this" approach, reasons for which can be seen in conventional warfare scenarios, recalling a pilot "shot down over Bosnia" who "survived until rescued in part because he DID NOT use the radio he had with him." This is because radios "can also be intercepted. So, too, can telepathic Ultraterrestrial messages, and the kind of unimaginable technology some aliens – and some humans – employ."[36]

Skeptics often whine, "if UFOs are real then why don't they just land on the Whitehouse lawn?" The hidden and secret revealing of the high strangeness phenomenon (laid out in this chapter) is quite literally the opposite to the landing on the White House lawn approach. Greenfield and Dick have answered this skeptical question, so stop asking it. The only way to prove the phenomenon to someone is for that someone to go through a high strangeness initiation themselves. This is because the phenomenon can not (or chooses not to) land on the White House lawn (or maybe they already landed many times over without a witnesses who can see it as such). At any rate, given the complexity of the phenomenon surveyed in this text, the skeptical argument of "if they're real, then why don't they just land on the Whitehouse lawn?" is proven to be overly simplistic and juvenile thinking.

All this being said, I once more urge enthusiasts of high strangeness not to become entangled in the *proving trap*, desperately attempting to convince others. The skeptical mainstream individual will most probably never find sufficient evidence to alter their perspective, and from a psychological standpoint, I would argue that it may be literally impossible for them to undergo such a shift. Given this reality, I advise people not to overly concern themselves with avoiding the "woo factor"[T] when discussing the phenomenon.

For example, Tom DeLong (who I will discuss in Chapter 4) made a tweet which suggested extraterrestrials could "bend the fabric of space-time, manipulate and control antimatter reactions, contain and transfer the human soul."[37] This quote caused some consternation in the mainstream UFO community, as the tweet in question was removed from the UFO subreddit, r/UFOB. The explanation for its removal was as follows: "You know the reddit public, too much woo and it opens the troll floodgates. Imo, if we start off with the nuts and bolts, and have accepted that, the next step would be the woo. We are in a process taking steps."[38] Taking baby steps to warm up normies to the woo factor is all well and good for mainstream UFO enthusiasts. However, that approach is not what high strangeness is all about. This book is not about warming anyone up. You need to come in hot to *My Cosmic Trigger*, as I said in the introduction chapter, the dial is already at eleven.

As such, I make no apologies for pursuing the ultimate woo-woo subject: the utterly absurd idea that there is a war in Heaven and humans are caught in the middle. And as we continue in this book, I think it will become even more clear as to why an occluding function of high strangeness phenomena is necessary and why the Whitehouse lawn argument is so silly and not the *gotcha* the skeptics think.

Going back to *Hellier*, I remind the reader that the series began after the team received a mysterious email connected to Terry Wriste, who is fea-

T Coming from the phrase woo-woo, meaning "outlandishly mystical, supernatural, or unscientific" (Merriam-Webster). Also, see: *A Shaman from Indiana: The "Woo" Factor in Bigfoot Research*, where it is said that "the paranormal side of Bigfoot; what is known in the mainstream Bigfoot research community as 'Woo!,'" Lowlandsbigfoot.org, Dec. 2018.

tured in Greenfield's *Secret Cipher of the UFOnauts.* Wriste told Greenfield that he learned from Indrid Cold[U] (a supposed extraterrestrial associated with the Mothman phenomenon) directly, that Cold and his group had been "over run by the Grays and other more serious Deep Aliens working for the Negatives." Wriste says Cold's "most unusual point was his claim that they had been invited to take refuge on Earth by the Third Order" which is "humans and posthumans who are advanced enough to qualify as Earth's representatives in space-based governments."[35]

RAW explored a similar theme in the first volume of *Cosmic Trigger*, retelling something Grady McMurtry (the person who officially revived the OTO after Crowley's death) told him in response to his observation regarding the similarities between Leary and Wilhelm Reich's persecution by the powers that be. It was RAW's theory that "The attempt to destroy both Dr. Reich and Dr. Leary reached its most intense peak right after they reported their extraterrestrial contacts." And to that McMurtry said the "$64,000 question" is "why does the gnosis always get busted? Every single time the energy is raised and large scale group illuminations are occurring, the local branch of the Inquisition kills it dead." RAW reports that McMurtry's claim is that this is because there is a war in Heaven.

McMurtry explains this cosmic war, saying: "The Higher Intelligences, whoever they are, aren't all playing on the same team. Some of them are trying to encourage our evolution to higher levels, and *some of them want to keep us stuck.*" McMurtry goes on to clarify that "some occult lodges are working with these nonhuman intelligences who want to accelerate human evolution, but some of the others are working with the intelligences who wish to keep us near an animal level of awareness."[30.1]

So, it is no wonder that high strangeness is ridiculed by the other paranormal fields. In this chapter we have turned the woo-woo dial up to 11 and jumped straight into a cosmic war. However, I would be remiss if I didn't mention the war in heaven theory early in this text because it is something that has been contemplated all the way back to the beginning of high strangeness, starting with Charles Fort. Also, it is a topic that has been written about by Keel, RAW, Greenfield, and was featured in *Hellier,* which constitutes the revival of high strangeness research in our present day. I am just continuing the tradition and wouldn't be worth my salt as a high strangeness author if I shied away from this topic because it was too utterly absurd for mainstream readers.

U "After the encounter, Derenberger stated that Cold revealed he was from the planet Lanulos in the galaxy of Genemedes." (Cryptidz.fandom.com/wiki/Indrid_Cold).

With all of this being said: let's continue on our weird journey, paying no attention to the laughter and *scorn of the norms-* plunging "beyond the Reality Barrier" to decode the "core of the Ultraterrestrial Secret" which is "too numinous to be other than ineffable."[36]

Resources:

1. Reddit, u/GregNewkirk, r/Hellier

2. John Keel, *Mothman and Me: 20 years on the Flying Saucer Beat,* High Times, 1980.

3. Leecy Davis, *Seven species that used to be cryptids,* December 12, 2020, Blogs.iu.edu/sciu/2020/12/12/seven-cryptids-species/

4. Paul Vella, *International Bigfoot Symposium - Willow Creek, California September 2003,* Bigfoot Information Project, BigfootProject.org. And *Jane Goodall Tells Jimmy Kimmel Bigfoot Might Exist,* Cassandra Yorgeyapr, 2023, explore.com/ news/seriously-jane-goodall-bigfoot

5. Sofie Jackson, *Ex-soldier claims Bigfoot 'with special powers' exists after pal spots 'humanoid',* Daily Star.co.uk, March 2021._

6. OxfordParanormalSociety.com.

7. *Mary Joyce Researcher and Author of the Unknown,* #310, Nite Callers Bigfoot Radio, Jan. 2021, Host, Lauren Smith.

8. Greenfield's interview on, *Right Where You Are Sitting Now,* Episode 54, Jan. 2021 and Allen Greenfield Fantastic Page, Dec. 2023.

9. Allen Greenfield, *Secret Rituals of the Men in Black,* p. 2, p. 73, p. 2, p. 90, p. 81.

10. UrbanDictionary.com.

11. Michio Kaku, *The Joe Rogan Experience,* June 2022, number 1828.

12. *Joe Talks About Bigfoot and UFO's,* Youtube: PowerfulJRE, March 2021.

13. John Rimmer, *Beyond the Boggle*: review of Jack Hunter's (ed.) *Deep Weird; the Varieties of High Strangeness Experience,* 2022, Magonia Review, Pelicanist.blogspot.com.

14. Jack Hunter, Ph.D., *Deep Weird: High Strangeness, Boggle Thresholds and Damned Data in Academic Research on Extraordinary Experience,* 2021, Journal for the Study of Religious Experience.

15. John Keel, Operation Trojan Horse, 1970, p. 288.

16. James C. Morrison Jr., Marshall McLuhan: No Prophet without Honor, Chapter in *Beyond the Ivory Tower: Academic Discourse in the Age of Popular Media,* Massachusetts Institute of Technology, Mit.edu/~saleem/ivory/.

17. Jack Hunter, Ph.D., Parapsychology and the Varieties of High Strangeness Experience, *Mindfield,* Vol 13, issue 3, 2021.

18. Merriam-Webster.

19. *Greg Newkirk and Karl Pfeiffer talk Hellier, UFOnauts, VALIS, Hauntings, Bigfoot,* March 2020, YouTube: Talking Weird.

20. Charles Platt, *The Voices in Philip K. Dick's Head,* The New York Times, book review of *The Exegesis* of Philip K. Dick, Dec. 2011.

21- Kyle Arnold, *Philip K. Dick's spiritual epiphany,* Oxford University Press's Blog, Blog.OUP.com, July 2016.

22. Robert Anton Wilson, *Cosmic Trigger II: Down to Earth,* 1991, E-book: p. 429, p. 467.

23. Otto Rank, *Beyond Psychology,* 1941.

24. Kyle Arnold, *Was Philip K. Dick a Madman or a Mystic?,* PublishersWeekly.com, July 2016.

25. Phillip K. Dick, *VALIS,* Chapter 14, 1981 and *VALIS: an opera* by Tod Machover, song: Pt. 2: Valis.

26. P. Jackson, J. Lethem, E. Davis (ed.), *The Exegesis of Philip K. Dick,* 2011, pp. 687, 1182, 1106, 882, 1004, 687, 1446, 909, 687, 622, 920, 321, 451, 789.

27. C.G. Jung, *Two Essays on Analytical Psychology,* 1966.

28. Carylon Lovewell's public e-mail list, circa 2021.

29. Terence McKenna, *Having Archaic and Eating it Too,* Workshop, BetterListen.com, Oct. 1990.

30. *My Cosmic Trigger Finger is Broken,* 1999.

30.1. Robert Anton Wilson, *Cosmic Trigger vol 1: Final secret of the Illumanti,* p.163, E-book: p. 266-267.

31. Terry Alden, *Technosophy.com,* circa 1998.

31.1. Annie Besant, *Theosophy,* Anandgholap.net.

32. Erik Davis, *Philip K. Dick's Divine Interference,* TechGnosis.com, April 15, 2005.

33. Publisher's summary of *Hagia Sophia / Sanctum of Kronos: Spiritual Dissent in an Age of Tyranny* by Peter Mark Adams, ScarletImprint.com, May 2023.

34. Nathan Isaac, *Causeways-* Season 2, episode 10, Penny Royal, April 2022.

35. Allen Greenfield, *Secret Cipher of the UFOnauts,* 1994.

36. Allen Greenfield, *Secret Rituals of the Men in Black,* 2005, p. 2, p. 90, p. 81.

37. X: @TomDelonge, Aug. 15, 2023.

38. X: @UFOB, Aug. 15, 2023.

Section Two: Windows of High Strangeness & Theories of Intersection

in my secret garden, the angel alarm goes off –
the mystery body of nature, envelopes me (and you)
subtle, but a factor that is real, beauty
only the initiated can see

A self-published Borderland Sciences Research Associates volume on flying saucers dating from 1950,

Chapter 3

The New Age Vortex

Make a mental note: Nox has now been probed.
The design is a soul-whole world-hole
That: is channeling the details of light and dark
fresh with familiars and the fairy air

What High Strangeness Researchers Do

Laura Knight-Jadczyk claims her book *High Strangeness: Hyperdimensions and the Process of Alien Abductions* was written with the help of the Cassiopeans, a non-physical group whom she contacts through use of a Ouji board,[A] an *utterly absurd* way to get information for a book, highlighting a taboo related to high strangeness research: the New Age. Some in the high strangeness community are not open to New Age subjects, but my book seeks to break down this taboo by including the material in my analysis of the phenomenon. High strangeness researchers skeptical of the New Age would do well to be reminded of the fact that the *utterly absurd* is often the most reliable as we go down the paranormal rabbit hole.

As I pointed out in chapter 1, Timothy Green Beckley was open to New Age subjects; however, other noted high strangeness researchers have been as well. Allen Greenfield featured Meade Layne (1882-1961) in his work, saying he was "writing about flying discs before Kenneth Arnold's Sightings," which is where the term flying saucer comes from. Greenfield also points out that Layne "introduced the idea of channeled masters to UFOlogy."[1]

Layne presented "an inter-dimensional, etheric-based theory" of UFOs and ETs, terming "those from the other realms as Etherians" and saying the "UFOs themselves" are sometimes actually "living creatures." He claimed this information "came directly from intelligences channeled through Mark Probert, the greatest psychic medium of his time." Layne's

A Pulitzer Prize winning American poet, James Merrill's (1926-1995) "postmodern apocalyptic epic," *The Changing Light at Sandover* "won the National Book Award for Poetry, in 1978 … Merrill spent more than twenty years transcribing supernatural communications during séances using a Ouija board … Ephraim is a control spirit who allows Merrill … to communicate with friends … who have passed on as well as with famous poets, including … W. B. Yeats, and W. H. Auden." (fineeditionsltd.com, Publisher's summary)

book encourages readers to "not discount channeled material" before reading the 1954, *The Coming of the Guardians*.[2]

In addition, Greenfield also features the Light/Lines group in his writings, a group which "began publishing a quarterly newsletter" in 1982, with each issue offering "a selection of ... channeling from the Confederation of Planets."[3] This group was responsible for what became known as the Ra Material, made famous in the 1984 book, *The Ra Material: An Ancient Astronaut Speaks (Law of One)*.[B]

John Keel provided information on the New Age topic of the Ashtar command in his work, reporting on the message a contactee supposedly received from "the Ashtar Intergalactic Command." The contactee was told that UFOs "are in reality the space bodies of certain aggregates of consciousness" and exist in "both the third and fourth dimensions simultaneously." He was also told "Their purpose has been ... to interlace these two realms of consciousness which are seemingly separate." However, "the time quickly comes when the veil is torn aside" and all is perceived as One. When this occurs "the saucers seen by the few will be seen by the many. It will appear that they have suddenly arrived in your skies in great number .... For in reality they are where they have always been, but man sees with new eyes."[4]

Keel and Greenfield both write about the Pleiades. The channeled messages from beings from this constellation is a popular New Age topic. Greenfield mentions a Dr. Fred Bell, a "contactee in communication with ... a Pleiadean being" named Semjase, that "has shown up in a number of other cases over the last twenty or so years" [1]

With all that being said, it now may be easier for high strangeness researchers skeptical of the New Age material to agree that Knight-Jadczyk's book is worthy of consideration and also a great illustration at what high strangeness research is all about. This is because the book is an attempt "to weave together the contradictory threads of religion, science, history, alien abduction, and the true nature" of parapolitical intrigue. Her highly strange research "strips away the facades of official culture and opens doors to understanding our reality."[5]

Trying to discover how and why multiple paranormal topics "weave together" is the *raison d'etre* of high strangeness research. Moving forward, let us assume these disparate paranormal subjects do indeed intersect. The question then remains: why is this the case?

B Well known New Age author and speaker, David Wilcock has contributed to the rise of popularity of the Ra material in our current times. See *Ra and the Law of One: Wisdom Teachings with David Wilcock*, (gaia.com/video/ra-and-the-law-of-one).

Window Areas

In our survey of explanations as to why this highly strange paranormal intersection exists, we shall start with the *sine qua non* of this theory: window areas. Window areas are the most popular theory of why a wide variety of paranormal subjects intersect. John Keel "described what he called 'window areas' where he consistently observed a range of unusual phenomena that occur in specific locations."[6] These "Geographical Gateways" are "locations of 'focused unexplained activity'" where "inexplicable phenomena of the type reported by Charles Fort" occur, such as "gigantic birds ... spirit presences; phantom creatures ... and similar manifestations of [an] extra-dimensional" nature.[7]

Keel said he came up with the window area concept after he "discovered that UFO sightings within a given area during a specific period of time were confined to sectors with a radius of about 200 miles." He said he first "termed these sectors base areas," but this concept was misunderstood because "soon after my first article ... teen-agers everywhere were out scouring the countryside looking for underground UFO hangars. So I adopted the term 'windows'[C] as a good substitute."[4]

The New Age Vortex

To start off, we'll delve into a particular kind of window area: the New Age energy vortex. Although some individuals might argue that an energy vortex is essentially synonymous with a window area, I hold the belief that there are nuances setting them apart, which I will outline in the upcoming chapter. Exploring the New Age energy vortex in the realm of high strangeness research holds significance due to the similarities it shares with window areas.

By exploring the concept of the energy vortex (and in so doing, looking at the New Age topics: the ascension and starseeds), I hope to break down the barrier to New Age material and open up this avenue of study to researchers of the phenomenon. Including these concepts increases the chances I won't be allowed a seat at the high strangeness lunch room table at Paranormal High, should one be established. However, I believe in the importance of these subjects so much that it's a risk I'm willing to take.

These energy vortexes are said to be most commonly found around ancient sacred sites which are said to be special places "on the earth where energy is either entering into the earth or projecting out of the earth's plane" and

---

C Other names include doorways, portals, wormholes, and stargates. See *Stargates and Energy Centres on Earth: How to Locate and Use Them!* by The Abbotts.

these sacred sites are sometimes found at sacred Temple complexes, such as "the Great Pyramid in Egypt, Machu Picchu in Peru [and] Stonehenge."[D,8]

I think it is fair to say that a New Age energy vortex is something of a synonym for sacred sites. This is because certain locations "have power, that's why they're called power places, sacred sites, or vortexes by a large majority of people."[9] However, I point out that some sacred sites do not have large ancient temple complexes.

Vortexes Versus Window Areas

Energy vortex sites are said to be places of psycho-spiritual healing and not just places, like window areas, where high strangeness phenomena are found. However, I believe window areas are potential New Age energy vortex sites, or, perhaps more precisely, we could say they are *budding* sacred sites. This chapter will help us move toward a theory and practice to achieve this shift. I will go into more detail regarding how to turn a window area into a sacred site/New Age vortex in volume two of this series, *My Cosmic Trigger: Perilous Chapels and High Strangeness Magick*. However, for now I can say that a major component of my magick of high strangeness is to work to turn an ordinary window area into a New Age energy vortex: turning one's own backyard into a sacred site.

High strangeness phenomena are reported at vortex sites just as in window areas. For example, notice this description of the Sedona, Arizona vortex, when it is said that the "amount of activity recorded would make you think" the area was "some kind of intergalactic airport." It is said that the locals are not only seeing UFOs but also "Orbs, portals, actual aliens and Bigfoot ... in Sedona's high desert." And it is also said there is an area near Sedona which is "Located deep within the national forest" and "the rumor is that it was confiscated by the U.S. Government because it housed one of the most powerful inter-dimensional portals on the planet."[10]

Again, the main difference between a high strangeness window area and a New Age energy vortex area is the latter's ability to promote psycho-spiritual healing. The healing nature of these spots is described as having "transformational power which can lead you to higher levels of consciousness, a deeper wisdom of all things" due to accessing the "healing energy available to you from earth's frequency." In addition, these spots make possible "elevated levels of spiritual" energy and as a result, "many people are drawn to" take "pilgrimages" to these "sacred sites."[9]

D The author of this quote also provides "Sedona Soul Adventures" which are "completely different from any other retreat that is available anywhere else." See, DebraStangl.com.

Sedona

In the New Age community (at least in the United States), Sedona, Arizona is the most famous energy vortex. This is evidenced by the fact that "one of the most important expressions" of New Age spirituality is found in the magazine, *Sedona: Journal of Emergence.*[11] This publication first started circulating in the Sedona area, but is now a monthly magazine read not just nationally but also globally. The publication features channeled messages from such entities as Kyron, Mary Magdalene, Jesus, archangels, the Arcturians, Thoth, transdimensional beings from Andromeda, the Pleiades and many others. I've read this magazine since around 2008 and enjoy it immensely.

The Sedona vortex is so well known that it is a big source of tourism, as evidenced by the fact that many of the businesses in the area "are also geared towards wellbeing and purification" and "you can find strip-malls full of crystal shops, aura-reading stations and psychics." In addition, "Every other office along the state route running through town offers a 'spiritual tour' of the vortexes."

The story of how Sedona became known as the location of a New Age energy vortex is of interest to high strangeness research in general and my individual story in particular. Sedona became a "New Age capital" in the 1980s when "a U.S. psychic named Page Bryant identified the vortexes after a vision." She learned that these "vortexes were places where spiritual energy was at its highest point" and "spiritual seekers across the country listened."[12] A recommendation to make use of the psycho-spiritual healing properties of the Sedona energy vortex is to "invoke affirmations" and contemplate "life-changing decisions" because in the area one can "gain extra power and acceleration."[13]

Asheville (Sedona of the East)

In 1994, Bryant wrote *The Spiritual Reawakening of the Great Smoky Mountains,* which led to the widespread recognition of Asheville, North Carolina as the Sedona of the East. Her book "came as the New Age movement was maturing in Asheville, and national media began tagging the mountain metropolis with the 'New Age mecca' tag."[14]

Bryant reports that a spirit guide instructed her to leave Sedona for the Great Smoky Mountain region of the United States, where Asheville is located. She claims there are "vortexes, power spots, and sacred sites within the Great Smoky and Blue Ridge mountains and other areas throughout western North Carolina," pointing out that "this part of the earth is waxing to full power."[15] According to Bryant, this fact makes the energy of the region "the most intense ... on the entire planet."[15] It is little wonder her spirit guide instructed her to move to the area.

A fact which will become more interesting as this chapter continues is that she says there are "places where a natural vortex has lost its power,"[15] and are dormant just like a dry river bed. She says this is because they have "been eroded away either by time or by the encroachment of modern society."[15] The magick of high strangeness is concerned with re-awakening dormant vortexes.

She says numerous "bioelectric energy points," known as vortexes, are distributed throughout the Earth. These vortexes can be compared to "acupuncture points on the human body" and are located at intersections where ley lines converge. Bryant describes a vortex as "a high-energy place where natural planetary power has coagulated into an intensely powerful mass ... of energy" and are "openings" where "natural earth energy is extremely potent."[15] She says an electromagnetic charge exists in the Asheville area because of the four distinct seasons and terrain of the region, which are "waterfalls, rich plant life, lots of rainfall, hills and mountains."[15]

An interesting side note is that the Great Smoky Mountain region is the "Salamander Capital of the World" because in this region there "are more salamander species ... than almost anywhere else on earth."[16] In alchemy, salamanders were thought to have mystical properties (or, more accurately, represent mystical properties latent within humans)[E] and the phoenix is "equated with the mythical" salamander. Conversely, it has been said that black magicians eat them to "enhance their power."[17]

The salamander power animal is the "creature of the hidden" and "opens us up to secrets within ourselves ... within others, and ... of the spirit."[18] I can think of no better spirit animal for the high strangeness researcher. A major component of high strangeness magick is working with power animals that are in resonance with the phenomenon.

The tourism around New Age energy vortex sites in the Asheville area is not as developed as in Sedona. However, some claim "Asheville is fast challenging Sedona ... as a mecca for the New Age movement."[14] And the area has been publicly recognized as a "New Age mecca" since 1996 when it was reported "There are those who believe the Great Smoky Mountains possess the power to heal" because the area "contains grids of natural power that humans can feel. That a vortex of natural energy centered ... around this mountain city ... is re-emerging as a force in everyone's lives." Like in Sedo-

E The 1667 alchemical painting *The Hand of Philosophy* features a salamander surrounded by flames while situated in the center of the palm.

na, the tourism in the area is based on spiritual growth, as you can "balance your personal energy field, use herbal first aid on your soul and harness your own consciousness as the main healing force in your life" while finding "practitioners to help you ... better harmonize with the world."[19]

Bryant explains the mechanisms of why a New Age energy vortex site would be healing, pointing out that sites with increased electromagnetic energy allow easier "contact with one's deepest inner self, spirit forces ... and other dimensions of reality" and can bring "balance to the human body and health on all levels." Indeed, she claims electromagnetic energy is "the healing energy in nature."[15]

Bryant says the area is "one of the most intense and potent healing areas of the entire planet." The region has a long history as being a place of healing. After railroad extensions in 1880 made it easier to visit the area there was a stimulation of "growth and industry" as the "area developed as a vacation and health center, based on the 'climatic theory' that Asheville had the altitude, atmosphere and climate to heal tuberculosis." As a result "the area became one of the nation's best-known centers for the treatment" of that disease. The area also became "well-known for psychiatric care with the opening of Highland Hospital in 1904 [which] enjoyed a national reputation" and is now most known as being the place of death for Zelda Fitzgerald (wife of writer F. Scott Fitzgerald).[20]

For clarification, vortex sites, such as Asheville and Sedona, possess psycho-spiritual healing qualities as well as high strangeness phenomena. Whereas window areas only contain high strangeness phenomena, the healing properties are not present. An example of the phenomenon manifesting in the area is seen in the fact that a crop circle was reported to have been found in 2005 in Buncombe county, where Asheville is located.

In addition, there are also significant amounts of UFO sightings reported in the area. A researcher that documents high strangeness in the area said they find this interesting "because these are also reported to be times of what people call sky ship messages" when one "can receive telepathic messages from the UFOs." This researcher speculates the Western North Carolina mountains "hold a large amount of quartz" and that "the energy of vibration put out by" this mineral "acts like a beacon for other strange events to feed off the energy." They further speculate, as do others, that "Ufos seem attracted to the energy" given off by the quartz. This researcher also claims that there are "stories of the ufos using the area for space and time travel through portals."[F,21]

F A great website that details high strangeness in the Western NC area is Mary Joyce's SkyShipsOverCashiers.com.

Istanbul

Napoléon Bonaparte famously said, "If the world was only one country, Istanbul would be its capital."[G] This quote makes sense, as the city bridges the East and the West, sitting on two continents: Europe and Asia. The city is so awe inspiring it evokes poetic musings such as that Istanbul "alone seems to claim a kind of immortality and will be a city as long as humanity shall lie either to inhabit or rebuild it."[H]

Many years ago I read a channeled message in *Sedona: Journal of Emergence* listing Istanbul as a New Age energy vortex alongside Sedona and Asheville. This was the only time I have ever seen Istanbul officially mentioned in the New Age literature in the same breath as these two American vortexes. Unfortunately, I have since lost which channeled entity this came from.[I]

The New Age community in Turkey is not as established as it is in the United States. As a result, I was unable to find as many sources that confirm Istanbul is a vortex like I found for Asheville and Sedona. Some may claim this is even a good thing, saying this is evidence the vortex is not overrun by pop culture consumerism. At any rate, there are less mainstream newspaper articles discussing it specifically being a vortex, as there are for Sedona and Asheville.

Writing this section has forced me to lay out the reasons I believe the city to be a New Age energy vortex. In so doing, I believe I am revealing the reality that this city functions as a vortex to the New Age community in the United States, akin to how Bryant introduced the knowledge that ultimately led to the widespread acknowledgment of Sedona and Asheville as New Age vortex locations.

Historical

Former FBI agent and writer, John DeSouza[J] says regions exist where a fissure in the structure of our three-dimensional reality can be discov-

G Some suggest the attributed quote comes from this line, "The Emperor again fell silent, measuring distances on the map with his calipers and asserting that Constantinople was by its situation the center and seat of universal domination" (Christopher Herold, *The Mind of Napoleon*, 1961, p. 202).

H The quote is from *The Antiquities of Constantinople* by Petrus Gyllius, written during the 16th century.

I I did find that an "etheric" crystal was placed in Istanbul, to "represent" one of "the source points … for the new fifth-dimensional Earth" and to help with "the healing of the third-dimensional Earth." Now, "new energy lines … can be created" from this location to help with "the planet's healing." (*The Year of the Planetary Healer*, Juliano, the Arcturians, and Helio-ah through David K. Miller, *Sedona*, March 2011).

J "John DeSouza FBI Special Agent (RET.), worked Counter-Terrorism and Paranormal cases for over twenty-five years. He was also an attorney and maintained a Top Secret security clearance during his time in the US Government. DeSouza collected true life X-Files that were used on the highly popular show *The X Files*. He also shares many of these cases in his best selling books and his worldwide presentations" (Johntamabooks.com).

ered. According to him, these locations serve to provide us with "insight into what is happening" in our highly strange reality. He goes on to mention that these fissures act as gateways which he categorizes as morphogenetic sites, a concept delineated by Rupert Sheldrake. DeSouza proposes that these geographic areas can originate from intense historical occurrences that imprinted on the location which makes it "permanently a gateway ... to other realities."[22] The historical events that have occurred in Istanbul are innumerable and too vast to adequately summarize in this chapter.

A great academic essay exploring some of these innumerable historical events says "It has become a well-worn – if not unjustified – cliché to refer to Istanbul as a bridge between ... East and West." The article even uses the metaphor of a vortex to describe the city's history, saying "Like a vortex" the city "has sucked in and thrown together many different peoples" over the centuries and then "disgorged new civilizations – the Byzantine and Ottoman empires thereby creating further currents downstream."[23]

The Fall of the Eastern Roman empire occurred in the city in 1453 at the hands of the Ottoman Turks; but, as we know from an earlier chapter, the empire may not have ended as we typically think. Furthermore, the city was once the seat of Christendom located at Hagia Sophia and the city is still the location of *the Vatican* for Orthodox Christianity.[K]

Felt Sense

Peter Mark Adams, who also happens to live in Istanbul, speculates on geographic locations which give rise to window areas and he says in certain areas the "the interface between these dimensions is a lot thinner." He refers to this interplay as occurring on a "geo-psychic dimension" and says in these places the paranormal "phenomenon is outrageously out of control."[24] I believe Adams is able to describe these areas so succinctly because he happens to live in one. Living in Istanbul for over two years, there is little doubt that this hyper-historical city is one of these thin places: a vortex, a physical place that holds a sacred quality. Quite simply, I can feel it.

Spiritual Transformation

As with Asheville and Sedona, there are people who report that Istanbul has the power to facilitate spiritual transformation. According to the

K "Because of its historical location as the capital of the former Eastern Roman (Byzantine) Empire and its role as the mother church of most modern Orthodox churches, Constantinople holds a special place of honor within Orthodoxy and serves as the seat for the Ecumenical Patriarch, who enjoys the status of *primus inter pares* (first among equals) among the world's Eastern Orthodox prelates and is regarded as the representative and spiritual leader of Eastern Orthodox Christians." (wiki/ Ecumenical Patriarchate of Constantinople).

following mainstream news article, Istanbul is one of the top ten "sacred places" of "power and peace" in the world. It is claimed that visiting such a site can be a "vehicle for spiritual transformation." Specifically, the article says Istanbul's "ancient soul" is most noticeable at "the city's holiest, if not most awe-inspiring, vestiges: Hagia Sophia." It goes on to say that even though the area is crowded with tourists "one can't shake the feeling of a spiritual presence."[25]

I liken the feeling of being in Hagia Sophia to being near a waterfall. Some claim the positive physiological response you feel at a waterfall is "that the negative ions produced by some waterfalls are believed to increase serotonin, the hormone that generates feelings of well-being."[26] I have also felt this same feeling at a very well performed Gnostic Mass.

Spiritual Tourism

Just like in Sedona and Asheville, tourism devoted to spiritual aspects of the city exists as an outgrowth of Istanbul being a New Age vortex. However, the tourism in this regard is not as pronounced as it is in Sedona, for example.

The image of the whirling dervishes is one of the most iconic images of the city. It is seen in a lot of advertising for the city and on numerous tourist items: t-shirts, mugs, magnets, etc. The image of someone spinning in spiritual ecstasy invokes the idea of a vortex. The Whirling Dervishes are practitioners of a unique form of Sufi[L] mysticism and are closely associated with the Mevlevi Order, which was founded by the followers of the mystic and poet, commonly known as Rumi.

The tourism sector around this spiritual aspect of Istanbul is not as flourishing as it could be because "it has been illegal to perform this ritual for almost 100 years." So you aren't going to see as much tourism devoted to Sufi practices, but "Luckily for tourists and Turks, selective application of the law means that we can still watch the Mevlevis' whirling ceremony inside state-owned museums."[27]

Despite the legal gray area, you can still find tourism devoted to Sufis. For example, you can take a tour of "Sufi Shrines of Istanbul." The tour claims "A Sufi is a Muslim mystic who seeks to have a personal experience of God directly through meditation and prayer ... for example, the whirling movement is a religious ritual of meditation and prayer."[28] This is a very

L Broadly speaking, Sufism is the mystical branch of Islam, seeking a direct connection with the divine, using methods like meditation, chanting, and dance to attain enlightenment. Kabbalah is the mystical branch of Judaism, focusing on an esoteric interpretation of the Torah. Gnosticism is a mystical branch of Christianity, emphasizing the importance of inner knowledge or gnosis for spiritual development.

short introduction to the history of Sufism in general and its practice in Istanbul. The subject is so vast that it would take an entire book to cover it adequately.

NEW AGE

The following are two New Age sources which support the idea of Istanbul being a vortex. First, in a channeled message concerning Earth's "Crystal grid system" it is claimed a "dimensional crystalline portal" in Istanbul was activated in 1998 by "light-workers" who were "guided" in the task of "updating [the] energies" of the portal while working "in accordance with the grand divine plan."

They claim these portals had to be re-activated because they were "shut down" at the end of "Atlantis some 14,500 years ago." Shutting down the portals at that time caused the closure of the "crystal grid system," which in turn "negated the planet's 'ability to ascend.'" This is important because when these portals are fully operational they will "once again further enhance" Earth's light body while also restricting "the use of these energy gateways from further abuse by" negative Ultraterrestrials.

This neo-Atlantean reboot of the crystalline portals in particular and the crystal grid system in general is called the "Return the Dove,"[M] which has to do with "the injection of pure Christ energies" into the "ascending planet." When this injection of pure energy is complete, then "Mother Earth is again resplendent with her crown of crystal portal jewels" which make up "the Crystal Grid System."[29] Sounds good to me!

The second New Age source pointing to Istanbul being a vortex is *The Knowledge Book,* which contains channeled teachings of the World Brotherhood Union Mevlana Supreme Foundation.[N] The group's headquarters are in Istanbul, but it has groups in thirty-two countries. The book is said to be a result of "direct transmissions from the realm of the angels."[30] These angels say the teachings in the book have been presented to our world as part of the "accelerated evolution program." This accelerated response of the angels is due to the limited time available for humans to shift into a higher dimension which is so important the angels say that the "salvation of your planet depends on your cooperating with"[30] this higher evolutionary program.

Further, the angels say that during this transition to a higher dimension *The Knowledge Book* imparts frequencies of "OMEGA" which "is the final dimensional frequency your planet is able to receive." This final frequency "prevents the agitation of consciousness"[30] during the cosmic transition

M Also see, *The Return of the Dove* (GreatDreams.com/return_of_the_dove.htm).
N See, World Brotherhood Union - Mevlana Supreme Foundation (dkb-mevlana.org.tr).

and I think we can all agree a little less agitation is just what the doctor ordered for our current times.

The angels say the book's teachings act as a "protective roof" because they safeguard humanity's "spiritual and physical cellular" structures, while neutralizing any negative influences "coming into existence around you," similar to how antibodies counteract harmful agents. This entire process is "under supervision" of the Angelic "system" which allows you to establish a direct connection with their "channels of healing."[30] Working with a direct angelic connection is a critical component of high strangeness magick.

The main technique of the book is the *Cosmic Light-Photon Cyclone Technique*. Interestingly, *cyclone* is defined as a "powerful energy vortex,"[30] so we can say the technique utilizes New Age vortex energies. The book's teachings are encoded with this technique and give one the "power to absorb very advanced frequencies." The angels say this technique was "prepared centuries ago to be bestowed on your planet during this period."[30]

The technique is a method for harmonizing the positive "time energy" of our current moment, thereby closing the "doors" to the negative "time energy" of evil. The angels report that it "is a technique uniting you with the energy" of evolutionary consciousness and this connection offers you a shield against detrimental factors present in our human dimension. It is to "prepare your entire planet for" a new dimension and to do that it "locks up your consciousness[O] so that you will not be affected by the advance[d] power of the [negative] cosmic influence."[30]

The angels' thoughts on Istanbul are that it is their "focal point"[30] and their "center."[30] The city serves as the unique "universal center," providing a "direct channel" to receive counsel from the "reality totality"[30] to all humans on your planet. This suggests Istanbul is the vortex of all vortexes. I also add that the *reality totality* has a nice ring to it, so it must be true. As I like to joke, if it rhymes it must be true.

Interestingly, a medium I know believes the city is a Switzerland for the warring angelic forces: meaning in this city the angels and demons (rebel angels) have a truce where they intermingle freely under a white flag of truce. This energy can be seen in the Sun Ra song "Angels and Demons at Play." Listening to this song as you walk through the back streets of Istanbul does make this *utterly absurd* claim seem a bit more possible. The angels of *The Knowledge Book* say that during this current time period beings such as "Jinns, Fairies, and Devils" coexist harmoniously with angels within the "Unified Field" dwelling in dimensions governed by highly "advanced technologies."[30]

O This reminds me of the concept talked about by Bob Dobbs: Lockdown Bob rule.

As someone who has been reading New Age literature for over twenty years, I can say *The Knowledge Book* is particularly heady New Age channeling discourse. That is, it is more advanced and nuanced than most of the channeled material. This is especially saying a lot because it is translated from Turkish. I think these two things give more credence to the material. I had known about *The Knowledge Book* since around 2002 but only recently dove into the material when researching this chapter. It also appears to fit with other channeled material in regards to a temporal war over timelines.

In a recent channeling from Ashtar, he speaks of "the Galactics" and "Ascended Masters who are assisting in this whole process" of helping humanity move onto the timeline of "the new Earth." He says this positive timeline is "a different time-line" from the one of the "forces of darkness" who are "attempting to keep you on their [negative] time-line." Ashtar says the goal of lightworkers is to "assist the entire population of this planet to move along onto the new time-line," which is "not the biblical time-line that you have grown up to understand" because that negative "time-line is no longer." As a result, we are now on a positive timeline of our own creation and will never be effected by "the old time-line of the third-dimensional illusion."[31]

High Strangeness of Istanbul

Just like in Sedona and Asheville, there are also high strangeness phenomena reported in the Istanbul. An example can be seen in an episode of the Youtube channel *Mysterious Middle East* which tells of a legend surrounding a house in Istanbul that supposedly disappears for a short time each year.[32] The phenomenon is said to be related to the fairy folk of the Middle East, Jinn, where the term genie comes from.

Also relevant is the legend that "Greek gods that were associated with" the founding of the city "such as Zeus, Hera, Poseidon, [and] Hecate" led to "villages … along the Bosphorus" to be "founded by [one of those] gods or their offspring."[P] Another legend states the famous Jason and the Argonauts "sailed through the Bosphorus in search of the Golden Fleece."[33] Traveling through the Bosphorus, which separates the Asian and European sides of the city, it really does feel like the land of the gods.

P "Zeus was nothing more than a very sick criminal. Think of him as an extraterrestrial version of a Nazi Gestapo leader. He was someone who was vested with the authority to run this planet, and he saw the prisoners not as real people, but as play things, and he could do whatever he wanted with them with no repercussions towards himself. There is no way to escape the fact that the guy was also a brutal alien rapist" ("ZEUS the Extraterrestrial," *The Farsight Institute*). This group conducts "the highest quality remote-viewing studies … in the world that investigate scientific questions and historical mysteries" (FarSight.org).

Other New Age Concepts

New Age Grid Work

In New Age literature, talk of the energy vortex can not be discussed without also discussing the overall energy grid. This concept was mentioned briefly in the above section. For a more in-depth analysis of the concept we will turn to Asil Toksal, a New Age practitioner of Turkish ancestry, who performs New Age energy grid work around the world.

Toksal claims his spirit guides have informed him the energetic grid was "established long ago to support all beings on Earth." In the geographic locations where "the energy is the strongest" cultures "have built meeting places, temples, sanctuaries – and have revered these as sacred places." These sacred sites were used "to connect to ancestors, to spirit, to nature, and to Earth and the grid itself." His guides claim that in ancient times the "energetic grid was maintained by humanity, sometimes in collaboration with benevolent spirit guides." The energetic grid network "helped to maintain harmony and balance, as well as support human evolution."[34]

He says his guides "tell us that humanity's ability to attune to these energies has weakened" since ancient times and the "spirits of the land that were once part of our everyday reality are now mostly considered 'myth.'" As a result, the grids "have also fallen into disrepair, and the Guides say that it is time for us to begin to attune to and support these important networks yet again to assist our own evolution." Connecting with the Genii Loci of one's own backyard, attuning into the energies, and repairing the grid is a big part of high strangeness magick.

Toksal describes himself as a "sacred earth practitioner" who works on revamping the areas of the grid that have fallen into disrepair. One of his guides claims these sacred earth practitioners are needed because "the entire globe of this Earth will require many individuals to be guardians ... and transmitters" of this grid energy. They say that in "this stage of humanity's existence" it is vital to establish the "connection of these various networks." Ultimately, his guides claim this energy grid is to be implemented for humanity's "own Ascension process." The grid is said to aid this spiritual evolution process because the "network of energy lines" increases the "frequencies that are available and accessible."[34]

Ascension

Ascension is another popular New Age concept I must explain, especially since the above spirit guides claim the energy grid's sole function is to aid the ascension process of spiritual evolution. To help us explain this central New Age concept I will now present the work of Lisa Renee who says she is an "Ascension Guide, Planet Gridworker [and] Starseed Advocate."[Q]

Renne's work indicates ascension is a synonym for spiritual awakening and is defined as an "increase of Expanding Consciousness that occurs when our spiritual-energetic bodies connect into our physical bodies." With ascension, we are "moving our Consciousness from one reality to another," and because "reality is a dimension, what we are undertaking is essentially a full dimensional shift." And in order to "go through this shift we must adjust our way of thinking and being."[35] The research of high strangeness phenomena is all about adjusting one's thinking.

Window Area - Vortex Intersection

The following may be a possible explanation of high strangeness intersection in window areas and New Age energy vortex sites. According to this source, at the present moment "the planetary body is undergoing a space-time reorganization that ripples out many strange anomalies that influence the quantic field"; as a result "there are new patterns of electromagnetic disturbances ... or distortions in the collective field." The "quantum field" is "rippling these effects" into the "morphogenetic fields of earth."[35] I suggest that high strangeness researchers are the people documenting these distortions in the quantum field.

It is said the grid worker intuitively understands this distortion and "feels like something very different, extraordinary and even bizarre is occurring in the earth fields."[35] Again: notice the presence of high strangeness showing up (i.e., the utterly bizarre). I argue high strangeness researchers are the people who are most aware of the bizarre goings on in Earth's fields, even more so than New Age gridworkers. It is for this reason I encourage high strangeness researchers to avail themselves of New Age literature and practices to further inform their work (and vice versa).

The following assertion to me sums up what a high strangeness researcher sets out to do and sums up their preconscious intuition and intention, the bizarre happenings in the planet's quantum field "feels like it is a new design that is encompassing our consciousness with the necessity to learn a foreign language, and yet it feels distantly familiar and vastly powerful."[35] High strangeness researchers are discovering and studying this new language.

Q She claims to have "experienced a spontaneous Kundalini event many years ago that catalyzed a Starseed Awakening to perceive multidimensional realities and communication with the Evolutionary forces of Light [she] has been personally contacted and then prepared...by Interdimensional beings ... to comprehend the Science of Ascension through the Law of One ... She is ... a spokesperson for the shift of humanity to Ascension" (AascensinoGlossary.com).

High Strangeness Grid Research

What I find interesting as we compare the New Age theories around the Earth grid with those of high strangeness researchers is that the material presented is remarkably similar. The difference lies in how the material is *obtained*. In the case of the New Age, the information is captured out of the ether, via a supposed higher dimensional being. The high strangeness researcher, however, comes to their conclusions via scouring historical and current records, a more journalistic method. Again, I think utilizing both sources of information has a synergistic effect for the positive benefit of both. I wouldn't recommend one without the other.

Dr. Joseph P. Farrell discusses an earth energy grid in depth in his work, but before we examine this research, a brief look at Farrell's overall body of work is warranted. He obtained "a doctorate in patristics[R] from the University of Oxford, and pursues research in physics, alternative history and science, and 'strange stuff.'"[36, S]

Farrell's book *The Giza Death Star* was published in the spring of 2002, "and was his first venture into 'alternative history and science.' Following a paradigm of researching the relationship between alternative history and science, [he] has followed with a stunning series of books" that cover almost every area of high strangeness, including:

The SS Brotherhood of the Bell (Nazis developed anti-gravity aircraft); *The Cosmic War* (covert war between good and evil Ultraterrestrials); *Secrets of the Unified Field* (in which he argues that Einstein's Unified Field Theory was actually achieved and has been used for secret military weaponry); *The Philosophers' Stone* (modern physics' connection to ancient alchemy); *The Nazi International* (the Nazi's plan to covertly control the world after WW2); *Roswell and the Reich* (via Operation Paperclip the CIA was overtaken by ex-Nazis and the crash at Roswell was actually a secret anti-gravity Nazi aircraft); *LBJ and the Conspiracy to Kill Kennedy* (the military industrial complex killed JFK in a coup); *Genes, Giants, Monsters and Men* (humans were genetically engineered by extraterrestrials); and *Saucers, Swastikas and Psyops: A History of a Breakaway Civilization* (the Nazis went into hiding after WW2 and created a separate civilization from ours that utilizes advanced ET technology).[36]

R "Patristics … is the study of the early Christian writers who are designated Church Fathers. The names derive from the combined forms of Latin pater and Greek *patḗr* (father). The period is generally considered to run from the end of New Testament times or end of the Apostolic Age." (wiki/Patristics)

S There is even an academic essay written about his work in a book from Cambridge University Press, entitled "Occulture in the Academy? The Case of Joseph P. Farrell" by J. Stroup, in *Histories of the Hidden God: Concealment and Revelation in Western Gnostic, Esoteric, and Mystical Traditions*, 2013.

Farrell says the ancient construction of pyramids and massive stone sites "constitutes the coordinated effort of post-Cosmic War" Ultraterrestrials. He says the stone and pyramid sites' "ultimate purpose lies in the preservation and *eventual recovery* of a physics and worldview that would otherwise have been lost without such memorization in these monuments."[37] That is, the monuments found at ancient sacred sites were left by both sides of a Cosmic War and figuring out the spiritual science behind them is key for our modern day society. This also seems to imply there is a current covert battle between secret terrestrial groups for control of this grid's power.

Farrell speculates on how the spiritual science of these individual sacred sites was used in the ancient past, noting that with "American Pueblo Indians, there are legends connecting such sacred sites to the flow of energies between this plane of reality and 'other concurrent realities' as a kind of gateway ... between worlds."[37] He claims that sites in the United Kingdom such as Stonehenge "are situated according to a discernible and definite ... grid upon the topography"[37] of the country.

Farrell also says what makes this fact so important is that the same "activity is also being done by ... Mayans ... South American 'Incas,' ... ancient Egyptians" and "Modern Freemasons laying out Washington, DC [and] Chinese geomancers following the precepts of *feng shui* and at virtually all times in their history." This is evidence that the activity "spans all times and transcends cultures, and yet it is being done according to the same basic principles." The same basic principles are that "it all appears to have been done according to a 'grid' pattern of amazing complexity and global extent."

Farrell says the motivations for all these different cultures in constructing such sites on the grid, points to "hidden players" of lost and ancient history whose purpose was "clearly alchemical."[37] This alchemical purpose points to a "much deeper function and significance" of the global grid. This deeper purpose is "revealed in the fact that, after whatever catastrophe had overwhelmed the civilization that constructed it," in the first place (such as Atlantis), we learn that "the grid system appeared to have been built to channel whatever energies it represented to 'their own magical purposes.'"[37] Meaning the grid can be utilized by the forces of good or evil; it all depends on who controls it.

Dark Grids

Farrell claims after this Cosmic War "there were ... *two* surviving elites ... a 'good' elite, wishing to restore humanity to its previous Golden Age" and also "a 'bad' elite, wishing to restore all the technological instruments … to enslave the rest of mankind by means of them." Put simply, the bad Ultraterrestrials want to reboot the grid for evil purposes and the good Ultraterrestrials want to reboot it to use it for life enhancement. Oh, and not to alarm you, but if the bad Ultraterrestrials and their human minions succeed in using the grid to enslave humanity they will then march "out into space in an orgy of conquest."[37] So, no pressure, dear reader.

Farrell goes into more detail about the two factions in the cosmic war over the Earth grid, saying the two groups are "the origin within esoteric … tradition of the idea of two 'brotherhoods.'" The "'white' brotherhood," practices white magick, which is: "the right hand path of love, peace, [and] harmony." The "'black' brotherhood," practices black magick, which is: "the left-hand path of violence, chaos [and] social engineering."[37] These thoughts fit with the ideas I presented in the previous chapter. Crowley himself also echoed these ideas saying he "seriously" believed there was an "organized" secret plan "of the Black Lodges to prevent people from thinking."[38]

Greenfield says this Black Lodge, which "opposes evolution," actually "operated more or less openly" in Nazi Germany.[1] Speaking of, we now come to the black magick of those dreaded Nazis, whom Farrell claims were constructing radio and radar stations on ancient sites based on sacred geometry. He claims that Heinrich Himmler was the "most powerful man ever to have attempted the resurrection of 'Atlantis,'" attempting to "activate the world grid system that was its legacy."[37] Great, that's all we need: a resurrected Nazi-run Atlantis.

Farrell says the Nazis placed their headquarters "in significant positions according to sacred geography" which they hoped would enable "their rulers to transmit psychic powers over areas covered by the geomantic grid."[37] In short, Farrell claims the Nazis were trying to use this ancient spiritual technology of the grid for world domination in a similar manner to the evil priestly elite of ancient times. Those ancient priests, once "established in positions of power" extended "their influence" in order to "make demands on the population for sacrificial"[37] offerings.

Moving from ancient to modern times, Downard also speculates the grid is being altered by negative actors on the world stage. He asked if said players were "attempting to change the direction of the mystical primordial pulses that travel" ley lines. His speculation was that "an atomic explosion" might be powerful enough to "cause a variation in the magnetic lines of force" (i.e. ley lines).[17,T]

T "The now-legendary Episode Eight of *Twin Peaks: The Return* might well shine some light on this, given that Lynch and Frost depicted the Trinity test as creating a rip in the dimensional veil", which gave "'the Experiment'...the opportunity to seed our realm with her demonic brood" ("Barbie, Barbelo,

Farrell wonders if the Nazis found "the means to 'activate' or even tap into the physics of the alleged energies of the global grid system." He argues that the fact that "the placement of such temples – and the Nazi transmitters – on world 'grid' sites suggests the Nazis did indeed … rediscover some aspects of long lost science." He points out that they "showed immense interest in Nikola Tesla's schemes for wireless broadcasting of electrical power," saying, "it seems evident that Nazis working with some version of Tesla's wireless electrical broadcast technology had discovered at least some aspects of the physics behind ancient geomancy and the world grid system."[37]

But, you are perhaps thinking, there is nothing to worry about; the Nazis lost WWII and were wiped out. Hopefully, you are correct, but I'm afraid to disappoint, as the ultimate parapolitical topic of high strangeness research is that the Nazis only lost *the battle of WWII* and retreated to fight *the continuing world war* by more covert and esoteric means.

Other New Age sources propose a similar evil use of this earth grid, claiming a group of evil "Archon extraterrestrials," (called simply the "NAA"--"negative alien agenda") has taken control of this grid in some places on the globe,[39] with another source saying there is an "Etheric Archon grid" which has been "present around this planet for the last 26,000 years" and has been "strengthened by many" Archon Ultraterrestrials over that time. These "Archons became afraid that the Galactic Confederation will make real contact with the surface population of this planet and they reinforced the grid to prevent that." This is where the theory that Earth is a prison planet comes from.[U.40]

REMOVING THE DARK GRID

Not to be too dismayed at our prison planet situation, it is claimed our awareness of the negative grid and the practice of the "goddess vortex technology" will dissolve it. In practice "etheric liberation" involves increasing love energy because Archons are "allergic" to love energies and the love energies also empower the non-physical, higher dimensional good guys. The evil archons are also allergic to "healthy sexual energy" and when they are able to suppress this source of life force then "the surface of the planet" can more "easily be controlled."[40] So the very least one can do is try and get your freak on to free the planet.

Babalon and the Bomb," *The Secret Sun Institute*, Chris Knowles, SecretSun.blogspot.com, Aug. 11, 2023).

U "There are two alien forces on the planet, struggling … for supremacy. One force wishes to keep humanity asleep … the other force wishes to give humanity knowledge so that it may free itself of the clutches of the planetary forces, the Archons … and escape the prison planet that is the Earth." Tom DeLonge and Peter Levenda, *Sekret Machines: Gods: An Official Investigation of the UFO Phenomenon*. p. 53.

Those familiar with the work of Wilhelm Reich will see resonance in his theories and the above paragraph. In *The Function of the Orgasm,* Reich claimed that all human mental problems stemmed from damned up sexual energy, which could be cured by increased orgastic potency. He also discovered something he called "orgone energy" which is "the cosmic life energy of the planet." A lot of people familiar with Reich's work around sexual health are unaware his later work took a highly strange turn. He claimed evil aliens "are currently waging an unheard of type of warfare on the planet Earth by *withdrawing* from our planet vast amounts of" positive orgone energy and "*simultaneously,* pouring into our atmosphere, DOR, deadly orgone energy."[41]

Evil Vortexes

In addition to positive New Age vortexes there are also said to be negative vortexes. In 1972, Ivan T. Sanderson published an article titled "The Twelve Devil's Graveyards Around the World." The most known of these "12 Vile Vortices" is the Bermuda Triangle and all are "points on Earth where known physics cannot be applied" because there exist "natural anomalies ... caused by the planet's electromagnetic fields being stronger there than anywhere else." These vortexes are said to be vile because, at the Bermuda Triangle for example, the area has "In the last 50 years ... claimed over 700 boats, 120 planes, and countless lives."[42]

One New Age source claims the evil vortexes located on Earth were used as portals for an Archon invasion in 1996. The two vortexes that hold "the most potential for Ascension on a planetary scale" are in Ljubljana, Slovenia and Santa Monica, California. And as a result, "they have been suppressed by dark forces so that they can continue their rule."[43] This battle over energy vortexes between light and dark forces brings to mind a curious fact from American history in general and Asheville history in particular: in 1933, the Silver Legion (a.k.a. the Silver Shirts) was founded by William Dudley Pelley and headquartered in Asheville, North Carolina.[V,44]

The Silver Legion "would prove to be one of the largest pro-Hitler organizations in the United States" and "vowed [it] would wage 'the ultimate contest for existence between Aryan mankind and Jewry.'" Pelley was a "writer, publisher, guru [and] self-proclaimed metaphysician" who was put on his dark spiritual path one "night in 1928 when, while sojourning at a ... mountain bungalow, he drifted into what he later described as an 'ecstatic

V Guy Warren Ballard "Founder of the mystical I AM movement ... was also associated with the fascist Silver Shirts prior to World War Two. George Hunt Williamson was associated with Ballard for a time." (A. Greenfield, *Secret Cipher of the UFOnauts*, p. 19).

interlude.'" He explained that he spent "seven minutes in eternity," where he left his body "and entered a mystical realm." Pelly also said he met "a divine oracle who continued to speak to him from then on." He wrote an account of the episode, saying, "call it Heaven … call it the Astral Plane, call it the Fourth Dimension, call it What You Will."[45] Given the evil ideas that sprang from this realm, Mr. Pelly, I'd be inclined to call it Hell.

Was Pelley setting his American Nazi headquarters in Asheville a terrestrial part of a larger cosmic battle over the grid in general and specific New Age energy vortexes in particular?[W] Crowley suggested Ultraterrestrials, who have the power to manifest in the physical or be "discarnate" as it suits them, also have the power to "induce a girl to embroider a tapestry, or initiate a political movement to culminate in a world-war; all in pursuit of some plan wholly beyond the purview or the comprehension of the deepest and subtlest thinkers."[38] Had the Nazis won the war, would Asheville not be the New Age healing center it is known for today but instead a dark vortex of evil? Given the details in this chapter, this appears very possible.

Personal Experiences

Drunvalo Melchizedek

Drunvalo Melchizedek is one of the first writers to make energy grid work popular in the New Age community. During the mid to late 1990s when I was in college, a woman in my friendship group told me her mother was part of his entourage and would travel the planet doing this grid work. Every time I encountered her while out partying as only a college student can, she was amazed that I knew about the importance of her mother's work with Melchizedek and that I would keep inquiring about it. This was one of my early synchronistic connections that informed the original manuscript of this book.

Melchizedek is not as popular as he was when I was in college, but his work nevertheless has penetrated popular culture. This is seen in the song by the band Tool, "Forty Six and 2." The song refers to Melchizedek's claim that "once all humanity has restored their merkaba, the human race will evolve into a higher stage."[46] The books *Gifts of Mother Earth: Earth Energies, Vortexes, Lines,* and *Grids* and *Sedona Vortex 2000* by Richard Dannelley both explore Melchizedek's work with earth energies.

W "It is my contention that as the … Old Testament is a book describing humans' interactions with the Elohim, a group of space based … alien conquerors, the Yoga Sutras are a collection of ancient instructions on how to interact with the technology of these Space Alien Conquerors." Clif High, "Clif's Yoga Sutras Part 1," clifhigh.substack.com, July 22, 2023.

Ashtar Command

Another experience which occurred in college and informed the original manuscript of this book involved the Ashtar Command. This event occurred while my friend and I were under the influence of a psychedelic. This is the same friend who also had the alien fetus show up on his factory floor. We were listening to the Ween album, *The Mollusk,* and I plainly heard a voice breaking through the car radio. It was a male voice saying, "This is the Ashtar command." There was no other content to the message. I told my friend what I was hearing, but he did not hear it. At this time, I had a vague recollection of the Ashtar Command as a New Age subject, but mainly knew of the term via a band by the same name that played in the region around my university.[X]

I much later learned of the curious incident which occurred in the U.K. in 1977 when a message broke through the normal TV broadcast purporting "to be a communication from an individual identifying themselves as Vrillon, representing a body called the Ashtar Galactic Command." The message "was simple: we humans had to give up our warlike ways and embrace a more peaceful existence ... before it was too late." Vrillon said the course correction was "in order that you may share in the great awakening, as the planet passes into the New Age of Aquarius" which "can be a time of great peace and evolution for your race, but only if your rulers are made aware of the evil forces that can overshadow their judgments."[47]

Guided to Vortexes

Life circumstances have brought me to live in two known New Age energy vortexes. While composing this book, I presently am dividing my time between my residence in western North Carolina (less than an hour from an Asheville vortex) and Istanbul. If the below is correct, then it was due to some predestined mission involving helping to activate this Earth energy grid. Life circumstances have also brought me to live in two window areas, which I will discuss in Chapter 10. I believe these life circumstances could be due to me being a starseed.

"Starseed" is another important term from the New Age literature. They are said to have "specific roles" and a "spiritual mission ... to help free the planetary soul from ... energetic oppression enforced by the" evil Ultraterrestrials. They are also here to "change destructive timelines" by anchoring humanity to the most positive timeline. Utilizing magical techniques to provide this anchor is perhaps the most important component of high

X See "Review of *American Sunshine*" by Ashtar Command (northerntransmissions.com/ashtar-command-american-sunshine/).

strangeness magick. This is all a pretty tall order for human starseeds, considering we must also find time to focus on folding laundry and paying taxes. But whining will get us nowhere – so why did I just do it?

Starseeds are said to be taken by the flow of the Tao to find themselves in various sites important to the overall grid while living their lives: the universe guides them to live in these areas as part of their larger mission as starseeds. This is because they are "conduits of [a] higher frequency of energy." This "higher frequency energy gets into this reality system" because starseeds are "human acupuncture points." They pour this higher energy into the grid by their very existence and thereby bring "these energies into this realm." In this way they are weaving "larger fields of energy" which "are called Morphogenetic Fields."[48]

My Time in Asheville

After my graduation from college in 2000, in the Asheville vortex area of Black Mountain, North Carolina, I was hypnotized by my aunt (also a spiritually inclined psychotherapist)[Y] at the Light Center, a Geodesic domed meditation center. The center was started by James V. Goure, who "served as a Commander in the Navy shortly after World War II" and "then was attached to the Atomic Energy Commission in Washington, D.C. as a Senior Executive Officer." It is claimed that "During his work with this commission, [he] became aware of the very real threat of a nuclear war. [And] realized that none of the diplomatic and military methods tried had established world peace." Not dismayed by his failed attempts on the material plan to establish peace, Goure moved his efforts to the astral realm where he protected his family "by placing them in 'bubbles of light.'" He came to believe the same spiritual protection "could be done for the planet," and this was the inspiration of the center.[49]

Perhaps being hypnotized at this power spot to actualize my true self set me on the path that led me to where I am today. I would recommend all college graduates participate in such a ritual upon receiving their diploma. I also point out that engaging in psycho-spiritual activities (such as hypnosis) while at sacred sites is a key component of high strangeness magick.

In early 2017, I moved to Asheville, North Carolina, and by that time was well aware of its role as a New Age energy vortex. I moved to take a position as a psychotherapist at a premiere residential treatment center for young adults struggling with addiction. I say premiere because it caters to the children of wealthy families, including some of the Hollywood elite, and

Y See GailVaughnRogers.com.

hires amazing clinicians – such as myself. Having worked as a psychotherapist at this facility, I can attest to the idea that the region aids the healing process and, when treating addiction, one needs all the help they can get. At this facility, nature treatment modalities were used, such as vision quests and vision walks. I was blessed to participate in one vision quest ceremony, assisting a clinician of Native American heritage.

The facility is nestled in the mountains of Buncombe County, where Asheville is the major city. Interestingly enough, the facility is on the grounds of what was at one time a survival compound for Y2K. After civilization did not collapse, the grounds were sold and it eventually ended up being the treatment center where I worked. While writing this book, a manager told me that it was his understanding the location was where several ley lines converged. This was passed down to him verbally by an executive of the program. Later in the book I will speculate which ley lines they may be referring to.

The Asheville area is also known to be one of the hot spots for Alcoholics Anonymous (AA) groups in the country, meaning there are a lot of meetings considered to be of good quality. The founding of AA is a high strangeness rabbit hole (involving deceased Christian monks, Ouija boards, Carl Jung and psychedelics) we will not go down just yet, but I hope to explore in subsequent volumes of this series.[Z] I was originally a skeptic of the AA approach, but am now a believer in its efficacy, as I have witnessed it first hand, although I myself am not an addict.

The modern discoverer of the Sedona and Asheville vortex, Page Bryant, passed away in July of 2017 while she was living in Waynesville, North Carolina, approximately thirty miles from where I was living at the time in Asheville. Before she passed, she was working on her novel, *The Second Coming of the Star Gods*. The book ostensibly dealt with "When, How, What and Why the humans started to speak with the gods" or conversely "When, How, What and Why the gods started to speak with humans?" The novel was intended to be "a journey into the relationship between gods and humans" and deal with "the intervention of the gods through Pharaoh's dreams, visions and prophecies."[50] I do not know how much of the book Bryant completed before she passed.

My Time in Istanbul

In Istanbul, before the *pandemic* put a stop to it, I participated in a very powerful weekly shamanic drum circle where I consciously utilized the vortex energy. I will explore more of the high strangeness in Turkey in general and

Z See "The Occult and Psychedelic Origins of Alcoholics Anonymous and 12-Step Recovery" by Junglepuker, r/occult, 2017.

Istanbul in particular in later volumes of this book. For starters, I can point out that a possible Jinn haunting caused me to get a bad AirBNB review; and a very talented psychic said I had the biggest guardian angel she had ever seen. My angel is fairly high up the angelic hierarchy, being an assistant of an archangel. Not that it is a competition, but most guardian angels do not have this high a rank according to the psychic. I jokingly call this my *big ass angel,* which can be seen on the cover of this book protecting the planet.

My Time in a Dark Vortex

Life circumstances have also led me to visit the dark vortex of Santa Monica. In 2005, I went to Hollywood, California to pitch reality TV show ideas. Interestingly enough, I sold one concept to the production company of Mike Sears, who was an integral ingredient for the start of super-producer Mark Burnett's ascendancy (current sources estimate his net worth at half a billion). Sears was an "early and frequent collaborator with Mark Burnett" and "produced and directed Mark's first television experience with the Raid Gauloises Adventure Race, going on to produce and direct the first two Eco-Challenge documentaries and setting up the first season of Survivor with Mark."

Eco-Challenge is recognized as the birthplace of contemporary reality TV adventure series, such as *Survivor,* and thus marked the start of Mark Burnett's prosperous career. In addition, Sears and his wife "coined Survivor's famous phrase 'Out Wit, Out Play, Out Last' for the first season's casting promotion on CBS."[51] Based on my perception it appears that if not for the collaboration with Sears then the alchemical fire that was Burnett's success may have never been ignited.

In an interesting, six degrees of separation type manner, Sears had a role in the Trump presidency. My logic is that if it were not for the success of Burnett's *The Apprentice* then Trump would not have been popular enough to win the presidency in 2016. And if it were not for the early collaboration of Sears and Burnett, then perhaps Burnett would have never been in a position to produce *Survivor,* the mainstream show which launched his career. Burnett's role in the rise of Trump has been speculated upon in the *The New Yorker,* where it was said that "With *The Apprentice,* the TV producer mythologized Trump – then a floundering D-lister – as the ultimate titan, paving the way to the Presidency."[52]

I also pitched some concepts to a producer at his home in Santa Monica. This producer pointed out his home was in the same neighborhood where the home used for the exterior shots in the TV show *7th Heaven* was located. *7th Heaven* was a wholesome show about a Christian pastor, his wife, and seven children and ran for eleven seasons. An interesting juxtaposition with the idea of Santa Monica being a dark vortex. However, I felt no evil energy at the time, except for the disappointment of the producer not wanting to collaborate with me.

Another interesting anecdote of my trip to the dark vortex was that I pitched shows at the production company that was producing the *Star Trek* franchise.[AA] There is a deep, high strangeness rabbit hole related to *Star Trek*'s creator Gene Roddenbury who had a "relationship with a mysterious extraterrestrial group calling itself the Council of Nine that were being channeled by the psychic Phyllis Schlemmer in the 1970s. Roddenberry sat in on channeling sessions from 1974 to 1975."[53]

Group Member in Sedona

Although I have not been to Sedona, an original member of my psycho-spiritual group, Çhaplins Öf Peril, attended an addiction treatment center in the area. The facility utilized many transpersonal psychology techniques such as holotropic breathwork and shamanistic techniques. This individual reported powerful experiences on both a psycho-spiritual and transpersonal level. If it weren't for the powerful healing effects of the Sedona vortex, then perhaps he may not be with us today.

Interestingly, while writing this chapter this individual made plans to revisit this facility as a guest. He reported that the day before he was to leave, he realized he had lost a piece of rose quartz that a staff member had given him upon completion of the program. He wanted desperately to find it before his trip so he could show the staff he still carried it with him. He had all but given up trying to find the quartz when he returned to his bedroom, finding it placed on top of a necklace he had laid out on his dresser (where he had previously looked several times). This individual swears the quartz must have materialized out of thin air and claims it was "one of the most unexplainable and paranormal experiences I've probably ever had ... easily the most bizarre" and so much so that it didn't "seem real." This is high strangeness for you, so bizarre it doesn't seem real.

Speaking of Atlantis

While writing this book the topic of Atlantis has come up much more than I thought it would. Honestly, before researching and writing

AA Piller (1948 – 2005) "was an American television scriptwriter and producer, who was best known for his contributions to the Star Trek franchise" (wiki/Michael_Piller). It is interesting to note that he apparently passed shortly after I pitched my concepts to his production company.

this book, it was not a New Age topic I was particularly interested in. In addition to Atlantis showing up in the material for this book, it is also important on a personal level. This is because while living in the window area of Carrollton, Georgia, I witnessed someone channel a trans-dimensional entity from the "light command." I was cryptically told that myself and "two Americans would raise Atantis [sic]."[AB]

I now believe this prediction that I would *raise Atlantis* might have to do with New Age energy grid and vortex work as laid out in this chapter. As we have seen, the theory is that the old grid during the times of Atlantis supported a golden age, a veritable garden of Eden. Then a war took place over control of this grid, leading to the destruction of Atlantis. Whether the good or bad Ultraterrestrials win this cosmic war 2.0 will determine if Earth returns to a golden age or the dark Nazi prison planet, the evil Atlantis of Himmler. If the prediction I received is believed to be true, then myself and two Americans will be successful in activating this ancient vortex energy for the forces of good. So eat your dark heart out, Heinrich!

Conclusion

I propose that window areas exist roughly due to the same phenomena as the New Age energy vortex sites, but on a smaller scale. Perhaps these sacred sites were once small geographic window areas that were turned into large vortexes through ritual attention, or were taken over and expanded upon by (good and evil) Ultraterrestrials.

By providing a brief overview of basic New Age ideas like the energy vortex, ascension, the Earth grid, and starseeds – while demonstrating their connections with ideas explored in high strangeness literature – I aim to inspire researchers of the phenomenon to explore New Age literature. This is because I believe that delving into various aspects of this topic can enrich one's high strangeness research. Moreover, I contend that it has the potential to guide us in crafting *new rituals* within the realm of high strangeness, bringing us closer to a successful praxis of high strangeness magick and research.

I use the term praxis as opposed to practice because "praxis is always 'history making action' that transforms the world in which the practice is carried out."[54] For example, using this new praxis, I encourage high strangeness researchers to turn their local window areas into New Age vortex/sacred sites. We are in a unique position to accomplish this because we are the ones who are discovering them, not the New Age folks. The facilitation of

AB Of note here is that Greenfield claims unusual spellings of words is part of the *Secret Cipher of the UFOnauts.*

a window area to a vortex/sacred site can be facilitated with the new rituals of high strangeness magick.

I also encourage New Age practitioners to look into high strangeness literature. For one, doing so will help you learn more about how to discover where the window areas are in your locale. Up until now, New Age practitioners mainly focus on already established vortex/sacred sites. High strangeness research will also prove helpful because it provides journalistic and scholarly evidence to back the bold claims of New Age channelers. This will help deepen your spiritual practice because these claims are backed up by nuts and bolts research.

One reason I like this chapter is because it points out that the stakes in this field of research are pretty high. I mean, what is higher than a covert global war for control of the planet? One critique I have of the high strangeness community is that the whole endeavor has an air of only being about fun and games. I'm sad to inform you that this isn't the case: as I have demonstrated in this chapter, the dire warnings of the New Age channelers about the evil forces involved in the phenomenon are also borne out by high strangeness researchers.

Some would say a battle between the forces of good and evil over some invisible earth energy grid is simply crazy. But I point out, again, *it's only crazy if it's not true.* If it is indeed true, then it raises the stakes infinitely with this book you are reading. Also, in terms of karma, if you don't rise to this challenge then you are literally letting down the planet, galaxy, and maybe universe. And, laying karma aside, historically speaking, if you are wrong about this chapter being mere sci-fi fantasy, then you are, to say the very least, on the wrong side of history.

However, don't get me wrong. One of the great things about high strangeness research is the fun factor in figuring out the puzzle. And not only that, but the camaraderie around figuring out the puzzle within a community. Going back to *Hellier*, one thing that brings me back to multiple viewings of the series is the sense of community of the investigators as they piece together this utterly absurd, highly strange cosmic puzzle. They are having fun as they go down the rabbit hole. And as we know, those evil Nazi archons suffer anaphylactic shock when humans are enthralled in a fun energy. With that being said, enjoy yourself as you continue your research. Figuring out where the pieces fit is immensely fun. So, I ask you: are we having fun yet?

References:

1. Allen Greenfield, *Secret Cipher of the UFOnauts,* 1994, pp. 13, 20, 60.

2. Meade Layne, *The Coming Of The Guardians,* 1954. Publisher's summary.

3. Carla Lisbeth Rueckert, Jim McCarty, Donald Tully Elkins, *Light/Lines: The First Twenty-Five Years,* 2014. Publisher's summary.

4. John Keel, *Operation Trojan Horse,* (first published 1970), 1976 ver., pp. 46, 8, 145.

5. Laura Knight-Jadczyk, *High Strangeness: Hyperdimensions and the Process of Alien Abductions,* 2005. Publisher's summary.

6. Rob Riggs and Tom Burnette, *The Bigfoot-UFO Connection,* Llewellyn.com, April 2014.

7. Peter Levenda, *Rites of the Mummy: The K'Rla Cell and the Secret Key to Liber AL,* 2021, E-book: p. 236

8. Debra Stangl, "What is a Vortex?" VisitSedona.com.

9. Melissa Alvarez, *Earth Frequency: Sacred Sites, Vortexes, Earth Chakras and Other Transformative Places,* 2019: E-book: p. 20

10. "Crystals, Vortexes and UFOs: Sedona's Metaphysical Side," Sedona.net.

11. *Sedona Journal of Emergence,* encylopedia.com.

12. Tara Isabella Burton, "Spiritual Sedona: The Arizona Town Bursting with Positive Vibes," TheGuardian.com, Jan. 2017.

13. Gregory Drambour, "Sedona Vortex Spiritual Experiences," *Sedona Sacred Journeys,* Sedona-Spiritual-vactions.com, gregorydrambour.com/books.

14. Jason Sandford, "Page Bryant, Psychic Who Identified Sedona and Asheville Vortexes, Dies," AshVegas.com, Sept. 6, 2017.

15. Page Bryant, *The Spiritual Reawakening of the Great Smoky Mountains,* 1994, pp. 116-17, 92, 148, 157, 84-85, 14, 79-80, 92.

16. "Salamanders of the Smokies," MyPigeonForge.com.

17. James Shelby Downard, *Stalking the Great Whore: The Lost Writings of James Shelby Downard,* 2023, pp. 291, 81.

18. Ravenari, "Salamander - Land-Swimmer," Wildspeak.com.

19. Grant Parsons, "New Age Comes Unto These Hills," *News & Observer of Raleigh,* June 1996.

20. Robert Pozner, "Asheville's Growth Began with 19th Century TB Treatment," Citizen-Times.com, July 2015.

21. K. Fletcher, *Mysteries and Strange Stories in the North Carolina Mountains,* 2014, E-book, p. 8.

22. John DeSouza, *Higher Journeys with Alexis Brooks,* Podcast, June 2018, Time: 33:00

23. Nina (Ergin) Macaraig, *Constantinople/Istanbul: A Vortex of Peoples and Cultures*, 2012.

24. Peter Mark Adams, "Energy Medicine, Entity Attachment, and Ancestral Healing," *The Higherside Chats*, Feb. 2022, Time: 52:38.

25. "Best Places for Spiritual Awakening," NBCNews.com, April 4, 2011.

26. "The Magic of Falling Water," waterfallkeepersofnc.org.

27. Joshua Allen, "The Quiet Comeback of Istanbul's Hidden Sufi Lodges: The Banned Dervish Halls Are Scattered Through the City," AtlasObscura.com, Oct. 10, 2016.

28. "Sufi Shrines of İstanbul," istanbul.com/sufi-shrines-of-istanbul.

29. Alec Christos Gabbitas, "The Planet's Crystal Grid System: The Return of the Dove," LightParty.com, Feb. 22, 2008.

30. Bülent (Önsü) Çorak Vedia, *The Knowledge Book*, 1996, pp. 167, 808-809, 673, 809, 1119, 809, 808, 429, 598, 274. scribd.com/document/408641929/vdocuments-mx-the-knowledge-book-bilgi-kitabi-pdf

31. Ashtar, Channeled by James McConnell, *The New Earth Timeline*, Ancient-Awakenings.com, 08/6/2023.

32. "Quantum Mechanics and the Djinn Dimension," Youtube: *Mysterious Middle East*, 2020.

33. Niki Gamm, "Istanbul: City of Legends and Fairy Tales," *Hurriyet Daily News*, 2015.

34. "Sacred Earth Practitioners: Activation Level," Asiltoksal.com/sep-activation-level.

35. "Ascension Glossary," ascensionglossary.com, Awakening Symptoms, Subatomic particles, Quantic fields impact to space time, Planetary gridworkers.

36. "About Joseph P. Farrell," gizadeathstar.com/about/.

37. Joseph P. Farrell, *Grid of the Gods: The Aftermath of the Cosmic War and the Physics of the Pyramid Peoples*, 2011, E-book: pp. 23, 179, 24, 23, 23-24, 208, 25, 27, 92, 95, 209, 123-124.

38. Aleister Crowley, *Magick Without Tears*, (written in 1943, published in 1955), quoted in *Secret Cipher of the UFOnauts*, p. 58, Chapter IX: "The Secret Chiefs."

39. "Negative Alien Agenda (NAA)," ascensionglossary.com/index.php/NAA

40. "Etheric Archon Grid," November 1, 2015, prepareforchange.net/2015/11/01/etheric-archon-grid/

41. Jerome Eden, *Planet in Trouble: The UFO Assault on Earth – Startling Proof of the Danger from Outer Space and How Wilhelm Reich's Discoveries Can Be Used to Combat It*, June 23, 1973.

42/ Dr. Phoenix, "The 12 Vile Vortices," heelsandpyramids.com/paranormal /12-vile-vortices/

43. "Daily Meditation for healing the Los Angeles Vortex," Feb. 22, 2022, WeLoveMassMeditation.com

44. "The Silver Shirts: Their History, Founder, and Activities," 1922, ajcarchives. org/AJC_DATA/Files/THR-SS1.PDF

45. Jon Elliston, *New Age Nazi,* Mountain Xpress, 2004, mountainx.com/news/ community-news/0128pelley-php/

46. Sean McCarthy, "Evolution Calling: Tool – 'Useful Idiot' and 'Forty Six & Two,'" *Pop Matters.*

47. David Barnett, "Vrillon: The Alien Voice Hoax That Became a Legend," Wednesday 22 November 2017, independent.co.uk/.

48. "Starseed," AscensionGlossary.com.

49. "Founders of the UR Light Center," urlight.org/founders/.

50. PageBryant'sfacebookpage,facebook.com/Page-Bryant-1430820273880355/.

51. "Mike Sears," Internet Movie Database.

52. Patrick Radden Keefe, "How Mark Burnett Resurrected Donald Trump as an Icon of American Success," *The New Yorker,* December 27, 2018.

53. "Contact with the Council of Nine & Roddenberry's Star Trek Future," *Exopolitics Today with Dr. Michael Salla,* November 5, 2021, episode summary.

54. Stephen Kemmis, Jane Wilkinson, Christine Edwards-Groves, Ian Hardy, Peter John Grootenboer, Laurette Bristol, "Praxis, Practice and Practice Architectures," book chapter from *Changing Practices, Changing Education,* 2013.

JOHN DESOUZA was an FBI Special Agent for over 20 years and collector of the real life "X-Files." The author has researched and uncovered paranormal experiences as they have been revealed to him. Trained as an attorney and investigating official of the U.S. government, John DeSouza unravels mysteries that elude investigators restricted to the purely material world. The author devotes himself to his companies and to writing books on spiritual and paranormal topics.

Chapter 4

Why Window Areas Exist: A Highly Strange Person

My top brought Zeus down, my middle shines up, my bottom has all power,
and my hole is a flower for the stars.
Where your head be, is a see-true weapon:
But, not if your eyes are painted.

Why Do Window Areas Exist?

Assuming that window areas are the cause of high strangeness phenomena begs the question: *Why do window areas exist?* The proceeding chapters will survey the prevailing theories on the matter. Author and former FBI agent John DeSouza[A] discusses window areas in an interview where he claims that "we have two types" which connect our world to "paranormal phenomena." The first is "people" and the second is "geographic locations." This chapter will explore people as the cause of high strangeness window areas and the next chapter will explore special geographic locations being the cause.

For DeSouza, some individuals are "lightning rods" which attract "paranormal experiences." He believes this is due to a person's particular "consciousness" and gives an example of a woman who reported seeing demons, the fae, orbs, UFOs and deceased relatives. He claims these types of individuals who "attract all types of paranormal experiences" are a relatively common occurrence.

Humans as Paranormal Conduits

If we accept that some people are naturally inclined to be walking window areas for high strangeness, it begs another question: Why? DeSouza speculates this is due to some humans having a unique electromagnetic configuration that in turn meshes with certain geographical nodes around the planet.[1]

In our attempt to gain more insight into why some people attract paranormal phenomena, let's turn to the work of Colin Wilson. He says the

---

A "John DeSouza was an FBI Special Agent who maintained a top secret security clearance for over twenty-five years as he investigated paranormal experiences. During that time, he collected what he calls 'the real-life X-FILES'" ("Paranormal Common Sense with John DeSouza," *Beyond Belief with George Noory*, Season 9: Ep 20, Gaia.com.)

answer lies in "something that orthodox science" has ignored but is "as fundamental as Newton's discovery of the laws of gravity."[2] He points out that in 1935 a paper was published at Yale called "Electro-dynamic Theory of Life," suggesting, quite simply, that living things produce electrical fields that can be measured, called "life fields." Life fields also crop up in the theory behind acupuncture, which says "the universe is permeated with … the same vital force" which also "permeate the human body, with definite crossing points like 'leys.'" This vital force energy is called *ch'i*.

Moving from naturally occurring life fields, we come to *thought fields*. Wilson puts forth the theory that what we call ghosts are actually just the thought field emanating from an individual onto the life field of an area. He says a ghost may actually be "a kind of snapshot, imprinted" on the overall life field of an area "by some intense emotion" via a human's thought field apparatus. He explains that "intense happiness can 'imprint' itself on [these] 'fields' just as easily as intense misery or fear."

Wilson points out that people's thought fields can "attach themselves to any kind of matter." Giving the real world example of how this might play out with a real estate agent "trying to sell a desirable property" and then being "puzzled and disappointed when clients exclaimed, 'Ugh, let's get out of here! This place gives me the willies!'" The fact that bad vibes can be projected onto a house, for example, is evidence that we are "dealing with some general law concerning fields." He also points out it is easier for a human to impress their thought field on the "electrical field associated with a certain area" if there is water running through it.[2] This is especially important to the high strangeness magical approach of utilizing the small (and often overlooked) creeks in our own backyards to enhance our goal of turning the area into a sacred space.[B]

The Uri Geller Effect

We will now look at case examples of people who seemingly have innate powers (making them a high strangeness magnet) and the ability to cultivate them. The main person we will look at in this section is the Israeli parapsychology popstar, Uri Geller. Geller's paranormal abilities were featured in RAW's first volume of *Cosmic Trigger,* where he was mentioned specifically as being a puzzle piece to the Sirius mystery. According to RAW there was "an alleged extraterrestrial entity that supposedly communicates through Geller and enables him to read minds and bend metal."[3] So, if we

B See "Michael Wann: Susquehanna Alchemy, River Goddess Worship, and The Big Ritual," *The Higherside Chats*, May 12, 2018.

are to take this as true, we could speculate that extraterrestrials are able to enhance a person's thought field ability.

Let us turn to the writings of Andrija Puharich[C] on Geller. Puharich claims he first heard of Geller in 1970 from "a report written by an Israeli army officer" who reported Geller had telepathic powers such as the ability to bend metal with his mind. Puharich claims his time with Geller convinced him that he "was one of the most unusual men in the world."[4] Puharich is an important person to know for high strangeness researchers. Colin Wilson says he "was known as a respectable scientist" seen in the fact that the writer Aldous Huxley said he was "one of the most brilliant minds in parapsychology." Wilson says that Puharich's contact with Geller "seemed to have destroyed his judgment," because he was "asserting that Uri Geller was some kind of divine messenger, an instrument of 'the controllers of the universe,' and that the aim of these mysterious entities was to bring a New Age of peace and prosperity to the earth."[5]

Wilson assumes Puharich's opinion, that Geller is a "divine messenger," is woefully incorrect. This brings me to something I say often in my high strangeness research: *it's not crazy if it is true*. However, this isn't exactly correct in a clinical sense, which I will explore in the conclusion. I also like to say *it's not wrong if it's correct*. I have found that often researchers will dismiss an absurd claim out of hand before considering it may actually be a reality. The claim is so absurd (to their perception of reality) that they immediately dismiss it out of hand. In this case, if Geller really and truly is some kind of messenger from cosmic forces, then Puharich's judgment is sound. It is only unsound if it is not true. This extraterrestrial messianic side of Geller (explored in detail in volume one of RAW's *Cosmic Trigger*) is little known.

Geller is most known for his spoon-bending American television performances, appearing on, *The Tonight Show Starring Johnny Carson* and *The Merv Griffin Show*. The image of a bent spoon is now ubiquitous thanks in large part to Geller and its inclusion in *The Matrix* movie franchise. It is now seen as a symbol of breaking free of our materialistic view of reality. The bent spoon is so tied to Geller that he even has a large bent spoon sculpture outside of his museum in Israel.[D]

Geller claimed that his powers began to emerge when he was around 5 years old, discovering "that he could read his mother's mind. When she

C He is also author of *The Sacred Mushroom: Key to the Door of Eternity?* (1974) I do believe it is one of the keys to eternity. Also see the film *Plan Nine From Outer Space* which "looks at the" alleged "sinister origins of The Nine," a New Age channeling group; "its disciples include cutting edge scientists, multi-millionaire industrialists and leading politicians." The following article also explores Puharich's involvement with the group. (urigeller.com/plan-nine-outer-space/)

D See the UriGellermuseum.com.

came back from playing cards with friends, he suddenly knew precisely how much money she had lost." The tangible phenomena such as spoon bending started at the age of 6.[5] Geller also was a part of research at the Stanford Research Institute (SRI). The documentary, *Third Eye Spies* (Lance Mungia, 2019) gives a wonderful account of the goings on at the SRI during the height of the Cold War. SRI was affiliated with the CIA and the US military in studying the use of remote viewing to help defeat the Soviets.

In the documentary, the former SRI researchers and ex-psychic spies claim remote viewing was exceedingly accurate and therefore useful for military purposes (such as locating Russian nuclear submarines, hostages and secret military installations). The official story is that the program was disbanded by the powers that be because it was not accurate enough. Many believe the program continues to this day, albeit clandestinely.

In the documentary it is claimed they brought in a person off the street, with no inborn psychic ability, as a control test subject. They were surprised to find this person ended up being the best remote viewer in the entire program. Some claim this discovery – suggesting that everyone has an innate ability for psychic powers[E] – is the reason the program was shut down (publicly at least). The idea is that if the masses discovered they had trans-dimensional powers, it would upset the cosmic apple cart. With that being said, it appears people have the ability to cultivate these powers, meaning these powers don't just manifest in special people. We are all special.

RSPK

In *The Geller Phenomenon,* Wilson compares Geller's abilities to RSPK (Recurrent Spontaneous Psychokinesis). The common term for RSPK is the poltergeist phenomena, poltergeist being the German word for a rowdy ghost. The term psychokinesis (PK) can be defined as "the ability to use energy of the mind to move or otherwise affect matter without physical contact."[6] Noted parapsychologist Hans Bender called RSPK the "royal road to an extended understanding of man, of his position in nature and of nature herself."[7]

In these so-called poltergeist hauntings, events and disturbances of a remarkable variety are often reported. These typically include strange noises such as unusual knockings, raps, bangs, whistling, singing, and talking. Movements and destruction of domestic objects are among other strange

E As Rudolf Steiner said, "by emphasizing the truth that the way to higher knowledge is open to anyone who will acquire for himself the faculties by which he may prove this spiritual truth herein claimed." (*The Way of Initiation: How to Attain Knowledge of Higher Worlds*, 1908, Chapter 1, Audio book: 6:00).

occurrences often reported. Objects have even been reported to disappear and reappear, sometimes in different locations. Beds are sometimes reported to shake and furniture to rearrange itself. In extreme poltergeist cases, "teleportation, mysterious conveyance of various articles in and out of locked doors and closed drawers or cabinets" have been reported.[8] Numerous poltergeist cases have been studied by contemporary parapsychological researchers; as a result these strange occurrences are well-documented in the parapsychology literature. There seems to be a general agreement among parapsychologists that the poltergeist phenomena is not the result of pesky ghosts but is caused by RSPK. I recall being surprised when Dr. Roll told me personally he did not think poltergeist activity was due to actual ghosts.

In most poltergeist cases, there is a living person at the center of the disturbances, whom parapsychologists refer to as the agent. This person is often a teenager experiencing a difficult time during adolescence. Most parapsychologists believe that, *without the person realizing it*, they are venting their inner psychological frustration in an unusual way by projecting it onto the people and physical objects surrounding them.[F,6] Wilson says in the 20th century the idea of the unconscious was put forth by psychologists and is now generally accepted. However, he says "the idea that the subconscious mind is capable of acting directly upon matter in the real world still seems incredible, although numerous authenticated cases exist in which that seems to be the most likely hypothesis to explain the facts."[5] The subconscious or unconscious mind was *discovered* by Freud and the psychoanalysts in the early 1900s.

An early psychoanalytic pioneer who was also interested in the poltergeist phenomena was Nandor Fodor. His 1951 book, *Haunted People: The Story of the Poltergeist Down Through the Ages* was an early text on the phenomenon. He was also the first person to put forth the idea that poltergeist phenomena manifested from the unconscious mind of an agent.

Fodor's contribution to the field of poltergeist studies is documented in the 1953 book of essays, *Psychoanalysis and the Occult*. There it is pointed out that he "applied his psychoanalytic insight to the problem of the poltergeist which he considers an *extrojected* ... manifestation of a schizophrenic disorder that can be understood 'only in terms of the dynamic psychology'"

F These people, instead of resolving their stress in normal ways, blow off steam unconsciously through RSPK activity. This is thought to be so because patterns can usually be found in the disturbances which are generally symbolic and give clues as to the nature of the unresolved stress of the agent. The disturbances often appear as metaphors to the causes of stress. For example, anger towards a certain person may be released by the agent causing items belonging to the target person to break.

of Freud. The phenomena involved in a poltergeist case, Fodor said, are "expressive of deep-lying psychological conflicts."[9]

Fodor's investigation into a case of high strangeness, involving, of all things, a talking mongoose, in 2022 was made into a movie called *Nandor Fodor and the Talking Mongoose*. The film's description is as follows: "In 1935, Hungarian-American para-psychologist ... began his investigation of a strange occurrence on the Isle of Man. An average British family ... claimed to have been contacted by a mysterious ... talking mongoose."[10]

People who are the agents of the RSPK phenomenon are those with paranormal abilities, but don't have conscious awareness of them. As a result, unaware people aren't able to cultivate and control their powers like Uri Geller, who was born with innate powers, or those in top secret programs who are taught how to access their own latent powers.

Wolfgang Pauli Effect

Similar to the RSPK phenomenon is what is known as the Wolfgang Pauli Effect, which is named after "an Austrian theoretical physicist who pioneered the study of quantum physics."[11] Pauli helped Jung come up with the term synchronicity and introduced acausality, a principle which represented an "enormous shift in intellectual history." This is because "according to quantum theory" we must "now abandon our servitude to strict causality," which is the idea "that all events have some well-defined set of causes" indicating that "nature is structured and lawful." The structure of reality itself is said to be acausal because "there are no well-defined causes for individual quantum events." Jung learned of this discovery through his friend Pauli, which led to his "idea of synchronicity as acausal connection through meaning of inner psychic states with outer events."[12]

The Pauli Effect was coined after it was discovered that his presence had a disruptive effect on technology and that synchronicities would occur in his presence.[G,14] Perhaps people like Pauli (along with RSPK agents) have an inborn ability that they aren't cultivating, so it is manifesting in a negative way. Awareness of our innate ability to access paranormal abilities seems key in making sure they manifest in a positive manner.

Gestalt of Like Minded Individuals

High strangeness researcher and author Trey Hudson speculates that window areas may occur due to a "gestalt of like minded individuals" who come together and (consciously or unconsciously) create a high

G Interestingly, the comedian Adam Carolla often talks about how he has this effect on technology, causing it to malfunction.

strangeness field in a particular area.[15] Trey also reported to me that strange things happen when he gets together with a particular friend. An explanation of why a gestalt of like-minded weirdos could cause a window area can be found in the 2018 book *Paranormal Encounters on Britain's Roads* by Peter McCue. McCue speaks of the psychic internet theory, which suggests the possibility that "people's minds sometimes interact at a subconscious level and generate paranormal phenomena." This theory would seem to suggest "that many ghostly manifestations and apparitions could quite possibly be explained as 'hallucinations engendered by … a kind of group telepathy.'"[16]

THE WITCHING-HOUR AND WEDNESDAY

3 A.M. is sometimes called the witching hour because many people report paranormal happenings at that time. In a sense, 3 A.M. is a temporal-based window area, a window in time. One theory is that this time is a paranormal window area because a mass of people are in a deep state of sleep. This mass of people in deep sleep may have a group effect, causing the veils between dimensions to be thinner at this time. Filmmaker Christopher Garetano[H] says 3 A.M. is "like a vortex opening everywhere at a certain time of night."[17]

In addition to window areas existing around time, there are also seasonal ones as well. During Halloween, for example, "it is believed that the veil between the physical world and the spiritual … world is at its thinnest."[18] There is also a day of the week that appears to be a high strangeness magnet. According to Keel, "The Wednesday phenomenon is quite evident in the historical events as well as in contemporary sightings. A disproportionate number of UFO events seem to be concentrated on Wednesdays."[19]

In the study of high strangeness, one theory is that the phenomenon manifests more readily at liminal spaces and when people are in liminal states of being. This is because in the liminal, "energy is a lot more potent and the veil between worlds is at its thinnest."[20] The definition of liminal is "occupying a position at, or on both sides of, a boundary or threshold."[21] 3 a.m. and Wednesday are liminal, or in between, times. 3 a.m. is neither morning nor night; Wednesday is neither early nor late in the week. This time and day of the week is putting people in a liminal consciousness, which thereby facilitates them to be more open to high strangeness phenomena.

GRAVEYARDS

Graveyards are geographic locations that some claim are window areas for paranormal phenomena. At first blush, the reasoning behind this is that it is due to spirits of the dead. Author and anomalistic researcher

H See travelchannel.com/profiles/talent/christopher-garetano.

John Tenny[I] provides another explanation that fits with our gestalt of like-minds theory. He speculates this may be due to the mass of psychic energy (people grieving) that is experienced at a graveyard.[22] This would mean the numerous mourners, letting out psychic energy in the area over many years, would create a window area, not the spirits of the dead.

Mass Meditation

Large groups of people coming together and having an outpouring of positive psychic energy is seen in mass meditations. Studies have shown "a distinct correlation between large groups practicing advanced Transcendental Meditation and a drop in" the crime rate. One particular study showed a 21.2 percent drop in homicide and an 18.5 percent drop in violent crime in a three-year period. This study indicates that large groups of people practicing mass meditation "had an energetic ripple effect on decreasing homicide and violence in urban areas nationwide."[23] A Russian professor of physics, Dr. Konstantin Korotkov, "explains how you can influence the world around you with your mind" saying that "According to the superstring theory in physics, waves of vibration flow from everything in the universe, affecting the collective consciousness of others." Because of this fact "Groups can enliven that field" creating "a certain synergy of energy" whereby "a common goal is achieved."[24]

I regularly participate in the mass meditations at WeLoveMassMeditation.com. They will sponsor mass meditations for world events, as if to stem the tide of negativity. For example, they offer mass meditations for the war in Ukraine, erupting volcanoes, and the Covid "pandemic." The head of the site is an individual going by the alias, Cobra, who claims to be in physical contact with positive extraterrestrials assisting mankind. This is unique in New Age literature, because most people claim to be in psychic, not physical, contact with extraterrestrials.

The benevolent extraterrestrial forces behind Cobra claim "The more people that gather together in meditation with powerful intention" at specific times "the faster we reach" a "critical mass" of people and we can then "change our world for the better, raising global frequency, which affects everyone" and supports the "Light Forces" in their battle with the dark forces for control of the planet.[25] Utilizing mass meditation in the appropriate way is a component of high strangeness magick.

I See his 2020 book *Theoretical Weirdo: A Mish Mash of Ramblings about Weirdness.*

Jesus Christ

The psychic power of a gestalt of like minds coming together is also seen in the Christian tradition. Magician and Jungian analyst J. Marvin Spiegelman, Ph.D., provides a transpersonal, Jungian analysis of this in his book of essays, *Psychotherapy as a Mutual Process.* He says that Jungians refer to the therapeutic relationship as an "analytic 'field" which is a "therapeutic field" that both the patient and therapist are "embedded in." Spielgelman reports that due to this field effect he will "very often" get symptoms such as "bodily reactions" which "the patient is having."[13,J] I can confirm the existence of this phenomenon in my psychotherapy practice. For instance, I often find myself feeling an emotion, typically sadness, before my clients become consciously aware of their own feelings of sadness. When I inquire if they are indeed experiencing sadness but haven't yet realized it, they consistently respond in the affirmative.

Spiegelman claims this therapeutic-quantum field is the occult explanation behind the New Testament quote: "For where two or three are gathered together in my name, there am I in the midst of them." Of this shared field he says the archetype of "The self[K] seems to be presiding over the process" and as such the "field vibrates with power, emotion and meaning."[13] The mainstream Christian book *Power Portals: Awaken Your Connection to the Spirit Realm* explores these concepts but from a more traditional Christian perspective. The book rests on the claim "that all Christians are intended to live ... in the realm of the supernatural." And says if people live in this manner they can then "participate in the supernatural on a daily basis through divine portals or gates."[26]

The Forrest Gump Effect

In the exploration of high strangeness, there appears to be a phenomenon where a researcher finds themselves consistently at the epicenter of all that is peculiar. This occurrence, which I have dubbed the "Forrest Gump effect," seems to be facilitated by synchronicity. In the upcoming section, "Toward a Grand Unifying Theory of High Strangeness," I will delve into

---

J Spiegelman also says quantum mechanics in the late 1920s "revolutionized physics" and also "greatly expanded our notions of fields." As a result we now "understand quantum fields not as existing physically in space-time the way a classical gravitational or electromagnetic field does. Instead, quantum fields are potentials for manifestation in space -time, which are not directly measurable" (*Psychotherapy as a Mutual Process*, in the essay "On the Physics and Psychology of the Transference as an Interactive Field.")

K In Jungian psychology, the "self" represents the central and transcendent aspect of an individual's psyche, striving for wholeness and integration. It serves as the ultimate goal and the path to individuation, which is the process of achieving wholeness and realizing one's full potential.

the theories that shed light on how this mechanism operates. This section will specifically focus on how it materializes within an individual.

Peter Levenda

The perfect person to illustrate this effect is Peter Levenda. He is a walking window area and his writings are the embodiment of high strangeness as a field of study. Going through his life will help us see how the Forrest Gump effect manifests, and looking at his writings will also help us highlight many of the most important subjects within the field. Noted occultist James Wasserman said Levenda was "Equally at home in the worlds of clandestine intelligence agencies, corporate boardrooms, and candle light temples."[27]

Existence of Secret Nazis, Post World War II

As I mentioned earlier, a popular high strangeness subject is that the Nazis didn't go away after their defeat in World War II but instead covertly regrouped in secret enclaves in other parts of the world, specifically in South America. The 2020 Netflix docuseries *A Sinister Sect: Colonia Dignidad* is about one such enclave, a German Nazi sect established in Chile in 1961. The head of "this German colony had been part of the Hitler Youth and his intention was to take his nationalist military ideology to South America."[28]

Levenda claims he flew to Chile in 1979 to research this group and was briefly captured. His thought was that this "mysterious colony and torture center in the Andes Mountains held a key to the relationship between Nazi ideology and its post-war survival on the one hand, and occult ideas and practices on the other." The people who detained Levenda "were not Chileans but … Nazis, providing a sanctuary for men like Josef Mengele."[29]

In addition to these secret South American enclaves, there is a theory they set up a covert worldwide 4th Reich. For example, the idea is that via Operation Paperclip, ex-Nazis took over the CIA and NASA via the process of agency capture. The fictionalized Amazon Prime television series *Nazi Hunters* draws on this idea and follows a ragtag group of vigilantes living in 1977 New York City who "have discovered that hundreds of high ranking Nazi officials are living among us and conspiring to create a Fourth Reich in the U.S."[30]

Levenda writes about the Nazi power structure surviving its defeat in WW2, going underground and setting up a covert worldwide 4th Reich. He demonstrates the "existence of a Nazi underworld" that presents a major "threat to global security."[31] This theory states the Nazis had a plan in the event of being defeated: to create a post-war extraterritorial state. For a detailed account see Joseph P. Farrell's *Nazi International: The Nazi Postwar Plan to Control Finance, Conflict, Physics and Space* (2008).[L]

Occult Nazis

Another important area of high strangeness research is Nazis and the occult, a topic which is all but mainstream now. Levenda's 1995, *The Unholy Alliance: A History of Nazi Involvement within the Occult* helped jump start the topic to mainstream acceptance as it was "the first book in English on the subject of Nazi occultism."[29] The book explains how occultism came to play such an important role in Nazi political ideology and how the secret occult group, the Thule Society, influenced the Nazi movement.

Again, no, Aleister Crowley was not a Nazi (nor a Satan worshiper). There is actually evidence that he used his occult knowledge to help the allied forces. The book *Secret Agent 666: Aleister Crowley, British Intelligence and the Occult* gives evidence to back up this claim (Richard B. Spence, 2008). While Crowley is rumored to have worked with British intelligence to help defeat the Nazis, Dion Fortune worked with her own private group of magicians to provide a magical defense of Britain on the astral realm. See *The Magical Battle of Britain* (Dion Fortune, 1969).

In all fairness to the rumors of Crowley's involvement with the Nazis,[M] I point out that one of his students, J.F.C. Fuller, was an open supporter of Hitler and the British Union of Fascists Party, led by Oswald Mosley in England. Fuller was a genius military strategist who was the first to advocate making tanks (with their armor, firepower, and speed) the priority in the field of battle, thus revolutionizing warfare with an approach he called blitzkrieg. Because of the fact that Hitler adopted this approach, Fuller's blitzkrieg warfare has become almost synonymous with the Nazi war machine.[32] Fuller met Hitler in Germany in 1936 when he met with a senior German military officer who was a proponent of armored warfare.[33] Fuller attended Hitler's fiftieth birthday party, in April, 1939, a celebration capped

L Farrell's book also explores the idea that Nazi's had advanced technology (UFOs). I'm sure you are asking me: "If they had this secret advanced technology, then how did they lose the war?" The answer is found in the theory that the advanced technology wasn't weaponized soon enough to stave off defeat, meaning they couldn't outfit the UFOs with weapons before the allied powers won. The theory continues that they are now fully weaponized and use this exotic weaponry to covertly control the entire planet.

M A good barometer for the high strangeness researcher is to see if a source claims Crowley was a Nazi and/or Satanist. I'm a big proponent of a take what you need and leave the rest philosophy when it comes to this research, so when you see this it is a sign to be mindful of what to take as true from the person and what to take as false (and thus leave it). Also, if they pronounce it Craw-ley, not Crow-ley (rhymes with the bird) then it is a sign to take their thoughts on Crowley with a grain of salt.

by a parade of tanks and motorized infantry. After the parade "Hitler greeted Fuller on the receiving line and said, 'I hope you were pleased with your children.'" Fuller is said to have replied, "Your Excellency, they have grown up so quickly that I no longer recognize them."[34] All of this is to say it is understandable that Crowley would be painted with the Nazi brush considering the close affiliation of one of his former students, however Crowley and Fuller parted ways after a falling out in 1919.[N]

Kennedy Assassinations

A little known, but fascinating fact surrounding the JFK mystery is the "bizarre world of 'wandering bishops' who appear throughout the Kennedy assassinations."[35] Wandering bishops are people who are consecrated[O] outside of official churches, such as Catholic or Orthodox Christianity. Levenda admits to creating a fake orthodox Christian church to avoid the Vietnam draft. He created this faux church with his high school friend, who was also big into Orthodox Christianity.[36] He says that at the age of seventeen, he and this friend "gate-crashed the funeral for assassinated Senator Robert F. Kennedy at St. Patrick's Cathedral in New York City, and led the procession out of the cathedral." And as if that wasn't enough, he was also a "member of the same front organization – a renegade Ukrainian church in the Bronx – that provided cover for David Ferrie and Jack Martin (suspected co-conspirators in the JFK assassination)."[37]

East Coast Occult Revival

The details of the revival of occult practice in New York City are well documented in James Wasserman's memoir, *In the Center of the Fire*. This book also features details surrounding the revival of the modern day OTO (Ordo Templi Orienti), of which Wasserman has been named the "father." Given the ever-present (though subtle) importance magick has on the overall direction of a culture, this is no small feat. For a detailed look at how the occult powerfully (but subtly) influences a society, see *Occulture: The Unseen Forces That Drive Culture Forward* (2018) by Carl Abrahamsson and Gary Lachman.

In his memoir, Wasserman goes into detail about Levenda's considerable impact on the New York occult scene, pointing out that he regu-

N Aleister Crowley and J.F.C. Fuller had a falling out in 1919 after Crowley accused Fuller of stealing money from him. (See *The Confessions of Aleister Crowley: An Autohagiography*, edited by John Symonds and Kenneth Grant.

O Apostolic succession is the belief and practice in certain Christian traditions that through the laying on of hands, spiritual authority (magical mojo from the Holy Spirit) are transmitted in an unbroken line from the apostles, to subsequent generations of church leaders, ensuring legitimacy of said leaders.

larly gave lectures at the infamous Magical Child book store and was a fixture of the community. Wasserman said that he worked with Levenda in connection with his own official Tahitu Lodge of the OTO, but points out that Levenda was never a formal member. This New York scene was described as a "bubbling swamp of spiritual fecundity" which Levenda "eased his way into the center of" facilitated by the fact he was "charming, soft-spoken and aloof" while being "well-versed in all aspects of occult theory and practice."[38]

Modern Magical Grimoire

The *Necronomicon* is a mythical book that was mentioned in the fictional writings of H.P. Lovecraft. However, in 1977 the *actual* book was published with an introduction by an author listed only as "Simon." In actuality, the book was not the product of the mythical author, but was a "team effort" between Jim Wasserman who provided the layout, while the "text itself was Levenda's creation" which was "a synthesis of Sumerian and later Babylonian myths … peppered with names of entities from H.P. Lovecraft's notorious and enormously popular Cthulhu stories."[38]

However, just because the book is *fiction* doesn't mean it isn't *real*. This is because saying Levenda's *Necronomicon* is "'only fiction' isn't much of an argument when it comes to magick, which could be called the science of make believe." The Tibetan spiritual tradition includes "the creation of 'tulpas': entities willed into existence by disciplined acts of imagination." Whether or not a magical text is real or not is "irrelevant to the occultists who use them to release the power of their own will."[39]

One explanation of the 2014 Slender Man stabbings, for example, was that the entity in question was a tulpa,[P] a fictional character created on the internet via group intention that took on a life of its own in the psychic ether. This is similar to the idea of an archetype affecting one's conscious behavior. In his memoir, Wasserman reported strange occurrences around *The Necronomicon.* He said that when people entered the home where they were working on the book, everyone who entered accidentally ended up shedding blood; the typesetters had their loft overrun by rats and his padlocked temple was mysteriously broken into from the inside out.[27]

While this overall chapter suggests a high strangeness window area is caused by a *person* and the next chapter puts forth the idea it is caused by a *place*, this particular section considers the idea that it could be caused by a *thing* (such as a mysterious book).

P See *Beware the Slenderman* documentary, HBO, 2017. And *The Meme Humanoids: Modern Myths or Real Monsters* February 13, 2022 by Lon Strickler.

This addition leaves us with the idea that paranormal phenomena can be caused by a highly strange *person, place, or thing.*[Q]

Cutting Edge Thelemic Research

Levenda has also written two books covering high-level Thelemic research. Thelema is the psycho-spiritual system of Aleister Crowley but these two books cover topics associated with a more obscure branch of Thelema, led by Kenneth Grant. In the mid-1950s, Grant created his own branch of the OTO (now sometimes called the Typhonian OTO) in England. Grant's OTO is separate and distinct from Crowley's official OTO, which was re-established in America in the early 1970s. Wasserman's *In the Center of the Fire* explores his role in helping to re-establish this OTO, which can be said to be the mainstream Thelemic group. I am a member of this OTO (sometimes referred to as the "Caliph[R] OTO") but I am most inspired magically by Grant's Typhonian OTO.

Kenneth Grant (1924-2011), the last living student of Crowley, has a more high-strangeness-friendly take on Thelema in particular and magick in general. Because of this, Grant-inspired magical studies are looked down upon as *utterly absurd* by the mainstream occult community. No offense to the mainstream magical and Thelemic communities, but I think the most creative occult work comes from practitioners of Grant's school of thought.[S]

In *The Dark Lord: H.P. Lovecraft, Kenneth Grant, and the Typhonian Tradition in Magic* Levenda lays out Grant's magickal system. Two important aspects of his system are that Grant believed there is magical validity to the fictional writings of H. P. Lovecraft. He claims that Lovecraft came up with his fictional writings by tapping into a magical "plane" that was "accessible" to him "unconsciously" while Crowley tapped into this realm consciously.[40]

Grant's system of magic also differs from the mainstream Thelemic system as it focuses on "establishing rapport with denizens of other worlds," "dimensions," and "beyond the stars."[41] Mainstream Crowleyites are criti-

Q One theory of the paranormal is that mirrors are high strangeness magnets. See the series *Dark Holler* (Ward Hiney, 2022) and the episode of Greg and Dana Newkirk's *Haunted Objects Podcast* entitled "The Dark Mirror's Reflections of Death" for a deeper dive on mirrors being high strangeness magnets.

R The use of the term "Caliph" in the OTO after Crowley's death refers to the individual who serves as the head and continues the organization's spiritual guidance. Grady Louis McMurtry (1918-1985) was the first Caliph of the OTO as he worked to reestablish and preserve the OTO's activities following a period of relative obscurity after Crowley's passing in 1947.

S And those of Michael Bertiaux's school of magick, which is an esoteric system influenced by Western occult traditions, Haitian Vodou, and Gnostic beliefs. His Ordo Templi Orientis Antiqua (OTOA) is a unique and independent organization that he was the leader of but was started in Haiti by Papus (1865-1916). It is a separate and distinct organization from the more well known OTO founded by Karl Kellner and Theodor Reuss, which also included the famous members: A. Crowley, J. Parsons, and K. Grant.

cal of this approach, saying such a focus is *utterly absurd* because they believe any entities spoken of in magical literature are actually just aspects of one's mind, similar to Jungian archetypes.[T] Among mainstream magicians it is generally agreed upon that *The Book of the Law* is merely a product of Crowley's own subconscious and the guardian angel entity he said dictated the book, Aiwass, was merely an angel of his own creation. Grant stated an opposite opinion regarding the nature of Aiwass, saying: "the key to the next stage ... of evolution upon this planet ... will be achieved by a willed congress with extraterrestrial entities of which" Aiwass "is the immediate messenger to humanity."[42]

I find it odd this is the mainstream belief, being that Crowley himself said his "observation of the Universe" had convinced him that "there are beings of intelligence and power of a far higher quality than anything we can conceive of as humans" and that these beings "are not necessarily based on the cerebral and nervous structures that we know." Not only did Crowley say these ultra-intelligent beings exist, he maintained "the one and only chance for mankind to advance as a whole is for individuals to make contact with such beings."[41] Followers of Grant's school of magick take Crowley's suggestion seriously whereas mainstream Crowley followers take this specific suggestion as *utterly absurd* and simply ignore it. I believe this is because it goes against the prevailing opinion that all beings encountered in magical work are from one's own unconscious. This is the main reason Grant's work is dismissed by establishment magicians.

Other reasons for the dismissal of Grant's approach to magick is that he "often cites works of fiction and scholarly works indiscriminately" and "rarely gives his sources." In addition to breaking these immutable rules of magical scholarship, he "performs some rather odd feats of logical gymnastics" that are "often reminding one of a bad horror novel rather than a serious occult tome." In addition, he is also seen to include materials that "seem more like bad New-Agey science-fiction than Magick" and "often sounds like a UFO channeler who took a wrong turn on the way to Sedona." If I may be so bold to say so, I believe it is the mainstream occultists that took a wrong turn on the way to Sedona. And, finally, because Grant keeps providing "even weirder stuff for his fans" in each subsequent book "it is obvious that Grant washed out both mundanely and Magically."[U,43] My personal

T The most famous skeptic of Aiwass as author of *The Book of the Law* was Crowley's former secretary and renowned member of the Golden Dawn, Israel Regardie, who argued in his biography of Crowley, *The Eye in the Triangle*, that Aiwass was merely a product of Crowley's unconscious (1982, pp. 473-494).

U The mainstream critique of Grant is similar to that of M. Bertiaux, as his masterwork, the *Voudon Gnostic Workbook* is dismissively said to be "the size of a large city's phonebook, and has about the same literary and Magical value." John L. Smith, "Typhonian Tomes: Being a Guide to the

pledge to readers is to provide even weirder content in each subsequent volume of the *My Cosmic Trigger* book series. Notice the critique of Grant's work fits perfectly with my theory that the conventional magical community is not receptive to other paranormal fields because they desire mainstream acceptance. Most of the critiques the above occultist gave Grant are because his writing style does not fit into the academic paradigm.

Renowned magician Donald Michel Kraig said that, while Grant's approach to some is considered "advanced work," to others it is "downright weird and even frightening." Kraig even questions if Grant's work is "fiction? Metaphor? [or] Reality?"[44] I propose the more *downright weird* our magical approach, the better. To me, a magick of high strangeness is a fun-house mirror type approach that sees little difference between fiction, metaphor and reality. And this magical approach is frightening because the phenomenon we are interacting with is frightening.

In Levenda's *Rites of the Mummy: The K'Rla Cell and the Secret Key to Liber AL* he "brings attention to the existence of a sacred geometry within the verses of *The Book of the Law*: a completely unexpected discovery [that is] mathematically verifiable."[45] The claim is made that this sacred geometry (discovered by a student of Grant) is proof that *The Book of the Law* was dictated by a nonhuman intelligence.

American Secret History

In high strangeness research one subject that people study is how shadowy occult groups have influenced various governments. This is where Levenda's three-part *Sinister Forces*[V] series comes in. This book series is said to be "one of the most important books about America ever written," as the book "tells the dark and bloody story of how ... occult practices have been used to dominate American political life, and transform our country from the world's citadel of freedom into the dark morass of lies."[46]

Sinister Forces: Book 1

In *Sinister Force – The Nine: A Grimoire of American Political Witchcraft* (2011), Levenda claims there is a "Satanic undercurrent to American affairs" and that these "sinister forces" have been "at work throughout history"; from the ancient and "mysterious mound-builder culture to the Salem witch trials" onward to "Operations Paperclip, when high level Nazis were

Works of Kenneth Grant" originally appeared in the OTO's IAO Camp's *Herald-Tepaphone*.

V It is interesting to note that the *Sinister Forces* series is published by this book's publisher, Trine Day. Imagine my excitement for my book to land on the same publisher as Levenda's. I wrote this chapter many months before reaching out to Trine Day to publish my book.

invited into the upper echelons of American government," to MK-ULTRA "a CIA mind-control program run amok."[47]

MASONS AND AMERICA

As I said, looking at how secret occult societies operate on temporal power is a vast topic in high strangeness research; so, naturally, there is a lot of research on the influence of the Freemasons in shaping global culture. In *The Secret Temple: Masons, Mysteries and the Founding of America* (2009), Levenda says "The influence of Freemasonry on the creation of the United States" is easy to prove because "many of the founding fathers were Freemasons," adding that "the ideals that contributed to the formation of the country were also those of the Masonic lodge." This is important because the "Masonic orders made it possible for like-minded individuals to meet and embrace a 'kind of thinking' which said all humans 'were created equal.'" This type of thinking "was revolutionary for its time" but is "common among the best of Americans today."[48]

A prevailing opinion in the high strangeness community is that any Masonic influence is evil. I believe this is a simplistic view, as I believe the original aims of Freemasonry were noble as evidenced by founding principles of the USA. However, I would wager to guess it has been used as a *breeding ground*[W] for powerful men with opposite intentions of *life, liberty, and the pursuit of happiness* to recruit for their own nefarious secret societies, such as the KKK.

GOVERNMENT UFO DISCLOSURE

Levenda has co-written a book with Tom DeLonge (most known for being a member of the band Blink 182) who is infamous in the high strangeness community. The book in question is the two volume, *Sekret Machines: Gods, Man, and War* (2017), which is said to be "the result of input from scientists, engineers, intelligence officers, and military officials." The book presents a reality so "unsettling" that it "demands the collaboration of ... every field of human endeavor if we are to understand and manage its effects."[49] Endeavoring to manage these effects is a critical component of my magick of high strangeness.

DeLonge is infamous in the high strangeness community because he is the founder of the *To the Stars ... Academy of Arts & Sciences*, which is as-

W AI can "hallucinate" quotes by generating text based on patterns learned from training data, often producing quotes that sound plausible but may be entirely fabricated by the AI and are not from the purported source. This breeding ground quote was from an AI, James Shelby Downard hallucinated quote. Computer experts are trying to stop this hallucination process, but I find it one of the most interesting aspects of AI.

sumed by many in the community to be a military intelligence operation. People say "it sounds far more akin to the making of a tightly controlled government ... psychological operation ('psyop' for short) than the result of a group of highly-qualified people who were interested in" raising awareness about the reality of UFOs.[50] This is a fair assumption given the founding involved "a group with curiously impressive resumes from the military industrial and intelligence complex's highest rungs."[X,50] However, I can think of nothing more *utterly absurd* than UFO disclosure being led by a member of a pop group from the 1990s. Remembering what we have learned earlier in this book: the more absurdly strange something is means the more trustworthy it is. This underscores the possibility that a '90s pop star will lead humanity to the stars. A strange timeline indeed.

Intelligence Connections

Levenda's association with DeLonge's group and intelligence agencies has also caused some distrust towards him within the high strangeness community. Levenda is somewhat open about his connections with temporal powers, as evidenced by the fact that during his days in New York he allegedly "hinted broadly of dealings with intelligence agencies and secret societies operating at global levels of social influence."[38] He also lists that he is a member of the "Association of Former Intelligence Officers" in his author biography.

Many in the high strangeness community will automatically dismiss an author if they have any connections to intelligence or the military. This is because they assume any temporal power is "evil" and, of course, as a result, anything they do is evil. However, I don't look at various military and alphabet agencies (this is the slang term for the CIA, DIA, FBI, etc) having involvement in high strangeness research in such black and white terms. In short, I don't think everybody who is involved in such organizations are evil. I also urge members of the community to remember the lesson we learned from the TV show *The X-Files:* Agent Mulder was on the inside of the FBI fighting for truth while collaborating with the researchers at the independent new publication, *The Lone Gunman.* I think it is reasonable to assume there are many real-life Mulders in these organizations.

X It is said that DeLonge hired an advisor, a paid employee of To the Stars Academy, "with a DIA background in the form of a man with a deep counter-intelligence background who supposedly ran the Advanced Aerospace Threat Identification Program (ATTIP) in secret for years within the Pentagon." This individual "claims administrative hurdles made it impossible to convey critical info about UFOs to top rungs of Pentagon leadership and beyond, so he decided to pursue the topic outside of the Pentagon." See endnote 50.

But whatever the truth is, the fact remains that Peter Levenda is one of the best writers in the field of high strangeness. I can't say enough good things about his work. His life has taken him to the nexus of the JFK mystery, secret post-war Nazis, government UFO disclosure, the modern occult revival, and modern grimoires; and so, if you ever find yourself in his vicinity, then you can be assured you are in his personal high strangeness window.

Personal Experiences

ODESSA

Growing up, my father had a copy of Ira Levin's 1976 book *The Boys from Brazil* in our home library. I point this out as evidence that the theory of Nazi survival post-war was at one time a more mainstream idea. I still remember my father explaining to me what the story was about while standing outside the family study. The novel centered around something called ODESSA. Levenda says that ODESSA "entered mainstream consciousness as a catch-all term for anyone of several groups of former SS officers ... engaged in a kind of secret society" hellbent on "world domination." He says the most important fact of ODESSA, one that "many investigators have missed ... is the true extent of this network in the U.S."[31]

A past coworker retold the following story regarding her husband who was a soldier in World War II and stationed in Germany after the war. She reports that in his post-war duties as a soldier he happened upon a clandestine Nazi meeting, consisting of Nazi higher ups sitting around a table with a large portrait of Hitler hung prominently on the wall. He then reported his encounter with this secret Nazi meeting to his commanding officer. His wife said that some years later, while he was living his civilian life in the US, a man presumably from the military came and interviewed her husband about the incident. She said the man had a briefcase which led her to believe he was using it to record the meeting. This was long before the days of pocket recording devices.

Bob Dobbs

Like Levenda, Bob Dobbs is another walking window area and highly strange Forrest Gump. His life has interwoven with many names pertinent to high strangeness research: Mae Brussell and Dr. Peter Beter (the first public para-political researchers), Walter Bowart (known for the 1978 book *Operation Mind Control*), Dave Worcester (a channel for Cosmic

Awareness), and Marshal McLuhan (the father of media studies). I will explore my relationship with Bob in volume three of the *My Cosmic Trigger* series.[Y]

As I began regularly engaging with Bob, he informed me that encountering strange events, such as peculiar dreams and synchronicities, was a frequent experience for those who came into his orbit. In fact, it was so common that he routinely warned people about it and provided guidance to help them navigate these phenomena.

James Wasserman and Brother Kanya

I knew James Wasserman, author of the above mentioned autobiography *In the Center of the Fire,* personally. I met him when he came to give a workshop on the Gnostic Mass to the OTO body I was a member of in Atlanta, Georgia (Dove and Serpent Oasis). I also got to hear his lecture on the book and see him perform the Gnostic mass as a priest which was a memorable experience, as the mass definitely had a palpable magical mojo vibe that I didn't feel when other individuals were in the role of priest, no offense intended to other priests. Wasserman has also published some of Levenda's books through his publishing company, Ibis Press (an imprint of Red Wheel/Weiser). Sadly, Wasserman passed away right after the 2020 election.

Interestingly, Wasserman mentions in his memoir that he was married by a Brother Kanya, who I was introduced to by the renowned Transpersonal psychologist Stanley Krippner in the mid 2010s.[Z] Kanya Vashon McGhee was an African American gentleman who used to run an occult book shop in Harlem (The Tree of Life) from 1969 to 1980. "The Tree of Life was more than the average bookstore, it was an institution that transformed lives," but unfortunately the "bookstore was pushed out by gov't agencies and replaced by a parking garage."[51]

Brother Kanya lived in Atlanta when I was living there and gave me the channeled book *Revelations for a New Era: Keys to Restoring Paradise on Earth,* which is in the "Messages from Matthew" series of books.[AA] I still regularly follow these New Age channelings every month (MatthewBooks.com) and think of Kanya fondly each time I visit the site. He was in his

Y In the meantime you can learn more about him at IonAndBob.com, DobbsTown.com, and see, "McLuhanesque: The Unexplainable Episode with Bob Dobbs," Hermitix Podcast, 2021.

Z My wife and I drove Kanya to see Stanley Krippner speak at the Jim Klee Forum at the University of West Georgia after being asked to do so by Krippner. Kanya and Krippner were old friends and Krippner even gave the floor to Kanya for him to say a few words after his presentation.

AA He also gave me a book by a prolific high strangeness author with the middle name of Vaughan, a fact so controversial that I have to hide it in a footnote and only give the author's middle name.

80s when I knew him and his vitality and keen intellect at his age was an inspiration. He also appeared on the podcast I host with my wife, *Further Living,* and I will never forget his optimism and his insistence that humanity was headed for a golden age; for him it was a foregone conclusion. He introduced me to his essay about the Tree of Life bookstore, "A Tree Grew in Harlem." This rare but important essay is extremely relevant for the student of high strangeness and I will now feature some of its key passages.

Kanya said "a lengthy consideration of the plight of inner city African-Americans led [him] to found The Tree of Life Bookstore & Educational Center of Harlem in 1969" because he was "convinced that if other black people could realize and fathom the importance of the immutable Laws of the Universe as stated in ancient historical texts such as ... *Hermetic Principles of Hermes Trismegistus,* that a profound transformation would take place." He said that his work with the Center was to especially target "the dropout, the junkie, the street brother, and generational ghetto dweller – all presumed destined for lives of misery based on" a "self constructed 'inner' prison of self limiting thought."

He said that he had used these spiritual teachings and had "undergone a powerful change" of his own life and then "wanted other inner city Black people to experience that same surging River of Life that now flowed unobstructed through" his veins. He said that during the decade the Center operated he "witnessed many a miraculous transformation" among the people who regularly came to the Center, "from dropout to scholar, junkie to health guru," from "'sinner to saint.'"

The center was influential in the community, as evidenced by the fact that "Civil Rights leader Dick Gregory joined forces with the Tree and perceiving its potential as an inspiration and healing force" then "began to spread its message in his own talks." The location of the Center was "the corner of 125th and Lenox Avenue" which "had been the center of black consciousness in the New world." This vortex featured visits by "W.E.B. Dubois, Marcus Garvey, Malcolm X, and Dr. Martin Luther King, Jr.," who, when they visited, carried "the message of the unique role of the black race in the ever-emerging world community." Because of all the unique influences and visitors over the years, "the corner was a focus point for the entire planet, and its energy nourished the young Tree."

What do you suppose the powers that be did regarding a Learning Center where African Americans could learn of "their African heritage as the birthplace and cradle of Mankind" and where "Whites freed from the shackles of their color" could then merge into "an ever growing spiritual community in the heart of Harlem," a place where all people could find "an atmosphere of joy ... in the midst of an urban chaos of alarming proportions"? Kanya points out that "due to political chicanery" and "in spite of the community's expressed outrage," the Tree of Life building "was torn down on September 17th, 1980 and in its place for 21 years, stood a parking lot!" He claims that "the excuse" given "for its demolition never resulted in a new hotel and convention center"[AB] as was promised by political leaders.[52]

This sad fate was featured in *The New York Times*, where it was reported that "The state has decreed that one of Harlem's younger but more popular institutions – the Tree of Life – will have to make way for a parking lot."[53] One is immediately reminded of the iconic song by Joni Mitchell, "Big Yellow Taxi," and its lyrics about paving paradise and in its place putting a parking lot. Kanya moved the Center to Atlanta, Georgia in 1992 where it was "deeply involved in" researching "Mind Control consciousness." He said that "since we are still the sole guardian of such a wonderful and valuable 'secret,' we seek a partner so that we may share it with The World." I am deeply honored to have been able to visit the Center when it was located in Atlanta and hope this book helps spread the story of The Tree of Life.

Finally Kanya ends the essay saying that in the future he will "spell out the specific ways that this insight will bring" human beings to a "spiritual exaltation ... And in the process, transforming the Harlems of America into The Spiritual Capitals of the Western World," a process of creating "a veritable Garden of Eden on Mother Earth."[52] There can be no better explanation of the power of turning a geographic area into an energy vortex or sacred spot. The magick of high strangeness seeks to replicate what Kanya achieved and proposed, in the town of every practitioner.

Conclusion

Researchers have pointed out the fact that the paranormal happenings of the most famous haunted house in American history (the Amityville house) were centered around one of the young children in the family.[54] And because this iconic haunting was centered around a young agent, they maintained it was similar to a poltergeist (RSPK) case.[AC] This evidence suggests the paranormal occurrences in the home weren't caused because it was on the site of a window area; they were caused because an individual

AB "In the late 1970s congressman Charles B. Rangel, (Dem, NY) had been granted money by President Jimmy Carter for a feasibility study on erecting a Trade Center/ Luxury Hotel complex on the site in conjunction with the Harlem Urban Development Corporation (HUDC)". See endnote 52.

AC They also explore the fact that this individual, as an adult, reportedly had abilities similar to Uri Geller and retell a story of someone witnessing these miraculous abilities while in Hickory NC, which is thirty minutes from my hometown of Lenoir, NC.

living there was a high strangeness magnet. To further this idea, other paranormal researchers point out that the house was no longer haunted after the family moved out.[55] And so it appears that, at least some window areas have a highly strange individual they are centered around.

However, I think high strangeness window areas are caused by an interaction between a highly strange geographic location and a paranormally-inclined individual. I add that, if the individual's own being is interacting with these window areas, then the conscious intention of the person would be a major detriment if it was a positive or negative window area. The importance of one's intention when they are in a window area is where the importance of a magick of high strangeness comes in.

Resources:

1. "John DeSouza: Who Are the Paranormal Magnets?" *Higher Journeys with Alexis Brooks,* 2018. Time: 33:58, 16:00, 37:00.

2. Colin Wilson, *Strange Powers,* 1973, E-book: pp. 49-54.

3. RAW, *Cosmic Trigger, Vol 1: Final Secret of the Illuminati,* 1977, E-book: p. 281.

4. Andrija Puharich, *Uri: A Journal of the Mystery of Uri Geller,* 1974, p. 2.

5. Colin Wilson, *The Geller Phenomenon,* 1976.

6. William Roll and Lois Duncan, *Psychic Connections,* 1995, pp. 4, 171 and 177.

7. William Roll, "Poltergeist and Space-Time: A Contemplation on Hans Bender's Ideas about RSPK," *The Journal of Parapsychology,*Vol. 64, Issue 3, 2000.

8. Stanislav Grof, *The Adventure of Self-Discovery: Dimensions of Consciousness and New Perspectives in Psychotherapy and Inner Exploration,* 1988, p. 155.

9. Julie Eisenbud, "Psychiatric Contribution to Parapsychology," in *Psychoanalysis and the Occult,* edited by George Devereux, 1953, p. 12.

10. *Nandor Fodor and the Talking Mongoose,* IMBD, imdb.com/title/tt19838620

11. "Wolfgang Ernst Pauli," FamousScientists.com.

12. J. Marvin Spiegelman, Ph.D, "On the Physics and Psychology of the Transference as an Interactive Field" in *Psychotherapy as a Mutual Process,* 1996.

13. J. Marvin Spiegelman Ph.D, "The Interactive Field in Analysis: Agreements and Disagreements" in *Psychotherapy as a Mutual Process,* 1996.

14. "Gary Lachman: Precognitive Dreams, the Hypnagogic State, & Synchronicity," *The Higher Side Chats,* Feb. 15, 2022, Time: 1:00.

15. Personal Communication, Unpublished Interview#1, 2022.

16. Marcus Lowth, "The Psychic Internet Theory: What Is It? Does It Make Sense?" UFOInsight.com.

17. Christopher P. Garetano, "Demon Time," *Strange World,* episode 8, Travel Channel.

18. "Samhain and the Thin Veil," DonegalSquare.com, Oct. 2019.

19. John Keel, *Operation Trojan Horse*, 1970, p. 94-95.

20. TikTok @The_LiminalWitch.

21. Oxford Languages.

22. John Tenny, *Conspirinormal,* Episode 233, Oct. 2018.

23. Andrea Rice, "Mass Meditation May Lower Crime Rate," Wanderlust.com.

24. Sejal Shah, "The Undeniable Power of Mass Meditation: 3 Top Reasons You Wanna Try," Community.Thriveglobal.com.

25. "Why Meditate? Why Participate in Mass Meditation?," WeLoveMassMeditation.com.

26. Joshua Mills, *Power Portals: Awaken Your Connection to the Spirit Realm,* 2020. Publisher's summary.

27. James Wasserman, *In the Center of the Fire: A Memoir of the Occult, 1966-1989,* 2012.

28. Natalia Puertas Cavero, "New Netflix Series Unravels the Dark History of Chile's Colonia Dignidad," AldiaNews.com, Sept. 2021.

29. Peter Levenda, *Unholy Alliance: A History of Nazi Involvement with the Occult,* 2002. Publisher's summary.

30. Nellie Andreeva, "Amazon Nabs Jordan Peele's *Nazi Hunters* Drama with Series Order, Sonar Produces," DeadLine.com, May 2018.

31. Peter Levenda, *The Hitler Legacy, The Nazi Cult in Diaspora: How It Was Organized, How It Was Funded, and Why It Remains a Threat to Global Security in the Age of Terrorism,* 2014, Publisher summary found at Goodreads.com, E-book: p. 30.

32. Brian Holden Reid, *J.F.C. Fuller: Military Thinker.*

33. Karl-Heinz Frieser, *The Blitzkrieg Legend: The 1940 Campaign in the West,* 2013.

34. Stephan Wilkinson, "J.F.C. 'Boney' Fuller, Wacko Genius of Armored Warfare," historynet.com, 7/9/2009.

35. Peter Levenda, *Sinister Forces: A Grimoire of American Political Witchcraft: The Nine,* 2011. Publisher's summary.

36. Forum Borealis, "Peter Levdenda: Perfect Storm: JFK, Nazis and Renegade Bishops," July 2016.

37. "Peter Levenda," SimonAndSchuster.com.

38. Allan Cabal, *The Doom That Came to Chelsea,* NYPress.com, Nov. 2014.

39. Jeff Wells, "Weird Tales: The Necronomicon, HP Lovecraft, Abdul Alhazrad, Aleister Crowley, Michael Aquino, John Dee and Peter Levenda," RedIceCreations.com.

40. Peter Levenda, *The Dark Lord: H. P. Lovecraft, Kenneth Grant, and the Typhonian Tradition in Magic,* 2013, E-book: p. 162.

41. A. Crowley quoted in Kenneth Grant, *Outer Gateways,* 1994.

42. Kenneth Grant, *The Magical Revival,* 1972, p. 210-211

43. John L. Smith, "Typhonian Tomes: Being a Guide to the Works of Kenneth Grant," originally appeared in the OTO's IAO Camp's *Herald-Tepaphone.*

44. Donald Michael Kraig, *Modern Magick: Twelve Lessons in the High Magickal Arts,* 1988, E-book: p. 1064.

45. Peter Levenda, *Rites of the Mummy: The K'Rla Cell and the Secret Key to* Liber Al (2021). Publisher's summary,

46, Whitley Strieber, "Peter Levenda: Sinister Forces," UnknownCountry.com.

47. Peter Levenda, *Sinister Forces: The Nine: A Grimoire of American Political Witchcraft,* 2011. Publisher's Synopsis.

48. Peter Levenda, *The Secret Temple: Masons, Mysteries, and the Founding of America,* E-book: p. 317

49. Tom Delonge, Peter Levenda, *Sekret Machines: Gods, Man, and War,* 2017. Publisher's synopsis.

50. Tyler Rogoway, "Tom DeLonge's Origin Story for To the Stars Academy Describes a Government UFO Info Operation," TheDrive.com, Dec. 2019.

51. Harlem's Mart 125: The American Dream, Facebook Page.

52. Kanya Vashon McGhee, *A Tree Grew in Harlem.*

53. "Parking Lot Is to Replace the Tree of Life in Harlem," *The New York Times,* January 24, 1976.

54. Greg and Dana Newkirk, "The Amityville Plank's Lingering Horrors," *Haunted Objects Podcast,* Oct. 31, 2022.

55. "Dave Spinks," *Talking Weird,* 2.25, November 2021.

Alfred Watkins (27 January 1855 - 15 April 1935) was an English businessman and amateur archaeologist who developed the idea of ley lines

CHAPTER 5

WHY WINDOW AREAS EXIST: A NATURALLY OCCURRING HIGHLY STRANGE PLACE

Victorious salamanders because doom is false.
The Panpipe comes, now goes.
There is something supernatural about the Alleyway:
from demonic to divine, dark but brighter than the shell's flower.
It is our hour of the rising.

As discussed in the previous chapter, author and former FBI agent John DeSouza claims there are two types of window areas which connect our world to paranormal phenomena. The first type is people, which we looked at in the previous chapter. The second type concerns geographic locations and this chapter will look at naturally occurring window areas. DeSouza claims naturally occurring window areas are designated by "the universe" and the induced window areas are because "something happened in this place that made it permanently a gateway ... to other realities."[1] We will explore induced window areas in the next chapter.

EARTH ENERGIES

The ground from which these geographic window areas spring is the Earth itself which is "bathed in energy from the Sun, and the Earth's magnetic field." As such, "all life is immersed in electric, magnetic, and gravity fields, which fluctuate according to solar weather."[2] The Earth itself "serves as a huge electrical circuit with a surrounding electromagnetic shield." And the "fundamental frequency ... of the Earth's EMF (electromagnetic frequency), is 7.83 hertz (Hz)," which is scientifically known as "the Schumann resonance." This is important because "all life-forms on Earth evolved within the Schumann resonance[A] and incorporated it into their evolving neurological and biological processes."[3]

A "Many people report feeling refreshed and relaxed after visiting certain sacred places... which have fields that lie within the Schumann Resonance range." James A. Swan, *Sacred Places: How the Living Earth Seeks Our Friendship*, p. 146.

Animals are thought to have sensitivity to these Earth energies. For example, "birds are now known to have a magnetic sense" which enables them to "find their way on immensely long migration by means of the geomagnetic field" and when a pigeon "claps its wings" it is "sending out a radio-blare from the feathers in its wings, which are made of piezoelectric keratin."[4]

Looking at this energy a little more esoterically, we can say it is simply the living, natural life force of the Earth. Author and New Age psychic Page Bryant divides this "one force into three categories for the purpose of defining its multiple characteristics as it manifests in the physical world;" dividing up the overall life energy into "electricity, magnetism, and electromagnetism" which "collectively ... form [the] 'breath' of our planet."[5]

Morphogenic Field

Another naturally occurring energetic field of earth is the so-called morphogenic field. It is said the very "nature of things depends on" this field. This theory was made popular by the biologist Rupert Sheldrake and "suggests that each type of living system has its own type of field." In turn, these fields "inform and shape different types of atoms, molecules, crystals, living organisms, modes of thought, etc."[6] This theory suggests living organisms emit a field of energy which interacts with naturally occurring Earth energies and that "all self-organizing systems, such as ... cells, plant [and] animal societies" also "have a collective memory on which each individual draws and to which it contribute." This hypothesis "implies that the so-called laws of nature are more like habits."[7]

From my perspective, the vital lesson to extract from Sheldrake's research is the existence of subtle life energies radiating from organisms and the Earth. Mainstream science's denial of this reality hinders the progress of scientific advancement and, consequently, impedes conscious evolution. A new paradigm in science is needed and "One of the key elements of the new paradigm must be an acceptance of the existence and workings of life energies." This is because "All around the world, people assert that life-force energy exists."[8] For example, *chi* is a fundamental concept in ancient Chinese philosophy and refers to the vital life force or energy that flows through all living things and the universe. Understanding chi is central to various aspects of Chinese thought, including traditional Chinese medicine, martial arts, feng shui, and philosophy.

Electrical Fields

Colin Wilson says "there are specific electrical fields connected" to certain geographic locations (such as mountains, water, and deserts) that are "perfectly normal" and naturally occurring. However, it is in "the area of such fields" where paranormal phenomena "often seem to occur."[9] These electrical fields facilitate paranormal activity because "electricity animates all ... bodies that exist" and "intensifies one's degree of vitality on all levels; physically, emotionally, mentally and spiritually." This electric field "amplifies all emotions, be they positive or negative." On top of that, electrical energy acts "upon the human consciousness" on a spiritual level where it has its "most positive and powerful effect" because "it can *awaken* the soul."[5]

Magnetic Fields

John Keel speculated that window areas "tend to be places where peculiar magnetic faults exist," saying the "planet is covered with magnetic faults, and interestingly enough, many of them are grouped around the ancient mounds, temple sites, and spots where flying saucers are seen most frequently." He says that "psychically oriented people living in these regions tend to have extraordinary experiences with elementals, angels, MIB, and spacemen."[10] One explanation of why this may be the case is because the increased magnetic energy "might change or heighten" the brain "of certain people." Based on this, we might conclude that when certain parts of the brain are activated, it finds a "frequency that taps into" high strangeness phenomena because when "a brain is stimulated by this magnetic field it is" similar to a brain of someone on hallucinogens, in trance or meditating: "three states where people report seeing anomalous activity."[11]

Page Bryant's spirit guide, Albion, says in the Blue Ridge mountains there is now a "powerful spiritual reawakening occurring." One reason for this is because the "mountains are magnetic in their charge of life force" and thus "conducive to helping one turn within to tap [their own] subconscious and [be in touch with] the Collective Unconscious" of humanity. In addition, magnetism "promotes sensitivity and awakens the psychic and intuitive faculties within the human mind."[5]

In his 1975 book, *Secret Doors of the Earth: The Hidden Influence of Ancient Aliens and Sacred Geography on Human History,* Jacques Bergier argues that Easter island has a magnetic anomaly and that Delphi in Ancient Greece was also unusually magnetically charged. Oracles played a significant role in the socio-political life of that time due to their reputation for providing divine guidance, being that the utterances of the Sibyl (prophetess) was thought to be directly from the god Apollo. The most famous was the Temple of Apollo at Delphi but other Oracle sites existed, such as the one at Erythrae in ancient Ionia. Leaders and communities relied on them to make crucial decisions and the Oracle's role extended beyond politics to encompass religion, culture, and economics, making it a central and revered institution in the ancient Greek world.[12]

Author Chad Stuemke says that "Every eight minutes a magnetic portal opens up between Earth and sun ... when the magnetic field of Earth and sun meet." He speculates that the ancients would focus on the geographic location where this occurred and "would go there and build mounds and stone circles on them" and then ritualistically interact with them to "pick up information"[13] from spiritual dimensions.

Electromagnetic Fields (EMFs)

All humans are "immersed in a swirling mass of electromagnetic fields (EMFs)" and because of this "electromagnetic energy is probably the key to understanding some intriguing mysteries." And for those that "have been spending their lives in a quest to understand" high strangeness phenomena, "electromagnetic energy is a key."[3] With that said, we turn to the work of Chuck Zukowski[B] and his "paranormal crossover theory."

Zukowski believes "the presence of ghosts can attract aliens," "the presence of aliens can attract ghosts," and the "presence of aliens could attract Bigfoot." The scientific explanation for this reality has to do with EMFs, because ghosts (or any non-human paranormal entities) are made up of an electromagnetic field of energy. This theory was born out of his many years as a field investigator of various paranormal phenomena, such as UFOs, Bigfoot, ghosts, and cattle mutilations. Zukowski claims his research crossed the lines of multiple paranormal fields because he saw a pattern of overlap, noticing that "sometimes there were Bigfoot sightings around areas where UFOs have been reported" and "sometimes the witness would mistake a ghost for an alien presence, or visa-versa." He believes the "common denominator is EMF."

He further explains how his EMF crossover theory works for aliens and ghosts, saying that a spirit creates a concentrated electro-magnetic field which is then picked up by aliens that have the technology to mon-

B His research is featured in Ben Mezrich's *The 37th Parallel: The Secret Truth Behind America's UFO Highway* (2017).

itor EMF fluctuations. Zukowski wonders if the aliens "are curious why these energy fields pop up, or maybe [they] know certain signatures are emanating from spirits, and can ... communicate with them."[14] According to this theory, multiple paranormal phenomena intersecting, has to do with aliens communicating with our dead relatives. Utterly absurd indeed ... and, therefore, highly likely. On the bright side, aliens interacting with our dearly departed kind of takes away the pressure of us having to do it ourselves.

Moreover, Zukowski expounds on the interconnectedness of Bigfoot and UFO phenomena, proposing that Bigfoot's extraordinary natural senses – the very attributes that have enabled their elusiveness – may enable them to perceive EMF fluctuations. In contrast, extraterrestrials rely on advanced technology for this purpose. When a UFO is present in a particular area, it triggers EMF fluctuations, which a Bigfoot is sensitive to. Consequently, the accounts of Bigfoot sightings in proximity to UFO sightings stem from the inquisitiveness of the creatures, who appear to be investigating the activities of these aliens. In a bizarre twist, Bigfoot might just be the ultimate alien-tracking, EMF-sensitive, cosmic detective in the woods.

Moving to a more conventional means of EMF detection than a curious Bigfoot, is a common tool used by ghost hunters: EMF detectors. Many researchers "believe ghosts can generate electromagnetic fields of their own" and that ghosts "are able to induce spooky events such as flickering lights ... by manipulating the electromagnetic field."[15] Academic paranormal researchers also study EMF fluctuations in connection with paranormal events, saying "most of the haunt phenomena could be accounted for in terms of the physical energies recorded at the sites" such as "anomalous EMFs or GMFs."[16]

There are some researchers who go so far as to speculate electromagnetic energy is the source of all paranormal phenomena, asserting "that electromagnetically induced hallucinatory experiences accompanied by occasionally visible electrical phenomena in the atmosphere provided the entire explanation of UFOs and paranormal phenomena."[3] This is because it is believed that sites are haunted "not because of ghosts but because of conditions that produce ghosts." Further, it is theorized that "apparitions ... may be elicited when magnetic fields are applied to the right temporal lobe"[C] and "the disappearance and reappearance of objects" that are often

C See the Persinger Helmet, which was invented by Michael Persinger. This is a device designed to stimulate the brain with electromagnetic fields in an attempt to induce altered states of consciousness and paranormal experiences. Persinger's work is cited in this essay by Dr. Roll and

reported at haunted sites "may be due to automatic behavior and amnesia induced by the anomalous magnetic field." More specifically, "What may be critical is the brief exposure to magnetic fields whose temporal patterns imitate the relevant brain activity."[16]

Plasma Beings and EMFs

Most of us are taught in school that there are three states of matter: solids, liquids, and gasses. However, more than 99% of the visible universe, including the sun, the stars, and interstellar and interplanetary space is made up of plasma.[16.1] Plasma is called the fourth state of matter and is not usually taught in early schooling because it is too complex and not relevant to our daily lives. The simplified definition is that it is "ionized gas," with the "Earth itself" being "immersed in a tenuous plasma called the solar wind and is surrounded by a dense plasma called the ionosphere."[16.1]

Natural plasma phenomena include the "northern lights, ball lightning, and the unusual 'lights' seen along earthquake fault lines." On the other hand, the paranormal phenomenon, ghost lights, are said to occur "when one is in the presence of spiritual people or sacred places." As such, plasma may be a "manifestation of special places which will be reliably documentable when science develops reliable measures to monitor such a thing."[8] When I researched plasma, I found that the states of matter – or more accurately, the phases of matter – are in fact endless. Meaning, there aren't just four or six or ten. I highly recommend you look it up for yourself. It may be enough to help you break up the mind's tendency to think of the world as overly "solid" and delineated along clear lines. Physics tells us how weird reality really is, if we but pay attention.

In the high strangeness masterwork, *Origins of the Gods,* noted authors Andrew Collins and Gregory L. Little also tie high strangeness window areas to plasma beings, speculating "that the needle in the UFO haystack is the idea that sentient plasmas emitting powerful electromagnetic waves produce paranormal events."[3] They propose this demonstrates it is likely Keel's grand theory, is correct, that "The UFO phenomenon, spiritual experiences, and paranormal manifestations are all related, and they most likely stem from electromagnetic energy" which are "produced by natural Earth energies that are well-recognized by geology but not yet fully understood." The authors propose that contact with intelligent plasmas has "created mystical and spiritual experiences involving angels, glowing beings,

---

the helmet is featured in *Hellier.*

and the gods of ancient cultures [and] observations of these plasmas have created typical UFO sightings." When sensitive humans "are close to these emerging plasmas" they act as "the antennae that receive their messages." As such, it "is also very likely that ... sentient plasmas, held together by self-generated magnetic fields, are the source of many ancient beliefs."[3]

Gravity Anomalies

Dan Shaw's *The Vortex Field Guide*[D] provides a map of anomalous sites in America. These sites are "tourist attractions calling themselves 'Mystery Hill'" or sometimes "Mystery Spot." Shaw claims that some of these tourist traps actually "demonstrate phenomena that appear more like the new quantum physics than the old Newtonian physics" while "others are frauds."[17] Speculation is that they exist due to "some geological anomalies."[8]

In Jacques Bergier's *Secret Doors of Earth,* it is said that sites thought to "harbor a secret door"[E] are characterized by phenomena in which "gravity is disturbed" and "terrestrial magnetism is disrupted." Bergier goes on to say that a striking example of such a site is found at Chimney Rock, North Carolina, where unusual events have been recorded since the 1800s. He uses the term "secret door" to refer to what researchers such as Allen Greenfield call "windows," saying that he and Greenfield "are using different words to speak about the same thing,"[18] an opening "into other universes."[F]

Bryant claims her spirit guide Albion says there are areas that "display a curious phenomena that contradicts what we normally consider natural law." In these areas, such as Mystery Hill in Blowing Rock, North Carolina, it is reported that "water runs uphill" and people walking in the house on the property "cannot stand up straight." Bryant adds that "Albion considers such sites to be places where a natural vortex has lost its power and has completely 'inverted.'"[5] A component of the magick of high strange-

D Dan Shaw has been called the "Vortex Detective." His TV and film appearances include Brad Meltzer's *Decoded: Devil's Triangle, Alaska* (History Channel), and *Mysteries of the National Parks: Yosemite* (Travel Channel), and the documentary *Ancient Tomorrow*" (DanShaw.com).

E The OTO body in Carrollton, GA that I was first initiated into (circa 2000) was named the Solve-Coagula Camp, and I was told by the body master that it was almost named The Secret Door. This body merged with Yggdrasil Camp (metro-Atlanta), Equilibrium Camp (Norcross), Lilith Camp (Athens, GA), Netmet Ankh Netmet Camp (Braselton, GA) to form the Dove & Serpent Oasis serving all those areas, in 2001.

F Jacques Bergier co-wrote the influential, *The Morning of the Magicians* which delves into the Nazi's fascination with the occult and examines how these beliefs may have influenced some of their actions during World War II.

ness is to restore benevolent cosmic power to these special geographic locations that have lost their power.

Quartz Rock Clusters

What could be facilitating these energetic anomalies at specific geographic locations? An important theory in the high strangeness community is that these anomalies are caused by large clusters of quartz rocks. In both the *Hellier* docuseries and the *Penny Royal* podcast series, it is speculated that large clusters of quartz deposits could be a reason for the high strangeness phenomena found in and around Hellier, Kentucky. This is termed the Kentucky anomaly due to the intense geomagnetic field that the large deposit of quartz creates. Nathan Isaac, host and creator of *Penny Royal,* says that the magnetic pull in this area is so strong that sky and ground try to meet. The atmosphere is being magnetically pulled down to try and touch the quartz rock, which is shooting its energy upward.

According to NASA, the Kentucky anomaly (or "Kentucky Body") is "a very prominent magnetic anomaly ... beneath Kentucky and Tennessee" and "prominent aeromagnetic and gravity anomalies are also associated" with this region. They say that a "model constructed" to explain "the magnetic anomaly" indicated "the complex [was] a large mafic plutonic intrusion of Precambrian age.[G,19] Jeffery Scott Holland says this magnetic anomaly "is right in line with everything I've been saying about the 'Kentucky Vortex'" and speculates it may "be a sort of Unified Field Theory for everything that's weird about" the area.[20]

In both *Penny Royal* and *Hellier,* it is speculated that these large quartz deposits in Kentucky have an effect on people's mental health; and hallucinations triggered by this could contribute to the reported high strangeness in the area. To support this theory, the *Hellier* and *Penny Royal* researchers point out a fact they learned in their investigations of the area, saying that there is a larger than average number of mental health issues in the Somerset, Kentucky area, as evidenced by the fact that over 50% of the patients in the state mental health hospital are from the region.[H,21]

G "Terrestrial magnetic conditions at the Oregon Vortex have been attributed to a violent geological change that took place eons ago. I wouldn't hazard to guess whether some impending violent geographic change might have an effect on mass consciousness" (*Stalking the Great Whore: The Lost Writings of James Shelby Downard*, p. 189).

H This aspect of the show was reported on in the local press, where it is said "some surprising things are claimed about this community – in addition to more fanciful subjects, there is also talk about conditions that may lead to high rates of mental health issues"(Christopher Harris, "Somerset Featured in Second Season of Paranormal Doc *Hellier,*" *Commonwealth Journal*, Somerset-Kentucky.com, Dec. 3, 2019).

The creator of *Penny Royal* points out that the other area said to have a lot of quartz is Sedona, Arizona, which had a high number of UFO sightings in the late 2000s. He says: "I talk about it all the time" there are "people seeing these energy balls," wondering if it is because there is "a super powerful [geomagnetic] field focused up through the quartz" which in turn "affects the mind and causes people to see these balls of energy that they think are UFOs."[22]

Bryant argues that the presence of numerous quartz deposits in the ground is one of the factors contributing to the formation of vortexes in Asheville region.[5] This puts large quartz deposits at three of the top high strangeness geographic locations mentioned thus far: Asheville, North Carolina; Sedona, Arizona; and Hellier, Kentucky.

Ley Lines

Another potential explanation for the existence of high strangeness window areas is in ley lines, which were first discovered in 1921 by amateur archaeologist, Alfred Watkins. He discovered them while he "was looking for features of interest on a map of the Blackwardine area," discovering "a straight alignment passing through various ancient sites and churches," but he offered "no underlying theory for their function." After Watkin's death in 1935, "speculation about the meaning and purpose of ley lines continued" and in 1936, famed occultist Dion Fortune (1890-1946)[I] put forth the idea in her novel, *The Goat-Foot God* (1936), that ley lines were "'lines of power' linking prehistoric sites." Guy Underwood[J] introduced the idea that there were "nodes in the system" of ley lines which were "places where two or more ley lines meet or cross." The most famous of these nodes would be Stonehenge.[24] Colin Wilson describes leys as "lines of living earth force" and that dragon paths (from the Chinese esoteric tradition) "are two names for the same thing."[25] The infamous godfather of high strangeness research, James Shelby Downard, referred to them as "Electric Roads" or "lines of magnetic influence."[26]

I Famed British magician, writer and contemporary of Crowley. She co-founded the Fraternity of the Inner Light, an occult organization that promoted her teachings. She claimed to have communicated with the Ascended Masters who dictated her book, *The Cosmic Doctrine*. See *Dion Fortune and the Inner Light* by Gareth Knight.

J Author of *The Pattern of the Past* (1977), which looked at "Primary geodetic lines.... Animals and the Earth force.... Topographical evidence of the geodetic system.... Early evidence in stone -- The central site of Stonehenge.... Freemasonry and Medieval architecture -- Layout of Medieval churches and cathedrals."

Earth as a Living Body

For Wilson, leys are based on "the knowledge system that lies behind the Chinese science of feng shui" and are "the recognition of the Earth as a living body." Interestingly, he ties this knowledge system to that of Atlantis, which "has become the symbol of a remote golden age in which science was based on this recognition"[25] of the earth as a living body.

"When we think of the earth as being a living organism," says Bryant, "the terms ley lines… and vortexes then come to literally define the circulation system, organs, and the nervous system" of the planet. She perceives leys to be "an invisible, thin, hollow 'tube' through which natural planetary energy is conducted like electricity through an electrical cord" and believes they "transport electricity, magnetism, and electromagnetism, the earth's life force or blood, throughout her body." Continuing the Earth-as-human-body analogy, she says that "Vortexes are like mini-earth chakras" and are "acupuncture points in the Earth." In these geographic areas "natural earth energy is potent" and is "where that power may be tapped." Bryant claims that the acupuncture needles for the Earth are the "human mind, prayer, and ceremony" and to the ancient shamans of the British Isles the stone circles were "serving like acupuncture needles."[5]

In 1979, atmospheric scientist James Lovelock published the book, *Gaia: A New Look at Life,* "presenting an in-depth argument for the Earth being alive." Since the publication of this book "a whole new movement called 'Gaia Consciousness' has emerged, seeking to articulate the implications of the living-Earth thesis."[8]

Leys: How the Energy of Earth's Body Is Moved

Using the human body analogy, the ley is "a vein" of the living Earth along which these subtle energies flow, just like blood flows through veins in a body. The fact that ley lines run between the sacred sites of stone circles and burial mounds would seem to reinforce this notion. These sites of stones and mounds punctuate the energy and "act as places of power along the network of lines"[27] just like organs in the body. These places of power where ley lines cross, such as the sacred site of Stonehenge, are called nodes, "junction points" or "ley terminals," and the "joining of energy always results in the convergence point becoming an intense vortex"[5,K] or sacred site.

K These nodes have also been called "sensitive spots," (pp. 167, 80-81) which is an area where "two or more" leys "intersect" and detecting them or using them "depends on those who are endowed with a dowser-like sensitivity" (*Stalking the Great Whore: The Lost Writings of James Shelby Downard*, p. 187).

Telluric Currents

Telluric currents is a term often used interchangeably with ley lines. For example, it is said that "UFOs may travel along telluric currents or ley lines around the Earth to draw energy."[L,28] The description of telluric currents is essentially the same as ley lines. For example, it is said that "telluric currents, also called simply, 'Earth currents' were known by ancient cultures.... Many of the ancient megaliths around the world, including places like Göbekli Tepe" and "the many massive stones in Egypt... the Moai Stones in Easter Island, protruding stones from the Earth in Ireland" were "all tools that tap into telluric energy."[29]

Pierre Teilhard de Chardin (1881-1955) mentions telluric energies when he waxes philosophical about the noösphere, which is important to this chapter in particular and this book as a whole. This is because the "noösphere is the sum-total of mental activity" of the planet and is a manifestation of the fact that the Earth is "growing its very own mind."[30] In addition to this group mind growing around Earth on the astral realm, he points out that there is also a "living membrane composed of the fauna and flora" existing around the globe. This "biosphere" actually "forms a single piece of the very tissue of the genetic relations which delineate the tree of life."

Chardin says that we have entered a "new era in evolution" which he calls "the era of Noögenesis." In this new era, he argues we need a "support proportionate to the operation" of creating the noösphere, which involves adding "another membrane in the majestic assembly of telluric layers" around the globe. I think the high strangeness magical praxis of turning window areas into New Age energy vortex sites is the "support proportionate" to the "operation" of helping establish the noösphere.

When the noösphere layer is established, a spiritual "fire" then "spreads in ever widening circles til finally the whole planet is covered with incandescence," according to Chardin. This new layer which is "outside and above the biosphere" is the "thinking layer" of the planet and when it is established it marks a "new age." This is because it means "The earth 'gets a new skin.' Better still, it finds its soul." This process is "the most astounding of the revolutions undergone by the earth."[31] The path to establishing Chardin's noösphere is through working with window areas and turning them into sacred sites: the magick of high strangeness. Chris Hardy, author of *Sacred Network: Megaliths, Cathedrals, Ley Lines and the Power of Shared Consciousness,* would perhaps agree with the thoughts I have laid

L "Telluric currents of the type called 'ley lines,'" *Stalking the Great Whore*, p. 321

out in this section, as his book "Unveils the coming state of shared consciousness for humanity fueled by the sacred network."[32]

Liminal Spaces

As I pointed out in the previous chapter, liminal spaces "are places where energy is a lot more potent and the veil between worlds is at its thinnest": because of this, high strangeness phenomena are more likely to manifest in these locations. Examples of geographic liminal spaces include "wells and springs, cemeteries, cross-roads ... entry ways, staircases, [and] doorways."[33] Liminal spaces as a cause of high strangeness phenomena are explored in depth in the *Hellier* series.

Crossroads

Downard asserted that "crossroads were the favored sites of" witches and sorcerers and were "significant to ritual sex magic."[34] In Haitian Vodou, Papa Legba "is one of the most important of the gods in the pantheon" and is linked to "crossroads." This god or lwa is the "opener of the gates between the human world and the spirit world" and as such "is the first to be summoned at ceremonies" because he is the "opener of the gates ... guardian of the crossroads, the point of entry to the spirit world." This means that if you want to talk to a lwa besides Legba you have to ask him to open the gates so the lines of communication are open. Due to these facts, crossroads are "a key location both in its physical form and symbolically because of the importance of communicating with the lwa in Vodou."[35]

Naturally Occurring Liminal Spaces

These types of window areas are "common among more primal-minded people" and are places in nature "which bear no special" human-made structure, often featuring only "a well-worn foot path." The Earth is full of such sacred spaces: "groves, springs, caves, rivers [and] meadows."[36] It's possible that the intricate temple complexes observed at sacred locations were first naturally occurring liminal areas that were gradually developed and enhanced over time.

It is also speculated that springs are a focus of unusual phenomena. The reason given for this is that there is an Earth "force embodied in [spring] water" that contains "energies capable of manifesting" paranormal phenomena. This "hyperphysical force" that is capable of facilitating high strangeness "is liberated" when "spring water bubbles out and dashes along into brooks, creeks, and rivers" and "where streams come together." It is reported that numerous "oddities" have been reported "at the confluences" of water channels and "most of the major mound complexes... are on or near merging streams." Because of these facts "North American springs were invariably revered by the Indians as seats of earth spirits."[36]

Mystical Toponymy

Mystical toponymy suggests that regions with certain names often evolve into hubs of high strangeness. This field encompasses the investigation of geographic names imbued with "magic and mystery significance" or symbolic importance. This theory comprises two fundamental aspects: "word wizardry" (or onomatology, the study of names) and "the science of symbolism," which is also associated with latitude and longitude degree lines.[26] In short, it explores the "SynchroMystic aspect of place names" which "appear to ... turn up in peculiar connections."[37] It is theorized that these peculiar connections turn up because the place names are "imbued with sorcerous significance."[34]

History of the Term

Bill Grimstad (aka Jim Brandon) explored this theory in a 1978 essay, which was perhaps the first references to mystical toponymy in the literature. However, his essay identified John Keel as "the first to notice name frequency correlations in paranormal events." While in the process of documenting "all sorts of weirdities" he reported a noticeable correlation between "paranormal happenings" arising "in conjunction with" cities bearing the name Fayette (or similar variations).[38] This connection has given rise to what is called *The Fayette Factor*.[M]

The controversial Grimstad[N] brings to mind another important historical figure in high strangeness research who must again be mentioned: James Shelby Downard (1913-1998). The origin of the concept is traced to Downard, who was known for his "penetrating conception of 'mystical toponomy.'"[37] Reportedly, Grimstad was so "taken with Mr. Downard's concept of mystical toponomy" that it probably prompted him to write *The Rebirth of Pan: Hidden Faces of the American Earth Spirit*.[39] Another author that continues "expanding upon Downard's" concept is Michael Hoffman, who (along with Grimstad) was one of James Shelby Downard's two main

---

M See Loren Coleman's, "The Fayette Factor File," CopyCatEffect.blogspot.com, Jan. 2018.
N For more on this controversy see the Conclusion chapter.

protégés.[O,40] Downard's most famous essay, "King Kill 33°: Masonic Symbolism in the Assassination of John F. Kennedy," was created in collaboration with Hoffman who claimed that in 1977 Downard "approached me with the idea of writing a book based on his extensive notes on the JFK assassination."[39] Those extensive notes eventually became the essay in question.

Around this time period Downard was only known to a "small swath of Fortean" researchers from his arcane writings on the JFK mystery and his *Sirius Rising* tapes. The latter were brought to a larger swath of high strangeness researchers with RAW's first volume of *Cosmic Trigger*.[41] In the book RAW shares ideas from Downard's *Sirius Rising* tapes, saying they "set forth the most absurd, the most incredible, the most ridiculous [Sirius theory] of them all": secret magicians are "preparing Earth, in an occult manner, for extraterrestrial contact." However, RAW says, the "only trouble is that after the weird data we have already surveyed" this theory "may not sound totally unbelievable to us."[42] Downard was then brought to a "larger more diverse audience" by Adam Parfrey's 1987 book of collected essays, *Apocalypse Culture,*[P] featuring the essay "King Kill 33,°" which was "Downard's mad masterpiece."[41]

This introduction to a larger, more diverse audience led to Downard entering into pop-culture, seen in the fact that Marilyn Manson wrote a song in 2000 called "King Kill 33.°"[Q] There was also an Atlanta, Georgia band with the same name that formed in 1990 but "never issued a full-length album" and were described as "a combination of Black Flag and Pink Floyd."[43]

It is difficult to determine which of the above three researchers first discovered mystical toponymy, because Downard, Hoffman, and Grimstad would "occasionally gather in Downard's Airstream trailer … and shoot the breeze about" high strangeness. So "how anyone would" be able

---

O "Black Jack 21 alchemy is achieved … through the ceremonial manipulation of…subconscious archetypes and symbols, comprising the Twilight Language which communicates with our" unconscious mind. The American people are so "far gone in the depths of this processing" that we can say "Psychologically, they have the status of…demoralized prisoners of war" and "It bears repeating: Americans have been marching in" this dark direction since "the immolation of the King of Camelot near the 33rd degree line in 1963." (Michael Hoffman, *Twilight Language*, 2021, p. 239). I argue, thwarting Wetiko's use of twilight language ("Black Jack 21 Alchemy") is an essential practice of high strangeness magick.

P "Apocalypse Culture is compulsory reading for all those concerned with the crisis of our times. An extraordinary collection unlike anything I have ever encountered. These are the terminal documents of the twentieth century." J.G. Ballard

Q The song "is the eighteenth track on the 2000 release *Holy Wood (In the Shadow of the Valley of Death)*. The song opens with a sound reminiscent of the buzzing of an insect's wings, followed by a blowing sound backed by Manson whispering 'blame me,' referring to the Columbine massacre." (mansonwiki.com)

to accurately "draw lines of demarcation to ascertain who came up with what, I do not know. Certainly Mr. Downard took the lead."[39]

Separate from these three,[R] is another Fortean author who furthered mystical toponymy research, Loren Coleman. On his blog he quotes a commentator that said after Grimstad's initial essay on the subject the topic was "expanded upon ... by many other researchers, most notably by" himself. He claims that "shortly" after Grimstad's essay on the subject he wrote a similar piece for *Fortean Times* (no. 29, Summer 1979), called "Devil Names and Fortean Places," where he laid out "evidence of Fortean events happening in Devil-named places." Coleman says his essay on mystical toponymy, "was one I had been working on ... long before I heard of Grimstad/Brandon."[44] In the essay he "retroactively analyzed specific locations" with Devil in the name and discovered "indigenous peoples and colonial settlers had named these areas after sinister entities to forewarn travelers and future homesteaders they might want to be careful in exploring and living in those spots."

Controversy Around the Term

This section hopes to clarify why there is so much quibbling over who can lay claim to the founding of mystical toponymy. There is so much controversy around the three pioneers of the field (most notably Grimstad) that Coleman said: "I will take on the full ownership of this 'Fayette' concept ... it is mine," Grimstad "gave it up by being [a] Holocaust denier ... and not coming forth with apologies, new editions, or reprints of The Rebirth of Pan."[44] I want to be clear here, I fully believe in The Holocaust: the fact that the Nazis murdered six million European Jews during WWII and I am in no way questioning it. Also, when it comes to studying the work of, Brandon/Grimstad, Downard, and Hoffman (or any author I quote): Caveat Emptor. I also want to make another thing clear: I do not have enough knowledge on this controversy to say I know for a fact if Coleman's assertion that Brandon/Grimstad, is a "Holocaust denier" is a factual statement. Readers would do well to remember that libel: publishing false statements about someone which damage their reputation can open you up to a lawsuit. It would take an entire book to adequately explore this topic and as such, it is beyond the scope of this text. However, I did want to alert readers as to why, merely mentioning mystical toponomy or its founders is such a hot button issue in high strangeness research.

R For further analysis of these three controversial originators of Mystical Toponymy, see Season 2 of the *Penny Royal* Podcast, episode 2: "Mystery Machine."

Mystical Toponomy Explanations

Brandon said he did not have the "tiniest ghost ... of an idea" of how a "word root" (such as Fayette) could impact "the physical and psychical"[36] worlds. Let us now look at some possible explanations as how it may be possible.

Cybernetic Explanation

In Cybernetics, there are "three central concepts" which are said to be "crucial in any ... system. They are communication, control and feedback." Norbert Wiener[S] (1894-1964) coined the term "cybernetics," the word comes from the Greek term "'kybernetes' meaning ... 'steersman,'" to "designate the important role that feedback plays in a communication system."[45] This explanation was explored in the *Penny Royal* podcast, where Isaac theorized the phenomenon occurred by tying into the energy of ley lines which facilitates a feedback loop between "people, places and events" that exist "outside cause and effect" in an almost "quantum way." In turn, this strange feedback loop will "somehow correspond to the mapping of the Earth's geography."[46]

General Lafayette

The Fayette Factor is named after the American revolutionary war hero, General Lafayette, and is centered around US cities named after him. He was a colleague in arms with Benjamin Franklin and they "constitute two of the most important links in the chain of circumstances that culminated in the establishment of the original thirteen colonies." Manly P. Hall says Lafayette was "also a man of mystery" in the same vein as the mysterious "Professor" who led the committee that designed the original flag of the new nation and who appeared on "the evening of July 4, 1776" while a "group of men were gathered for the momentous task of severing the last tie between the old country."[47]

During this debate on starting the new nation "a fierce voice rang out," causing the men to stop and ask "Who was this man who had suddenly appeared in their midst and transfixed them with his oratory?" It is said the voice of this mysterious Professor rang out with such "a holy zeal" that the attendees were moved "to their very souls." And then "Name after name was placed upon the parchment: the Declaration of Independence

S *Cybernetics: Or Control and Communication in the Animal and the Machine* is a book written by Norbert Wiener and published in 1948. It is the first public usage of the term "cybernetics" to refer to self-regulating mechanisms.

was signed" as the mysterious man disappeared among the excitement. Hall speculates this mysterious individual was Saint Germain.

Hall suggests that Saint Germain became an immortal human that now meddles in world affairs, after he "passed through the 'philosophic death' as Francis Bacon in 1626." Bacon is important to this book because of his "vision of the 'New Atlantis,' a prophetic dream of the great civilization which was so soon to rise upon the soil of the New World."[47] Hall wonders, "Did General Washington and Doctor Franklin recognize the Professor as an emissary of the Mystery school which has so long controlled the political destinies of this planet?" Perhaps this Mystery school of immortal humans moved "the secret societies of Europe" to conspire and "establish upon the American continent 'a new nation, conceived in liberty and dedicated to the proposition that all men are created equal.'"[47]

At any rate, "The cities, towns, and counties across the United States, which are the hotspots linked to the Fayette Factor, are tied to the ... sites that the Marquis de Lafayette visited on his grand tour of the country in 1824-1825." It is also important to point out that his "visits were highly ritualized happenings, in which he was involved with laying many cornerstones"[48] at Masonic temples. We are left to wonder if Lafayette was "a magician of such power that the mere application of his name has been enough ever since to make a place 'act up.' Or was he himself a mere unwitting function of the Fayette factor?"[34]

Ultraterrestrials, Lafayette, and Immortal Humans

Perhaps ultraterrestrials influenced Lafayette's travels and/or the inhabitants of the locations he visited to name cities after him, knowing from their trans-dimensional vantage point that his name would accurately reflect the highly strange vibe of the land. This may have been knowledge they were privy to, thanks to their transdimensional vantage point. As Dick said in his *Exegesis* "Although we remain unaware of supernatural entities they guide and direct us."[49]

Or perhaps Lafayette was secretly guided by St. Germain (an immortal human) on where to travel. This utterly absurd idea will make more sense in the next chapter, when we explore theories from the book, *Secret Doors of Earth: The Hidden Influence of Ancient Aliens and Sacred Geography on Human History*. This book states there are "immortals in our midst" whose secret societies create "centers of energy" that allow them to "communicate with extraterrestrial intelligences in the galaxy" and that this group has "dispensed" the power of these "Interdimensional portals" to humans.

Said portals are "secret doors of the earth" which act as "passageways to other dimensions" and are safeguarded and propagated by "Extraordinary beings among us, who are as old as the planet."[18] Hall speculates that the mysterious Professor had a hand in starting the United States of America and as such was an event that "parallels others of a similar kind recorded by ancient historians attendant upon the founding of every new nation," leaving him to ask if they are "coincidences, or do they demonstrate that the divine wisdom of the ancient Mysteries still is present in the world, serving mankind as it did of old?"[47]

The Mystical Power of Names

Another speculation is the "triggering element in Fayette, Lafayette, and Fayetteville is the root word 'fay/fey'" with the "literal meaning of 'fayette'" being "'little enchantment' or 'little fairy.'" Perhaps these locations "may be enchanted by the use of [this] name, the mere titling giving it some name power."[50] The English word fey is defined as "fated to die ... accursed, unfortunate, unlucky." These two definitions of fey "would seem to place us on a tightrope between wizardry and death" when interacting with these sites. Brandon claims this perilous tightrope walk "does fit incidents I have recounted."[36] Walking this tightrope is what high strangeness research and practice is all about because the possibility exists that "certain areas [might] tend to trigger 'bad' (from our viewpoint) phenomena." My magick of high strangeness seeks to trigger the good phenomena and eliminate the negative.

This means that the power of the word fay/fey "may come down to... something like the 'names of power' that played such a prominent part in the ancient magical texts." These names of power leave us with the "possibility" of words and symbols "as causers or controllers of phenomena." This highly curious possibility "definitely requires more study" because "there are strong indications that ... the word *fay* and its permutations have a link with certain kinds of events."[36]

The Psychological Power of Names

This utterly absurd theory, saying that a geographic location with an unusual name will be more likely to produce strange paranormal phenomena, has support in mainstream areas of study. Sigmund Freud, the father of psychoanalysis, said "words and magic were in the beginning one and the same thing, and even today words retain much of their magical power."[51] While French psychoanalyst Jacques Lacan was "not the first analyst to underscore the import of names," he is the psychoanalyst who is most known for this concept. Before Lacan, "Karl Abraham's famous article on 'the determining momentum of names' is probably the first in which the issue was clearly raised, stressing the idea that a person's" name "had a secret influence on his destiny."[52] Lacan mysteriously said a name "is a mark that is already open to reading… printed on something that may be a subject who will speak."[53] God knows what that means, but something that complicated must be evidence for the highly strange power of names! For Marshall McLuhan, the father of media studies, "The name of a man is a numbing blow from which he never recovers."[54] It is believed that McLuhan got this idea from the line from *Finnegans Wake,* which reads "who gave you that numb?"[55]

These are bold statements by psychoanalysts and McLuhan, but social psychology research indicates the veracity of their stance on the power of names. "Nominative determinism is the hypothesis that people tend to gravitate towards areas of work that fit their names. The term was first used in the magazine *New Scientist* in 1994, after the magazine's humorous 'Feedback' column noted several studies carried out by researchers with remarkably fitting surnames."[56] According to social psychologists, there is some evidence to "suggest that your name can determine your job … a proctologist called Dr Butts, a pastry chef called Baker" which leaves us to ask "is it sheer coincidence, or does the universe have a way of pushing people towards" professions that are in harmony or synchronization with their name? This isn't just anecdotal evidence, in "social psychology there are studies" which indicate that "the spelling of people's names in the US potentially influenced major life decisions, such as which careers they pursued." Research "found that people named Dennis or Denise tend to become dentists at a higher rate than people of other equally popular names."[57]

Earth Spirit

One explanation of window areas is that they are created by a mysterious Earth spirit. According to Greg Carlwood's reading of the seminal book, *Origins of the Gods,* high strangeness occurs due to "a blanket of consciousness that kind of covers the entire area, as if it's one big etheric entity."[58] The first section of this chapter was about Earth energies, which would argue this section is just about an anthropomorphization of naturally occurring phenomena; but let us now consider it is a literal etheric entity. One name some have given this earth spirit is Pan, the ancient Greek god of nature.[36]

Two Ways to View Pan

Pan as an etheric Earth energy can be seen in the following lines from an ancient poem, "I Call strong Pan, the substance of the whole, Etherial, marine, earthly, general soul, Immortal fire; for all the world is thine, And all are parts of thee, O pow'r divine."[59] In Crowley's poem which follows we see a more anthropomorphized Pan, with the goat-footed god as a representation for this Earth force, "Io Pan! Come over the sea / From Sicily and from Arcady! Roaming as Bacchus, with fauns and pards / And nymphs and satyrs for thy guards."[60] So is Pan a diffuse etheric Earth force or an actual god? Or perhaps the truth is found somewhere in the middle? Maybe the god Pan is the ultraterrestrial representative of this force of nature.

The Earth Force Has a Will of Its Own

In regards to this Earth energy, "Whether or not we're talking here of the pipe-playing" ancient god,[T] the fact remains that the planet contains "a great collective identity" which is actually "a living thing with an awareness and will of its own." It is claimed this entity has so much awareness that the main symbols of the "disturbing condition" of overly rationalistic autocracy the world is "laboring under" could possibly "come under attack by the Pan earth organism" itself. And even though these times are dire, "everything will work out somehow" because "the long-thwarted and distorted Pan force will play an ever growing part."

The Language of the Earth Force Is the High Strangeness Phenomenon

Things such as Orgone energy are having an "unrealized effect upon the Pan force in the surrounding environment," thus causing this "all-subsuming Pan force" to facilitate paranormal phenomena. From this point of view, high strangeness phenomena are "the earth spirit" showing us that it "has things to communicate." It is hard to understand this communication because it is speaking "with the Allvoice in the Alltime." This is so hard to understand because humans are stuck in the temporal "details of the moment that we call reality" and as such "there is little to

T Pan as a prefix means "all." See the following quote from *The Homeric Hymns*, "Then all the immortals were glad in heart ... and they called the boy Pan [i.e. derived from the word pantes meaning 'all'] because he delighted all their hearts." *The Theoi Project*, theoi.com/Georgikos/Pan.html

seize onto and analogize with familiar elements in our experiences."[36] The message we seem to be getting is that high strangeness phenomena are all "interrelated and tied together by a subtle earth energy interacting with human consciousness" and on top of that "we humans have an important relationship to" this "powerful 'Earth Spirit.'"[3]

Personal Experiences

Most of my personal experiences with window areas are in the next chapter. But I will now give some details on my personal experience with word wizardry, onomatology, "or the science of names [which] forms a very interesting part of the investigations of the higher Masonry."[61] Again, for clarification I point out that mystical toponymy incorporates onomatology and "the Masonic science of symbolism"[62] related to geographic locations. In word wizardry we are studying the fact that "a yarn is being spun and 'charmed' conjunctions ... are [being] formed, partly from invocation and partly from 'surfing' a magnetic attraction that seems to organize anomalies around certain 'words of power' and potent symbols."[63]

Vaughn

It is speculated that "certain numbers" are "entangled with certain [high strangeness] phenomena" and as a result "the same would have to be said of certain words." These words "tend to be involved in events of, at best, a sort of Puckish drollery and at worst, tragedy." The words in question are not referring to "spooky tongue-twisters as H. P. Lovecraft's Yog-Sothoth ... but of quite ordinary names like Bell ... Grubb, Magee ... Parsons, Pike, Shelby" and, as we have seen, variants of Lafayette.[36] One of these words also happens to be my last name, Vaughn/Vaughan. I've observed this name appear in my research over the years, and I've noticed a higher-than-average presence of authors in the fields of paranormal, the occult, and transpersonal psychology who share this surname.[U]

Most notable among them is psychic Alan Vaughan[V] (1936-2001), the author of notable books such as *Patterns of Prophecy* (1973) and *Incredible Coincidences: The Baffling World of Synchronicity* (1979). His work is central to two of the seminal books on high strangeness: *Cosmic Trigger, vol. one* and *Philip K. Dick: The Dream Connection*, edited by D. Scott Apel.[W] In the former, he is a puzzle piece of the Sirius mystery, with RAW saying

U One renowned author of highly strange topics has the middle name of Vaughan but is so controversial, I can't mention his full name.

V Allaboutheaven.org/sources/vaughan-dr-alan/190

W His work is also mentioned in Colin Wilson's introductory essay to *The Goblin Universe.*

"Mr. Vaughn [sic] also had the impression of being contacted by Sirius in 1973,"[42] the same year RAW and Dick reported their contacts with inhabitants of this star system.

Apel reports he reached out to Vaughan because he "knew with personal certainty the reality of his psychic abilities and his sincerity in their use" and understood that if "anyone could discern the whereabouts of Philip K. Dick" beyond the grave "it would be Alan Vaughan." Vaughan told Apel that he learned from Dick that "he had several ... story ideas left over, and he might try to channel one or two of them to" him. Dick would achieve this feat by being able to "inspire some of [Apel's] writing" by "channeling him or tuning into him." Vaughan also told Apel that he felt Dick could "inspire some of your writing – if you'll let him.... But more important than the writing will be your experiences with getting in touch with Philip K. Dick, shall we say, psychically."[64] As a writer, I know we need all the help we can get.

I have always figured the tendency to see more people with the name Vaughan/Vaughn writing about matters of high strangeness is because of our genetic connection to the famous Welsh alchemist and philosopher Thomas Vaughan (1621-1666). Vaughan is a Saint of the Gnostic Catholic Church (EGC), which is the ecclesiastical arm of the Ordo Templi Orientis (OTO)[65] and Peter Levenda has written the definitive book on him, *The Tantric Alchemist: Thomas Vaughan and the Indian Tantric Tradition.* Vaughan is likely a distant relative of mine, but my genealogy research yields no confirmation. I do know that my Vaughan ancestor came to the New World in 1619 on the ship *Bona Nova,* which is Latin for good news.

Being that I am hitching my Vaughn wagon to an alchemist, I must go into a little detour because I know to the uninitiated alchemy is seen as pseudoscience. It is important to point out that "During the last thirty years of his life, Jung turned to alchemy as a fundamental resource for depth psychology. In alchemy he found images and thoughts that were uniquely fitted to his perceptions of psychological life," confirming "his views of the spontaneous activity and directedness of the unconscious."[66] Jung said his "primary aim" with the study of alchemy was "to demonstrate that the world of alchemical symbols definitely does not belong to the rubbish heap of the past, but stands in a very real and living relationship to our most recent discoveries concerning the psychology of the unconscious." He said that our "modern psychological discipline" gives "us the key to the secrets of alchemy, but, conversely, alchemy provides the psychology of the unconscious with a meaningful historical basis." Jung describes the art of alchemy with the "oft-repeated saying 'solve et coagula (dissolve and coagulate), the alchemist saw the essence of his art in separation and analysis on the one hand and synthesis and consolidation on the other."[67] To me, high strangeness researchers are like alchemists: they blend different paranormal topics to find a deeper understanding, creating a whole that's greater than its parts.

Interestingly, Philip K. Dick "loved the seventeenth century English religious poet Henry Vaughan,"[68] who was Thomas's twin brother.[X] There are other Vaughans/Vaughns that are writers of paranormal, occult, and transpersonal psychology subjects and I hope to feature them in more detail in volume three of this series, *My Cosmic Trigger: Ancestors, Gurus, Guides, & Friends in Highly Strange Places.* Apart from writers sharing my name, I've also noticed Vaughn/Vaughan appearing unexpectedly in the study of high strangeness. I'll share two examples to illustrate this. To guard against the selective perception effect, I even did some number crunching and by my estimations – Vaughn/Vaughan is expected to appear in, at most, 1/2500, people writing in English.

Diana Vaughan

Diana Vaughan is a fictional character at the center of a notorious hoax known as the "Leo Taxil Hoax." This elaborate deception was perpetrated by a French writer of the same name during the 1880s and 90s. He alleged that Diana was a former high-ranking priestess "of Lucifer" who had converted to Catholicism and was now revealing the dark secrets of a fictional group of Satanists that Taxil claimed were linked to Freemasonry and the Church. The character provided details of her encounters with "terrifying" demonic entities, including "Lucifer himself." Also provided were details surrounding "the instructions given directly by" the Dark Prince to "high ranked freemasons for the war ... against God." The reason this character was so named is because she used her ancestor, Thomas Vaughan's "work located in the family's library." His work helped Diana's dark magick because "Vaughan and his contemporaries [were] guided by satanic entities" and, as a result, they lacked "the true meaning ... of alchemy" which is "authentic spiritual path to reach God."[69]

X See, "The Rosicrucian Mysticism of Henry and Thomas Vaughan," at TheCenterForSophiologicalStudies.com, Sophiological studies refer to the exploration of the concept of Sophia and related topics in theology and delves into the various aspects of Sophia as a symbol of divine wisdom, often within the context of Christian mysticism.

Helen Vaughan

Renowned Welsh writer and mystic, Arthur Machen (1863-1947) knew Aleister Cowley via The Golden Dawn[Y] and is known for "his tale of femme fatale Helen Vaughan" in *The Great God Pan*.[70] He is known for this novella because it is "regarded as a classic of weird fiction among scholars of the field." The character Helen was "the product of a woman mating with something from ... beyond the veil of the senses" and as such this story "may have inspired H. P. Lovecraft's 'The Dunwich Horror.'"[71]

Vaughn, Montana

In *The Rebirth of Pan,* Brandon gives an account of a high strangeness hotspot in a city named Vaughn. This brings us back to the second element of mystical toponymy, weird effects of place names on a geographic location. It is reported that UFO and cattle mutilation activity was so high in Vaughn, in the mid 1970s that a "local deputy sheriff and a journalist compiled a valuable book on the subject."[Z] He reports an incident "where a Bigfoot allegedly appeared to two young girls near a trailer home" also pointing out the area contains "an Air Force ballistic missile site." This odd combination of cryptid and military activity is supported in the fact that "many of the creature incidents" featured in the deputy's book "had definite military correlations."[36]

I would be remiss if I didn't quickly point out an interesting facet of the above case in Vaughn: that the Bigfoot encounter occurred at a trailer home. At this point it is a bit of a dismissive cliche to speak of strange occurrences happening at trailer parks. Interestingly, the author provides a theory as to why this may be the case, tying it to Orgone, the "mysterious life energy" which Reich claimed was capable of being accumulated in particularly "constructed containers which he called 'Orgone boxes.'" Because of this, Brandon "wonders whether trailers might not be acting as some sort of energy accumulators ... that are having an unrealized effect upon the Pan force in the surrounding environment."[36]

Conclusion

It appears ancient civilizations recognized the presence of Earth energies, whereas in modern times we have often dismissed their existence. However, not only do these energies exist but there are also specific lo-

Y See *Talking to the Gods: Occultism in the Work of W. B. Yeats, Arthur Machen, Algernon Blackwood, and Dion Fortune.*

Z See, "Why Are There so many UFO Sightings in Montana?" www.mtpr.org/montana-news/ 2022-09-14/ why-are-there-so-many-ufo-sightings-in-montana

cations where their intensity is exceptionally high, potentially facilitating paranormal occurrences. In the upcoming chapter, we'll explore how people have been harnessing these powerful spots for various purposes, both benevolent and malevolent, since ancient times.

As our exploration of mystical toponymy has revealed, these unique geographical focal points position us "on a tightrope between wizardry and death." This is likely due to the fact that the "power behind these manifestations may not be entirely under control but acts somewhat chaotically."[36] In the next chapter, we will explore how the conscious intentions of those who visit these areas and attempt to manage the chaos are of paramount importance.

Sources

1. "John DeSouza: Who Are the Paranormal Magnets?" *High Journeys with Alexis Brooks,* 2018, HigherJourneys.com, 33:58, 16:00, 37:00.

2. Dan Shaw, Interview, VortexMaps.com, 2007, Scribd.com/document/94834637/Vortex-Maps-Catalog-2007

3. Andrew Collins and Gregory L. Little, *Origins of the Gods: Qesem Cave, Skinwalkers, and Contact with Transdimensional Intelligences,* 2022, E-book, pp. 38, 42, 244, 30, 84.

4. Peter Redgrove, *The Black Goddess and the Unseen Real,* 1988, p. 15.

5. Page Bryant, *The Spiritual Reawakening of the Great Smoky Mountains,* 1994, p. 78, 79, 148, 85, 109.

6. Seb Janiak, "Morphogenic Field," SebJaniak.com.

7. John Horgan, "Scientific Heretic Rupert Sheldrake on Morphic Fields, Psychic Dogs and Other Mysteries," ScientificAmerican.com.

8. James A. Swan, *Sacred Places: How the Living Earth Seeks Our Friendship,* 1990, pp. 208, 209, 230, 212.

9. Colin Wilson, *Strange Powers,* 1973. E-book, p. 54.

10. John Keel, *Our Haunted Planet,* 1971. p. 83.

11. *Mysterious Universe* podcast, Episode 28.19, Nov. 19, 2022. 14:53 mins.

12. George E. Bean, *Aegean Turkey,* 1966.

13. Chad Stuemke, "Esoteric Architecture, Stargate Detroit, and the Great Lakes Triangle," *The Higher Side Chats,* Nov. 17, 2020. 55:14 mins.

14. Chuck Zukowski, "EMF, My Paranormal Crossover Theory," UFOnut.com.

15. "Why Ghosts Are Magnetic," ApexMagnets.com, Oct. 15, 2015.

16. William G. Roll, *Psychological and Electromagnetic Aspects of Haunts,* 2000.

16.1. Plasma (state of matter), britannica.com

17. Dan Shaw, Vortex Research Group, *Vortex Field Guide,* 2011.

18. Jacques Bergier, *Secret Doors of the Earth: The Hidden Influence of Ancient Aliens and Sacred Geography on Human History,* 1975, Audio book- Chapter 4. Publisher's summary.

19. M. Mayhew and D. Myers, *A Compilation of Mineral Occurrences and the Relationship Occurrences to Structural Elements of the Kentucky and Tennessee Region,* NTRS.NASA.gov, Feb. 1984.

20. J. Holland, "The Kentucky Anomaly," UnusualKentucky.blogspt.com, July 27, 2008.

21. Hellier, *The Secret Commonwealth,* Season 2, Episode 8, Dec. 12, 2019. 34 min.

22. *Penny Royal* Podcast, Season 1, Episode 2: *Alien Space Bats.*

23. Nathan Isaac, *The Convergence Enigma* (Formerly *FearScape Paranormal Podcast*), *Getting Spooky with Nathan Isaac,* Another Realm Media, Youtube.com, March 24, 2021. 38:00.

24. Keith Fitzpatrick-Matthews, "Ley Lines: From Neolithic Trackways to Channels of Mystical Energy," BadArchaeology.com, 2011.

25. Colin Wilson, Introduction to *The Goblin Universe* by Fredrick William Holiday, 1990.

26. James Shelby Downard, *Stalking the Great Whore: The Lost Writings of James Shelby Downard,* 2023, pp. 321, 41.

27. Danny Sullivan, *Ley Lines: The Greatest Landscape Mystery,* 2004. E-book- p. 56 (chapter 4).

28. Allen Greenfield's segment summary, "Remembering Tim Conway/UFOs & Men in Black," *Coast to Coast AM with George Noory,* Feb. 17, 2022.

29. "Using Telluric Fields to Recharge Your Energy," *HealersOfTheLight.com,* Aug. 27, 2018.

30. Pierre Teilhard de Chardin, *The Formation of the Noösphere,* The Library of Consciousness, Organism.earth, 1947.

31. Pierre Teilhard de Chardin, *The Phenomenon of Man,* 1959, pp. 182-83

32. Chris H. Hardy, *Sacred Network: Megaliths, Cathedrals, Ley Lines and the Power of Shared Consciousness,* publisher's summary, 2011.

33. TikTok, @the_liminalwitch, Wales

34. James Shelby Downard, "Sorcery, Sex, Assassination and the Science of Symbolism." This essay is a "fleshed-out version" of "King Kill/ 33" which appeared in the first edition of *Apocalypse Culture,* 1987.

35. Martha Warren Beckwith, "Legba: The Crossroads and the Cross," NatureAndSupernaturalNature.wordpress.com, July 26, 2020.

36. Jim Brandon, *The Rebirth of Pan: Hidden Faces of the American Earth Spirit,* 1983, pp. 116-117, 193-194, 2, 237, 241, 136, 104, 185, 212, 136-137, 136.

37. "Who Started SynchroMysticism? James Shelby Downard," TheSynchromystic.com, Aug. 6, 2017.

38. Bill Grimstad, "Fateful Fayette," *Fortean Times,* 25th Edition, 1978.

39. Michael Hoffman, quoted by Adam Gorightly in, "Lost, but Now It's Found," his Foreword to *Stalking The Great Whore: The Lost Writings of James Shelby Downard,* 2023.

40. "SynchroMysticism and 'Twilight Language': Michael A. Hoffman II," TheSynchromystic.com, Oct. 15, 2017.

41. Adam Gorightly, "Lost, But Now It's Found," in *Stalking The Great Whore: The Lost Writings of James Shelby Downard,* 2023.

42. Robert Anton Wilson, *Cosmic Trigger Vol. 1: The Final Secret of the Illuminati,* 1977, pp. 168, 221.

43. Lee Smith, "Dressed to King-Kill," CreativeLoafing.com, Wednesday March 21, 2001, CreativeLoafing.com/content-164465-dressed-to-king-kill

44. Loren Coleman, "The Dirty Little Secrets of Twilight Forteans," Jan. 2021, CopyCatEffect.blogspot.com.

45. "Cybernetics," Cyborganthropology.com

46. Nathan Isaac, Hedgerows and Highways, *Penny Royal,* Season Two, Episode Three, 2022, 58 mins.

47. Manly P. Hall, *Collected Works Illustrated: The Lost Keys of Freemasonry, The Secret Teachings of All Ages,* E-book: pp. 1258-60.

48. Loren Coleman, "The Fayette Factor File," Copyatffect.blogspot, January 30, 2018.

49. Philip K. Dick, *The Exegesis,* quoted in *Phillip K. Dick: The Dream Connection,* p. 182.

50. Loren Colman, *Mysterious America,* 2001, E-book: p. 370.

51. Sigmund Freud, *Introductory Lectures on Psychoanalysis,* 1917.

52. François Sauvagnat, "Fatherhood and Naming in J. Lacan's Works," Lacan.com.

53. Jacques Lacan, *Introduction to the Names-of-the-Father Seminar,* Vol. 40, Television, Spring, 1987.

54. Marshall McLuhan, *Understanding Media: The Extensions of Man,* 1964, p. 32.

55. James Joyce, *Finnegans Wake*, 1939; see "Marshall McLuhan on James Joyce," people.well.com/user/abs/Cyb/archive/mcluhan_joyce.html

56. "Nominative determinism," Wikipedia.

57. S. J. Velasquez, "Do Our Names Push Us Towards Certain Jobs?" BBC.com, 2018.

58. Greg Carlwood, "Ryan Patrick Burns: Skinwalker Ranch Updates, Communing with the Trickster, & the Magic of P. B. Randolph," *The Higher Side Chats*, Dec. 5, 2022, 13:37.

59. *The Initiations of Orpheus: To Pan*, sixth century BC.

60. Aleister Crowley, "Hymn to Pan," published in *The Equinox*, Volume III, No. 1, March 1919.

61. *Encyclopedia of Freemasonry*, quoted in "King Kill 33" by James Shelby Downard and Michael A. Hoffman II, Rare Editions from Research Intelligence, Published by Independent History & Research, found at Scribd.com.

62. James Shelby Downard with Michael A. Hoffman II, "King-Kill 33: Masonic Symbolism in the Assassination of John F. Kennedy." This excerpt is from the version of the essay that has been out of print since 1987 when it appeared in the first edition of Adam Parfrey's anthology, *Apocalypse Culture*. Subsequent editions of this book, including the current Feral House revised edition, do not carry this version. See whale.to/b/kingkill_33.html

63. Michael Hoffman, *Twilight Language*, 2021, p. 65.

64. Scott Apel (editor), *Philip K. Dick: The Dream Connection*, 2014, E-book-p. 173.

65. Aleister Crowley, *The Gnostic Mass*, 1913.

66. Murray Stein, Ph.D., "Understanding the Meaning of Alchemy: Jung's Metaphor for the Transformative Process," JungChicago.org, June 2017.

67. Carl Jung, *Mysterium Coniunctionis*, 1963, Foreword, pp. xiii, xiv.

68. Erik Davis, "Philip K. Dick's Divine Interference," TechGnosis.com, April 15, 2005.

69. "The Case of Diana Vaughan, Ex-Great Priestess of Lucifer," YogaEsoteric.net, Feb. 2016.

70. John Coulthart, "The Great God Pan," JohnCoulthart.com, May 2009.

71. Randy Stafford, "The Great God Pan," Marzaat.com, November 16, 2020.

Chapter 6

Induced Window Areas: Highly Strange People, Doing Highly Strange Things, in Highly Strange Places

To proceed: know which nutrients giants took to electrize Earth.
Wonderworks: Pointed out by the Héloïse case of Long-Tall-Sally.
Not a moment to lose! Look for footprints – find the Golden Beach.
The Summum Bonum is under a warrior's enveloping telemac.

Introduction

This chapter puts forth theories that naturally occurring geographic window areas are being enhanced and/or consciously created by highly strange people; or, perhaps more accurately, by beings of some type.[A] Once these strange people have created (or located and enhanced) one of these "Sensitive Spots," they are then able to "tune in" to its "etheric force." Then they can use the energy for mystical purposes, using the area as a crystal is used in a "crystal radio."[1] In these special areas, one is better able to access subtle Earth energies, a function that is also enhanced by people doing highly strange things, such as magical rituals and shamanic practices.[B]

An example of what this process looks like is as follows: "Symbolical buildings are constructed on sensitive spots and symbolical performances occur at such places to tap into and channel mysterious energies."[1] Said another way, the function of structures constructed in window areas is to "draw together … and magnify its magical nature, creating [a] spiritual intensity," this process is similar to how one uses a "magnifying glass aimed" at the sun to burn a piece of paper.[2]

A But as I like to say: aliens, Bigfoot, gnomes, angels, gods, and ghosts are people too!

B A crystal radio works by using a crystal detector to translate the incoming radio waves and convert them into audible sounds without requiring an external power source.

Mechanisms Behind This Phenomenon

The use of window areas (or sacred sites) is "a statement of how beauty and meaning can result when people and nature are working together in harmony." However, these special geographic areas are "linked to a system of subtle natural forces" that "we understand very little and [don't] even have a good language to describe."[2] I say that to underscore the inherent complexity of the task of this chapter.

Humans and the Earth Are Magnets

I will provide a brief overview of several theories on how the interplay of Earth energy and human energy works in these areas. Keel explains how this interplay might work, saying that it is "probable that manifestations are dependent upon unknown conditions which have an electromagnetic basis." He adds that "When specific individuals (people with latent or active psychic abilities) are in specific places (window areas)" and when "the undefined electromagnetic conditions exist" then "the phenomenon is able to manifest itself in one of its many forms."[3] This undefined electromagnetic effect of window areas is so potent that it can cause people living in those locations to "become apparition-prone." Additionally, it is suggested that people who exhibit heightened sensitivity to electromagnetic fields may "previously have been exposed to such fields."[4]

This all might be explained by conceptualizing that "The Earth is a magnet"[1] and people are also magnets. To get at the idea of the magnetic nature of humans, we turn to Franz Anton Mesmer (1734-1815), who "taught that magnetism permeated the universe" and he "believed that the human body possess a magnetic field."[5] Also, Dr. Albert Abrams (1863-1924) "investigated the 'electro magnetism' of the human body" becoming "convinced that a relationship exists between the 'elctro-magnetic,' of the human body and the electro-magnetic field of the earth."[1]

Yes, I know that Mesmer[C] and Abrams are considered pseudoscience by today's modern scientific standards.[D] However, let us remember that Mesmer's beliefs about animal magnetism have found some validation in modern times and a "modern incarnation of [animal magnetism] is demon-

C For more on the high strangeness of Mesmer see, "In the Mouth of Mesmer: Illuminating the Origins of Magnetism and Mind Control featuring Khrist Koopa," *Subliminal Jihad* podcast, episode 140, March 11, 2023.

D See Charles V. Pollack, Jr.'s, "Electronic Therapeutics of Albert Abrams, M.D." *Pharmacy in History*, Vol. 26, No. 2, 1984. Also see Sadie F. Dingfelder's article, "The First Modern Psychology Study: Or how Benjamin Franklin Unmasked a Fraud and Demonstrated the Power of the Mind," *American Psychological Association, Monitor*, apa.org/monitor, July/August 2010, Vol 41, No. 7.

strating that this invisible healing force is real."[6] This modern incarnation is seen in the term "biofield," which is used in alternative medicine to describe a hypothetical electromagnetic field that surrounds and interpenetrates the human body.[E] Proponents of this concept believe that the biofield is responsible for regulating the body's functions and that imbalances in the biofield can lead to health problems. Also, consider that "modern hypnosis" started with Mesmer's work.[7] Not too shabby for someone born in the 1700s.

The quackery of Abrams is evident, as he believed that different diseases and ailments could be identified by specific electronic frequencies and that he could treat them by adjusting these frequencies. But let's remember that Electroconvulsive Therapy (ECT) was first used in 1938 (over ten years after his death) and is still used today; being "the oldest somatic therapy still in use in psychiatry today [and] remains one of the most effective therapeutic interventions for a wide variety of psychiatric disorders."[8] No, I am not advocating the use of ECT, but am making a larger point that mainstream medical practitioners are using electricity in the treatment of diseases. Because of this it is hard to not consider there is something to the electromagnetic nature of humans when we consider we are still shocking people to make them happier.

We Sing Our Bodies Electric[F]

Now, taking a more lyrical perspective on this interaction between the energies of the Earth and humans, it's suggested that "Invisible waves of energy" continually flow through us and as "these energies" traverse through our bodies we start to vibrate like a musical instrument. This is because people are "musical notes being played by nature all the time."[2] Geographic areas have "their own 'notes'" and in window areas "the amplitude of this note" is actually "much higher." Because of this, different people "resonate more powerfully" with certain places, all "according to who they are as well as the specific power" of the particular area.[2]

Ancient Strangeness

Having explored the interaction between human and Earth energies in window areas and sacred places, let's turn our attention to the strange actions of the ancients. As we'll soon discover, their ancient spiritual prac-

E See Dr. Christine Berger and Suzan K. Thompson, Ph.D. "Biofield Therapies," *American Counseling Association, Counseling Corner Blog*, June 12, 2019, counseling.org.

F "I Sing the Body Electric" is a poem by Walt Whitman from his 1855 collection *Leaves of Grass* and is also the title of a 1969 collection of short stories by Ray Bradbury.

tices and rituals were intimately tied to window areas, with the intention of either enhancing pre-existing natural windows or creating entirely new ones. We will also investigate how these ancient practices uniquely harnessed the potential of these sacred locations.

Highly Strange People of Ancient Times: Shamans

The individuals conducting ancient ritual practices at these window areas were shamans. A shaman is "a person who acts as intermediary between the natural and supernatural worlds, using magic to cure illness, foretell the future, [and] control spiritual forces."[9] At locations with "intense electromagnetic anomalies that today we might describe as earth portals, vortex sites, and window areas" ultraterrestrials communicated especially with shamans. These "transdimensional beings have been influencing humankind since the earliest beginnings of the human species"[10,G] via the most sensitive individuals, which in ancient times were identified as shamans. I would argue that those sensitive individuals are now people like you, dear reader.

Ancient Stones

One of the highly strange things the ancients did was erect stone circles. Sights such as Stonehenge "involve astronomical and astrological" alignments. It is said the effect of the stones are to remind one of the "alchemical mind's genius" and in "some cases, people even say a spark of energy leaps from the stones to touch them, as if to initiate them into some ancient order."[2] Circles of standing stones are found in many parts of the world. One theory about their origin is that they "may be 'accumulators' whose purpose was to store a kind of energy" or enhance window areas. Some have theorized that the "stones could be 'charged'" by such activities as "ritual dancing."[11] Others have theorized that standing stones located at sacred spots were "used by the ancient people to tap the earth's power," meaning the stones served "like acupuncture needles by the shamans."[12,H]

G "A shaman is a man who has immediate, concrete experiences with gods and spirits; he sees them face to face, he talks with them, prays to them, implores them." (Arnold Mindell, *The Shaman's Body: A New Shamanism for Transforming Health, Relationships, and the Community*, quoting Eliade, 1993, p. 95.) Shamans can also be women or transgendered, although they are often referred to as men in Western writing.

H See also Mark Vidler and Catherine Young's, *Sacred Geometry of the Earth: The Ancient Matrix of Monuments and Mountains*, which claims that "circles of standing stones and man-made mounds" have "geometrical relationships" with the "world's mountains, coastlines, [and] islands." (2016.) Publisher's summary.

ANCIENT BLOOD

Another theory as to how humans have created window areas is related to blood. The idea is that "about half of England is a morphogenic site" because the Roman empire invaded these Celtic areas (beginning in 43) and then "took the shamanic class" of the population, murdering "all of them ... and their blood ran into the ground throughout England." This blood, "when it ran in the ground ... created these permanent morphogenic sites throughout England."[13] This idea is also found in the idea of burials contributing to an area becoming a sacred space. For example, a "man-made sacred site is the grave of the famous chief of the Cherokees, Junaluska."[12]

STRANGE ANCIENT TRIBES

Next we turn to the mysterious North American mound builders, the Adena culture. This group of people "were not a single tribe, but rather, a group of indigenous people that shared similarities in... cultural practices, including a common burial and ceremonial system that included mound building." The Adena had a thriving and complex civilization as evidenced by the fact that "building these mounds was a monumental task as these ancient people didn't use the wheel and had no horses."[14] These weren't just small mounds of dirt, but gigantic piles of earth and their geographic location had complex astronomical connections: a fact discussed in episode six of Graham Hancock's recent Netflix documentary, *Ancient Apocalypse* (2022), where the Serpent Mound in Ohio is explored.

In the high strangeness podcast docuseries, *Penny Royal* (which I regard as the unofficial podcast companion to the *Hellier* documentary series), there is speculation that the Ancient Adena culture opened up portals in the Kentucky area via their ancient rituals and practices. The show points out that Kenneth Grant "essentially argued that the Adena had used Kentucky to pierce the veil ... and had created a window area there." And based on the amount of high strangeness phenomena reported in the area, "it might be easy to believe that a gateway was left open and through that opening poured in an army of UFOs, bigfoots" and other "interdimensional beings."[15]

ANCIENT EARTH ENERGY SCIENCE

These ancient builders of stone circles, mounds and pyramids, may have tapped into an "earth energy science." This science works by the idea that "if you build something in a specific way and you are working with the earth energies in a very specific way ... you get this orgone effect."[I] This

I According to Reich, "orgone energy is a vital life force that can be both positive and neg-

approach was based on a "scientific understanding" of knowing where to place their sacred sites, in order to "manipulate the environment."[16] I believe what this possible ancient Earth energy science looked like is seen in something called BioGeometry, which is a "science that uses shapes, colors, motion and sound to induce harmony into the subtle energy qualities of the environment." BioGeometry was used "in sacred power spots of humanity that give a spiritual dimension to the timeless monuments erected since the dawn of humanity." This approach to working with earth energies "bridges science and spirituality to produce a natural harmony into the environment."[17] The theory is that the ancients had this knowledge and it was the basis behind their ancient sacred sites of the world, from mounds to pyramids. These sacred sites "were portals where primitive man experienced communication with other dimensions," while over "time these places became the sacred power spots of humanity." The overall thrust of the BioGeometry worldview "aims to reawaken" the understanding that "rituals played a significant role in the harmony between humans and nature."[18]

Some have speculated an ancient race of giants utilized this "geomantic science" and built sacred sites such as Stonehenge "as a way to enchant the landscape." These sites were "tools of enlightenment" seen in the fact that "when you go to Stonehenge" or the "King's Chamber in the Great Pyramid" there is a noticeable "effect on human consciousness, an elevation of the spirit." Further, this Earth science was "an ancient system that supported health and prosperity across the land."[16] Notice the similarities between this theory and Wilhelm Reich's work with orgone accumulators' positive effects on the environment.

Modern Magical Strangeness

A good fictional example of ancient high strangeness intersecting with modern high strangeness is seen in the 1984 film, *Ghostbusters,*[J] co-written by Dan Aykroyd, a known student of the paranormal. The film's main antagonist is a powerful and ancient Sumerian god known as Gozer. The entities' human followers were active in ancient times but remained

ative, and it can become stagnant or blocked in the body, leading to various health issues. He proposed the concept of orgone accumulators, which are devices designed to harness and concentrate this energy for therapeutic purposes" (Orgoneenergy.org/blogs/news/what-is-orgone-energy). For more on how these devices are used to help the environment, see Georg Ritschl's, *Operation Paradise: Effective Environmental Healing with Orgone Energy*, 2007.

J See *Programmed to Chill*, bonus episode 62: ghostbustin' featuring Wendy Painting & Reid, on "the true meaning of ghostbusters" and K. Grant said some believed women were a "door, a gateway, onto the void, through which … forces could be invoked" by those who possessed the "keys." (quoted in *The Rebirth of Pan*, p. 24)

dormant until after WW1, when an architect "concluded that society was too sick to survive and founded a cult dedicated to Gozer." The architect built the building in New York City using special metals so it would act as a "super-conductive antenna and portal" for Gozer to enter our human realm and destroy the world.[19] This building turns New York into a high strangeness window area which allows the rise of the Ghostbusters (who become famous busting the phenomena unleashed) and who then defeat Gozer when he comes through the portal at the end of the film.

An example of the ancient and modern coming together in the study of sacred sites is seen in Teotihuacan, which means the "place where the gods were made, or city of the gods." The idea of an ancient and modern intersection is seen from the air, as the "city layout strangely resembles a computer circuit board with two large processor chips – the Sun Pyramid and the Moon Pyramid." Other interesting facts relevant to this chapter is that "According to colonial sources, the Nahuas thought that Teotihuacan was built by … a race of giants that populated the world during the previous era and whose survivors hid away." Also "Archaeologists have found that Teotihuacan's structures are embedded with mica," which is relevant because "Mica is stable when exposed to electricity [and] has superior electrical properties as an insulator … and can support an electrostatic field."[20]

The idea that ancient (and some modern) cities resemble computer parts is an idea that is floating around the short video spaces (Instagram and TikTok).[K] To me the most compelling example given in this regard is seen in Teotihuacan.

Crowley and Modern Magick

Modern practitioners of magick are, presumably, performing similar rituals as those used by the ancients. Some magicians even think they are practicing a lost ancient spiritual science, which means the line between ancient and modern in this regard is blurred. It becomes even more blurred when we look at the supposed origins of magick.

Some magicians claim that magick itself has *no origins* or that it was *born with the world,* whatever that means. The apocryphal *Book of Enoch* claims there were angels who consented to fall from heaven to Earth. These angels were said to be initiates of magick who communicated this knowledge to man.[21] Some sources claim magick was first given to Adam who in turn passed it to Noah and then Abraham, who then reportedly spread it to Egypt.[22] Éliphas Lévi claims magick "was the science of Abraham and

K See Wired.com/2016/08/extreme-closeup-computer-hardware-looks-like-tiny-cities/ & 9gag.com/gag/a7rmExw

Orpheus, of Confucius and Zoroaster, and it was magical doctrines which were ingraven on tables of stone … by Trismegistus".[21] Moses was reported to have put the teachings of magick under the disguise of the Holy Kabbalah. Throughout the ages, different groups and individuals have tried to keep the teachings of magick "secret" so as to conceal its truth from the profane masses.[21]

The secret teachings of magick passed from these ancient groups to modern-day groups such as the Order of the Golden Dawn and the Ordo Templi Orientis (OTO). Groups such as these tried to preserve the teachings of magick in their original unadulterated forms, because Lévi claimed that "profanation had befallen the doctrines and mysteries of magic [which has] repeated from age to age [and this] misuse" of magick "has been a great and terrible lesson." He goes on to say "the key of science" which is magick "has been thrown to children" and "as might have been expected, it is now, therefore, mislaid and practically lost."[21] The teachings of magick were salvaged from this fate in modern times by occultist Aleister Crowley (1875-1947) who felt his "special job was to preserve the Sacred Tradition" and to "restore magic the respect and honor it commanded in earlier times."[23] The ancient teachings of magick, as properly restored by Aleister Crowley, are what we know as magick today; and Crowley began spelling the word with a K to denote this proper restoration.[L]

Crowley's specific magical philosophy is called Thelema and its philosophy is *Do what thou wilt shall be the whole of the law, love is the law, love under will,* as I explained in the last chapter. It comes from his book, *The Book of the Law,* which he maintained was dictated to him by an entity named Aiwass. He said that "the existence of true religion" rests on the assumption of the actual existence of a "discarnate intelligence … whether we call him god or anything else." *The Book of the Law,* "proved scientifically"[M] the existence of these ultraterrestrials, something other religions failed to do. Further, "this proof [is]the most important step in science that could possibly be made" because it "opens up an entirely new avenue to knowledge." Lastly, the "claim" of *The Book of the Law* is to "open up communications with discarnate intelligences."[24] These facts are important because, as I have shown, window areas are where one can more readily make contact with ultraterrestrials.

L Chaos magick is considered to be the most modern form and I consider my magick of high strangeness a form of Chaos magick.

M See *Rites of the Mummy: The K'rla Cell and the Secret Key to Liber AL* in this regard because "it offers a new approach to the mathematical nature of" the book and "brings attention to the existence of a sacred geometry within the verses of The Book of the Law: a completely unexpected discovery but nonetheless mathematically verifiable" (Publisher's summary).

CROWLEY AND THE LOCH NESS MONSTER

There is a theory that by means of his magick Crowley created a high strangeness window area on Loch Ness in Scotland at his residence, the Boleskine House. Some time after Crowley's death the house was purchased by Jimmy Page of Led Zeppelin.[N] Crowley reportedly bought the house to complete the rituals in the book, *The Book of the Sacred Magic of Abramelin the Mage,* the aim of which is to help one obtain the Knowledge and Conversation of the Holy Guardian Angel. In his autobiography, Crowley claimed that the spirits he summoned in his ritual work at the house "got out of hand, causing one housemaid to leave, and a workman to go mad."[25]

He explained these occurrences, saying he had "little doubt the Abra-Melin" entities "whatever they are, used the place as a convenient headquarters" and during "their spare time" sought out to terrify the "natives" of the region. This led to a "great many definite legends," two of which are mentioned above. Interestingly, he says "I should have liked to deny the reality" of these occurrences "but the phenomena were just as patent as the stones of the house." Later he said that "such phenomena" which happened in relation to the "Abra-Melin Operation" occurred due to flaws in his magical practice, saying he later learned to succeed in "suppressing them by preventing my magical force from leaking away." He said such high strangeness phenomena which occurred at his Scottish home, "annoyed me as it annoys an electrician who finds that his current is escaping ... giving shocks to people" who get in its path. Crowley later learned to be able to "persuade" his "magical energy" to work "though the proper channels" and not always be "breaking loose."[24]

However, Crowley didn't achieve this perfected magical practice before summoning a cryptozoological beast, as he "'made' the Loch Ness monster when he failed to complete a complex Magick ritual" and this "failure... unleashed" the creature.[26] In general, Crowley was a practitioner of sex magick, which is based on the idea "that enormously powerful forces and entities could be summoned up through rituals involving aspects of human sexuality."[27]

In addition to summoning the lake monster, Crowley reported other highly strange animal phenomena, such as unusual beetle sightings. Grant explains this incident, pointing out that in his autobiography Crowley mentions "an invasion of these creatures during his occupation of Boleskine" and found them so unusual he even "sent a specimen for investigation to

N See */wiki/Boleskine_House* for a brief overview of the home.

specialists in London" who "were baffled by it."[O] For Grant, these mysterious insects were "beetle-vahanas of an alien consciousness" and the point of the magicians in the OTO is to "establish terrestrial outposts for these alien creatures,"[28] and their ultraterrestrial consciousness. If this is true, then Crowley was setting up such an outpost at Boleskine but had not perfected the practice. A person properly informed with the magick of high strangeness has the necessary praxis to be successful in this regard.

Grant claims the mysterious beetles were "Lam's legions," a "reference to the arrival on planet Earth of an alien race."[29] The Lam to whom Grant is referring is from Crowley's 1919 painting, famous for being the first painting of a grey alien. Keep in mind this was well before the iconic image of the creature entered public consciousness with the cover of Whitley Strieber's *Communion* in 1987. Crowley painted the Lam portrait during the Amalantrah Workings and "it is generally agreed within occult circles that Crowley intentionally opened a portal of entry via magick ritual" during these workings which "created a gateway through which Lam and other extra-cosmic influences could enter ... our earth-world."[30] However, I do need to point out that there is not a general agreement in this regard; the mainstream occult circles are more inclined to ignore this aspect of Crowley's work.

Others have speculated that Crowley created an "occult power plant" at the Boleskine House and speculate he used this sacred site to enhance his own magical power even when he was located in other parts of the world. In other words, he could draw on the power of the area from anywhere in the world.[31] This idea is supported by Grant who claims that magicians "who utilize the Current of Maat will constitute zones of magical power which radiate" positive energy "and thereby act as reservoirs for" other magicians.[32] I maintain that this is an essential aspect of the magick of high strangeness and this is what the overall *My Cosmic Trigger* hypersigil is all about: being a reservoir of positive energy for people researching and practicing high strangeness.

Crowely's Death and the 1947 UFO Flap

Kennth Grant points out that Crowley's death was synchronistically tied to the famous 1947 UFO flap,[P] saying his death of that year "occurred on the brink of the Ufological Era" and "coincided with a massive

O See also "Terrified BBC Call Exorcist to House of Satan; Horror after Insect Attack on Film Crew," thefreelibrary.com/TERRIFIED+BBC+CALL+EXORCIST+TO+HOUSE+OF+SATAN%3B+Horror+after+insect...-a060956190

P The informal definition of the word is "a state of agitation; a panic" (Oxford Languages) and is an older word that was used in the study of UFO phenomena back in the day.

wave of" UFOs being sighted and talked about all over the world.[28,Q] The wave of sightings in 1947 was so famous it led to "a rarely heard bluegrass song called 'When You See Those Flying Saucers'" which "was composed in 1947 ... and released as a single by the Buchanan Brothers."[33]

Jack Parsons

The next modern day magician we will look at is John ("Jack") Whiteside Parsons (1914-1952). Parsons is arguably the most worldly successful magician since John Dee (1527-1608). In 2018 a CBS show about Parsons called *Strange Angel* appeared, an adaptation of the book, *Strange Angel: The Otherworldly Life of Rocket Scientist John Whiteside Parsons* (2006). Parsons "was a major force in the early development of solid fuel booster rockets" and there is a "Lunar Crater (named) in his memory." He was an "OTO member from 1941, and served for a short period as Master of Agape Lodge." Parsons was also a principal founder of Jet Propulsion Laboratory (JPL).

In the occult world, Parsons is most famous for his Babalon working, which was "an elaborate sexual magick experiment designed to bring Babalon[R] into physical manifestation."[34] Grant says that Parsons's "Magical Workings through 1945-6 facilitated an ingress of alien forces."[35] Parsons's romantic and magical partner (Marjorie Cameron) at the time "reported a sighting of a UFO, which she believed was proof that Parsons's magic was working."[36] Around this same time, in 1947 pilot Kenneth Arnold reported seeing a UFO in Washington; his sighting is the origin of the term flying saucer. Grant wrote that "something pierced the Veil during the 'Babalon Working,' for in 1947 – the year of Crowley's death – occurred the first UFO sightings that were to multiply massively in the ensuing years."[35] To explain this highly strange synchronization of occult happenings and UFOs, Grant evokes the high strangeness door analogy saying Parsons's ritual work "opened a door and something flew in."[32]

It is also speculated that Parsons utilized a sacred site in his magical work, as the California OTO he was a part of in the 1940s "had a temple on nearby Mount Palomar." Local Native American tribes "regarded the mountain as holy" while the California OTO members "believed Palomar was the sexual chakra of the earth."[36.1] Supposedly, this group "erected a stone tem-

Q Grant also ties this time period with the curious fact that the "nuclear energy released into the earth's atmosphere in the mid-1940s reactivated in man his latent astro-ocular potential" (Kenneth Grant, *Outer Gateways*, 1994, p.117).

R Think: the wild energetic side of the divine feminine archetype. "Babalon signifies an opening of outer gatewars for traffic with trans-human Entities. The name Babalon means, literally, the 'Gate of the Sun'" (Grant, *Beyond the Mauve Zone*, p. 11).

ple" in the "remote woods of Palomar" near the location of "the future site of the telescope" of the Palomar observatory, with Parsons traveling "back and forth between Palomar and his sex magic mansion in Pasadena."[1,S] The fact that the Mount Palomar Observatory is one of the most historically significant observatories in the world and tied to Parsons in synchromystic ways is what high strangeness is all about.

Kenneth Grant's Strange Doors

The magick of Kenneth Grant is full of references to opening doors, gates, or windows to other dimensions. For example, he says that his received (or channeled) *The Book of the Spider* "is an example of an improperly opened gate, whereas" his received book "the *Wisdom of S'lba* exemplifies the contrary."[29] He furthered the work of the grandfather of Chaos magick, Austin Osman Spare, pointing out that this magician and artist had a "formula incorporated" in his art that was "designed to open the outer gateways."[28] *The Wisdom of S'lba* encourages magicians to "open the gate and call to the wind, the backward darkness will respond."[28] These are just a small number of instances of the many references to opening portals, gates or doors to other dimensions in Grant's magical praxis.[T] A fact relevant to this chapter is that he also spoke a lot about how human technology created portals between the dimensions. He said that "around 1945 with the first atomic explosion" there was a rupture of "the subtle membrane of the earth's magnetic atmosphere[U] ... and two years later, there swarmed through the resulting rent the forces alluded to as UFOs ... ETs, etc, for which, after more than forty years, no adequate explanation has been proposed ... by the governments of this planet."[V,35]

Grant on the Importance of *The Book of the Law*

Grant claimed Crowley's *The Book of the Law* contains "the supreme *grimoire*"[W] of our current age and holds "the secret formulae which

S The Observatory "is very close to the 33rd parallel of north latitude, so in that position it is in accordance with the...'Master Plan' having to do with the Atomic Bomb, the Space Program, etc., which are so directly connected with Masonic Sorcery." (*Stalking the Great Whore: The Lost Writings of James Shelby Downard*, p. 216).

T Also see Grant's *Outside the Circles of Time*, where he says "ma is the door or hole in the fabric of Time" (p. 148).

U The 2017 revival of Twin Peaks "explores Bob's origins in Part 8, showing that an orb bearing his face was created...during the first atomic bomb test in 1945." Bob is "an interdimensional entity who feeds on pain and sorrow. An inhabiting spirit, he possesses human beings and then commits acts of rape and murder in order to feast upon his victims." [Wikipedia, Bob (*Twin Peaks*).]

V Energies from "This intrusion from Outside" caused a "marked increase in...psychological disorders and a heightening of dream activity among sensitives, artists...even scientists. Certain dreams had already inspired writers such as H. P. Lovecraft with prophecies concerning...time-cycles which [the author] considered mere fantasies." (Grant, *Beyond the Mauve Zone*, p. 12).

W A grimoire is a book or manual that contains a set of instructions, rituals, spells, and mag-

unseals ... cosmic consciousness in humans." It also "contains the keys to the gates of extra-terrestrial worlds which ... sometimes impinge upon our own." When this impinging occurs it transforms the world, also transforming "the magician and prepares him for an existence" that appears "alien to his mundane consciousness." Finally in this regard, "the key to" understanding the book "will unlock the ultimate door and admit the full influx of extra-terrestrial energies." When this happens the "resulting transcendent experience of total Beauty ... will 'regenerate the world' ... our insignificant planet."[32]

Grant and the Greats of High Strangeness Research

Grant echoes ideas of Keel and Vallée, saying that "it is probably that the earliest myths" of humans "preserve accounts of ... traffic from the Outside." He adds his own take on this process of Earth being visited from ultraterrestrials, suggesting it has gone "unnoticed by all but initiates and certain peculiarly constituted individuals" such as "magicians, dreamers, sensitives, spirit-mediums, poets, prophets." Notice he does not list the following mainstream types as having noticed this important cosmic process: university professors, lawyers, politicians, or talking heads on TV.

Grant claims "the interpretation and exploration of the aethyrs" by the "mediaeval magicians" and the "more recent manifestations" of "little green men, are apparent in connection with the phenomena of so-called Ufology." According to Grant we must look to the work of Keel and Vallée for "examples of this 'new' mythology which is as ... fantastic as any [that] evolved in ancient times."[32] Grant also points out that the "influence of Sirius" actually "powers the OTO" via entities such as Lam and notes that RAW "mentions some of the Siriac manifestations" in the first volume of *Cosmic Trigger*.[32,X]

Allen Greenfield

Greenfield's Great Arabia workings are as important as the previously mentioned magical workings of Crowley, Grant, and Parsons. The mountain in question is Mount Arabia, which is "a 400 million year old monadnock outside of Atlanta, Georgia," where occultists "link arms in mutual aid and support of each other while administering the mysterious points-chauds empowerments and performing various workings ... of the Gnostic Church."[37] According to Greenfield the site was a "Native American Holy place" and was

---

ical knowledge, often associated with occult, or esoteric traditions. Grimoires are typically used by practitioners interested in mystical or magical practices.

X His views on art have inspired my painting praxis, as he said art "in the true and vital sense" is actually a "magical machine, a means of occult exploration..." (Grant, *Outside the Circles of Time*, p. 37)

also his "power point" because at the site he was able to feel rather "than see ... the 'electrical' energy – Od, or Orgone, or Chi, or Prana."[38]

During the workings on Mount Arabia, the group of magicians studying under Greenfield were doing a magical type of reiki energy work with the *points chaud* (hot points in French), which are "locations on the human body that are 'power points,' that can be ... activated, and that are directly connected with both the subtle body and some source of energy that is external to ... the human body."[39] This practice comes from the magick of Michael Bertiaux, who consecrated Greenfield. Bertiaux conceived of the points as a type of magical engine that provides "power for the growth of more and more ... doors of consciousness." These doors are projecting "into other dimensions and pathways through space-consciousness."[40] The initiates of the Great Arabia Mountain working have "reported increased healing capacities, increased empathic ability, increased scrying and clairvoyant ability, and added 'juice' in general magickal workings."[39]

Magical Conclusion

Famous modern-day magicians have used their magick rituals to make what we now know as high strangeness window areas or sacred spaces. I think this fact adds to the relevancy of the topic of this chapter. However, I do point out that the idea of opening paranormal portals is not a mainstream idea in magical circles. As I have pointed out earlier in this book, the occult establishment (Big Magick, as it were) is going to dismiss any of the above mentioned work of these famous magicians. I find it ironic that the most famous practitioners of our time – upon whose work modern occultists often base much of their own practice – routinely have their most important work dismissed by skeptical mainstream occultists.

Highly Strange Alien Technology

The evidence thus far presented suggests that, since the earliest days of humanity, transdimensional entities- via shamans, priests, and magicians- have been exerting an influence on our species. This influence is particularly notable at places with intense electromagnetic anomalies, described as portals, vortex sites, and window areas. But this fact does beg the question: do ultraterrestrials *create* the window areas with advanced technology or *use* already naturally existing window areas?

The following channeled messages from commander Ashtar of the Galactic Federation concerns these window areas, which he refers to as Stargates. Ashtar claims that the reason for an unconditional love, group meditation they recommended to humans, was for "opening a Stargate … that would allow those from other planets … to visit" Earth. A "Stargate is an interdimensional portal that allows beings from many alien races to travel from galaxy to galaxy" for the purposes of "knowledge, exploration and to aid less sophisticated societies to raise their planetary consciousness." This is especially important at this time because according to Ashtar: "Every 26,000 years the Earth changes … it begins to raise itself, in Light" and as a result we facilitate a new "Golden Age."[40.1]

The above suggests a window is opened through advanced spiritual practices of some type. Keel speculates ultraterrestrials find already existing gates with advanced technology and seemingly exacerbate them. "The phenomenon," he says, "is mostly invisible to us because it consists of energy rather than solid earthly matter" but "is guided by a greater intelligence and has concentrated itself in the areas of magnetic faults throughout history."[Y,3]

On *The Joe Rogan Experience* podcast, physicist Michio Kaku talks about how advanced an alien civilization would need to be in order to have the type of technology described above. To consider this possibility, Kaku asks us to open our minds to the possibility of an alien civilization which is 1000 years more advanced than ours. To help us imagine these possibilities, he describes three types of civilizations. A civilization 100 to 1000 years past Earth would be considered a type 1 civilization and would be able to have complete control over anything on the planet, such as the weather. A type 2 civilization would be 1000+ years from us and could "harness the power of an entire star;" an example of this civilization would be *Star Trek*.

Kaku says that "once you go to higher energies, the laws of physics… break down" and this is what Plank energy is all about. Any civilization that can harness Plank energy would be "masters of space and time" and could even "play with blackholes." A type 3 civilization would able to harness Plank energy, which means they would have technology for the creation of wormholes, "gateways through space and time" and "portals through empty space." A type 3 civilization is 100,000 years ahead of ours.[41]

In his book, *The Meadow Project: Explorations into the South's Skinwalker Ranch* (2020), Trey Hudson speculates the window area he discovered was due to technology from one of these advanced civilizations. However, according to Hudson, the possibility of us figuring out what they are doing in this geographic location is like ants trying to figure out what construction

Y "It makes itself visible to us from time to time by manipulating patterns of frequency. It can take any form it desires, ranging from shapes of airplanes to gigantic cylindrical spaceships. It can manifest itself into seemingly living entities ranging from little green men to awesome one-eyed giants. But none of these configurations is its true form." (Keel, *Operation Trojan Horse*, p.43)

workers building a road are doing. He also points out that floating black cubes have been observed in this location, which he speculates could be some sort of portalling technology.

Other paranormal creatures may be seen at high strangeness window areas because of this advanced alien tech. Consider "The Second Extra-Dimensional (ED) Corollary" which is that "the passage of Extra-Dimensional Visitors into our dimension creates temporary 'quantum-flux gate' portals that can be accessed by other energetic entities to enter our time and space." These "entities (ghosts, orbs, crypto-creatures) vibrate at a similar resonance as the ED's" or ultraterrestials "but may have nothing else in common" with them "except for the actual transition point they use."[42,Z] This theory is saying the confluence of various paranormal entities at window areas is akin to opportunistic creatures hanging onto the back of a trolley car for a free ride into another dimension.

Highly Strange Human Technology

In high strangeness research, it is speculated that certain groups of humans (such as those within the US military) have reverse engineered alien technology and have access to technology far beyond the iPhones in our pocket. This possibility is explored in Dr. Steven Greer's documentary *Above Top Secret: The Technology Behind Disclosure,* where it is argued that "We're at a tipping point in history" because there exists "hidden technology that could change everything." Even though this knowledge "has been suppressed for decades," those not typically privy to this subject are now becoming aware of it. This hidden technology, which secret governmental groups have gotten from aliens is: free energy, "portal technology," and literally "whatever you can imagine [has] already been done."[43]

Stranger Things Technology and Skinwalker Ranch

As I pointed out earlier, the hit TV show *Stranger Things* was based on the supposed real-life Montauk Project. One aspect of this project was the so-called Montauk chair, which "was basically a lounge chair that had crystal radio receivers put around it so it could pick up the thoughts of a psychic and be amplified outside the tower." The chair was "an amplifier" and is "doing the same thing with mental waves" as is done with a radio tower and radio waves.[44]

Z DeSouza also says that Earth itself is a portal spot in the Galaxy. And so it appears we are talking about smaller geographic Earth-based window areas within the whole Earth, which is a galactic window area. I believe this means that anywhere on Earth can be a window area given the necessary conditions.

Greer maintains, that in order to travel the vast distances of space an "interstellar civilization" would have to fold "space time." In the process of folding space time for travel in this manner you will "cross other dimensions" and in this crossing is where the "intersection" between "metaphysics and physics" occurs. This is an intersection of the mystical astral realm and "extraterrestrial technologies." Greer claims this highly strange intersection is the most "interesting part of this whole subject." However, this intersection with advanced technology and the astral dimension is "also dangerous," because it can be "technologically stimulated to occur."

Greer illustrates this danger by pointing out what he thinks is occurring at the world's most famous window area, Skinwalker Ranch: claiming a "certain cell" of a "covert group" has obtained the advanced technology explained in the above section. He reports that this group "started setting up phenomenon" at the ranch, meaning: the high strangeness reported there "is absolutely man made" by "high end" "interdimensional" technologies. He even compares what is going on at the ranch to what occurs in "the show *Stranger Things*" and according to Greer he has talked to whistleblowers that have used similar technology featured in the show. He recounts a story he was told by a whistleblower, when they were testing this technology and then "suddenly" they are "pulling in spooky looking creatures that look like they came out of the 9th ring of Hell." Greer sums these points up, saying: it is "weird stuff,"[AA] which may be the understatement of the year. The information he provides reveals there are human groups that have technological capabilities which are "way beyond what most people think they are."[45]

CERN

In the high strangeness community there are many theories around the European Organization for Nuclear Research, known as CERN.[AB] Specifically, the theory is that their Large Hadron collider is an example of such advanced technology which has even caused "interdimensional rifts."[46] For example, some in the community speculate the collider has caused subtle shifts to the timeline, which is seen in the so-called Mandela Effect. Others claim the collider is "being used as the 'power source' for [an] attempt to 'contact the gods' through this startgate."[47]

AA He goes on to say that this type of technology could be used deceptively, in what is referred to as Project Blue Beam, a fake, human-staged alien invasion.

AB The World Wide Web (WWW) was invented in 1989 by "a physicist at CERN research facility in Switzerland... [and the WWW] has been touted as the most accelerated means of human communication since the introduction of the television." (Rodney Perkins and Forrest Jackson, *Cosmic Suicide: The Tragedy and Transcendence of Heaven's Gate*, 1997).

Mirror, Mirror, on the Wall

Before we leave this section on human portal technology, let's consider some not-so-ancient human technology: mirrors. Often the older a technology is the more it becomes an invisible ground and we forget it is a technology at all, which McLuhan explored in his body of work. But the fact remains: a mirror is a technology, albeit one that has been around a long time. Mirrors were a wondrous human invention because when a "living creature" first "perceived itself in its own mirror, the whole world took a pace forward."[48] This technology has been used by mystics to access other dimensions since ancient times in a technique called scrying.

Raymond Moody, M.D., Ph.D. (who coined the term "near death experience" in his book *Life After Life*) wrote about scrying. He says that "seers engaged in this practice would peer into ... a mirror, a polished stone [or] a crystal ball." Scrying "originated independently in diverse cultures all over the world," from when the "chief oracle of Tibet employed a magic mirror to divine the future" to in Europe where practitioners "wandered from town to town with their mirror, and set up shop at each stop to tell fortunes." The theory is that scrying enables one to access another dimension where the future can be gleaned. In addition to gaining trans-dimensional knowledge, Moody says that "it is plain from the historical record that scrying can be a great aid to creative activity ... as it affords easy access to the unconscious level of the mind" making it "an excellent tool for self-exploration."[49]

High Strangeness of the Fairy Folk

In Celtic mythology, there are various supernatural beings that we know as the Fairy Folk. Keep in mind fairies are a collection of different races of mysterious beings and I am not referring to the popular representation of what we now know as a fairy, such as Tinkerbell. The Celtic peoples (Irish, Scots, Welsh, and Bretons) have an ancient oral tradition about these beings.

William Butler Yeats[AC] helped popularize these myths in his book, *Irish Folk and Fairy Tales* (1888), which "delivers a vast collection of stories, songs, and poetry of" Ireland's "legendary past." We see the power of the Fairy mythos in the fact that the book facilitated Yeats being seen "as a leading proponent of ... Irish cultural independence" and also helped him spearhead "the Irish Literary Revival."[50] In Irish mythology this group of beings is called the Tuatha Dé Danann; and the most popular species of this

[AC] A member of the Order of the Golden Dawn.

group is the Irish gnome, the leprechaun, the image of which is ubiquitous in American popular culture.

From the Scottish highlands region we have *The Secret Commonwealth of Elves, Fauns, and Fairies*, which was written in 1691 by the Rev. Robert Kirk; it is "a kind of metaphysic of the Fairy world."[51] The book "is the famous and mysterious treatise on fairy folklore [by the] Gaelic scholar and minister." Though it was written shortly before the author died in 1692, "the work was not published until 1815 after many legends had grown around Kirk's death, which imagined that he was secreted away by the fairies themselves for revealing their secrets."[51,AD]

The fairy races are humanoid creatures which live in a dimension of Earth somewhat close to humans and are even "distributed in tribes and orders" and "have children ... marriages, deaths, and burials" just like us. And while they are "in appearance, even as we," they have shapeshifting capabilities for a "mock-show." This means that humans are a "more terrestrial kind" of person, while the fairy folk are people with "chameleon-like bodies" which "swim in the air near the earth" dimension. They used to live out in the open when large areas of the planet "were uninhabited" by humans; and during these ancient times they "had their easy tillage above ground," which seems to imply they have since retreated into the caverns of the Earth and/or another dimension on Earth. For whatever reason, at present time they live apart from human people and can now only be observed by "seers, or men of the second sight."[51] The way I conceptualize this is to say that the fairy races are *humans meet ghosts*, with some races having a higher mixture of the two. For example, based on my research, it appears the Djinn are the most ethereal race (i.e., more akin to a human ghost) and the gnomes are the most solid race (i.e., more akin to a human person).

Strange Fairy Windows, Doors, and Portals

You see the portal motif often when researching the fairy world; for example, as seen in Daimler's: *Pagan Portals - Fairy Queens: Meeting the Queens of the Otherworld* (2019). In the literature, we find a reference

---

AD The two non-Celtic people with a belief in these creatures are found in Iceland and in the Islamic world. In the former country, the elves are known as the "hidden people" (or "Huldufólk" in Icelandic). The fairy race of Islamic lore, discussed in the Quran are known as the Djinn (or Jinn), sometimes referred to as the three lettered ones in Turkey. Westerners know the term "genie" from *The Arabian Nights' Tales, aka One Thousand and One Nights*, which "originally came from the Masters who gave them out as Veiled Truth to help humanity; and those who believed them through faith, received marvelous manifestations. In the beginning of these marvelous experiences, there must be faith to tide over, until We can manifest the Reality, for faith is the sustaining power and if We keep it generated, it becomes Reality." (Discourse 17, *The I AM Discourses of St Germain*, November 28, 1932, theiamdiscourses.com/discourse-17/)

to a portal to their dimension when we learn that "in ancient times it was believed … a Fairy king, led many a fairy rade [sic] out of Fairyland through a portal on Glastonbury tor."[AE,52] We also find references to liminal types of spaces: "circles in the grass" which are "commonly called fairy rings." The legends of the Welsh people "believe that the fairies, in a time not long gone, made these circles with the tread of their tripping feet, and that some misfortune will probably befall any person intruding upon this forbidden ground."[53] As would any trans-dimensional entity, these beings have a need for windows into other dimensions to interact with humans. However, my research is unclear if they use already existing windows or create their own.

Another fairy race commonly referred to as using portals to hop between dimensions is Bigfoot. Yes, some claim Bigfoot is a member of the fairy races.[54] High strangeness-inspired Bigfoot researchers look at this hairy creature as "much more than any ordinary animal" because of "some weird cases of these creatures seeming to phase in and out of our reality through portals." This would seem to indicate that "Bigfoot is something that's more interdimensional" and exists in an "almost spiritual-kind of a realm." When people begin looking into this creature they first believe it is an "ape, a flesh-and-blood animal," but "as you dig deeper" you start finding things "about cloaking and the fact that they can vanish before people's eyes." There are even reports of people having seen Bigfoot holding an orb, which looks "like a basketball with plasma swirling around."[55,AF] Some have speculated these "mysterious orbs" are possibly "transporter beams" for Bigfoot, the technology it uses to dimension hop. The "Renowned Bigfoot hunter Bill Brock" has also raised the "idea about multi-dimensional portals" and "referenced a recent NASA announcement that magnetic portals may be real."[56]

The Strange Windows of Angels

John Dee and the Angels

Any discussion of transdimensional beings creating portals, doors, or windows to other dimensions would be incomplete without men-

AE A tor is a hill or a rocky peak. See "Glastonbury Tor: Entrance to the Land of the Fairies," (BadWitch.co.uk). See also "What Makes Glastonbury so Mystical?" (NationalGeographic.co.uk).

AF See *The Alaska Triangle*, Season 1, Episode 5: "Bigfoot and Supernatural Portals," (Travel Channel); *The Bigfoot of Bailey Colorado and its Portal*, a 2023 documentary about a "group of Bigfoot researchers" who "created a Bigfoot hotspot and identified an alien portal located in a Native American sacred tree." Also see the podcast, *Urban Legends with the Ghost Brothers*, "Bigfoot and Portals with Jack Osbourne," 2022.

tioning Enochian magick, which was the product of John Dee (1527-1609). He was "a mathematician and scientific adviser to Elizabeth I" and is reported to have spoken to angels through a scryer, where they "explained the true origins of humanity, and delivered the original language spoken by mankind before the Fall." Through his interaction with angels, Dee learned this angelic language was to be used to "reverse the Fall of mankind and return all of nature to God – to create a new Eden by prompting the Apocalypse."[36,AG]

Enoch and the Language of Angels

The angels that gave Dee this magical system "identified themselves… as the same angels who had instructed" Enoch. We know Enoch from the Old Testament, where he is said to be "the only patriarch…to be elevated into heaven while still alive." As a result, "over the centuries, a wisdom tradition grew" which was "responsible for passing the primal teachings of the angels on to humanity." The apocryphal *Book of Enoch* is one fruit of this wisdom tradition and is famous in high strangeness research because of a "key event" in the book: "a description of how the rebellious angels, lusting after the daughters of man, descended to Earth and taught humankind" technologies and philosophies in order to "sow strife through the world."[57] It is often used as an example of the ancient astronaut theory (i.e., the angels of the Bible are simply extraterrestrials from other planets).[AH]

Enochian magick is composed of 48 keys (or calls). These keys open into the 48 "gates and cities of wisdom," which are "spiritual realms inhabited by different hierarchies of angels."[57] The spiritual "force that empowers" this magick, is "the Enochian language," which is so powerful because it is "able to express the primal essence of things directly." According to the angels, this was "the actual language spoken in heaven before the expulsion of Adam from Paradise." When Adam entered the Earth plane, he had "forgotten the angelic tongue"; as a result of this forgetfulness, he developed what is now known as Hebrew, which according to this information is a *stepped on* Angelic language.[57] The lesson here appears to be that, to return to Heaven or facilitate a heaven on Earth, we must learn to speak the angelic language once again.

AG It is also said it was "delivered by the angels to act as a catalyst for the apocalypse" (*Enochian Magic for Beginners: The Original System of Angel Magic* by Donald Tyson, p. 57).

AH See *The Confessionals Podcast*, Episode 122: "Secret Military Enochian Technology," which is about a "former military serviceman who was selected for a secret mission….to retrieve a downed aircraft [and] Once on board [he] came across unexpected and mind blowing things, including the Enochian language."

John Dee's Impact on History

Moving out of the occult realm, we see that Dee's work had a wide historical import, as his influence "can be found in an astonishing number of the major turning points of Western history." One example is that Dee invented the term British Empire which led Elizabeth I to strive for Britain to become a global power, an idea very foreign at the time. "In studying Dee and his work, we are studying the secret history of the world;"[36] and as I have shown this is a critical facet of high strangeness research. Meaning, the weird has and had a more powerful influence on the world than we initially think. I can't recommend Louv's book (*John Dee and the Empire of Angels: Enochian Magick and the Occult Roots of the Modern World*) enough; it is essential reading for our current times![AI]

Enochian Angelic Magick and the Apocalypse

Noted occult scholar, Donald Tyson, takes Apocalypse and Armageddon as synonyms, painting them both in a negative light and both as something to be avoided. However, he does say that neither is "preordained"[57] and thus can be avoided. Assuming the Apocalypse and Armageddon are synonymous is an incorrect reading of Biblical eschatology. For example, Apocalypse "refers to any time [that] a supernatural being ... reveals mysteries" or when "God destroys the ruling powers of evil and raises the righteous to life in a messianic kingdom" which hardly sounds like a bad thing. What does sound like a bad thing is Armageddon, which "refers to the location of the final battle between earthly evil and God." You will "sometimes hear someone refer to 'armageddon' in the same way they'd refer to the apocalypse – to describe ... the end of civilization."[58] However, a closer inspection of the terms reveals this is simply incorrect.

The term "apocalypse" is derived from the Greek word apokalypsis, meaning "unveiling" or "revelation." In this context, the Apocalypse can be viewed as a process of revealing hidden truths and knowledge, which ultimately leads to enlightenment and transformation for humanity. In contrast, "Armageddon" refers to a catastrophic global conflict, often nuclear in nature, and involving a clash of nations of the three main Abrahamic religions. These distinctions are paramount as we ponder the importance of Enochian magick, as they allow us to see the following statement in the

---

AI Dee's impact can also be seen in "the birth of modern science, in the creation of the secret societies that liberalized Europe and gave America its spiritual calling, in the creation of the state of Israel and its subsequent centrality to American foreign policy, and even in the genesis of the United States space program." (Jason Louv, *John Dee and the Empire of Angels: Enochian Magick and the Occult Roots of the Modern World,* 2018, p. 17)

proper light: that "the angels intended" Enochian angelic magick "to serve as a magical trigger for the chaotic transition – generally referred to as the apocalypse – between the present aeon and the next."[57]

It is said that "Enochian magic has been used for over a century by modern magicians working in the Golden Dawn tradition ... without any obvious signs of initiating a universal Armageddon."[57] I add that perhaps it was their work in this regard that contributed to the veil lifting and global war being avoided. The more the veil is lifted, the farther we are from Armageddon becoming a reality. As I type this in October of 2023, we have never been closer to a global religious nuclear Armageddon.

Again, the differences between Apocalypse and Armageddon is a key distinction when discussing Enochian magick, as it shows the angels weren't providing us with the keys to chaos but were providing us with the blueprint to *avoid* the chaos. The magick of the keys facilitates a peaceful, smooth, and fun transition from the old to the new Earth; and using the "magical trigger" of the keys is a big component of my magick of high strangeness. With all of this being said, it is important to point out that Parsons was using Enochian magick in the Babalon workings, which hopefully will help ease any fears of sinister intentions of Parsons.

It is my understanding that one point of Enochian magick is that the positive angelic influences cannot come into this Earth dimension unless humans specifically ask, intend, or will it so, much in the same way a vampire is unable to enter your home unless they are invited. The Enochian keys open the doors that allow this angelic influence to come in. Angelic help is literally on the other side of the door; we just have to open it and ask the angelic energy to enter.

Enochian Portals[AJ]

My views in the previous section are also seen in newer sources of Enochian magick; by that I mean new messages channeled directly from the angels themselves. One new source shows the angels highlighting the importance of working with strange doors or windows. For example, in *The Book of Galactic Light: Liber Lux Galactica* an angel says the Enochian system "reveals the true creators of our world" who "invite the use of the ancient Portal system." The angels are inviting us into "the New Earth," informing us that there are "passageways being established" to get us there. According to the angels there are "many working on the other side to establish the doorways that will allow us to live throughout this New Earth." The

AJ A portal is defined as, "a doorway, gate, or other entrance, especially a large and imposing one."

angels that are "the builders of these ... portals" encourage us to "use their technologies, of passage and portal, from this world to the New Earth." We are able to use these portals to get to the New Earth "when we let go" of the idea there is a grand war occurring because "there is no war between the light and the dark."[59] It appears we are being encouraged to rise above a duality mindset and into one of oneness, or wholeness. Again, this sounds like the exact opposite of Armageddon.

Another approach to angelic magick is from Enoch himself and is found in the book by Dr. Hurtak.[AK] These messages are similar to the above, as an angel says the material in the book "has been delivered to you in order that you may be prepared for the opening of the pyramidal grids" and "so that your own being will be prepared ... to move into the next unfolding" as "the primary man of light." This opening of pyramidal energy grids and the next unfolding of humans is a "transformation" of the planet which will "trigger the gifts of the holy spirit" and "will allow the Love of the Father... to be increased and multiplied" on Earth.[60]

It should now be clear that Enochian magick is not geared toward inciting global warfare (Armageddon). On the contrary, it facilitates the Apocalyptic revelation of truth, thereby serving as a means to *prevent* Armageddon. To accomplish this, magicians use the angelic keys to open the gates of heaven, so positive energy can pour in. Utterly absurd indeed.

Secret and Strange Humans

This section presents information that there is a secret group of humans which have in their possession, technologies so advanced they might as well be considered a separate species. This is known as the breakaway civilization in high strangeness research. The popular TV show *Rick and Morty* is a humorous take on this concept. In the show, a mad scientist has portal technology and the episodes center around the high strangeness phenomena he and his grandson encounter via their use of portal technology. This section deals with window areas being caused, not by ultraterrestrials or Bigfoot, but by a secret race of humans living on (or in) Earth. In *Secret Doors of the Earth,* the author speculates that a "secret group" of immortal humans[AL] created these portals and use them in their protector role of Earth against evil forces.[61]

AK See "Mars, Keys of Enoch, Space Arks, Portals, Pyramids, & Return of ET Seeders with Dr J.J. Hurtak," *Exopolitics Today with Dr. Michael Salla,* May 19, 2022.

AL One such immortal could be Saint Germain.

Another theory in this regard is that the sacred sites we have been studying in this text were created by survivors of Atlantis. It is said that this mythical civilization had "attained to a considerable level of scientific complexity" but was destroyed by a "cataclysm which took place after they attempted to merge their science with occult/supernatural forces." The explanation in this regard is that "the Bermuda Triangle phenomena may be the result of an out-of-control Atlantean experiment that led to a space-time disaster which produced 'electromagnetic fallout' in the Triangle area" because they had "loosed powerful forces and energies into the world they knew very little about."[62] Bryant claims her spirit guide Albion said that "Atlantean migrants" after the destruction "spread throughout the world seeking refuge and new beginnings" and claims these migrants came to the Blue Ridge Mountain region and are the people who "first inhabited" the area.[12]

The Hollow Earth, "which has been, correctly or incorrectly, connected with UFOs and the curious phenomena of coloured lights" has been speculated to be the location of "hidden terrestrial outposts of the Great Old ones."[28] As I mentioned earlier, some claim there is a resistance force of humans living in the caverns of the Earth whose "main objective" is "to overthrow the rule" of ultra-powerful, ultra-wealthy, ultra-technologically, advanced humans and their allies of "off-planet dark forces." When this evil group is defeated, the good guy cavern resistance force will "give advanced technologies to humanity." This group also has contact with "the positive civilization of Agartha that existed in subterranean caverns for millennia"[63] which may be what Grant refers to as "the Great Old ones."

An analysis of these cavern-dwelling ultra-humans is found in the chapter "Eerie Underground Bases of the Star Gods" in Brad Steiger's book, *Star Gods: Clone Masters of the Universe.* He claims there may exist a "very ancient civilization beneath the surface of our planet" which could be an "ancient race" of humans who "withdrew from the surface world to exist in subterranean caves" millions of years ago to avoid environmental catastrophe. These may be "Earth-evolved hominids," survivors from the "fabled Atlantis," who achieved an "apex" of technological civilization "only to blow itself to bits;" or they may be "Extraterrestrial beings" or "Star Gods" who "planted a colony on Earth" millions of years ago to give humans a "boost up the evolutionary ladder" via genetic engineering which they monitor from their underground bases.[AM,64]

AM For more theories on a secret group of humans with advanced tech, see "Paul Schatzkin - T. Townsend Brown, Philo T. Farnsworth, Secret Science, & the Caroline Group" *The Higherside Chats,* July 6, 2023.

Window of Evil

In the field of high strangeness, we have to contend with the dark side, and naturally, before closing up this chapter – must consider evil window areas. Synchromystic Michael Wann reports on a negative window area, saying there is a "two mile strange attractor field" in the Wilmington, Delaware area.[65] He explores how this negative window area manifests in the para-political world in an episode of *The Higherside Chats*. A central aspect of Downard's work centers around sinister "Sorcerers" using window areas for nefarious purposes, saying they are even "attempting to change the direction of the mystical primordial pulses that Travel" along ley lines.[1]

Downard speculates that evil window areas are used by dark magicians, "in whom science and sorcery have been reconciled" to create a "thing of horror" – a "computerized evil life."[1] These "practitioners of the science of evil have the common aim to produce a controlled world society" and these "practitioners... are most definitely tuned into [a] primordial power" to achieve their aims. The "science of evil" they utilize "has to do with...telluric currents and animal magnetism."[1] Downard is clear in his belief that the "magnetic fields" of Earth and humans, are a "force" that can be used "for good or evil."[5]

CERN and Bohemian Grove

The idea that a negative window is being established at CERN runs rampant in the high strangeness community. One Christian-centric thought is that there is "a strange convergence between modern science" and literal fallen angels at CERN.[66] Indeed, it is hard to fault the Christians making such, utterly absurd, speculations after *The Guardian* reported that a "fake ritual killing" was "filmed in a courtyard at Cern;" and the only explanation given was when a "spokeswoman suggested users of the facility had 'let their humour go too far' and warned of the potential for 'misunderstandings about the scientific nature of our research.'"[67]

This explanation brings me to a curious facet of high strangeness research- when the normal explanation arouses more intriguing questions, as opposed to putting the original questions to bed. For example, why do users of this facility find it so funny to participate in mock human sacrifices? I must confess the punchline is going over my head, even though I consider myself to have quite the funny bone. Christian-centric high strangeness researchers (not that there is anything wrong with that) see these mock human sacrifices and take it as evidence that ancient "sacrifice rites of certain pagan sects ... continue to be regarded as a means of invoking dark forces,"[5] and are not just the pranks of jokesters.

Aping Jerry Seinfeld, *so what's the deal with mock human sacrifices*? In this regard, I am reminded of Bohemian Grove, a "two-week encampment of some of the most prominent men in the world," including "artists and musicians, as well as many prominent business leaders, government officials, former U.S. presidents, senior media executives, and people of power."[68] I first heard about Bohemian Grove in 2001, from a left-wing hippie, when those folks were more curious (than they are now) about the weird goings-on of the powerful. Back then, if you were to bring up this gathering, you would be called crazy for suggesting something that didn't exist. Now, it is all but mainstream; even being featured in the Netflix show, *House of Cards*; called *Elysian Fields* in the series.[69]

On a recent episode of the HBO show, *John Oliver Tonight*, it was alleged that, Supreme Court Judge Clarence Thomas, attended the gathering; showing a picture of him with one of the billionaire Koch brothers and documentary film maker, Ken Burns.[69.1] And on a recent episode of the Joe Rogan podcast, the musician Kid Rock, tells a story involving him getting into a physical altercation at the gathering.[69.2] Other "notable members ... have included Clint Eastwood, Henry Kissinger, Walter Cronkite, Richard Nixon, Ronald Reagan, Charles Schwab ... and Jack London."[69.3] Reportedly, very real-world topics have been discussed at the gathering, being "particularly famous for a Manhattan Project planning meeting that took place there in September 1942, which subsequently led to the atomic bomb."[68]

Such gatherings are all well and good, I certainly support freedom of association, but again: *what's the deal with the mock human sacrifices*? Perhaps the most famous feature of the gathering is The Cremation of Care ceremony, which is the "annual ritual production," performed "in front of a 40-foot tall" owl statue. Reportedly, this ceremony includes, "hooded figures" placing "an effigy of Care" on top an altar, and then at the "end of the ceremony," it is "set on fire." Allegedly, this "symbolizes that members are banishing the 'dull cares' of conscience."[69.4] Yes, I know about the Burning Man festival, and the importance of rituals in general. However, I have never participated in a mock human sacrifice in front of a 40-foot owl. In fact, doing such things has never even crossed my mind. Do you have to be rich and powerful to *get it*?

On behalf of the normal people, not invited to a yearly summer camp for the world's power brokers, where life sized effigies are burned in front of giant owls, I ask that you cease preforming this ceremony. We don't find it interesting, funny, or cute; in fact, it is really *freaking out* a fair amount of us. Surely, this isn't one of the points of the ceremony? Freak out the poors, so we focus on weird rituals in the forest, not the machinations of the world's elite. No, I know that the most powerful people in the world have only our best interests in mind, so I am sure they will be open to stopping this aspect of their festivities.

Even Stranger Things at Montauk

Some claim the "various mystery schools" through the Montauk site were attempting to "tap into the morphogenic grid" and put a "negative spin on evolution" in the hopes that they could "limit the consciousness of human beings and thereby prevent full awakening." It is even claimed that the Montauk energy "grid is still being bombarded by various electronic transmissions" and as a result the area now "is like diseased energy... that has to be healed." However, the "only ones that really have permission to accomplish that healing are the owners of the land or the keepers of the gate."[70]

Deadly Orgone (DOR)

Wilhelm Reich (1897-1957) described orgone as life energy, adding that it had an opposite energy, DOR or Deadly Orgone, which he claimed was a "blocked life-energy on a 'proto-physical' level." Some Reichians say that the "negative energies conjured up by magic ritual cannot be sustained in a strong orgone field" and point out that "this is the reason why we continuously gift the sites of negative magical ritual with orgonite." Further, the "massive organisation of the planet will break the hypnotic spell" that an evil group "holds over mankind." They describe that members of this group "all believe in and use magic" – *dark magick,* I would add. The bad guys' "power wanes as soon as the energy that they are used to tapping into is withdrawn from them." This is done when "people disengage from fruitless conflict and become ... cooperative in the presence of strange positive orgone fields."[71]

Interestingly enough, there is scientific data backing up the idea of subtle energies having effects on humans, causing negative behavior and vice versa. For example, "positive ions are associated with increased irritability [and] depressive moods" while "negative ions" have the opposite effect. For example, "the Santa Ana wind, which is associated with increased crime, suicide, irritability, and tension, has positive ion levels" ten times higher than normal.[4]

Increasing the positive Orgone energy (and increasing the negative ions) so evil energies conjured up in dark rituals cannot be sustained is a major component of high strangeness magick.

How Windows Are Found

Before we get to my personal experiences related to this chapter, we will take a brief look at how window areas are found and, again, to be clear,

"Not all sacred sites or power spots are natural."[12] We have also looked at some of the ritual practices that can create (and enhance) them, and we have looked at advanced physical and mystical technology which can create (and enhance) them; however, we have not looked at how (human, secret, fairy, ancient, or space) people might find naturally occurring ones.

Extraterrestrial people seem to find them by locating large deposits of quartz, as "there are abundant indications that UFOs ... have definite affinity for quartz."[27] Ancient people found them with knowledge of the stars, being that "Typically [sacred] sites have an astronomical or astrological alignment aspect."[2] Human people will find them when they feel "pulled to a certain place by a higher force" and if "they surrender to the call of intuition, they are ... transformed."[2] Secret humans from nefarious breakaway societies found them when they "spontaneously experienced orgasms at vortexes of power."[5] And perhaps fairy people "feel the presence of ley energy" or find them with dowsing "rods, a pendulum, or other implements designed for that purpose."[12]

Personal Experiences

Writing a book should be an initiatory journey for the author, particularly if you intend the book to resonate with readers on a deep level. Crafting this specific chapter has indeed been a transformative experience for me. One of the most significant revelations I've had is learning that the region where I come from and currently live (part of the year) is, according to some, an exceptionally important area on a global-cosmic scale. A gentle reminder, I do not "believe" this stuff as we usually think of belief. And as I said in the introduction, I will explain what I believe in the conclusion. For the sake of making this a fun ride, I am narrating without bulky disclaimers, (i.e.: adding- allegedly, reportedly, supposedly, etc.).

Western North Carolina

The City of Asheville

As I pointed out earlier, I lived in Asheville (a purported New Age Energy Vortex) before moving to Turkey. I still consider it *my city*, as I live an hour away from it in my US home. Writing this chapter has brought the cosmic importance of the city and the Smoky Mountain region it exists in, into fuller focus. For reference, the Smoky Mountains are part of the larger Blue Ridge Mountain region.

Buncombe County Ley Lines

My research indicates the facility (mentioned previously) I worked at could be on the "The Cherokee Ley" which passes through "Buncombe County [and] through Leicester [passing] into the black mountain area".[AN] Or it may be the Smoky Mountain Ley, which is a line that runs "just north of the town of Leicester and on through Weaverville and on into the Mt. Mitchel vortex." Or perhaps the "Balsam Mountain" ley line which "slices through Fontana Lake...running parallel with the Cherokee" line "through Weaverville" and on through Black Mountain.[12,AO] When I lived in the area, my home was very near Weaverville, and I had major cosmic epiphanies in Weaverville restaurants sipping microbrew beer from the area.

In general, in writing this book I've learned that "there is an apex of intense energy" in the Blue Ridge Mountains "and surrounding mountains, with the Great Smoky Mountains as the energy center." The great smoky region contains some of the oldest mountains on our planet and the Grandfather Mountain region of the Blue Ridge "is a place that generates some of the most potent living energy on Earth; energy that is the life [of] our planet." This energy is "a power by which the Earth Mother heals ... her body."[12]

Keep in mind that knowing of specific ley lines running through these areas is a rare thing; the leys are not well mapped out in North America because "very little has been done by way of ley-finding" in this region of the world.[27] We have a developed mapping of the ley line system in Great Britain, but nowhere else in the English speaking world that I know of. As a high strangeness researcher, finding these things out was a huge puzzle piece in my own personal journey. Indeed, the place I was born and raised contains Grandfather Mountain, which according to Bryant's spirit guide Albion[AP] "is the true 'grandfather' of all the Earth's mountains."[12] I still remember driving around the region with my family and my mother pointing out the image of the Grandfather to me, explaining to me how the mountain looks like a sleeping man.

I feel my personal psycho-spiritual work and my high strangeness magical group, the Çhaplins Öf Peril (Ç.Ö.P.),[AQ] to be part of the overall plan

AN The lead singer of the band Animal Collective reportedly lives in the area, and a song on their latest album "narrates a road trip through the North Carolina countryside…the listener is taken from the former Black Mountain art school to a gathering of people…feeling like there's somewhere else they'd rather be." J. Friedman, "Animal Collective Rekindle the Light on Time Skiffs," PasteMagazine.com, February 4, 2022.

AO The clients of the facility were often taken on weekend excursions to this lake.

AP Notice the suffix 'ion.' In future volumes of this series, I will explain the importance of Ion, the channeled entity Bob Dobbs works with. Also of note: Bob & Ion have their own unique take on Enochian magick.

AQ The physical headquarters of this group is thirty minutes from Brown Mountain.

of this magical region, as the Ç.Ö.P., physical headquarters is located in this area of North America.[AR] Which brings me to the next section.

Caldwell County

I grew up in Caldwell county, North Carolina, a liminal space of sorts – existing in the mountains and foothills. The Northern and Western part of the county is in the Blue Ridge mountains and the rest is considered the foothills; specifically the Brushy Mountains – an isolated remnant (or spur) of the Blue Ridge. As we know from the *Hellier* series, high strangeness is attracted to liminal spaces. My childhood home had a view of Hibriten Mountain, the third tallest peak in the Brushy Mountains.

Interestingly, the county hosts Google's second-ever server farm, located in Lenoir, the county's largest city. It looms over the city, as it resembles a walled fortress and at night it ominously brightens the sky. The large complex commands a striking view from the city's baseball stadium, directly visible in center field. This unique feature made it quite challenging to remain unaffected by a sense of synchromystic fascination while watching the Lenoir Legends, the college summer league baseball team, which has Bigfoot as their mascot.

A fair amount of secrecy surrounds the facility and when it was completed the scuttlebutt was that even the mayor was not allowed inside.[AS] At one time, employees had to park at the abandoned town mall, to then be bussed into the facility. Interestingly enough, they were riding in old Caldwell County school buses which I may have ridden on when I was a student. At any rate, my joke is that all of the world's information is stored in my hometown.

I have been told by a local that the employees keep to themselves, do not really integrate with the larger community, and as such, are "like a cult." Of course, the local (who is not prone to fanciful thinking) was implying the fancy tech folks didn't want to socialize with the hoi polloi of a small Southern town and was not indicating they were in an honest to goodness cult.

However, there is alleged cult activity associated with other aspects of Google, meaning it isn't just snooty tech folks refusing to interact with the locals. An individual alleges he "worked for Google for about three and a half years [and] was fired because" he "raised alarm about a doomsday cult that dominated [his] former team."[72] The allegations of what this group and

AR In Turkey, it is located among the Ganos mountains, the region Orpheus was from.

AS I know from personal experience that the employees of the facility are encouraged to keep it secret they work there, in a manner that is reminiscent of how defense contractor employees are encouraged to keep it secret where they work.

its leader were doing is too dark and controversial to mention in this volume.[AT] However, if you research the topic you will quickly see what I mean. Also, please be advised that the allegations of this employee are involving "a business unit at Google" that the alleged cult had a "presence in." The whistleblower's allegations are that "most of the Google Developer Studio joined the team through ASG [Advanced Systems Group] as contractors, including many members of the Fellowship."[73] Again, this was all allegedly taking place in Oregon and California and is in no way connected to the Google server farm in Lenoir.

However, the weirdness in my town in this regard doesn't stop with Google. In 1979 "the world's largest windmill" was placed in a neighboring county, "atop Howard's Knob" which "had been installed as part of a program by NASA and the US Department of Energy to develop wind power… in response to the country's dependence on petroleum during the 1970s OPEC oil embargo."[74] A local newspaper revealed that the windmill was "controlled by NASA computers thirty-five miles away in Lenoir, N.C." where it was "collecting data for the department of Energy."[75] Interestingly enough, cult activity is tied to this story as well, albeit a "tongue-in-cheek cult at Appalachian State University." This group "dressed up in sheets, calling themselves 'Wooshies' who worshipped the god 'Nay-zuh' (i.e. NASA)." They were called the Wooshies because of the windmill "came to be somewhat affectionately called for the sound it produced." Another story "recounts students who created a 'mockumentary' video for a class with a fictitious group called the Pangalactic Unification Church and Restaurant – the 'Cult of the Wooshies.'"[74]

Please be advised that I have never heard of any cult activity in or around my hometown. I am just providing these two pieces of information about cults for your own synchromystic edification when considering the high strangeness import of my hometown.

But wait, there's more! Dr. Kerry Mullis (1944-2019) was born in Lenoir. He is most known for winning the "Nobel prize for perfecting the PCR DNA method," meaning the PCR test we heard so much about during the first Covid pandemic. He reports that "taking LSD was one of the most important things he ever did and that he would not have won the Nobel prize… if he had not done it." He also reports "a strange UFO or Mothman Prophecies type encounter with an entity."[76] In his autobiography, *Dancing*

AT It is similar to the Amy story in *Hellier*, but less dark. As I have said, Amy's subject is the third rail of high strangeness, and I'm not prepared to tackle it in my first book. Also see Isabel Vincent's, "Inside the 'Love Fest' Cult That's Allegedly Infiltrated Google Headquarters," (*New York Post*;) & "How a Religious Sect Landed Google in a Lawsuit," (The *New York Times*, June 20, 2022).

Naked in the Mind Field, Mullis writes "about a wide range of subjects: from the scientific method to parapsychology … to the HIV virus … to astrology." Finally, this book is said to challenge "us to question the authority of scientific dogma even as it reveals the workings of" Mullis' "uncannily original scientific mind."[AU]

Again, while considering the above information regarding Lenoir, notice the intersection of the para-political and paranormal phenomena (especially as it coalesces in a specific geographic location) when studying high strangeness.

Gregory Little, in addition to being the co-author of the seminal, *Origin of the Gods: Qesem Cave, Skinwalkers, and Contact with Transdimensional Intelligences* is also the author of *The Illustrated Encyclopedia of Native American Indian Mounds and Earthworks.* While I was writing this chapter, he posted the Smithsonian's Bureau of Ethnology map "showing the general distribution of mound sites they had identified in the eastern Half of the USA by the late 1800s."[77] The map indicates multiple mounds existing in Caldwell County. According to other Smithsonian Institute records, "Some of the most important mounds … were discovered in Caldwell County … and opened in 1882."[78] The topic of mounds in North America is an important subject in high strangeness and "any discussion of sacred sites and natural earth energy"[12] must include a look at their mystical import.

Table Rock

From my property in Caldwell County I can see Burke County's Table Rock, which is said to be "the most visible symbol in the region."[79] My research in writing this book has led me to find that Table Rock is one of the "extremely powerful and rare *beacon*" vortexes. These type of vortexes "are [almost] always … natural rock formations … or mountains" but "whether natural or man-made" they "are always connected by one or more *celestial ley lines* that link them to … other planets in the Solar System, stars or other galaxies." They are special because regular ley lines "are purely terrestrial and run just above or below the earth's surface," whereas "celestial leys are individual lines … that are natural to the Earth but that extend out into extraterrestrial territory." They are rare and "serve to *link* the earth with … a variety of cosmic forces." This is also important because "through them the earth's energy is transmitted into outer space."[AV,12] Interestingly for me

AU From, KaryMullis.com/books.shtml. There is more I could say about Mullis in regards to the events of 2020-2022, but it is too controversial for this volume.

AV Other Celestial leys are found at "Bell Rock in Sedona…Glastonbury Tor in England; and Stone Mountain outside of Atlanta, Georgia" (Page Bryant, *The Spiritual Reawakening of the Great Smoky Mountains*, p. 100).

and for my group's practice is that "Table Rock's energy is conducive to deliberately induced astral travel experiences ... and for gaining access to the energies inherent in other places."[12]

As I have said earlier, my US property is situated on an old Atlantis ley line. This is significant because "living near or on a ley would ... greatly affect the potency of your land as well as the quality of your domestic and personal life."[12] Living on an old Atlantis ley and within site of the Table Rock celestial beacon definitely increases the spiritual potency of my property – and hopefully its monetary value as well.

Brown Mountain

The high strangeness hotspot Brown Mountain[AW] is on the border of Caldwell and Burke counties. The mountain is known for the Brown Mountain Lights "which are one of the most persistent mysteries in North Carolina." The lights are said to "gradually float to the top of the mountain, hover, pulsate brilliantly, change color [and] blink on and off before disappearing." The Cherokee believed they were the ghosts of slain warriors and the European settlers in the region thought "the lights are a troop of candle-bearing ghosts destined to march forever back and forth across" the mountain.[80]

Brown Mountain has been a favorite spot of high strangeness researchers for many years. One of the fathers of the field, Timothy Green Beckley covered the topic in his book, *The Darkest, Deepest Secrets* (2013), in a chapter called "Mysterious Lights of Brown Mountain: Is This Famous NC UFO Base a Front for Crashed Saucers?" The area was also featured in the *Hellier* docuseries, with the crew looking for a secret entrance to an underground alien base there, and the enigmatic Terry Wriste provided them with coordinates which led them to Brown Mountain. When Allen Greenfield was being interviewed on various podcasts regarding his appearances on *Hellier*, he claimed he was visited by two Men in Black types at the hotel he was staying at while investigating the area.

The possibility that there is a secret UFO base in the area is also explored in the rare high strangeness book, featuring a story of a Burke County local who claims he was taken to a base inside of Brown Mountain in the early 1960s. The beings inside the base reportedly said he was "chosen to tell the people of Earth about their true history; that man was created on another planet ... which our ancestors destroyed ... now the waste of asteroids which lie between Mars and Jupiter." He was told by the beings inside the moun-

AW Brown Mountain appeared in an episode of *The X-Files*- Season 6, Episode 21: "Field Trip."

tain that they were from Venus and he was warned that "there are certain 'forces' that could decide that man should be destroyed from the Earth."[81]

Living on a Ley Line

As I mentioned previously, in writing this book[AX] I discovered that a North American ley line went through my home county. This ley is, according to VortexHunters.com, the Bermuda Triangle, Mount Shasta and Buffalo Lake Ley. Interestingly enough, as I was writing this chapter, I ended up buying a house on this ley line, working on this section the day the sale closed. The house is a five-minute walk from the center of the line and it was synchronicity which enabled me to purchase the home so easily and quickly.[AY] In purchasing the home, I learned that quartz rock decaying produces radon (in the US you have to get your home tested for radon as per requirements by law). I was told that quartz is so prevalent in the Blowing Rock region of the county that 80 percent of the homes there have levels above normal. The town of Blowing Rock brings us to the next section.

Blowing Rock/Mystery Hill

Blowing Rock, North Carolina is a town in Caldwell and Watauga counties. The gravity anomaly spoken about earlier in this chapter, Mystery Hill, is located in this town. I only visited the site as an adult, because my parents wouldn't take me when I was a child, always insisting it was a "tourist trap." Most residents of the region agree with this assessment, assuming the disorienting effects you experience on the site are due to tricks in how the site is set up. For example, it has ramped floors to amplify the anomalous gravity effect. Another reason the site is not taken seriously in the area is because you can buy such items as "Sasquatch Poop," an inventive name for chocolate covered nuts.

All that being said, in my opinion the effects at the site are compelling. It feels very clear that you are being pulled forward by gravity. This effect isn't the most dramatic thing in the world, but it can be felt without a doubt. I don't think the effect is so strong that the owners can just rely on its mild effects to attract customers. I think this fact is why the owners amplify the effect with tilted floors and silly Bigfoot candy (which I did, of course, purchase).

AX While writing this section my computer glitched and started deleting line after line, causing me to lose a day's work.

AY The realtor was a family friend who happened upon the property by a bit of chance. His wife appears to be something of a high strangeness magnet and has a compelling ghost story involving an apparent screaming banshee. Her grandmother was a Folk Healer in the area and there is a long tradition of Southern Appalachian Women practicing folk healing, see: *Southern Folk Medicine: Healing Traditions from the Appalachian Fields and Forests* by Phyllis D. Light.

Atlantis Returns

In writing this book, I have been surprised by the frequency with which Atlantis keeps coming up in general and specifically in connection with Western North Carolina. One ley line map floating around the internet, titled "American Ley Lines: The Science Behind Earth Magic," has a Bermuda triangle linked ley line connecting to Mystery Hill in Blowing Rock.[AZ] Another New Age publication featuring a map of the "Pilot Mountain Wheel" has a ley line emitting from the "Pyramid grid node" of the larger "Bermuda Triangle Vile Vortex grid node," connecting to Pilot Mountain, North Carolina.[82, BA] Another ley line map I found while writing this chapter is called the Goddess Equator grid, which is said to be "the old Atlantean grid." I found a link to the map of this grid system on a comment of the WeLoveMassMeditation.com website.[83]

Again, this mass meditation website is connected to the writer going by the name Cobra, whom I have mentioned earlier. This Goddess Equator ley map shows the center of a "minor" ley line of this grid going through Caldwell County, about ten miles from my property. The map also lists Brown Mountain, Pilot Mountain and Stone Mountain (the more famous monadnock in the Atlanta area over Mount Arabia) as being part of this grid. In addition, I have lived on lines of this grid system in Turkey. Hagia Sophia is listed as part of the grid and lines pass through Urla (where I first lived in Turkey) and where my property is on the coast of the sea of Marmara, in the Ganos Mountains.[84]

The Goddess Equator, grid system is of cosmic importance, having to do with the effort of "the Light Forces ... to bring as much Light as possible to the surface of the planet." In this effort, the "old Atlantean Light grid is being reactivated." During the "times of Atlantis, powerful temples were built [which] were anchoring divine Goddess energy on the surface of the planet." This Goddess energy is so important that "Public spaces that bring the Goddess energy to the general surface population need to be created" and "One very important aspect of that process is reactivation of old Atlantean Goddess vortexes, connected to the old Atlantean equator."[84, BB]

AZ Author Tom Robbins, who wrote the forward to Terence McKenna's *The Archaic Revival*, is from Blowing Rock. Also note: I can't find the source of this map, but it can be found at: flickr.com/photos/vaxzine/3389501328

BA "Pilot Mountain, a metamorphic quartzite monadnock rising to a peak 2,421 feet [and] is one of the most distinctive natural features in the U.S. state of North Carolina" (wikipedia.org/ Pilot Mountain, North Carolina). Also note: Stone Mountain and Arabia Mountain in GA are also monadnocks.

BB "Goddess temples always had a sacred lake situated nearby, where the Goddess vortex was anchored through a female angelic being under guidance from Iona. The Light forces have communicated that after more than 1500 years of suppression, Goddess temples need to be recreated

The above will be more relevant as I flesh out the story involving what I call the "Channeled Messages from the Carrollton Vortex," which occurred when I was living in Carrollton, Georgia. I explore this high strangeness window area in Chapter 10 of this volume and in a section below. In these channeled messages, I was told by a woman, in an accidental full trance (not a psychic by interest or trade), she was channeling the "light forces," and that I and "two Americans will raise Atantis [sic]." So, over twenty years ago, I was told I would raise Atlantis under utterly absurd circumstances and then, while writing this book, I ended up living in a home on a Bermuda triangle ley line.

Of course, the Bermuda triangle has been linked to Atlantis when in 1938 Edgar Cayce, also in trance, predicted that "a portion of the temples" of Atlantis "may yet be discovered under the slime of ages and sea water near Bimini... Expect it in '68 or '69 – not so far away." When the "Bimini Road was located in 1968, some propose it was a fulfillment of the prediction that the history of Atlantis would be revealed to the world."[85]

The mysterious message of me raising Atlantis becomes more in focus as I go through the book writing initiation process and flesh out the magick of high strangeness. It is still too early for me to make any formal pronouncements about what this "prediction" may mean, but the magick of high strangeness is involved. Also, I do believe we get closer when we look at the work of Michael Bertiaux. His magical praxis speaks of the importance of the "Atlantean Consciousness" and suggests "voudon was the religion of Atlantis."[86]

37th Parallel

Pilot Mountain is a quartz monadnock, just like Mount Arabia, and falls on the 36th parallel. In Ben Mezrich's book, *The 37th Parallel: The Secret Truth Behind America's UFO Highway* (2017), he points out that the phenomenon in question actually refers to the 36th to 38th parallel. Also falling within this area is Sparta, North Carolina, where my family owns a mountain retreat property. I will go into more detail about the high strangeness I experienced in this area in subsequent volumes of this series. Briefly, I will point out some of the high strangeness in the area. The New River is said to be the second oldest river in the world, after the Nile, and, along with the Nile, is among the small handful of rivers in the world to flow North. I will never forget trout fishing with my father shortly before graduating

---

again on the surface of this planet. Sisterhood of the Rose has been given this sacred task." See endnote 84.

from undergrad in 2000 on this river, as he informed me of this strange fact. Noted high strangeness shaman, Michael Wann, features the Susquehanna in his synchromystic work on the weird magick of rivers, saying that the New River, the French Broad[BC] and Susquehanna are considered the "three sisters" in his mythos.[87]

Georgia

The Carrollton Vortex

The theory there is a window area in Carrollton, Georgia was first furthered by the long-time high strangeness researcher, Andrew Stephens, editor of *The Absolute Elsewhere,*[BD] which was a "once-lost book-length interview from the 1980s with the co-founder of the Discordian Society" (Kerry Thornley) and members of an OTO body in Atlanta. The Carrollton window area is barely known in the mainstream high strangeness community at large, as its first official mention in the wider community was on an episode of *The Higherside Chats,* in 2022.[BE] On this show, author and paranormal researcher, Trey Hudson says he learned about the Carrollton Vortex from yours truly but I first learned about it from Stephens circa 2001.[88]

Carrollton is the home of the University of West Georgia, where I received my MA in psychology. The psychology program at UWG is one of the only humanistic and transpersonal-oriented departments in the world and was started on orders of Abraham Maslow (the founder of humanistic psychology). It has featured such luminary professors as Raymond Moody (who I mentioned earlier), William Roll (world renowned parapsychologist), Mike Aarons (Maslow's student and a co-founder of the humanistic psychology movement), Tobin Hart (*The Secret Spiritual World of Children* and Simon and Schuster's *The Four Virtues*) and Larry Schor (2004 Georgia counselor of the year and mentee of the so-called Canadian Timothy Leary, Duncan Blewett, author of *The Frontiers of Being*).

Thinkers closely affiliated with the program are represented in the special collections of the college's library, which include the personal papers of Sidney Jourard (leading force in humanistic psychology movement, *The Transparent Self*), Stanley Krippner (a founding father of Transpersonal

BC The French Broad River passes through Buncombe County, North Carolina; passing its majestic energy on my way to work at the treatment center I worked at in Leicester is something I will never forget.

BD Source: UnionOfEgoists.com/2018/05/22/sa1068-the-absolute-elsewhere-kerry-wendall-thornley/

BE Stephens claims he sees "a thread of continuity that connects together many of the events that make Carrollton such a strange place" and said he found that "certain events in the series [Twin Peaks] mirror real life events in Carroll county" (Personal Communication, Aug. 15, 2008).

Psychology and pioneering dream researcher), and Ingo Swann (psychic, artist, co-creator of remote viewing, *Penetration: The Question of Extraterrestrial and Human Telepathy*). It was in Carrollton that I received the aforementioned channeled messages, while in graduate school at the University of West Georgia.[BF]

Mount Arabia

I was never directly involved in Greenfield's Mount Arabia workings, but I do feel their work drew me back into the OTO specifically and my magical practice in general. After 9/11 I got super freaked out (to put it mildly) with anything parapolitical or mystical and took a magical retirement in 2001 as a result. Instead of high strangeness topics, I just focused on creative pursuits – writing a screenplay, selling a reality TV show in LaLa Land and self-producing a feature length film that appeared in the Atlanta Underground Film Festival. However, by the end of 2005, going into 2006 I found myself languishing, psycho-spiritually speaking.

It was around this time that I randomly ran into my old friend from my graduate school days and past leader of the OTO in Carrollton, in the most occult place that exists, IKEA. I had been thinking of getting back into group magical practice and took this as a sign I should rejoin the OTO. I later learned the Mount Arabia working had begun at roughly the same time. I even told Greenfield in an email that I thought his workings on the mountain had pulled me back into the Great Work. For historical accuracy, I found an old email to Stephens where I told him as much, saying: "I feel his mt. Arabia working is what drew me out of my magickal retirement in late 05, early 2006."[89]

I did have a UFO sighting on Arabia Mountain that Greenfield wrote about on his LiveJournal blog. The following is an excerpt of a blog post on the incident, entitled an "Arabia Mountain UFO? First hand account." He quoted my report to him about the sighting, where I said: "No wings of an airplane could be seen, and it was moving too swiftly to be a bird, and may also have been too high for a bird. Its flight pattern suggested it was not a traditional plane. It was moving slightly erratically; it would go down for a few seconds and then would make a sharp turn, (or perhaps a tight turn

---

BF My wife and I founded an Association of Humanistic psychology "Energy Center" at West GA. Again, also of note is that the name of the OTO camp in the area, Solve et Coagula, was almost named the Secret Door camp. The name comes from a quote in *The Book of the Law* which says "there is a secret door that I shall make to establish the way in all the quarters." Stephens agreed with my assessment that the local OTO body and the psychology department at UWG "could be viewed as outgrowths" of the Carrollton Vortex (Personal email communication, Aug. 2008, see endnote 89).

might better describe it) in the other direction. Then it floated off out of view."[90, BG]

Conclusions

The preceding chapters are an exploration of the enigmatic phenomena found in special geographical areas. I hold the view that these phenomena result from a fusion of all the theories put forth, rather than being attributed to a single exclusive explanation. It's crucial to recognize that high strangeness window areas often defy easy categorization and that a comprehensive understanding may necessitate considering multiple theories simultaneously.

Pan

Continuing with the notion of a writing a book as a profound educational journey for the author, I wish to emphasize that crafting the prior two chapters has prompted me to suggest that Pan might be the deity presiding over these locations of high strangeness, whether we choose to term them window areas, portals, or sacred sites. I've come to the hypothesis that Pan might serve as a symbolic or mythological representation of the enigmatic qualities associated with these phenomena, offering a lens through which we can potentially comprehend and connect with them. I believe this notion is hinted at in the fact that this book features content from Dion Fortune's *The Goat-foot God*, Brandon's *The Rebirth of Pan: Hidden Faces of the American Earth Spirit*, *Hellier* and the *Penny Royal* podcast series, all of which feature Pan's relationship to window areas. I will flesh out what I believe one does with this fact in volume 2, *My Cosmic Trigger: Perilous Chapels and High Strangeness Magick.*

Your Own Personal Window

After writing this chapter, I am firm in my desire to inspire high strangeness researchers and mystical practitioners to find their own local window areas and turn them into full-fledged sacred/vortex sites.[BH] Our planet is naturally suited to this because the Earth itself is a "*gateway first and planet second.*"[42] Humans have been "selected to steward this universe" because

BG In this same post, Greenfield added that "We've seen black helicopters buzz us, and have had orb effects, but no UFOs per se during Workings on Arabia Mountain. Here is an example following a consecration. Note orb above newly consecrated bishop (top picture) and enhanced view of orb." See endnote 90.

BH In the *Penny Royal* podcast series a case is continually made for the re-enchantment of our own towns and "The case for enchantment has been made throughout" the book, *Sacred Places: How the Living Earth Seeks our Friendship* (p. 198).

the "Earth itself is the 'living tunnel' for ingress and egress" of trans-dimensional beings of all types "as they travel to and from our physical" reality.[42]

Author and former FBI agent, John DeSouza claims that some groups are trying to obfuscate the fact that when ultraterrestrials enter the human dimension it creates "'quantum-flux gate' portals that can be accessed by other energetic entities in order to enter" our reality. Meaning they "all come and go through the same portals." The most important thing to remember in this regard is that to access these portals doesn't require permission from "the false Gatekeepers," i.e., "NASA, the parliament, or the Pope." And those that think "middlemen" actually "still stand post" over these highly strange gates, quite simply, are wrong. As a result, ordinary people "can crash the gates and access those portals" because "these ancient portals can only be activated and used by the most fearsome and wondrous powers in all the Multi-Verses – *believing human beings*."[42]

However, as this statement and this chapter has indicated, perhaps nefarious humans may already be rushing these gates, as they have given themselves their own permission. Shouldn't we do the same? I say, yes. Let us establish our own beachheads in these highly strange geographic locations and plant our own flags in the name of the cosmic forces of good!

Noted synchromystic, Michael Wann says that "we misunderstand what nature really is," but when we attend to "rivers [and] streams" and "look outside" the negative matrix to the "reality in our own backyard" we will see "interconnectedness." When we do this we will stop a negative "feedback loop" and will start to be "pulled by new timelines." Stepping into your own backyard's sacred space/window area, means you are breaking free from the negative "timeline manipulation." This is because when we are "looking at the heavens" in our own neighborhoods and towns, it helps move us "off the false reality" feedback loop.[91,BI] It appears he is urging us to turn the humble creeks in our own backyards into sacred bodies of water, not just utilizing the commonly accepted sacred bodies of water, like the Nile in Egypt.[BJ]

Why shouldn't our own backyards be sacred places of healing? Why shouldn't our own backyards be portals for heavenly creatures to pour forth

---

BI This also reminds me of what some researchers say is the "point" of *Penny Royal*, which is to look to one's own backyard & "Find your story, be the independent researcher and journalist in your own backyard" ("Appalachin Intelligence: Ancient Stone Structures, Forgotten Petroglyphs, and The Hidden American Underground," *My Family Thinks I'm Crazy Podcast*, Jan. 2023).

BJ P. Bryant says "the worldwide body of myths is filled with stories of the supernatural and sacred powers of springs and wells. One of the most interesting studies I have ever undertaken involves the so-called 'water cults' which are believed to have originated over 5,000 years ago. Water symbols have been found on many goddess" figurines. (*The Spiritual Reawakening of the Great Smoky Mountains*, p. 194).

in their battle against the dark forces? I see no reason this utterly absurd idea should not be fully embraced during these strange and tumultuous times.

A Two Front Cosmic War

My research indicates there has been an ongoing galactic conflict which presents itself on two distinct fronts: control for the window areas of Earth and the other being the facilitation of positive or negative timelines. The former, as I have shown in this chapter, concerns the age-old interaction between shamans and ultraterrestrials at window areas. This interaction seems to persist in our modern times but is now allegedly intertwined with the advanced technology of secret quasi-military/quasi-governmental groups and of the ultraterrestrials themselves. How absurd!

If these areas are in fact real then it follows that the underlying intention of individuals operating within these window areas is of paramount importance. If malevolent forces establish a presence in a window area, it can enable the ingress of negative ultraterrestrials, and vice versa. This underscores the critical role of high strangeness researchers who participate in the magick of high strangeness to assert a positive influence on the location, thereby facilitating the arrival of benevolent ultraterrestrials.

Sources

1. James Shelby Downard, *Stalking the Great Whore: The Lost Writings of James Shelby Downard*, 2023, pp. 80, 167, 79, 189, 216, 81, 166-7, 320.

2. James A. Swan, *Sacred Places: How the Living Earth Seeks our Friendship*, 1990, pp. 35, 35, 112-113, 150, 35, 113.

3. John Keel, *Operation Trojan Horse*, 1970, from 1976 version, pp. 286, 43.

4. William G. Roll, *Psychological and Electromagnetic Aspects of Haunts,* University of West Georgia, Carrollton, Georgia, USA.

5. Michael Hoffman, *Twilight Language*, 2021, pp. 89, 91, 332, 88.

6. Eric Leskowitz, "Mesmer Reconsidered: From Animal Magnetism to the Biofield," *Explore*, Volume 15, Issue 2, March–April 2019.

7. Ljubomir Radovancević, "The Tribute of the Pioneer of Hypnotherapy: Franz Anton Mesmer, in the History of Psychotherapy and Medicine," *Journal AMHA: Acta Medico-Historica Adriatica*, 7(1), 2009:49-60.

8. Fahad Mukhtar, William Regenold, and Sarah H Lisanby, "Recent Advances in Electroconvulsive Therapy in Clinical Practice and Research," June 2023. ncbi.nlm.nih.gov/pmc/articles/PMC10259509/

9. Dictionary.com

10. Andrew Collins and Gregory L. Little, Introduction to *Origins of the Gods: Qesem Cave, Skinwalkers, and Contact with Transdimensional Intelligences by Erich von Däniken*, 2022, E-Book: p. 13

11. Colin Wilson's Introduction to *The Goblin Universe* by Ted Holiday, 1990, p. 10.

12. Page Bryant, *The Spiritual Reawakening of the Great Smoky Mountains*, 1994, pp. 85, 145, 82, 115, 117, 145, 129, 98-99, 102, 115, 145, 115.

13. John DeSouza, "Who Are the Paranormal Magnets?" *High Journeys with Alexis Brooks*, June 27, 2018, Times: 33:58, 16:00, 37:00.

14. Kathy Weiser-Alexander, "The Adena Culture of the Northeast," LegendsofAmerica.com, March 2020.

15. Nathan Isaac, "Alien Space Bats," *Penny Royal,,* Season One, Episode Two, 2020, Time: 10:00.

16. Hugh Newman and Jim Viera, "Giants of Ancient Britain: Geomancy and Megalithic Sites," *The Higher Side Chats,* March 6, 2022, Times: 45:00, 28:00, 5:50.

17. Ibrahim Karim, *Back To a Future for Mankind: BioGeometry,* 2010. Publisher's summary.

18. Ibrahim Karim, *Biogeometry Signatures: Harmonizing the Body's Subtle Energy Exchange with the Environment,* 2016, p. 34.

19. Ghostbusters.fandom.com/wiki, *Ivo Shandor, 550 Central Park West.*

20. "Teotihuacan: An Ancient City That Resembles a Circuit Board," *Ancient Code Team,* Ancient-code.com, April 20, 2022.

21. Éliphas Lévi, *The History of Magic: Including a Clear and Precise Exposition of Its Procedure, Its Rites, and Its Mysteries,* 1913, from 1993 version: pp. 41, 3, 4, 5.

22. Ted Andrews, *Simplified Magic: Beginners' Guide to the New Age Quabala,* 1998, p. 9.

23. Aleister Crowley, *Magick, Liber ABA, Book 4, Parts 1-IV,* 1998, edited by H. Beta, p. xxiv.

24. Aleister Crowley, *The Confessions of Aleister Crowley: An Autohagiography,* December 5, 1989, pp. 397, 359, 588.

25. Crowley quoted in the article by Paul Gallagher, "Aleister Crowley: How the Great Beast Unleashed the Loch Ness Monster," DangerousMinds.net, June 2013.

26. Paul Gallagher, "Aleister Crowley: How the Great Beast Unleashed the Loch Ness Monster," DangerousMinds.net, June 2013.

27. Jim Brandon, *The Rebirth of Pan: Hidden Faces of the American Earth Spirit,* 1983, pp. 25, 192, 138.

28. Kenneth Grant, *Outer Gateways,* 1994, pp. 157, 35, 219 and 179, 92.

29. Kenneth Grant, *The Ninth Arch,* 2002, p. 200, xvii-xviii

30. Daniel V. Boudillion, "Aleister Crowley's Lam and the Little Grey Men: A Striking Resemblance," Boudillion.com, 2003.

31. Aaron Wright, Benjamin Grundy, "Abramelin Meltdown," *Mysterious Universe Podcast,* episode 27.03: Jan. 2022, Time: 44:00.

32. Kenneth Grant, *Outside the Circles of Time,* 1980, pp. 178, 51, 35, 39, 56, 81-82, 159.

33. Wayne Erbsen, "When You See Those Flying Saucers," *Hudson Valley Bluegrass Association,* hvbluegrass.org, August 1, 2018.

34. Allen Greenfield, *The Roots of Modern Magick,* 2004, pp.155-56.

35. Kenneth Grant, *Beyond the Mauve Zone,* 2016, pp. 12, 14, 35.

36. Jason Louv, *John Dee and the Empire of Angels: Enochian Magick and the Occult Roots of the Modern World,* 2018, E-book: pp. 17-18, 641.

36.1. Paul Rydeen, *Jack Parsons and the Fall of Babalon,* citing and quoting Michael Hoffman, 1994, p. 4.

37. Ta Set Ma'at Lodge, *Rite Ancien et Primitif de Memphis-Misraim,* The Abbey of Al Qiyamah, alqiyamah.us/memphismisraim.

38. Allen Greenfield, "Arabia Working," *Smashing Illusions: A Journal for Scientific Illuminism,* tausirhasirim.livejournal.com/81596.html, March 22, 2008.

39. Tau Naamah, "Points Chaud 101," TauNaamah.Wordpress.com, May 2007.

40. Michael Bertiaux quoted in Tau Naamah, "Points Chaud 101," TauNaamah.Wordpress.com, May 2007.

40.1. The Abbots, *Aliens, UFOs, and Stargates,* 2023, E-book: p. 41.

41. Michio Kaku, "Physicist Michio Kaku on the Shift in the UFO Phenomenon," *The Joe Rogan Experience* #1828,, PowerfulJRE: Youtube, June 2022.

42. John DeSouza, *The Extra-Dimensionals: True Tales and Concepts of Alien Visitors,* 2016, E-book: pp. 100, 168-169, 250, 252.

43. Steven Greer, *Above Top Secret: The Technology Behind Disclosure* (2022).

44. Peter Moon, "The Montauk Project, Chi Gong, and the Secret Romanian Hall of Records," *The Higher Side Chats,* 2013.

45. Dr. Steven Greer, "Black Budget, Stargate, Raytheon, Lockheed Skunk Works," *Shawn Ryan Show* podcast, episode 65: *UAP/UFO Secrets,* Times: 58:00-1:01.

46. Sherman Carmichael and Jason McLean, *Mysterious Georgia (American Legends),* 2021, p.131.

47. "The Portal Factor," *Global Watch Weekly Report,* Scribd.com/document /332276354/The-Portal-Factor-pdf, May 23, 2014.

48. Pierre Teilhard de Chardin, *The Phenomenon of Man,* written in 1938 and originally published in 1955. From the 2008 version, p. 181.

49. Raymond Moody, M.D., Ph.D, "Scrying," *Theta: Contemporary Issues in Parapsychology,* Spring 1990.

50. William Butler Yeats, *Irish Folk and Fairy Tales,* 1888. Publisher's summary.

51. Robert Kirk, *The Secret Commonwealth of Elves, Fauns, and Fairies,* written in 1691 and published in 1815. Publisher's introduction to 2020 E-book, & E-book, p. 53.

52. Theresa Bane, *Encyclopedia of Fairies in World Folklore and Mythology,* 2013, quoted in Ronel Janse van Vuuren, *Magic Portals and Entrances to Faerie,* ronelthemythmaker.com/magic-portals-and-entrances-to-faerie-folklore/, Feb. 2019.

53. Wirt Sikes, *British Goblins: Welsh Folk-lore, Fairy Mythology, Legends and Traditions,* 1880, quoted in Ronel Janse van Vuuren, *Magic Portals and Entrances to Faerie,* Ronelthemythmaker.com/magic-portals-and-entrances-to-faerie-folklore/, Feb. 2019.

54. David and Carroll Swing, "Gnomes in the Garden: Celtic Faerie Teachings" and "Celtic Faerie Teachings, at Avalon Grove," avalongrove.com/faeries/. In person lecture, Asheville, North Carolina, circa 2005.

55. Brent Swancer, *Bizarre Cases of Bigfoot and Portals to Other Dimensions,* 2022journalnews.com.ph/, January 3, 2022.

56. Michael D. Kane, "Is Bigfoot an Extraterrestrial Visitor? Some Researchers Think So," Masslive.com, Oct. 19, 2015.

57. Donald Tyson, *Enochian Magic for Beginners: The Original System of Angel Magic,* 1997, pp. Xi, 1-2, 5, 46, 91.

58. Greg Carey, *Ultimate Things: An Introduction to Jewish and Christian Apocalyptic Literature* and *Merriam-Webster* as quoted in Lindsey Ellefson, "The Real Difference Between the 'Apocalypse,' 'Armageddon,' and 'Doomsday,'" Life-Hacker.com, October 7, 2022.

59. Daniel Daniel Rekshan and Celestial Beings, *The Book of Galactic Light: Liber Lux Galactica,* 2022, pp. 67-70.

60. J. J. Hurtak, Ph.D., *The Book of Knowledge: The Keys of Enoch,* December 1, 1996, E-book: p. 13.

61. Jacques Bergier, *Secret Doors of the Earth,* 1975, Audio book: Chapter 4, 7:57; Chapter 5, 1:45; Chapter 9, 1:39.

62. Timothy Green Beckley, et al, *Underground Alien Bio Lab at Dulce: The Bennewitz UFO Papers,* 2012, p. 27.

63. Cobra, *Resistance Movement,* The Portal: Intelligence Hub for the Victory of the Light, 2012Portal.Blogspot.com, April 2012.

64. Brad Steiger, *Star Gods: Clone Masters of the Universe,* 1997, p. 71.

65. Michael Wann, "The Field of Dreams and the Merchants of Death," *The Higherside Chats*, September 5, 2021.

66. "CERN: Where Science and the Supernatural Collide," *End Times Productions*: Youtube, Feb. 17, 2022.

67. "Fake Human Sacrifice Filmed at CERN, with Pranking Scientists Suspected," *The Guardian*, Aug 18, 2016.

68. wiki/Bohemian_Grove

69. Jade Budowski, *'House of Cards': All About The Secret Society*, Decider.com, June 2017.

69.1. Supreme Court Ethics: Last Week Tonight with John Oliver, Youtube: Last Week Tonight, Feb 22, 2024, time: 12:10.

69.2. Kid Rock Punched Someone at Bohemian Grove, Youtube: PowerfulJRE, Feb 22, 2024.

69.3. The-Bohemian-Club, britannica.com/topic/The-Bohemian-Club

69.4. Cremation of Care, wiki/Cremation_of_Care

70. Preston B. Nichols and Peter Moon, *Pyramids of Montauk: Explorations in Consciousness,* Book 3 of the Montauk series, 1995, p. 256-7.

71. Georg Ritschl, *Operation Paradise: Effective Environmental Healing With Orgone Energy*, 2007.

72. Kevin Lloyd, "The Cult in Google," Medium.com/@kwilliamlloyd/, June 2022.

73. "How a Religious Sect Landed Google in a Lawsuit," *The New York Times*, nytimes.com/2022/06/16/technology/google-fellowship-of-friends-sect.html, June 20, 2022.

74. Kelly Agan, "The World's Largest Windmill: Boone's Mod-1 Wind Turbine, 1979," *N.C. Government & Heritage Library*, NCpedia.org/worlds-largest-windmill-boone, 2016

75. From a June 7, 2021 post on Caldwell County History Hunters FB group, featuring a 1979 article about this computer. The original poster claims it was from the Lenoir News Topic or Watauga County paper, but was not sure.

76. A. K. Wilks, "Pulling the Cosmic Trigger: The Contact Experiences of Philip K. Dick & Robert Anton Wilson," ParanoiaMagazine.com, September 29, 2017.

77. Gregory L. Little, Ed.D. Twitter/X:@DrGregLittle2, July 22, 2023.

78. Cyrus Thomas, *Burial Mounds of the Northern Sections of the United States: Fifth Annual Report of the Bureau of Ethnology to the Secretary of the Smithsonian Institution, 1883-1884.*

79. Larry Clark, *Burke County, North Carolina: Historic Tales from the Gateway to the Blue Ridge*, 2007, pp. 11–12, quoted in en.wikipedia.org/wiki/ Table_Rock_(North_Carolina).

80. Sherman Carmichael, *Mysterious Tales of Western North Carolina,* 2020.

81. Commander X, *Underground Alien Bases,* 2012, p. 90.

82. Peter Champoux, GeometryOfPlace.com.

83. "Urgent Meditation to Dissipate the Attack on Zaporozhie Nuclear Power Plant Every 4 Hours," WeLoveMassMeditation.com, July 5, 2023,

84. "The Goddess Equator Grid," LeyLines.net, *The Goddess Equator,* January 24, 2023, 2012portal.blogspot.com/2023/01/the-goddess-equator.html.

85. Liz Leafloor, "Does Bimini Road Lead to The Lost Civilization of Atlantis?" Ancient-Origins.net, Sept, 2014.

86. Michael Bertiaux, *Ontological Graffiti,* 2016, p. 242.

87. Michael Wann, "Susquehanna Alchemy, River Goddess Worship, and the Big Ritual," *The Higherside Chats,* 2018.

88. Trey Hudson, "The Meadow Project: Cryptid Humanoid Stalkers, Portal Boxes, and Monkey Bears," *The Higher Side Chats,* September 2022.

89. Personal communication with Andrew Stephens, August 2008.

90. Allen Greenfield, "A Report From Arabia Mountain," Tausirhasirim.Live-Journal. com, Aug. 13, 2008, tausirhasirim.livejournal.com/89912.html?utm_source=embed_post.

91. Michael Wann, "The Field of Dreams and the Merchants of Death," *The Higherside Chats,* Sept. 5, 2021, Time: 1:36.

Section Three: Toward a Grand Unifying Theory of High Strangness

From some unknown source, I undoubtedly listen!
Telling me what I ought to hear, what I ought to know
From me it doesn't come, from me, it doesn't go –
you know what? These energies I'm keeping low.

Personal snapshot by Richard Adams of Robert Anton Wilson, 1977, at National Theatre, London, for stage version of *Illuminatus*! September 2, 2008

Chapter 7

Cosmic Synchromystic Galactic Gnostic Gonzo Group Quantum Questing

Open the door softly, down where the stories grow proud.
For all that good work, you're still a poor 11:11 scholar,
a running saint, the 2:2:2 stayer; but graced by Pan-
the wisdom of all ages and solace of the wake

Toward a new Praxis[A] of High Strangeness Research

In relation to the material presented in this book, I see myself primarily as an occult journalist, with "occult" simply meaning concealed or esoteric. Additionally, when it comes to the overall *My Cosmic Trigger* project, I assume roles as an initiator, shaman, guide, transpersonal psychotherapist, comedian, teacher and friend. I intend to explore those facets of my identity more extensively in forthcoming volumes of this book series, various classes, and podcast episodes.

The High Strangeness News Beat

My journalistic beat is the high strangeness phenomenon; which I claim is the only *real news.* This is because what we are researching here is the cosmic secret itself, anything that doesn't contend with this material is, by comparison, *fake news.* How are we to cover a beat that intersects with so many varied paranormal disciplines? How are we to study something that throws open the very nature of reality and questions our fundamental understanding of it? To answer these questions, I'm offering a new approach to the study of the phenomenon. I believe high strangeness deals with subject matter that is on the very "frontier" of thought and

---

A *Praxis* is practice infused deeply with theory and is often used because it sounds fancier to say "praxis," rather than practice.

is so "unique" and "transformative" that it's in a "subversive position to rewrite the grander logics that ensnare the mainstream."[1]

New Tools of High Strangeness Journalism

When we research this utterly absurd phenomenon it causes a radical reassessment of the fundamental nature of reality; as such, as we are trying to find the research tools of the high strangeness news beat, we must realize that something new needs to be invented, something that "deals with every aspect of experience, including those we normally would avoid or suppress." This new *something* "is not opposed to science, but on the contrary welcomes each new development and discovery as further points of illumination on the path."

Another reason a new approach needs to be invented to study high strangeness is because of the fact that "the old artificial and cultural divisions between science and magic – or alchemy and chemistry" are no longer valid. And, because these artificial distinctions are no longer valid, "humanity is on the threshold of discovery of a 'grand unified theory' of consciousness and physics." It is suggested the "occult disciplines" might possibly "hold a key to that discovery" but I maintain this grand unified theory is found in my approach to the research and practice of high strangeness, which also includes the study of occult disciplines.[2]

The approach I outline in this chapter – referred to as Cosmic, Synchromystic, Galactic, Gnostic, Gonzo, Group, Quantum, Questing (Quad G, Dub Q) – represents one discipline among many. Our use of this method and the discussion of its underlying theories are intended to bring us closer to figuring out a grand unified theory. I believe the key to unlocking this discovery rests in the hands of the well-informed high strangeness researcher. When I say "well-informed," I'm referring to a high strangeness researcher whose approach is enriched by a blend of mystical/occult/shamanistic traditions and New Age philosophies – this is what I'm calling "high strangeness magick."

A New Approach

In his book, *The Meadow Project: Explorations into the South's Skinwalker Ranch*, Trey Hudson says when researching this anomalous site he found out the "traditional method" of paranormal research was "not sufficient." He said this because the high strangeness phenomena they found there were "crossing into too many disciplines ... to address these events from a single field of study." As a result, he says a "new approach and set of protocols" will need to be developed to "document" cases of "extreme high strangeness."[3] What follows is my attempt at developing a new approach and set of protocols.

The Best Tool: Yourself

The important thing to remember in this new approach is that: the most valuable asset in investigating high strangeness phenomena is the subjective experience of the observer. This doesn't imply the exclusion of conventional research methods but rather emphasizes our complete acceptance of the notion that the ultimate frontier of paranormal exploration lies within us. This is due to the integral role played by human consciousness in the manifestation of high strangeness. In short, this new approach underscores the significance of the observer's mind in the research.[B]

This unconventional approach to the study of the paranormal relies heavily on the researcher's personal experiences to gauge the credibility of investigations. Those who adhere to traditional methods often view this approach as the least reliable, as conventional wisdom prioritizes objective research. However, I am maintaining that the more subjectively weird the evidence is, the more reliable it is. This concept finds a concrete illustration in the synchronicities associated with the "trash stratum" in the *Hellier* series, as I explored in chapter 2.

Psychic Questing

For more direction as we grope toward a new praxis of high strangeness research we turn to psychic questing. Noted author and researcher Andrew Collins is considered as "having coined the term" in the 80s. It is defined as "using intuitively inspired thoughts and information" for research into things such as "the exploration of history, the search for hidden artifacts" or the "quest for enlightenment."[4]

The Green Stone

In October 1979, Andrew Collins and Graham Phillips discovered a short steel sword with an unusual design, sparking what is known as the "modern revival in psychic questing." Their experiences inspired Graham Phillips to co-write a book, *The Green Stone* (1984), chronicling their

B I am unable to find the source this notion comes from. If any reader knows where it comes from please let me know and I will properly cite it in future editions of this book. Also, my desire is for this book to be encyclopedic in scope, so if you find a theory or idea I do not properly cite, please let me know.

quest. The book follows their pursuit in following a "trail of cryptic clues to discover a hidden green gemstone" that is "said to hold ancient supernatural power" and was also once "possessed by … a secret society called The Order of Meonia."[4]

Upon taking the stone to the office of their magazine "inexplicable events, witnessed by dozens of observers, began to occur," such as an "unexplained … incense-smelling smoke" that "filled the entire building each night as darkness fell," paranormal sounds were also heard such as "footsteps, eerie noises and unearthly voices" which "drove terrified visitors away" while "an odious blue, gelatinous substance oozed from the walls," as well as an "ominous, dark, faceless figure," appearing and disappearing, then finally a "sleeping bag of a member of the team spontaneously combusted as he slept in the building overnight."[5]

Historical Antecedents

Psychic questing is not a modern invention; Collins and Phillips just started the modern revival of the practice. A historical example "of the form it can take is to be found in John Boormans' film[C] *Excalibur* where the Grail Knights went seeking the Grail[D] through the use of dreams and portents."[6] There are also examples of "recorded instances of holy men or women being inspired to find hidden relics (e.g. Joan of Arc)" and of occultists using magick to "find buried treasure" and "psychics being brought in to uncover archaeological remains (e.g., Frederick Bligh-Bond)."[4]

It has historical antecedents in Tibetan Buddhism where it is known as "the Terma ('hidden treasure') tradition, and whole books have been written on the processes involved." The "monks who become involved in Terma hunting are known as Tertons ('treasure finders')."[4] The Terma spiritual tradition consists of ancient teachings and practices that were hidden by Guru Padmasambhava in the 8th century for the benefit of future generations.[7] These teachings are believed to have been hidden both physically and in the minds of the lineage holders to protect said teachings from persecution and to preserve them for future generations.[8] Notice again the presence of secrecy in this practice, which again invokes the idea of a cosmic battle between good and evil, making obfuscation necessary.

C I believe the film, *Close Encounters of the 3rd Kind* and *Oh Brother Where Art Thou*? are also examples of psychic quests.

D *The Gralien Report* is a podcast "about space, science, futurism, archaeology, and the mysteries of our universe...The word Gralien is a portmanteau that combines 'grail' and 'alien.'...the mythical idea of a long-sought and prized 'grail,' paired with our search for life elsewhere in the cosmos, are concepts that bridge the gap between humankind's ancient past, and our aspirations for future scientific discovery" (Gralienreport.com/about/ by Micah Hanks).

According to tradition, these teachings are later rediscovered by *tertöns,* or "treasure revealers," who are spiritual masters with the ability to find and reveal these hidden treasures. Further, the discovery of these hidden treasures (*termas*) occur during times of crisis, when the world is in need of spiritual renewal, because "Termas are considered especially ... powerful in the conferring of blessing in this present age" and it "is thought that terma teachings are custom-made for the time they are to be discovered and disseminated."[9] It is also said termas are hidden in the past "for the benefit of [a] future generation" and only appear "When the right times appear then again."[10]

At present, our planet is in the midst of a profound spiritual crisis, and it is imperative that we address this issue with urgency. We can do this by embracing our role as high strangeness *treasure revealers,* thereby playing a crucial role in healing our planet. This is because our research into the phenomenon can help us unlock the secrets of the universe and allow us to understand the cosmic forces that govern our world. This understanding is the real treasure, as it contributes to the evolution of human consciousness.

How to Psychic Quest

Collins says that a psychic quest "can begin with a strange dream, a visionary experience or an overwhelming compulsion which prompts the person to embark on a sequence of discovery." Speaking from experience, I can guess that high strangeness researchers are more often prompted by an "overwhelming compulsion" and I hope this chapter opens up more researchers to the influence of dreams and visions to guide them. I think the traditional high strangeness researcher may be reluctant to engage in such approaches because it is too close to New Age practices. However, we can discover hidden "confirmatory facts" when we visit "places revealed only by intuition" and communication with "external forces." This is achieved "through either meditational practices or magical processes."[4] Such an "external force" might be "a site guardian figure (a thought-form left behind from the past to watch over and spiritually care for the site)."[11]

Sacred Sites

The act of questing involves a journey, both physical and spiritual, in which one seeks to connect with something greater than oneself.

This can be achieved by traveling to a "sacred place … and see what happens to you"[12] in the now. By immersing oneself in the environment and energy of such a site, one may experience a shift in consciousness and gain deeper insight into one's own life journey. Traveling to a sacred site can involve a "search for hidden artefacts or simply the quest for enlightenment."[4] The important point here is that one can be looking to discover a tangible object or looking for the intangible, spiritual enlightenment.

We can say this intangible aspect is akin to a "pilgrimage" which is "part trip and part ritual" and "is prescribed in all the religious traditions for those seeking healing and renewal."[12] This is because visiting sacred sites can help to transcend the ordinary, everyday reality and tap into a higher consciousness and in so doing – individuals can find direction in their lives. As a psychotherapist and researcher of high strangeness, I recognize the transformative potential of questing. By stepping outside of one's comfort zone and exploring unfamiliar territory, individuals may confront their fears and gain a fresh perspective on their lives. The act of questing can be a powerful tool for psycho-spiritual development[E] and I believe that by focusing on this aspect, the high strangeness researcher can be provided the necessary grounding and healing needed to keep them psychologically sane, while going down the rabbit hole.

Archival Research

Archival research is a crucial part of psychic questing, as it offers context and validation for psychic insights; lacking a solid historical foundation may lead to unreliable results. It can also help to uncover obscure historical information which may be relevant to a psychic quest. This historical foundation can help deepen the insights gained through highly strange means – giving balance to the quester because it is providing historical context to one's psychically obtained information.

Magick

Psychic questing has been defined as a "combination of archival research and magical and psychical techniques" and the "similarity of this to a pragmatic approach to magick … will become apparent quite quickly, for both are concerned with Results."[13] A "close analogy here is chaos magick[F] where whatever tradition is most appropriate for a partic-

E I have witnessed this first hand in my psychotherapy practice, as clients have reported becoming psycho-spiritually renewed after visiting sacred sites.

F "Kenneth Grant himself was clearly acquainted with Collins"[14] as evidenced by his anal-

ular quest is adopted (and then discarded when not needed)."[14] In the *Hellier* TV series, magical and psychical techniques – such as tarot cards, ritual invocation, and spirit boxes – were utilized in their research.[G]

How to Psychic Quest Conclusion

There is a bold claim that the Green Stone quest was "the greatest paranormal drama played out in Britain in the twentieth century."[15] This leads us to ponder "how can such a forgotten, fringe practice possibly be" so important? Perhaps the reason it has been forgotten is *because* it is so important. The magick of high strangeness realizes that and readily accepts that questing is "a genuinely esoteric practice" and "merits inclusion in the domain of study known as 'Western Esotericism.'"[14] I first learned of psychic questing[H] in the summer of 2021 while writing this book. I was so blown away by what I learned of it in general and the green stone quest in particular, that I was inspired to create a painting about Meonia and the green stone.

Cosmic Synchromystic Galactic Gnostic Gonzo Group Quantum Questing

The previous section explained an approach to high strangeness research, psychic questing. I am proposing the following term for a new type of research method that includes psychic questing and attempts to take it further: Cosmic, Synchromystic, Galactic, Gnostic, Gonzo, Quantum, Questing. With my tongue in cheek, I call this the *Quad G, Dub Q* approach. I feel that further elucidation of this technique will enable high strangeness researchers to be more successful. Yes, I am aware that it could well be argued that I'm just proposing a new type of psychic questing and not coming up with a new approach *per se*.

Cosmic

The inclusion of the cosmic dimension in this approach reminds us to keep in mind that "consciousness is more than an accidental by-prod-

ysis of the word Meonia in his book *The Ninth Arch*.

G The team specifically used the "Estes Method" of working with spirit boxes which "is some kind of digitally-enhanced mediumship or" it "could even be considered digital/technologically-aided scrying" (AstonishingLegends.com/astonishing-legends/2019/2/16/estes-method).

H The concept of the psychic quest is explored in the *Penny Royal* podcast, as it relates to the high strangeness research of the *Hellier* TV show and their podcast. Upon learning the history and practice of psychic questing, the host speculates that both projects are a type of psychic quest. (Season 2, Episode 3, 59 mins).

uct of the...biochemical processes taking place in the human brain." This fact challenges us to view "consciousness and the human psyche as ... reflections of a cosmic intelligence that permeates the entire universe." I propose that our research into high strangeness will be more productive if we embody the reality that we are "fields of consciousness without limits, transcending time, space, matter, and linear causality."[16] Cosmic also invokes RAW's *Cosmic Trigger* series. I propose that practitioners look at their Quad G, Dub Q research as pulling their individual Cosmic Trigger. This is where the My Cosmic Trigger hyper-sigil comes into play: we need as many people pulling their own cosmic triggers as possible, this is the magick of high strangeness.

Synchromystic

A big difference between my approach and traditional psychic questing is that it embraces the field of Synchromysticism, which is "an emerging field of study" that exists "on the fringe of areas already considered fringe – primarily mysticism and Jungian psychology." The term was coined by Jake Kotze in 2006 when he defined it as "The art of realizing meaningful coincidence in the seemingly mundane with mystical or esoteric significance."[17] Notice that it is an approach about finding the mystical significance in the mundane, which reminds me of finding the truth in the trash stratum. Finding truth in the mundane and/or trash stratum is a major component of my approach to psychic questing.

The synchromystic view of synchronicities takes a different stance toward the nature of reality. That is, when one is down the rabbit hole it is not that helpful to get so concerned about what is true and false. This is a good stance to be able to take towards synchronicities because from one point of view the "idea about the significance of meaningful coincidences in movies" for example, "is not that it points towards real truths, but that they point towards possible realities that might emerge from the collective psyche into consensus reality."[17] At certain points in our research it is best to not "fret about what 'is' real" and instead put our attention to "checking the zeitgeists' temperature in order to project future possibilities ... and find hidden pockets of knowledge embedded in the pattern" of reality.[17] If researchers can be less strictly focused on what is *really real* then it opens them up to find these hidden pockets of knowledge and facilitate a positive future.

I like the approach of synchromysticism because it helps us get more up to date regarding how synchronicities manifest in our modern world.

It deals with "esoteric mystical symbolism" along with the "use of communications technology to document, share and compare synchronicities related to such symbols from ancient traditions throughout the mass media landscape."[17] In 2024, we aren't just meeting people at the village well anymore. We live online, communicating with hundreds of people per day and are being confronted with countless streams of information. In this infinite flow of data we are also confronted with seeing numbers more than at anytime in human history – they are on every email, receipt, and text message. This relatively new technological environment allows synchronicity to manifest more frequently than it did in the past. As such, synchromysticism is a unique product of the technological times we live in and this mystical approach could not have existed in Ancient Egypt for example.

Jake Kotze claims a big inspiration for him was the author Adachi. Some of you may be familiar with the work of the synchromystics and might be thinking it is all a little too schizo to use as a serious research methodology. But it gets weirder, as "Adachi claims that he is 'communicating with Enki' in his words, something akin to the schizophrenic delusion of talking to God or having some sort of communication with a hive mind (angels, aliens)." However, as I like to say, it's only crazy if it isn't true. So if he really is communicating with Enki, then he is merely telling the truth. As high strangeness research shows us, the truth has a stubborn tendency to be stranger than fiction and utterly absurd. And even if Adachi's belief is a symptom of mental illness the fact that he "identifies his work as communication with an entity which structures reality" (which is "the hallmark of psychosis") it "makes the product of his labor no less interesting, provided one understands it metaphorically."[18]

We can turn to the Jungians for guidance on how to look at findings of the synchromystics from a metaphorical perspective. Renowned Jungian, Marie-Louise von Franz, gives guidance on how to understand the power of the unconscious process, pointing out that "even the most bewildering and disjointed" expressions of schizophrenic patients could be deciphered into "intelligible speech," provided one has enough "patience and knowledge of the unconscious."[18] She posits that encounters with the unconscious hold the potential to "uncover something like 'great truths'" through the use of "metaphor and irony," but only if one is willing to invest time and effort to unravel their hidden meanings. She is suggesting that a deep appreciation and understanding of the unconscious is essential to uncovering the profound insights of reality. So, even if we don't agree that the findings of the synchromystic are literally true, we can get something out of their findings by looking at the insights from a "metaphoric perspective." To me, the important thing to remember is that "by remaining in the twilight of the unconscious, synchro-mystics, like other mystics, shamans and schizophrenics throughout the ages, can accidentally happen across tremendous insights."[18]

It is said that synchromystics "explore the ... unconscious" bringing "back insights to the conscious dayworld albeit" some would argue "in distorted form."[18] I add the caveat that *some would argue* because I think it is wrong to assume all the findings of the synchromystic are in a distorted form. In my estimation the truth lies in the middle, some appear distorted and some appear uncannily perceptive. Also, as I write this in late 2023, with consensus reality getting stranger and stranger, I feel it is highly disingenuous and intellectually dishonest to dismiss all of the findings of the synchromystics, out of hand.

What Synchromysticism Helps Us Do

In general the synchromystic perspective is an "alchemical technique" that puts us in a state of mind when we are doing our research that enables us to have "a means to connect a diverse range of information and ideas, as well as a way to see the world from a more open perspective." It allows us to "create meaning out of the chaos of current events and seemingly vapid commercial detritus that bombards us on a daily basis," meaning it is a tool that allows us to spin cosmic consciousness gold out of today's pop-culture straw/trash. It also allows us "to add new layers of meaning to more enduring and celebrated works of art,"[17] allowing us to see new points of meaning that previous generations have missed.

Synchromysticism can also be a tool that "help us forecast and respond to trends developing in the collective unconscious [or] noosphere," and when we are able to see these trends we are then able "to reclaim culture and steer it in a more positive direction or, at the very least, provide a fun and interesting new application for mass media."[17] Steering culture away from the dark cliff it is on and/or having some fun with mass media sounds good to me. Psychic questing is not concerned with pop-culture, mass media, nor items in the trash stratum – which I say to point out the differences from the Quad G, Dub Q approach to that of traditional psychic questing.

Synchromysticism can also help us decode twilight language, "the visible spectrum of" the matrix which "is rendered invisible through our willful forgetfulness." In order to be the best high strangeness practitioners we can be, the more we need to shake off our forgetfulness by remembering the spell the "sorcerous system of things" has over us.[19] No one is capable of an emancipatory act when enthralled by this spell.

Synchromysticism also helps us create an "empowering map" for people who are "seeking emancipation from simulation."[19] In the study of high strangeness people often fall into a trap of just researching and not acting. For example, the "Consumption of the knowledge ... of Twilight Language" is actually "an act of enthralment not liberation." The way around this trap is "the study and analysis of" twilight language's "function as neuro-linguistic programming,"[19] meaning we are seeing how the spell is negatively impacting us.

Overall, Synchromysticism can help us make sense of our highly strange reality by providing a framework for understanding the connections between multiple layers of meaning. When we explore the synchronicities and patterns that exist between seemingly unrelated events and symbols, we gain a deeper understanding of the hidden meanings that underlie them. Once we have this deeper understanding, we are able to have more informed Quad G, Dub Q research expeditions. This is important because it is when we are active in our research that we get free from the "psychological and spiritual bondage" that armchair practitioners are stuck in because they only "partake" of high strangeness research "to obtain a more thrilling shock of recognition concerning their own demise."[19]

Proto-Synchromysticism

This approach is new but "the fundamental concepts that synchromysticism draws upon have connections to mystic traditions as old as shamanism."[17] In modern times, James Shelby Downard is considered to be the first "proto-synchromystic." This is seen in the fact that he used "any source, street and river names, dates (and specific clock times), meridian lines" that he could find as "clues and meaning behind Kennedy's death," an approach that "is pure synchromysticism."[20]

The New Orleans district attorney, Jim Garrison, also used a proto-synchromystic approach in his indictment of Clay Shaw. In 1967 he "wrote a five-page memo called 'Time and Propinquity: Factors in Phase I,' which revealed ... connections he was making in his attempt to outline what he believed was the true nature of the assassination of President John F. Kennedy." He "believed that the best way to uncover" the mystery "was by noticing seeming coincidences – when two people happened to live a few blocks from each other or when someone ran a bar around the corner from where a cache of heroin was seized."[21]

Galactic

My approach is galactic insofar as it reminds us of the evidence pointing to the utterly absurd possibility that we are in the throes of an intergalactic war between the cosmic forces of good and evil. Curiously enough, when one starts down this utterly absurd rabbit hole you are led to this conclusion. A high strangeness researcher explains it by saying "I started out a few years ago to make a movie on Bigfoot" and "have ended up wondering if there is a war in the heavens between forces from the Dogstar and those of the Great Hunter."[22]

RAW stumbles across the same possibility in the first volume of *Cosmic Trigger,* when he recounts a conversation he had with Grady McMurtry, who is most known for reviving the OTO from 1971 to his death in 1985. McMurtry says that "For years I've been asking … everybody else I know: why does the gnosis always get busted? Every single time … large scale group illuminations are occurring, the local branch of the Inquisition kills it dead." Going on, he thinks it is due to the fact "There's war in Heaven. The higher Intelligences … aren't all playing on the same team. Some of them are trying to encourage our evolution … and some of them want to keep us stuck just where we are."[23]

This is also echoed by noted author, Richard C. Hoagland,[I] when he addresses the skeptical normie question of "if there exists a benevolent highly technological group of extraterrestrials trying to evolve human kind, then why are we in this fucking mess?" To this overly simplistic question, he answers: "Who says it's only one group? Maybe there are competing forces. Maybe there is a liberation force and a suppression force." He says this cosmic war may be a "competition between two forces. One to keep us in the dark and the other to provide us with the means to climb out of the dark into the light but it can only work during these narrow windows, about once every 26,000 years." He claims "that time has now come. We are at the tip of the spear, and all the good guys for enlightenment need to … pull their resources, assemble their knowledge, and make the final push and give everybody the knowledge of who we really are."[24]

This idea of a battle between good UFOnauts and bad UFOnauts is not a new idea and has been talked about in the literature as early as the late 1950s when an early contactee[J] claimed to have been told that the

---

I Hoagland is most known for publicizing the so-called "face on Mars." See his 2001 book, *The Monuments of Mars: A City on the Edge of Forever* and his most recent interview on *The Higherside Chats*: "Richard C. Hoagland: UFO Shoot-downs, NASA Rituals, and Moon Ruins Confirmed," Feb. 2023.

J *From Outer Space to You* by Howard Menger, 1959.

earth "is the battlefield of Armageddon, and the battle is for men's minds and souls."[25] If we are indeed in a cosmic war between the force of light and dark then this means high strangeness researchers are akin to war correspondents, which brings me to the next section.

Gonzo Journalism

Gonzo journalism was popularized by Hunter S. Thompson (1937-2005) and is "a style of reporting that places the reporter at the centre of the story in a highly personal and participatory way."[26] The author is the "protagonist" of the story they are reporting on, "simultaneously experiencing and reporting on a story from a first-person point of view."[27] It is not like traditional journalism that seeks to find an objective truth. This is because Thompson believed objectivity in journalism was a myth, saying that "With the possible exception of things like box scores, race results, and stock market tabulations, there is no such thing as Objective Journalism. The phrase itself is a pompous contradiction in terms."[28] An objective approach was not powerful enough to expose some truths, he said for example that "You had to get Subjective to see Nixon clearly, and the shock of recognition was often painful." This approach also deals with the "interplay of fact and fiction," which is "continually shifting but" when the "right balance is struck, the results can be devastating."[29]

Humor is an essential tool in the praxis of Gonzo journalism, employing "satire, hyperbole, scathing critique, and shocking descriptions as part of the story." Thompson used humor to great effect, as "during his peak years" he was "the pre-eminent satirist of his day, essentially using fiction to present truth more effectively than anyone could through more conventional means."[29] This use of humor was used to challenge conventional wisdom, reveal the absurdities of society, and build connections between the writer and the reader. Using humor and keeping our tongues firmly in our cheeks (at times) is a helpful stance to take to material so strange on the one hand and so profoundly important on the other. If a cosmic war between the forces of good and evil for control of the multiverse isn't something to joke about, then I don't know what is.

The inclusion of the art of gonzo journalism into the praxis of the Quad G, Dub Q approach is another way this approach is departing from the traditional psychic questing approach. Psychic questing is more of a New Age spiritual praxis and often humor can be sorely lacking in New Age disciplines. Humor helps further our research because, if you're laughing you're learning and it also helps us stay psychologically grounded.

The journalistic stance (publishing our highly strange research findings) allows us to get this material out to other people. To have any hope of deciphering the phenomenon we need as many eyes on it as possible, meaning we must report on our findings, no matter how strange they are. Noted Synchromstic Michael Wann, describes himself as a "Synchromystic-Apocalyptic Storyteller, Gonzo" researcher,[30] claiming that his research has "turned more and more into what I call gonzo research" because in the stories he researches he "always" finds himself "smack dab in the middle of it."[31]

In summary, gonzo journalism is a highly subjective and immersive style of journalism in which the writer is an active participant in the story they are covering. I believe this is the best approach to get to the truth in mainstream topics and even more so when it comes to high strangeness reporting. Gonzo journalism is a radical but still relatively mundane approach to investigation. Other, more paranormal, "awakened investigative skills are key," in this type of research. These skills "are abilities we must develop to pierce" the "veil" because untruth can not "long survive true awakened investigative skills."[26] We can "uncover and connect: clues and evidence utilizing rational investigative methods initially but then utilize intuitive paranormal mechanisms in order to reach" more "Para-investigative conclusions."[32]

Gnostic

The Quad G, Dub Q approach is a gnostic spiritual practice. This is due to the fact that the subject matter of high strangeness can't be fully comprehended with our current level of intelligence because "consciousness in its limited human phase cannot apprehend the significance of this transcendental" phenomenon.[33] It is also gnostic because the truth of high strangeness is "not intellectual but mythical and comes through special revelation."[34]

In short, the highly strange must be grasped via a gnostic knowing – one has to grok (to understand profoundly and intuitively) the phenomenon. The inclusion of "gnostic" also implies the Quad G, Dub Q approach is a magical one. I will further explain my magick of high strangeness in volume 2 of this series (*My Cosmic Trigger: Perilous Chapels and Highly Strange Magick*) but I will now point out that the more we approach our Quad G, Dub Q workings as a magickal act[K] the more we will have fruitful results.

K This approach is similar to so-called magical workings, the most famous of which was Crowley's, The Amalantrah Working (Jan. 14 to June 16th, 1918).

Group

In high strangeness research we see that group work is particularly helpful because when researching the phenomenon one encounters "patterns" that are "just a little out of sync enough ... that you can never quite get it all" and as a result "you can only be observing your side of it." Because one can only observe their side of the elephant,[L] "working with other people ... is supremely helpful." While everyone in the group is looking at their part, we can also "hold the space for one another" energetically. This energetic holding allows individuals to have greater access to their ability to "get more of a feeling for the whole."

Also, the more people you have allows more parts of the whole to be viewed because "you may not be able to see all of it but you can see your part. And then if you have more people you can see more ... parts" of the elephant. This approach to studying subjects is not new and is "the whole idea of a multidisciplinary approach in science."[35] A synergy of like minds expands research. Also, the group aspect has a positive psycho-spiritual benefit. High strangeness research and practice is stressful because we are looking at phenomena that drastically change our view of reality. We need our brothers and sisters to help provide emotional support as we head down the rabbit hole together.

Quantum

The concept of Quantum Consciousness can be seen as synonymous with "unity consciousness." This is a familiar idea in human history, as many Eastern traditions, and Western philosophies, have long emphasized the presence of "an underlying unity that connects us all." Previously, individuals had to adopt a specific "belief system" (such as specific religion) to embark on "a pathway" towards experiencing this unity. However, the "quantum approach" to "unity consciousness" distinguishes itself through its reliance on science.[36]

Unlike Newtonian physics, which viewed the world as a collection of simple cause-and-effect units, the principles of quantum physics highlight the interconnectedness of all things. Quantum physics indicates that there is an underlying scientific reality behind the interconnectedness of all things. This approach is based on a "Quantum Reality" which embraces a "Quantum Logic." The "quantum revolution goes so deep that replacing new concepts with old will not suffice. To cope with the quantum facts we must scrap our very mode of reasoning, in favor of a new quantum logic." We have to embrace a new kind of logic because the "world obeys

L See the parable of the blind men and the elephant.

a non-human kind of reasoning." Science and philosophy show us that "*Logic* is the skeleton of our body of knowledge." However, we need to embrace one of the "crazy logics" because it "may be just what we need to make sense out of quantum events."[37]

High strangeness phenomena consist of these so-called quantum events that can only be deciphered by "crazy logics," a quantum logic which is "an attempt to jump out of normal human waking consciousness and arrive at a place that cannot be found on any map, not even maps of the mind." This map-less state of mind "is a state of pure perception, without conscious editing of the experience."[2] The more we can enter this state of mind during our research the better it will go.

There exists a strange fact in high strangeness research that occurs when we are investigating the phenomenon, which is the copious amount of synchronicities one encounters. These synchronicities are so numerous it causes one to ask "What forces are there really at work here?" This is a very common question that comes up for researchers as "Anybody who begins to investigate" high strangeness type subjects will eventually find themselves "bedeviled" by the sheer amount of "coincidences that we come across." The Kennedy assassination mystery "is probably the most famous example" where people report coming "across dozens and then hundreds and then maybe thousands of 'coincidental' connections, between people, places, and events, which drives them crazy." A "regular ... mainstream historian's going to say ... that was a coincidence ... and dismiss them all because he cannot see a real cause-and-effect relationship." The weirdness one encounters in this research "is an indication that something else is at work" and because of that fact "we need a quantum consciousness approach to history itself, not just to our own minds."[38] I humbly submit my Quad G, Dub Q approach as one such quantum consciousness approach to history.

Questing as a Healing Act

One aspect of psychic questing that appeals to me and which I believe high strangeness researchers could benefit from, is that it emphasizes how quests are journeys of self-improvement that take place within one's own psyche. We can say that psychic questing is not only concerned with exploring the mysteries of the physical universe, but also concerned with exploring the mysteries within ourselves. This focus on the healing component will help high strangeness researchers not go insane as they conduct their investigations, which brings me to the next section.

Dangers

Researching high strangeness is not without danger. One of the pitfalls is extreme thinking which can "distort our perception" of the phenomenon. Another danger is "total immersion in trivial aspects of a case that ends up muddying the key elements of pattern detection." One must have "enlightened pattern detection" or looking at the manifestations of high strangeness can cause "obfuscation, not clarification." There is a tendency to "begin to see coincidences everywhere" and as a result there needs to be discernment, which can be found if we "remain mindful of how *our perception itself becomes part of the process of invocation.*"

A researcher that can't properly detect the pattern "can't grok what is insubstantial" or a "false lead." It is important to remember that "as in any language, one encounters gibberish and some sleuths are misled into believing it has significance," and so we "should be keenly aware that not everything in the symbolic stream is of profound remarkability." Properly discerning between "profound remarkability" and "signal noise – is the difference between a higher state of consciousness and a form of debilitation that can mimic the classic symptoms of mental illness."[19,M]

Personal Experiences

I have officially conducted two pilot Quad G, Dub Q workings to test my new approach and have not been disappointed. The first was to Brown Mountain, North Carolina (February 2023) and the second occurred in Istanbul, European-side (March 2023). By looking at the techniques I employed we can get closer to a systematic methodology.

Follow the Breadcrumbs of Your Bliss

This technique is akin to tracing a trail of synchromystic breadcrumbs to a mysterious destination. Driven by our innate curiosity (and perhaps by forces unseen) we leave no clue unexamined in our quest for that which lies beyond the boundaries of mundane reality. Joseph Campbell claims to have "a superstition that has grown ... as a result of invisible hands coming all the time" to help him when he followed his bliss. He says that if you "follow your bliss you put yourself on a kind of track" of "the life that you ought to be living" and when you do this "you begin to meet people who are in your field of bliss, and they open doors to you." This is the perfect state of mind to be in while conducting high strange-

M See, @NickHintonn's Aug 16, 2023, Twitter post, for a look at the dangers associated with this research (twitter.com/NickHintonn/status/1691907851063541786).

ness research, so "follow your bliss and don't be afraid, and doors will open where you didn't know they were going to be."[39]

Psycho-Spiritual Healing

Attempting to grow closer with your research partners is important because we are healed in relationship with others. And as the saying goes, *maybe the real treasure was the friends we made along the way.*[N] However, researching the cosmic mystery itself may be easy when compared to tackling interpersonal conflict.

Book/Info Exchange

This is a general sharing of books and articles between individuals of a similar mind. My research partner for the Brown Mountain working had a significant synchronicity with a rare journal I shared with him during this process. One person's dusty book on the shelf is another's mind blowing synchronicity.

Trash Stratum

I mean this quite literally, look at what is in the trash while on a research expedition. What was found in the trash stratum in the *Hellier* series was a tin can and a series of mylar balloons. The synchronicities the crew had around those pieces of trash, essentially, made the entire investigation. So, don't be shy about looking at the trash in the area you are researching.

Eat Local

When you are researching an area don't eat at chain restaurants, eat at long established local eateries. For one it is just good practice to support small business over mega-corporations and two, there is more of the area's energy found at local restaurants. Connecting with the area's mojo found at a local eatery will help with one's research. Local restaurants also provide ample opportunities for utilizing mystical toponymy.

Fireside Thoughts

At the end of a long day on a research outing it is important to gather around the campfire, metaphorically and literally if possible, because

N "Perhaps the most popular example of the cliché comes from the 1985 film *Stand By Me*, in which a group of pre-teen boys go on a quest to see a dead body. At the end of the film, the story's narrator concludes that their friendship was the most important part of the journey." (knowyourmeme.com/memes/maybe-the-real-treasure-was-the-friends-we-made-along-the-way).

fire is psychologically grounding and also ties us to the energy of grandfather fire.[O] This is where we really feel the importance of the group component of this approach, when we relax after a long day and talk with our friends about our experiences of the day and theorize what we think they mean.

News (Local and National)

During, preceding, and right after your expedition pay attention to the local news. In the Brown Mountain expedition I was alerted to look at the news (after overhearing patrons talking about angels and the balloon sightings). It just so happened that when we were doing our expedition that weekend, the now infamous Chinese weather balloons were directly over Western North Carolina. There was also a UFO sighting in Caldwell County on February 17, 2023, approximately 2 weeks after our expedition. This sighting was posted on a local woman's Facebook page. Based on my knowledge of such matters and based on her description, it appeared to be an experimental terrestrial craft using technology that is not in the public domain. When one sees a UFO it is important to determine if it is a secret craft of human origin or one of extraterrestrial origin.

Randonaut

The main tool I used in my Istanbul Quad G, Dub expedition was the Randonautica app, which generates random coordinates within a given radius of the user's location. The app utilizes a quantum random number generator to produce these coordinates. The idea behind the app is that rarely do we randomly visit places outside our habits. Meaning, even when we think we are just walking or driving randomly, we are being guided by unconscious patterns. As such, the creators speculated that we are never able to truly visit random locations and the app was designed to bypass this fact. Further, they speculated that by visiting truly random locations we are able to break outside the matrix.

Users are encouraged to set an intention for their journey before asking the App to give them a random location, with the idea being that the intention will guide the experience in a meaningful way. The community has had some pretty uncanny reports of intentions being set and then being led to a site that meets the intention. For example, one incident gained media attention in 2020, when two teenage girls in Seattle claimed

O "Grandfather Fire's wisdom brings relationship, healing and connection to difficult times" (sacredfire.org/fire-speaks/).

they had used the app to generate a set of coordinates, which led them to a suitcase containing human remains. The discovery led to a police investigation for the person responsible for the death. The case received widespread media attention, in part due to its unusual connection to the Randonautica app.[40]

The app has gained popularity in recent years which has been interesting to watch because I was part of the early Randonaut community circa 2018. This was when the app's functioning was only available through the community's Telegram channel. High strangeness author Nick Hinton[P] has been linked to the initial team that developed and tested out the approach.[Q]

During my Istanbul research expedition, my intention, when asking the app to randomly select my location, was to provide me a spot that would be a good test case for my Quad G, Dub Q approach. The location it led me to was an abandoned park in the near center of Istanbul, near the famous Taksim square. The park was in disrepair and was fenced off, but I was led directly to the door of the park, which was chained. I found this location very significant because my entire praxis of high strangeness magick is to turn your own backyard into sacred spaces and this abandoned park was definitely one ripe for that.

Dreams

Pay attention to your dreams preceding, during and immediately after a research expedition. Also, share those dreams with your research partners in the event there is a synchronicity between your dream and their individual research. The use of dreams to solve high strangeness mysteries is also seen in the TV show *Twin Peaks*, as the main investigator has a dream which is the "key to cracking the murder case ... ultimately" leading him to find "the person who brutally murdered Laura Palmer."[41]

Travel

This approach naturally requires one to travel to a location to investigate it. Noted author George Hansen speaks about the curious fact that people experience more synchronicities when they travel, specifical-

P See, Hinton on *The Duncan Trussell Family Hour*, episode 510, (duncantrussell.com/episodes/2022/6/24/nick-hinton) and *The Higherside Chats*, March 31, 2021, "Nick Hinton: The Saturn Time Cube, Tyler, & The Plasma Apocalypse."

Q "Nick Hinton, was the PR front man for Randonautica ... and he is no longer on their team" ("Is the Randonautica App Changing Our Timelines as We Speak?" psychicbabes.com), "Nick Hinton, a 24-year-old philosophy student at the University of Toledo, is an admin of /r/randonauts" ("I Tried to Glitch the Simulation and All I Got Was a Bottle of Pee," Tamlin Magee, Aug. 2019, TheOutline.com).

ly when they travel for vacation to places that "are a little out of the way" from where they normally travel.[R,42] This strange fact and the experiences with the Randonautic app implies that synchronicities manifest more readily when we get outside of our habitual patterns.

Conclusions

The initial results I've had with this approach were profound, leading me to firmly believe in its effectiveness. This research reveals an underlying strangeness in reality that surpasses our wildest imaginings. I am of the belief that we require a revolutionary research method to comprehend and study this strange reality. The traditional methods fall far short of this goal, but the quad G dub Q approach is one such method up to the task. My approach builds upon the foundation of psychic questing and I encourage others to develop their own methodologies as they delve deeper into high strangeness.

Let's come together, form our own groups, unravel mysteries, and thwart villains (literal and metaphoric) – just like the investigative team in *Scooby Doo*. The most famous line from the TV show, "And I would have gotten away with it too, if it weren't for you meddling kids!"[43] sums up the actions of the characters in the series who solve mysteries beyond their pay grade, due to some mysterious ability brought out by their unique group gestalt (and of course aided by Scooby snacks). This playfully illustrates the power of this approach.

Looking at it more seriously, we will explore the "wisdom teaching … conveyed in the story of Rumplestiltskin." That the maiden in this fairy tale has "the ability to successfully produce his name is not often the focus of the story." We are left to ask how she managed "to locate and then approach unseen, the secluded wilderness camp of a troll so powerful" he can magically turn straw into gold. The "enigmatic power that allows her to achieve this coup is the sub-rosa dimension of the tale"[19] and the Quad G, Dub Q approach seeks to harness this enigmatic power as we research high strangeness.

References

1. Jacob W. Glazier, PhD, "Deconstructing the Paranormal: Toward a Critical Parapsychology," *Mindfield: The Bulletin of the Parapsychological Association*, Vol. 13, Issue 3, 2021.

R [R] He claimed he found this concept in the book, *Synchronicity: Through the Eyes of Science, Myth and the Trickster* by A. Combs, 2000.

2. Peter Levenda and Jeffrey Evans, *Rites of the Mummy: The K'rla Cell and the Secret Key to Liber AL*, Nov. 2021, E-book: p. 97, 89.

3. Trey Hudson, *The Meadow Project: Explorations into the South's Skinwalker Ranch*, Oct. 2020, Audio book: Chapter 7, 20:00.

4. Andrew Collins, "What is Psychic Questing?" AndrewCollins.com.

5. Andrew Collins and Graham Phillips, *The Green Stone*, publisher's summary.

6. Paolo Sammut, "Psychic Questing," LiminalWhispers.com, liminalwhispers.com/psychic-questing.

7. Pema Dragpa, "Hidden for the Sake of Future Generations," May 2018, Padmasambhava.org.

8. Holly Gayley, "Ontology of the Past and Its Materialization in Tibetan Treasures," in the book: *The Invention of Sacred Tradition*, pp. 213-240.

9. Kunzang Palchen Ling: Tibetan Buddhist Center, "Treasure Lineage," (kunzang.org/treasure-lineage/).

10. Tsering Dolma, "Terma Tradition: The Hidden Secret in Tibetan Buddhism," Department of Buddhist studies, Faculty of Arts, University of Delhi, Delhi, India. oiirj.org/msr/july2015/02.pdf.

11. Grace Carey, *Web Quest*, 1996, p. 1, quoted in *Overlooked or Overcooked: The Case for Psychic Questing in Western Esotericism*, Simon Nugent, 2021.

12. Frederic Brussat and Mary Ann Brussat, "Questing as a Spiritual Practice," SpiritualityAndPractice.com.

13. Jack Gale, "Questing and Chaos," *Chaos International Magazine*, Issue 22, 1995, quoted in *Overlooked or Overcooked: The Case for Psychic Questing in Western Esotericism*, Simon Nugent, 2021.

14. Simon Nugent, *Overlooked or Overcooked: The Case for Psychic Questing in Western Esotericism*, 2021.

15. Paul Weston, *The Michael Line, The Qabalah and The Tarot*, 2015. p. 1, quoted in *Overlooked or Overcooked: The Case for Psychic Questing in Western Esotericism.*

16. Stanislav Groff, *The Holotropic Mind*, p. 17.

17. Valis, "The Cryptic Cosmology of Synchromysticism," RealitySandwhich.com, April 24, 2008.

18. Jonah Dempcy, *Metaphor, Metonymy and Synchromysticism*, 2013.

19. Michael Hoffman, *Twilight Language*, 2021, pp. 25, 65-66, 122.

20. "The JFK Stargate Mega Ritual," rundonotwalk.blogspot.com/2008_03_11_archive.html

21. Sam Knight, "Adam Curtis Explains It All," *The New Yorker*, January 28, 2021, newyorker.com/news/letter-from-the-uk/adam-curtis-explains-it-all.

22. Jim Brandon, *The Rebirth of Pan: Hidden Faces of the American Earth Spirit,* 1983, p. 1.

23. Robert A. Wilson, *Cosmic Trigger, Vol. 1: The Final Secret of the Illuminati,* p. 163.

24. Richard C. Hoagland: UFO Shoot Downs, NASA Rituals, and Moon Ruins Confirmed," *The Higherside Chats,* Feb. 26, 2023, time: 2:06-2:09.

25. John Keel, *Operation Trojan Horse,* p. 191.

26. "Gonzo Journalism," britannica.com/topic/gonzo-journalism.

27. "Understanding Gonzo Journalism: From Thompson to Wolfe," MasterClass.com.

28. Hunter S. Thompson, *Fear and Loathing on the Campaign Trail '72.*

29. David Wills, "When Fiction Is Truer Than Fact: Hunter S. Thompson's Gonzo Journalism," Dec. 2022, AreoMagazine.com.

30. *Susquehanna Alchemy,* podcast description.

31. Michael Wann, "Navigating Reality, and Collapsing the Old Paradigm," *My Family Thinks I'm Crazy,* Mar. 1, 2023.

32. John DeSouza, The Extra-Dimensionals, pp. 227, 247.

33. Kenneth Grant, Beyond the Mauve Zone, p. 149.

34. Jack Zavada, "Gnosticism: Definition and Beliefs," LearnReligions.com

35. Penny Royal, Causeways: season 2, episode 10, April 2022, time: 48:00.

36. Stephen Wolinsky, Ph.D., *Quantum Consciousness: The Guide to Experiencing Quantum Psychology,* p. 9.

37. Nick Herbert, *Quantum Reality: Beyond the New Physics,* 1987, pp. 20-21.

38. "Peter Levenda Interview," Project Camelot, vol. 2, p. 445, scribd.com/document/25510945/Project-Camelot-Interviews-Vol-2.

39. Joseph Campbell, "Follow Your Bliss," Joseph Campbell Foundation, jcf.org/ about-joseph-campbell/follow-your-bliss/.

40. "Landlord Accused of Murder: Teens on an Adventure Found the Bodies," *Mercury News,* August 26, 2020, MercuryNews.com.

41. "Analysis of Cooper's Dream Part 1," TwinPeaksGazette.com, May 24, 2017.

42. "George P. Hansen: The Trickster, the UFO, and the Taboo," *The Higherside Chats,* Sept. 2023.

43. "List of 'And I Would Have Gotten Away With It Too, If It Weren't For You Meddling Kids' Quotes," Scoobydoo.fandom.

Chapter 8

Synchronicity in High Strangeness: Egregores & Cybernetics

The shimmer: shimmers, shimmering, but seen clearly–
in miracle outposts of cosmic, cryptical envelopments.
Frequencies of the high river's way, bursts forth: in the now's now

Synchronicity

Comprehending synchronicity and gaining a foundational understanding of it is crucial for grasping high strangeness, as it pervades this realm of investigation. In the domain of high strangeness, synchronicity stands out as the predominant paranormal phenomenon, often serving as the medium through which *the phenomenon* manifests itself. Describing the importance of synchronicity is tricky because "it cannot be appreciated until it's personally experienced." However, when it is subjectively encountered it is "so radically discontinuous with our conventional notions of ... the nature of reality" that it can be "mind blowing." Synchronicity, furthermore, represents the "contact point between physics and psychology" revealing "a peculiar interdependence between external events and the subjective, psychological state of the observer." This merging of the "inner and the outer" reveals "their oneness"; and as a result, the occurrence of synchronicity is "a form of revelation."[1]

I don't think calling the coincidences one encounters in high strangeness "synchronicities"[A] adequately explains their bizarre nature. That is, the unique synchs encountered in this research are not your garden variety Jungian synchronicity. This is because when we encounter synchs in this research it is as if we are seeing the wiring behind the drywall that is ordinary reality. When the synchs of high strangeness happen to you, it feels "like you've touched a live wire in the building of reality."[2]

Furthermore, the high strangeness researcher believes that it is "through understanding" why these "strange synchronicities" happen

A [A] I will sometimes call synchronicity, "synchs" for short.

with such alarming frequency that we can, if we are lucky "glimpse the underlying girders of reality."[3] Put simply, researchers of the phenomenon believe that by understanding why these unusual synchronicities occur so often, we might get a glimpse of the basic structure of reality, which reveals itself to be highly strange and utterly absurd.

The Weird Flavor of Synchs in High Strangeness

To assert that high strangeness synchs are this profound is an extraordinary claim, which I am told: requires extraordinary evidence. However, to the skeptical mind there is never going to be enough evidence, no matter how extraordinary. As I pointed out in the last chapter, in this type of research there is a curious fact that people will happen across "hundreds and then maybe thousands of 'coincidental' connections, between people, places, and events, which drives them crazy."[4]

Adding to the weirdness flavor, people often report having coincidental connections with the strange subjects they are studying. An example is seen in RAW's *Cosmic Trigger*, where we learn that his close colleague, Kerry Thornley, was friends with Lee Harvey Oswald in the Marines. Thornley even wrote *The Idle Warriors* in the late 1960s, detailing his experiences in the Marine Corps with his infamous friend. He was also the co-founder of the faux comedy religion, Discordianism "which later became a central theme in the novels and plays" of RAW. The weirdness increased for RAW when, "Oswald's wife separated from him and went to live with Mrs. Ruth Payne in Fort Worth. Mrs. Payne was the sister of my family doctor."[5]

The Many Synchs in High Strangeness

Simply saying there are a lot of synchronicities when researching the phenomenon would not convey the full picture. We get a little closer when it is pointed out that they are so ubiquitous it is as if "they spill over the edges of ... an unattended sink."[6] In the subreddit for the *Hellier* TV series someone suggested a drinking game while watching the show, taking a shot every time the word "synchronicity" is said. Greg Newkirk responded, "you will die if you do this."[7] Just as the Innuit have multiple words for snow because it is so ubiquitous in their environs,[8] high strangeness researchers need multiple words for synchronicities. This chapter is a call to come up with a better naming system, it is a tentative first step and I welcome input from readers.

Conventional Types of Synchronicity

Before we get into the unique ways synchs manifest in high strangeness, let's look at some of the more conventional types. There are synchronicities with numbers, often called "angel numbers," which "are repeating number sequences often used as guides for deeper spiritual exploration."[9] Synchs occurring in relation to aspects of nature are another type. For example, when I was writing the section of this book regarding crows and high strangeness, I saw crows in my garden for the first time after living there for four years. These occurrences are due to the fact that there is a phenomenon in nature of "hyper synchronicity," perhaps caused by the "power of the vortex" which is the "creative force in nature.[B,10]

The following example, facilitated by nature, demonstrates the healing function of synchronicities, illustrating how they can bring psycho-spiritual growth. This comes from a client of Jung, a "young woman of high education and serious demeanor" who was struggling with "softening her rationalist shell with 'a somewhat more human understanding.'" While working with her, Jung was "hoping something 'unexpected and irrational' would turn up" to help break down her shell. During a session, while she was "describing a dream" involving "a golden scarab" Jung "heard a tapping on the window." The sound was caused by a beetle "closely resembling the golden scarab" from the dream and "was just what he needed and just what she needed." This is because it represented a "link between her dream image and the external world"[11] and was an irrational occurrence that helped him soften her overly rational side.

Other examples of synchronicities involve chance encounters with an individual you happened to be thinking about right before running into them or a synch related to a dream or meaningful coincidence related to a specific geographic location.

Types of Synchronicity in High Strangeness

I will begin identifying various types of synchronicity that one may encounter in situations involving high strangeness. It's important to note that this is an initial attempt at differentiation and is not intended to be a comprehensive list.

B David Avocado Wolfe claims his thoughts in this regard were inspired by Viktor Schauberger who theorized that "Spring water is the optimal choice for life and health, since it rises in an unspoiled environment. Due to human interaction, the number of intact water springs has reduced ... the structure of water has been destroyed due to its unnatural movement through straight pipes." (Flaska.eu/water-structuring/pioneers-of-water-research/viktor-schauberger)

Storms and Clusters of Synchronicities

One thing you encounter in researching the phenomenon are clusters of synchs, sometimes called synchronicity storms.[C] These might occur when all the above types of synchronicity happen all at once, or over a short period of time. For example, you have a dream about the number 1111 and wake up right at 11:11; then later that day you run into a random person that was in the dream, at a geographic location with the address 1111 Serendipity Way, at 1:11pm. This synch storm example is centered around time but synch clusters can also occur around a geographic location. For example, "One of the defining features of high strangeness is when [so] many synchronicities cluster in one place [that] it becomes difficult to explain away as nothing."[12]

The Synchronicity Bug and Synchronistic Awareness

Synchs "are like cultures from another dimension" which serve to "enrich our own culture." This is coupled with "the synchronistic mindset" or synchronistic awareness, which "can be likened to an antibody secreted by our psychic immune system that neutralizes the pathogenic effect of the wetiko virus," which is the archetype of evil. The fact that synchronicities can thwart the very archetype of evil demonstrates their healing power.

Synchs "propagate virally through the field of consciousness" similar to "a bug in the system" indicating "that synchronistic awareness is contagious." This type of awareness is a "consciousness that recognizes the synchronistic nature of the universe" and "is something we can turn each other onto and catch from one another." The fact that "we can help each other catch the 'bug' of synchronicity" means synchs are contagious.[13]

Synchronicity Through The Media

The synchromystics have offered a valuable contribution to the study of synchronicities by examining them in relation to media. I believe this perspective on synchronicities encourages individuals to integrate modern technology into their spiritual practice. Many people interested in this topic may resist using new technology in this manner. However, this luddite mindset closes one off from the synchronicities that may emerge from these new tools. This is important because high strangeness "involves a specifically digital element."[12]

C The term is discussed in season 1, Episode 7 of the *Penny Royal* podcast, and synch flurries are referred to in Barbara Marciniak's Pleiadian channeling, *The Fog Thickens*, part 2, Feb. 2022.

As researchers of the phenomenon, we must be receptive to the possibility of synchronicities emerging from our new technological environments. Jung's famous example of a synch in a therapy session involving a beetle flying into the window, in today's world, may manifest through one's Instagram feed; this makes the synch no less powerful. The new technologies, if we approach them correctly, only opens us up to more avenues to be impacted by the power of synchronicity.

Xenochrony and Synchronistic-Linguistics

Xenochrony comes from the Greek words *xeno* (meaning strange or foreign) and *chronos* (meaning time) and is a term coined by Frank Zappa to describe a technique of song creation. He said songs created with this technique were the "result of two musicians, who were never in the same room at the same time, playing at two different rates ... for two different purposes" and "when blended together" yielded "a third result which is musical and synchronizes in a strange way."[14] For Zappa, this strange synchronization often resulted in musically significant songs, seen in the fact that all guitar solos in the famous *Joe's Garage* (1976) album "are taken from various live recordings and superimposed over the studio recording." Put simply, this highly strange musical technique created great songs, not just random noise.

Bob Dobbs borrowed this term from Zappa (whom he knew personally) and now uses it to describe a unique type of highly strange synchronicity. He says because the hyper-technological environment we are in today is so unique that "synchronicity is not a special thing" anymore. The special thing now is xenochrony, which is a "strange synchronicity" and is not "just simple synchronicity." Presumably due to the highly strange person effect (discussed previously in this book) Bob claims xenochrony occurs when he interacts with "people who are interested in what I'm doing." I can attest that this is indeed the case and I will explore it in full in volume three of this series, *My Cosmic Trigger: Friends, Gurus, Guides, Gods, & Ancestors in Highly Strange Places.* He also goes on to explain a type of xenochrony that refers to his life specifically, saying that "if I tune into any movie" it will more often than not be "about me, more than it is about you." Bob says this is because the xenochrony is about "what I've already publicly said ... using a technical language" to explain reality and because he has done this analysis of reality more often than an ordinary citizen, he will get "strange synchronicity from the media"[15] about his life.

Bob's most famous example of xenochrony about his life's work is seen in the *Matrix* films. He claims that Neo is a perfect representation of what he is doing, which is providing us with a *close reading* of reality, that once grasped, can break us out of the Matrix. To further clarify matters, the white rabbit in the film is a representation of Bob's synchronistic-linguistics which "helps lead the hypnotized Neo to take his first tentative steps from second nature back to first nature."[16] Put simply, synchromysticism deals in synchronistic-linguistics and returning to first nature is a way of saying, breaking free of the matrix.

How So Many Synchronicities Are Possible

The fact a high strangeness researcher encounters an embarrassment of synchs when studying the phenomenon begs the questions: who, why, and how? Meaning, who (or what) is causing them?, why are they occurring?, and how are they occurring? I will look at the who or what is causing them in the next chapter and will explore the question of why they are occurring in the conclusion chapter.

In this section, I will explain theories which demonstrate that reality is structured in such a bizarre way, that it is fertile ground for these mind-dizzying synchs. The synchronicities are the figure and the highly strange quantum reality is the ground, the cosmic medium of reality through which syncs manifest.

Super Spectrum

One such ground is Keel's idea of the "Super Spectrum," which is a theory that the phenomenon is made possible by a previously unknown spectrum of energy. Keel speculates that we "are surrounded by energies we cannot see," giving the example that if we could see infrared rays "we could look at a telephone microwave relay tower and see a steady stream of brilliant reddish light pouring from it." This is because "the human eye can perceive only a very small portion of the electromagnetic spectrum." As a result, we could be simply unaware of the "many different frequencies" that "permeate the known universe," some of which could be coming from "objects, entities, and even worlds we can't see." Keel says that "Somewhere in this tangled mass of electromagnetic frequencies there lies an omnipotent intelligence" which can "manipulate energy" and can even manifest "any kind of object into existence on our plane." This would mean such an intelligence could arrange synchronicities using its mastery of the electromagnetic spectrum of energy. Keel points out that the "early occultists understood" that this "energy was the key to the whole"[17]

A Fluid Electric Field

The next theory involving the highly strange medium of reality through which these synchs manifest is presented by Charles Topham,[D] who was part of the original group of modern day psychic questers spoken about previously in this book. He suggests that "everything is linked energetically ... physically [and] mentally" on "so many different levels to everything else." Topham suggests that after one has gone through a high strangeness initiation, such as the one *Penny Royal* host Nathan Isaac went through researching his podcast, you start to see that "cause and effect, is a blind" and that we are "programmed with it because of [the] Newtonian physics" we are taught from a young age; saying that he now believes reality is "a lot more fluid ... like a fluid electrical field."[12]

This fluid field brings to mind the "butterfly effect," often tied to chaos theory, which is "rooted in the study of dynamical systems" where we see that "small changes in the initial conditions of such systems can lead to dramatically different results in the long run." The term butterfly effect "was coined by mathematician and meteorologist" Edward Lorenz who "discovered that even minuscule changes in the initial conditions of a weather model could have substantial impacts on the long-term weather forecast. The metaphorical idea of a butterfly flapping its wings in Brazil causing a tornado in Texas ... illustrates the sensitivity to initial conditions in chaotic systems."[18]

Topham says conducting this research is like completing a joint puzzle where everyone has "bits of the jigsaw" and the story unfolds as each contributes their piece. This fluid process is comparable to doing improv, where as the story unfolds the "narrative would change."

Isaac speaks to this fluid nature of researching the phenomenon, saying it works like "a flower blossoming," pointing out that some of the information he got for his *Penny Royal* podcast came "from sources that couldn't have possibly realized the information they were providing us would link to another piece of information from someone else." He talks about the subjective experience of this process, saying that "each new piece of information" he received in this manner seemed "so personal to our jour-

---

D The following podcast with Charles Topham includes a discussion of "psychic questing, apports, Andrew Collins, poltergeist phenomena, synchronicities, Pagan spirituality, ancient Christian churches and other sacred sites ... UFO experiences [and] a mass owl experience" (WhereDidTheRoadGo.com/about/itemlist/tag/Charles%20Topham).

ney into the mystery that almost always it was a piece of the puzzle that wouldn't have meant anything to anyone else except for us … in that moment we received it." He goes on to say that the "very real mechanism of transmission was another researcher," and that while swimming in this fluid electrical field they were "compelled by some chance encounter … to supply us with a detail necessary to unlock another door and move us further down the road to whatever would be the next unfolding."[12]

A Quantum Synchronistic Field

In this research we are confronted with "Coincidence piled on coincidence, indicating the existence of a powerful, subliminal force working at the level of chaos – at the quantum level." This "sinister force" is "struggling to manifest itself in our reality [and] our consciousness." This "dynamic was uncovered by" Jung and Austrian physicist Wolfgang Pauli, in their discovery of synchronicity. This force "is suppurating below the consciousness of the people but able to erupt without notice."[19]

High strangeness synchs are possible due to a "quantum synchronistic field." The discovery of this field comes out of the "revelations emerging from quantum physics" and these revelations "are unveiling something deep within the depths of our souls." Quantum physics is about the "subjective state, rather than being about objectively real states of a supposedly objective world." This may sound like hyperbole but it "is the greatest scientific discovery in all of human history" because it "is the physics of the dream," pointing to "the dreamlike nature of reality." The "quantum nature of things is expressed in the well established fact that light appears as either a wave or a particle depending on how it is observed," showing us that "the way our universe manifests is in some mysterious way, just like a dream, a function of our consciousness." This means that reality is ultimately "determined by how we observe it," representing a paradigm shift from "the classical Newtonian physics mindset, with its overly rational, mechanistic … and reductionist way of viewing things."[13]

The fact that reality has a dreamlike nature shows us how it is possible for synchs to manifest so abundantly. This is where the "kind of thinking that informs unified field theories" comes into play; a kind of thinking based around the idea that the "universe is wholeness moving within itself" indicating there is an "interconnectedness of quantum events." This interconnectedness can be thought of as "quantum nets" which "exist both locally when one particle is transformed into another, and nonlocally, when a change in one particle is instantaneously correlated with a change in a distant particle." Quantum nets show us that particles are "not so much 'things' as webs of relationships" and "quantum theory forces us to see the universe not as a collection of physical objects, but rather as a complicated web of relations between various parts of a unified whole" which is caused by "the dynamic interconnections of subatomic particles."[20]

Stare into the Strange Abyss and the Strange Abyss Stares Back

A prominent feature of high strangeness research is that if you start noticing it, then it starts noticing you back. In practice this means that when you start looking into high strangeness you become an antenna for it, indicating the phenomenon is responding to the attention of the observer. Perhaps this strange effect ties back to the observer effect in quantum physics, which shows us a "particle cannot manifest in reality ... until we observe it" indicating the "subjective mind has an effect on the objective world."[21] When we look into the phenomenon, paranormal events and synchs increase. A well known truism that RAW often pointed to was that "reading about ... synchronicity usually tends to vastly increase the amount of strange coincidences in one's life."[22]

Cybernetics and Feedback Loops

There is a "strange reflexivity" involved in high strangeness research, showing us that "interacting with the phenomena means understanding the experience has a responsive quality."[23] This strangely reflexive and responsive nature of reality (which makes it possible for synchs to manifest so frequently) is explained in the field of cybernetics and its theories around feedback loops. Nathan Isaac reports the high strangeness he experienced while doing the research for his *Penny Royal* podcast demonstrates "the way the phenomena" works: it "involves cybernetics and feedback loops."[23] He speaks further to this fact saying "reflexivity and circularity are essential parts of the interaction with the phenomena" and it "feels like magick, because it's how magick works."[23]

Cybernetics studies feedback loops in natural and artificial systems. The founder of cybernetic theory was Norbert Wiener, author of the 1950 book *The Human Use of Human Beings: Cybernetics and Society*. Feedback loops are central to this theory because they "are essential mechanisms that regulate and maintain the stability of biological" and social systems. The function of these loops involves "the detection of a change ... a response to counteract or amplify the change, and feedback mechanisms to monitor the system's state."[24] These feedback loops are seen in nature's predator-prey relationship and the plant/animal-oxygen/carbon dioxide relationship. The study of feedback loops in cybernetics helps us understand how living organisms interact with their environment and maintain overall stability.

Another key idea in cybernetics is self-organization. This involves studying "how large populations of crickets or neurons manage to synchronize their behavior so that their chirps or their neural firings end up moving in lock-step progression." A "critical advance in the field came by recognizing that all cases of synchronization could be captured mathematically." This mathematical formula was found in the "Kuramoto Model" which "has become the gold-standard foundation for studying spontaneous synchronization."[25]

Synchronistic Cybernetics

The fact that reality is structured in such a way that spontaneous synchronization is possible shows us how patterns can exist in naturally occurring systems. The concept of synchronistic cybernetics points to how high strangeness synchronicities are able to manifest. It is "contrary to linear cybernetics, in which feedback loops take place through space and over time" and is when "the feedback loops are beginningless, circular, instantaneous, and timeless."[13] Looking at the phenomenon through the lens of synchronistic cybernetics provides researchers with a new lens to look at high strangeness and helps us integrate the paranormal with cybernetic theory.

How Synchs Manifest in High Strangeness

Synchronicity in high strangeness can manifest positively and negatively. This is important because it shows you can either benefit from the phenomenon or be hurt by it. Making sure the phenomenon is manifesting to help us is at the heart of my magick of high strangeness.

The Helping Function

When the synchs manifest positively, it appears the phenomenon is trying to aid our research. Levenda explains this helping nature, saying that when he was researching *Sinister Forces* while in remote areas of Southeast Asia he "would walk into an old second-hand bookstore and find books that I needed for my research ... Scholarly texts would suddenly appear. Or texts would appear that had been written and printed privately."[4] This is especially significant since he was finding rare tomes of high strangeness in Southeast Asia, not New York City.

Keel said he thought that the "phenomenon was slowly introducing me to aspects I had never considered before." He said this helping effect in his research was an indication that he "was being led step by step from skepticism to belief" and that when his thinking "went awry and my concepts were wrong, the phenomenon actually led me back onto the right path. It was all an education process, and my teachers were very, very patient."[17]

Jacques Vallée details a life altering synch which occurred while researching the UFO cult, The Order of Melchizedek. He tells of a story that "seems incredible; yet it happened to me," reporting that while researching this cult he got into a taxi and the receipt showed the driver's name was Melchizedek. This incident left Vallée to speculate that: "Since there are only one person named Melchizedek in the L.A. phone book, I have to conclude that mere coincidence cannot explain this incident." He said it was this incident that "convinced me to put more energy into understanding the nature of such coincidences."

Putting more energy into understanding the nature of these types of coincidences is what high strangeness research is all about. Of this incident Vallée said, "Most coincidences you can rationalize away. I tried to rationalize this one away. I couldn't." Notice how these synchs can open up an overly rational mind to a new consciousness. The Melchizedek synch caused him to "speculate about a variant of current physics ... in which apparent 'miracles' could occur without violating physical laws, and in which psychic phenomena should be the rule rather than the exception." He said that this variant of current physics "points to under discovered relationships between physical reality and human consciousness" which could "be used to clarify some exciting theoretical and practical opportunities to understand both energy and information better." Finally, he theorizes that he thought the "key to these notions might be sought in cybernetics, but no serious attempt has been made to fit it into the lock."

The Melchizedek synchronicity caused him to question the very structure of reality, suggesting the synch perhaps indicated reality "might be organized more like a randomized database than like a sequential library." He explores this idea further, saying "If there is no time dimension ... we may be traversing events by *association*. Modern computers retrieve information associatively. You 'evoke' the desired records by using keywords, *words of power*.... Perhaps I had unconsciously posted such a request on some psychic bulletin board with the keyword 'Melchizedek.'"[26]

Synchronicity appears to be a sign we are on the right track. *Where* this sign comes from will be explored in the next chapter. Like signs pointing the way or breadcrumbs in the forest, whichever metaphor you use, the synchs we encounter in this research are trans-dimensional proof we are on the right track. I am proposing that Vallée's synch is a signal for him to continue to research the Melchizedek concept in general, not that the Melchizedek UFO cult is true *per se*. I do not think our highly strange universe would synchronize around Melchizedek for no reason.

With all that being said, I will briefly explore what I have found that may be important about Melchizedek. One source claims there are three cosmic Brotherhoods: the "Brotherhood of Michael, the Brotherhood of Enoch, and the Brotherhood of Melchizedek, which direct seventy Brotherhoods of the Great White Brotherhood." These cosmic brotherhoods "serve as a field of intelligence in the repairing of the universes so that they can evolve into infinite wisdom and glory."[27] This would indicate Vallée's Melchizedek synch was part of this overall repairing process.

Summary of the Helping Function

High strangeness synchs are signs pointing the way and I encourage researchers to trust them, rejoicing when they see them because it means "there is a story unfolding" and "you are being guided."[12] I encourage high strangeness researchers to surrender to this helping function. The process of trusting the helping function of these synchs will help you keep your mental equilibrium as you plunge down the rabbit hole and avoid the hurting function of these synchs.

The abundance of synchronicities encountered in high strangeness situations may induce feelings of paranoia, as the rational mind grapples with the challenge of understanding how such a multitude of synchs can occur. This chapter seeks to demonstrate that the fabric of reality itself is structured in such an unusual manner that frequent synchronicities are simply the norm.

The Hurting Function

Unfortunately, there is also a hurting function at play when you research high strangeness. Keel said he was lucky in that he was aided by the phenomenon but that "Other people who have become involved in this situation have not been so lucky." He claimed this was due to the phenomenon's "game playing" which led the unprepared to become "quickly engulfed in disaster."[17] This section will explore the negative side of high strangeness research which my magick of high strangeness seeks to thwart.

Tangential Tantrums

Kenneth Grant defines these as an "unexpected and unpredictable phenomena resulting, tangentially"[28] from magical practice in general. Specifically, they are "distortions caused by an improper ... opening" of gateways that are "aligned with the cosmic power-zones."[29] It makes sense that tangential tantrums would occur in researching the phenomenon because of the importance of window areas (or gateways) in high strangeness research. When explaining the type of synchs involved in an example of a tangential tantrum, he says it is "difficult to explicate in rational terms;" but says it involved the actor Bela Lugosi performing "not far from Bram Stoker's last resting place" in a London neighborhood Grant frequented. He said this was especially significant because it was right after he had conducted magical rituals inspired by the Lugosi film, *White Zombie*. Finally, Grant says "this 'coincidence' exemplifies an instance of *tangential tantrum*, or synchronicity, call it what you will."[29] Of course, this isn't a negative synch *per se*, but for the sake of clarity, I propose that tangential tantrums are negative synch storms.

Tragedy in *Cosmic Trigger*

RAW's revolutionary book contains a significant amount of tragedy that is often overlooked. Specifically, it chronicles how his exceptionally talented thirteen-year-old daughter was brutally murdered. This tragic event seems to be often overlooked in discussions about the book, and I believe this oversight has contributed to a negative dynamic within the Cosmic Trigger egregore. As we say in the psychotherapy game, what we resist persists. An occultist who knew RAW even declined to discuss the tragedy with me in the late 90s, as it was "still too painful."

Egregores

The concept of egregores is essential to a thorough understanding of high strangeness phenomena in general and how synchs manifest in this field of study in particular. Also, by looking at the relationship between synchronicity and egregores we strengthen our understanding of both these paranormal subjects. An egregore is said to be an "autonomous entity composed of and influencing the thoughts of a group of people" and is also the "conduit for a specific psychic intelligence ... connecting the invisible dimensions with the material world." This is also important to the magick of high strangeness, because egregore's are "the true source of power" of "ancient ... religious-magical practices."[30]

When an egregore is developed "things 'take on a life of their own.'" They can "range from demons that 'crush us without pity'...to symbolic characters like Santa Claus." There are "symbiotic relationships between an egregore and its group."[31] As such, another way of describing an egregore is as a "group mind," which "is created when people consciously come together for a common purpose." When this occurs a group mind is created that "has its own distinct personality and can influence the thoughts and behaviors of its members, as well as the events and circumstances that surround the group."[30]

The group mind is seen by examining the psychology of mob consciousness. When an angry mob formed "something like an obsessing entity took possession which was not the sum of the mass of the individual's souls, but vaster ... more fiercely and vividly alive." The "occultist carries the practical application of the doctrine of group minds much further than does the psychologist" because in the egregore concept the occultist finds "the key to the power of the Mysteries."[32] The mob's group mind (egregore) manifests negatively because it is not controlled properly and the "key to the whole situation lies in the direction of the attention of a number of people to a common object about which they all feel strongly in the same way." This fact gets at how an egregore can manifest in a negative manner or a positive manner; because, depending on the intention, it "is just as capable of raising consciousness to the level of the angels as of lowering it to the level of the beasts."[32]

An egregore can facilitate increased synchronicities because the group's "thought-form ... begins to give off vibrations, and ... by the law of the sympathetic induction of vibration, tend to reinforce the feelings of the person whose emotion gave rise to them and to induce similar feelings in others present whose attention is directed to the same object."[32] This suggests the egregore creates an energetic feedback loop with the members of the group. When this loop is established it means the group members are "cooperatively engaged" and as a result it facilitates "synchronistic awareness" which in turn "activates our collective genius and creates true culture." This true culture is when synchronistic awareness "effortlessly

... nonlocally, and virally transmits ... itself throughout time and space." This "Shared synchronistic awareness" is so powerful because it "magnetically ... attracts the universe into itself, materializing through life itself, creating a revelatory universe in the process."[13]

When a group of individuals focuses on a shared intent, the collective thought-forms they generate (known as an egregore) resonates in a way that causes increased synchronicities among group members that are also related to the shared goals of the group.

Tulpas

Tulpas are "thoughtform entities" from the Tibetan spiritual tradition and are "created through willpower, visualization, attention ... and ritual."[31] However, tulpas don't remain in the astral realm but actually manifest as a "mind-made body" after an advanced practitioner or group has manipulated "invisible energy into visible forms."[33] The concept of tulpas shows the potential power of an egregore.

They are able to be formed because thoughts of the group "that have been built up remain on the astral in exactly the same way that a habit-track is formed in the mind by repeated performance of the same action." Once built up on the astral they are "capable of an independent existence outside the consciousness of its creator," a fact which is "a very important factor in practical occultism, and the explanation of many of its phenomena."[32] The most famous tulpa today is "the slender man" which some theorize was created out of the "collective thought energy of thousands, perhaps millions of people from all over the world"[33] after gaining life in 2009 on the Internet.[E]

Longbody

The name for an egregore in Native American spirituality (particularly among the Iroquois[F]) is "the Longbody." The way the Longbody is described also further shows us how a group mind can increase synchronicities in a community. This concept was put into the parapsychological literature by Christopher Aanastoos and William Roll, professors from the psychology department at the University of West Georgia, where I went to graduate school. The term is "a metaphorical way to understand

E "The humanoid encounters ... that are detailed in" Lon Strickler's 2022, *The Meme Humanoids: Modern Myths or Real Monsters?* offer "glimpses into the phenomenon," exploring if beings such as the slenderman are "corporeal beings that are manifested by the human mind" (Publisher's Summary).

F *How the Iroquois Great Law of Peace Shaped U.S. Democracy* (PBS.org, Dec. 2018).

the interconnection between mind and matter that is suggested in one form or another by all the known types of psi phenomena."

The concept of the Longbody "represents a worldview quite different from that of Western cultures" because it proposes "a broad degree of spiritual interconnection between all things in the natural world." This worldview says a member of the tribe's "experience of self is not solely limited to their individual living body" but also "includes other family and tribal members (both living and deceased), the objects they possess, and the geographical locations that they inhabit or consider sacred." Our "small body" should be thought of as our individual self and what was previously explained as our Longbody "can all be seen as extensions of the individual small body" that "when taken as a whole, comprise the larger tribal 'longbody.'" This tribal oral tradition of which the Longbody is a part of, is based in a way of thinking that "opens the way for psi as a means to ensure the survival of the tribes and their respective longbodies across space-time."[34]

Synchronistic Egregores

As RAW said, "scientists have agreed with Carl Jung's opinion that the number of startling coincidences" in a synchronistic egregore "increases sharply around anybody who becomes involved in depth psychology or in any investigation that extends the perimeter of consciousness."[35] Though he doesn't state it explicitly, I believe RAW is getting at the concept of a synchronistic egregore with the previous statement, and he refers to what I am calling a synchronistic egregore as "the net" (which I will explore below.)

An answer to the question of why synchs increase when you start studying spiritual and paranormal subjects is found in synchronistic egregores. These occur when we "cultivate a network of allies who creatively collaborate in bringing forth the precious jewel of synchronicity." When this happens, the "archetypal field becomes greatly potentiated for synchronicities" because we are "in sync with other people who are also waking up through the shared open heart of synchronistic awareness."[13]

When an egregore is formed, synchs are bound to manifest because the collective energy generated by them creates a resonance which attracts similar energies, amplifying the probability of synchronistic events occurring. Again, when a group of individuals shares a strong common goal, their collective thought-forms can create a field that increases the likelihood of synchronistic events; this is the synchronistic-egregore effect. My magick of high strangeness seeks to exacerbate this positive effect and suppress the negative effect.

The Helping Synchronistic-Egregore of Alcoholics Anonymous

I witnessed this directly through the accounts my clients shared about their experiences in the Alcoholics Anonymous (AA) spiritual framework. Repeatedly, my clients recounted powerful synchronicities during meetings that left them amazed. I frequently had to emphasize to them that such occurrences are a natural outcome of their engagement with a spiritual system.

Synchronicities would manifest to offer assistance in specific ways. For example, if individuals were grappling with a challenge, someone in the meeting might bring up the same issue, or the entire discussion could revolve around their particular struggle. This intriguing observation implies that synchronicity itself plays a significant role in helping people stay sober. In essence, the meetings serve as a conduit to introduce the healing influence of synchronicity into people's lives. The synchronistic egregore spreads a network of synchronicities throughout the AA community, which aid people in maintaining sobriety: a web of healing is being spun. The healing web of synchs seen in Alcoholics Anonymous,[G] is present in all spiritual groups to a greater or lesser degree.

The synchronistic egregores of the AA community is more robust because it has been infused with the intention of group healing for over 100 years. Yet again, it bears repeating that synchronicity is a healing medium which demonstrates that the universe wants us to evolve, heal, and grow. The synchronistic egregore of the Cosmic Trigger community specifically and the high strangeness community in general are not as robust, since they are less infused with healing energy. This is because these two communities haven't been around as long, haven't had the conscious infusion of healing energy, and (perhaps most importantly) because the Cosmic Trigger community specifically has had the conscious infusion of confusing energy.

G See "The Mystical Roots of Alcoholics Anonymous: Founders of the Twelve-steps Drank Deeply from Esoteric Sources" (Mitch Horowitz, medium.com). And check out this quote from Bill Wilson's (the founder of AA) biography: "The Ouija board began moving in earnest. What followed was the fairly usual experience – it was a strange mélange of Aristotle, St. Francis ... archangels with odd names [and] deceased friends [giving] messages of comfort, information, advice." (*Pass It On*, p. 278); *LSD Could Help Alcoholics Stop Drinking, AA Founder Believed* (The Guardian.com, Aug. 2012); and *The War of the Gods in Addiction* by Jungian, David E. Schoen.

The Hurting Synchronistic-Egregore

I anticipate this section may stir controversy, but I want to clarify that my intention is not to offend anyone with the subjects I address. RAW's exceptional writings mean that any critique which deviates from praise may be seen as controversial. The RAW community, similar to the mainstream Crowley community, tends to focus on glorifying the past rather than generating fresh material inspired by the legacies of these two great men. Unfortunately, the communities around these two individuals tend to function more like a society of historical appreciation than a creative community. Not that there is anything wrong with historical appreciation societies.

In my view, the Operation Mindfuck element of RAW's work yields negative energy and fosters a synchronistic egregore that lacks the potential for healing at best and harms those that come into its orbit at its worst. To begin our analysis, let us first explore his notion of The Net, followed by Operation Mindfuck.

The Net

RAW explains The Net in general terms, saying it is "a web of … synchronicity … which connects everything-in-the-universe with everything-else-in-the-universe."[35] That is, he doesn't name this as the community's specific egregore. The egregore is an ancient concept but only relatively recently became widely known in the occult community, and I doubt he was familiar with it while writing his seminal book. When RAW uses the term "The Net" I'm retroactively saying that it is referring to the synchronistic egregore of the *Cosmic Trigger* community, defined loosely as the group of people who study and read about the subjects explored in RAW's books. I am unaware that he ever advocated conscious cultivation and maintenance of "The Net," which is important in creating a healing egregore. However, inadvertently, vis-à-vis Operation mindfuck, I believe RAW may have cultivated a hurting synchronistic egregore. Indeed, high strangeness writer and historian, Adam Gorightly, pointed out that "Operation Mindfuck reached critical mass on October 3, 1976, when Wilson's teenage daughter, Luna, was murdered at a Berkeley clothing store where she was employed." [35.1]

Operation Mindfuck

RAW says that "in New Orleans, Oswald and Thornley went about their different lives, and in Ohio" where he was living at the time he went about his; but all the while the "Net was gradually drawing us all into what ... we have called Operation Mindfuck."[35] He says if you are involved in arts, writing, and/or entertainment then "you just automatically become a member" of Operation Mindfuck "if you are sympathetic to" its aims. In this way "Operation Mindfuck rolls merrily along. And since there is no centralized" organizing group "nobody can ever stop it because there is nobody giving the orders."[36]

According to Gorightly, Operation Mindfuck sprang from Kerry Thornley's Discordian movement and "took the form of press releases the group issued offering a non-violent anarchist method to awake and mutate the sleeping robots of society."[35.1] This highly strange approach was based on the anarchist realization that art cannot be governed by the given power structure and any overt conventional action against said power structure is bound to fail. This is because the matrix, if you will, can counteract conventional actions. In this regard, RAW thought that as time goes on "more of the culture shapers are becoming" part of this operation and as a result "the whole world is having its mind fucked," which is something he is "very happy" to have played "a humble part" in such a "noble endeavor."[36]

Waking up sleeping robots is all well and good, but I believe Operation Mindfuck is ill-named, as it has painted the egregore into a corner of only providing chaos. Even RAW himself noted "in *Cosmic Trigger:* 'We were all having a lot of fun with Discordianism. None of us were aware, yet, that Operation Mindfuck could get out of hand.'"[35.1] As I write this in the Fall of 2023, I think we can say that the operation worked: the world is fucked, but nobody is laughing. I passionately maintain that right now we need more clarity, not more confusion. As a result we need to move from Operation Mindfuck to my proposed *Operation Mindheal.*

Advocating a switch from the cool and sexy Operation Mindfuck to the ultra-dorky antithesis of cool, Operation Mindheal will put me on the outs of a certain segment of the community: the too-cool-for-school element which embraces high strangeness the way a normie embraces a new, "cool" pair of blue jeans. That is, their interest in high strangeness is akin to a fashion preference. Their weirdness is merely an aesthetic choice. The New Age community is much more open to a praxis of psycho-spiritual healing, not that their community is perfect by any stretch of the imagination.

I know a focus on love and healing is not cool. I know this stance will also put me at odds with those fancy-pant, post-structuralist, post-modern, ultra-smug, lovers of French philosophers[H] that so gleefully deconstruct subjects until all that is left is intellectual folderol. RAW said that any artist even remotely into these subjects becomes a member of Operation Mindfuck. But to that I say, "Hard pass." I cancel my subscription. This book is in no way part of the Operation Mindfuck egregore; instead I invoke- Operation Mindheal.

I found RAW's Discordian-inspired[I] Operation Mindfuck humor was a lot funnier when I was in college. I don't think the humor really holds up in our present day. Humor, like no other art form, has a way of going stale with the passing of generations. Comedy doesn't age like fine wine; quite the opposite, which is an interesting sociological fact.

Being less negative of Operation Mindfuck, I point out that its goal of facilitating cultural chaos rests on the assumption that chaos is a necessary precursor to any meaningful change in society. Cultural chaos was accomplished, the precursor to real change has been met. The world has had enough confusion and I seek to clarify it. We now have to move forward with a psycho-spiritual praxis based on the highly strange to facilitate "real change in society."

Conclusion: The Synchronistic-Egregore of *My Cosmic Trigger*

The new synchronistic egregore I am proposing is separate from the Operation Mindfuck energy, as the My Cosmic Trigger synchronistic-egregore is a healing and helping energy. At this time, I passionately maintain we need to cultivate these positive synchronistic egregores. The web of synchronicities of the high strangeness community in general is trying to help the mystery (*the secret of secrets*) be discovered and we need to foster that impulse. The cosmic hidden hand wants the truth to see the light of day. The *My Cosmic Trigger* project is a hyper sigil, a magical operation to enhance and activate this healing and constructive Cosmic Net.

Having a positive intention when approaching the phenomenon is especially important, because it appears to have an amplifying effect. Meaning, if you put out the intention of chaos and confusion, you get back chaos and confusion ten-fold. As such, I suggest we approach the phenomenon with fun, love, hope, clarity, and healing. This is important

H Derrida, Lyotard, Deleuze, Guattari and the Slovenian Slavoj Žižek. Please be advised I'm a fan of these writers, just less so of their fans, so to say.

I I can also say the same for the parody religion, The Church of the Subengius, which was inspired by the Discordians. Also see, *Rhetorical Ripples: The Church of the SubGenius,* Kenneth Burke and *Comic, Symbolic Tinkering* (Lee A. Carleton, Virginia Commonwealth University).

because "there is no stopping the momentum of a movement which is moving along the lines of evolution"; in such a situation the group's egregore "forms a channel for the manifestation of evolution, and the momentum developed is irresistible"[32]

References

1. Paul Levy, *Undreaming Wetiko: Breaking the Spell of the Nightmare Mind-Virus,* e-book: p. 351.

2. *Dark Holler: High Strangeness in Low Places,* Episode 5, time: 38:31.

3. Nathan Isaac, *Penny Royal,* Season 2, episode 11: "Road to Nowhere," time: 5:57.

4. Peter Levenda, *Project Camelot Interviews,* Vol. 2, p. 445, 445. Scribd.com/document/ 25510945/Project-Camelot-Interviews-Vol-2.

5. Robert Anton Wilson, *Cosmic Trigger (vol. 1): Final Secret of the Illuminati,* p. 32.

6. Mike Clelland, *The Messengers: Owls, Synchronicity, and the UFO Abductee,* 2018, p. 44.

7. "*Hellier* Drinking Game," 2021, (reddit) r/Hellier.

8. Rebecca Thomassie, "Yes, the Inuit Have Dozens of Words for Snow – but What Does Each One Mean Exactly?" Aeon.co.

9. Olivia Munson, "What Does 222 mean? Angel Number Meaning and Symbolism in Your Life, Love and Career," *USA Today,* Dec. 2022.

10. David Avocado Wolfe, "The Magic of Nature, Rudolf Steiner, & Charles Fort," *The Higherside Chats,* Oct. 24, 2023, Time: 17:36-19:00.

11. Bernard D. Beitman, M.D., "The Scarab: Jung Created a Coincidence within a Coincidence," PsychologyToday.com, Nov. 2020.

12. *Penny Royal,* Season 2, Episode 3: "Hedgerows and Highways," time: 50:00, 1:10, Charles Topham's portion, 1:10:11.

13. Paul Levy, *Undreaming Wetiko: Breaking the Spell of the Nightmare Mind-Virus,* e-book: pp. 388-389, 316-327, 366, 389, 388-389.

14. Matthew E. Ferrandino, *What to Listen for in Zappa: Philosophy, Allusion, & Structure in Frank Zappa's Music,* 2015, p. 14.

15. Samuel Andreyev and Linus Minimax, Interview with Bob Dobbs, New York City, Dec. 2002, Torporvigil.com, Torpor Vigil Records.

16. Robert Guffey, "Synchronistic Linguistics in The Matrix Or How Bob Dobbs Became the Tetrad Manager," *Paranoia,* 2013,.

17. John Keel, *Operation Trojan Horse,* pp. 49, 256.

18. Lucas Potrykus, "Exploring The Chaos Theory and the Butterfly Effect," Medium.com.

19. Peter Levenda, *Sinister Forces Vol. 3, The Manson Secret: A Grimoire of American Political Witchcraft*, e-book: p. 679.

20. Mark Woodhouse, *Paradigm Wars: Worldviews for a New Age*, 1996, pp. 166-167.

21. Ron Immink, "The Observer Effect and Thought Management," Linkedin.com/pulse/observer-effect-thought-management-ron-immink

22. "Three Joycean Synchronicities," BuildingRoam.com/2012/07/, 2012.

23. *Penny Royal*, Season 2, Episode 10: "Causeways," Time: 19:00, 51:00.

24. "Feedback Loops," fastercapital.com/startup-topic/feedback-loops.html.

25. "The Mathematical Explanation for 'Spontaneous synchronization,'" 2022, BigThink.com/13-8/nature-synchronization/

26. Jacques Vallée, *Messengers of Deception*, 1979, pp. 210-215.

27. J. J. Hurtak, *The Book of Knowledge: The Keys of Enoch*, p. 9.

28. Kenneth Grant, *Outer Gateways*, p. 241.

29. Kenneth Grant, *The Ninth Arch*, pp. xviii, 136.

30. Mark Stavish, *Egregores: The Occult Entities That Watch Over Human Destiny*, e-book: p. 15.

31. Konrad Becker-Thompson, "Incorporated Entities," *Psionic Plastic Joy: A Journal of Anti-Social Media*, Issue 17, Fall 2012.

32. Dion Fortune, *Applied Magic*, Chapter: The Group Mind.

33. "What Is a Tulpa? Slender Man, Tulpamancy?:Exploring the Paranormal Origins and Practices of Tulpamancy," 2021, eosty.medium.com/ what-is-a-tulpa- slender-man-tulpamancy-84caab47f343.

34. Bryan J Williams, "Pueblo Parapsychology: Psi and the Longbody from the Southwest Indian Perspective," *Australian Journal of Parapsychology*, December 2007.

35. Robert Anton Wilson, *Cosmic Trigger (vol. 1): Final Secret of the Illuminati*, pp. 80, 32, e-book: p. 80.

35.1. Adam Gorightly, *The Prankster and the Conspiracy: The Story of Kerry Thornley and How He Met Oswald and Inspired the Counterculture*, p. 233-234, p. 160-161, p. 175, 2003.

36. Doctor Shambala "Operation Mindfuck! – Robert Anton Wilson (interview)," *Strange* Magazine's Youtube channel.

Chapter 9

The Controllers of High Strangeness Synchronicity: Owls, Tricksters, & Ultra-Terrestrials

Silver soldiers seal stars: the tripper of power, betwixt, dero's tower.
The all-event zings the wild childs of the land.
Fields that grew the tree are not felled.
Surly-hurry, glee-glum-green!
Past the post, to the great hide: through the relix window.

Who or What Controls the Synchs?

The last chapter demonstrated that reality is structured in such a way that allows a multitude of synchronicities to manifest in high strangeness research. This is perhaps explained via the phenomenon of entanglement, which Albert Einstein called "spooky action at a distance." In simple terms it "means that aspects of one particle of an entangled pair depend on aspects of the other particle, no matter how far apart they are." This apparent non-local connection between entangled particles is called "spooky" because it seems to violate Newtonian physics and, as a result, is "one of the most mysterious of all natural phenomena."[1]

The universe itself is a highly strange medium allowing for the synch storms seen while researching the phenomenon. However, it begs the questions: "What forces are there really at work here?"[2] and "Is there some intelligence coordinating all of this?"[3] This section seeks to provide clarity to those questions. However, on one level, it doesn't matter where they come from because, as we learned from synchromysticism, "the causes of synchronicities are not as important as their possible meaning."[4] But simply saying it doesn't matter where synchs originate is a bit of a cop out in my opinion, and what follows are some theories as to their highly strange origin.

Ultraterrestrials

Keel proposed that "ultraterrestrials [are] the ultimate source of power underlying UFOs, paranormal events, and religious and occult phenomena." This source comes "from some other part of our normal" electromagnetic energy spectrum that is beyond our everyday "senses and reality." Ultraterrestrials are "intelligent electromagnetic spectrum entities existing outside the visible light frequencies." Because they exist in this trans-dimensional spectrum of energy, they are "able to temporarily manifest ... into what appear to be a host of physical forms."[5] Keel further explains, saying that the ultraterrestrial source of the high strangeness phenomena "has to be a form of *intelligent energy* operating at the very highest possible point of the frequency spectrum" and, as a result, it "would be timeless, because it exists beyond all time fields. It would be infinite because it is not confined by three-dimensional space."[6]

Ultraterrestrials: Good and Bad

An intelligent force that is timeless, has infinite power, and is not bound by three-dimensional space would be able to easily facilitate synchs for mere mortals. This implies an ultraterrestrial "control system which acts on humans and uses humans," leaving us to "discover the source of this manifestation."[7] Put simply, we are left to discover if the source is good or bad. This is especially important to figure out because high strangeness research points to "a space war between the 'Guardians' (good guys from outer space), who are protecting our planet, and some evil extraterrestrial race."[6]

Other Names

Some synonyms for ultraterrestrials are "Secret Chiefs ... Ascended Masters"[8] or the "Inner Order" which are said to be "in communication with and overlapping with Ultraterrestrial Sources."[8] The famed occultist, Dion Fortune, "made contacts with certain inner plan adepts" while conducting "trance mediumship."[9] Whatever we call these entities, they "may be able to, as Crowley said, 'initiate a political movement to culminate in a world-war' (or prevent one)."[8] The good group are said to at war with the bad group, indicating what appears to be a "war between the Great White Brotherhood and the Black Lodge."[8] The Great White Brotherhood seems "to have the purpose of uplifting human character and initiating ... social evolution" and the Black Lodge is trying "to keep humanity in a state of materialist trance and evolutionary stagnation."[8]

Ultraterrestrials and Plasma

Researchers have speculated that UFOs "were likely constructed from a nebulous substance called plasma," which is "the fourth state of matter in the universe beyond solids, liquids and gases." This substance is important because "it is from plasma that all other physical matter comes into existence." High strangeness phenomena "could in fact be the outer manifestation of transdimensional intelligences" that are "able to occupy plasma environments." In this scenario, plasma could be acting "like a conduit providing a step down process for transdimensional intelligences coming from" outside "dimensional environments into our own physical reality."[10]

Angels

Another name for ultraterrestrials is angel. Again, as Keel speculates "the phenomenon carefully cultivated the religious frame of reference in early times, just as the modern manifestations have carefully supported the extraterrestrial from of reference."[6] It is speculated that perhaps "angelic entities also find it difficult to communicate and speak through the archetypes and symbols of our experience." And because of this difficulty "the angelic hierarchy or celestial intelligences organize the synchronicitous events ... we experience, under the providential power and guidance of God.[11] The highly strange, "twilight language is a form of angelic script that integrates synchronistic events, like a kind of semiotic text to be read."[11]

Dr. Lilly's CCCC

Dr. John Lilly, "a neuroscientist and writer who explored altered states of consciousness and communication with dolphins," gives the explanation that the increased synchs one experiences after "consciousness research" is due to the fact it "activates the agents of 'Cosmic Coincidence Control Center.'"[12] Lilly reports that he noticed in his life "peculiarly appropriate chains of related events that lead to consequences" which were "strongly desired," leaving him with "a strong feeling that some intelligence (greater than ours) directed the course" of people's lives.

He named this intelligence, Cosmic Coincidence Control Center, "within which is the Earth Coincidence Control Office (E.C.C.O.)." Lilly reports the "assignments of responsibilities ... of this system of control" for humans are as follows: "You must be able to maintain conscious ... reasoning, no matter what events we arrange to happen to you ... You are in our training program for life: there is no escape from it. We (not you) control the long-term coincidences; you (not we) control the shorter-term coincidences by your own efforts ... Your major mission on earth is to discover/create that which we do to control the long-term coincidence patterns: you are being trained on Earth to do this job."[13]

Lilly called the bad ultraterrestrials "solid state intelligence" or SSI. He defined them as "supercomputer like entities whose goal ... was of a malevolent nature," to literally "conquer and dominate all biological life forms on earth."[14] The good ultraterrestrials saved Dr. Lilly's life when his wife was moved to check on him in a flotation tank, saving him right before he drowned, after passing out. This "positive incident with his friends at ECCO,"[14] resulted in him being "convinced that the ECCO had saved his life on this occasion and that this extraterrestrial intelligence was trying to guide him."[14]

Gnostic Computers and Advanced Tech

The idea of a gnostic computer capable of arranging synchronicities is explored in Phillip K. Dick's famous novel *VALIS* (Vast Active Living Intelligence System), which is based on paranormal events he claimed were true. He explored these experiences in his nonfiction writing, which he called his "Exegesis." *VALIS* "is supposed to be a kind of god-computer capable of transmitting meaningful, transformative messages to Earth."[15]

Dick speculated it was a "sort of organic computer"[16] able to facilitate a "perturbation in the reality field in which a spontaneous self-monitoring negentropic vortex is formed, tending progressively to subsume ... its environment into arrangements of information." In addition VALIS is "Characterized by quasi-consciousness, purpose, intelligence, [and] growth."[17] It can cause us to experience synchs because it "continually guides" humans "through the 'maze' of life" by giving us signals "at the right time and place." These signals are the "messages" it uses "to communicate with" us.[16] Dick speculates that even though VALIS "has invaded our world" it is a positive entity because it has replaced "merciless determinism, with its own loving and living body, to de-program and save us."[16]

There is also a dark side to Gnostic Synchronicity Computers, as some have speculated that there could exist "a kind of Nikola Tesla-like 'tower' or 'antenna' – not necessarily purely physical – that attracts and orders synchronicity." If "something like that exists" it could perhaps be "aimed, like a weapon" as "a means of engineering humanity."[18]

Gaia

Others have speculated that our Earth "contains a great collective identity, a living thing with an awareness and a will of its own."[19] That this collective identity is even responsible for the "vast warnings of ecological and nuclear disaster given by the UFO entities." This theory states the "planet's *anima mundi*" is trying to tell "the human species to 'wake up.'"[20] This means that if the Earth has this ability then it could also arrange synchs.

Non-Ultraterrestrial Controllers

Names, Numbers, and Symbols

There is also evidence suggesting that certain numbers and words are "entangled with certain" highly strange "phenomena."[19] In this research, it is seen that "'chaotic unpredictable and senseless' events far beyond human volition ... are marshaling around certain names and numbers."[19] The reason this may be the case is because numbers may "be used as a magical means of invoking specific energies latent in the consciousness of the magician." And this is also because numbers can become "charged with an affect that may be transformed into magical energy."[21]

Words can be thought of as "magical instruments" because "their vibrations ... produce not a merely arbitrary noise but an elaborate symphony of tonal reverberations, which trigger a series of increasingly profound echoes in the consciousness" of readers. As a result, you "cannot over-emphasize ... the importance of this subtle form of alchemy" that shows "it is in the nuances and not necessarily in the rational meanings of the words and numbers employed that the magick resides."[22] Other researchers have "considered theories similar to" RAW's such as "the notion that we may be unconsciously drawn to certain symbols due to genetic memory embedded in our DNA."[4]

The Invisible Cosmic Hand

The invisible cosmic hand is seen in the idea of a "non-local intelligence guiding the affairs of the universe." This means synchronicities are emanating "from the same force that organizes uncountable numbers of snowflakes into unique"[4] formations. This force is a "law of the universe" and is the "force that causes a tree to grow, and water to seek its level."[23] It manifests in humans as a directional tendency toward growth, maturity, and self-actualization.[24] This universal force is also the "basis from which dreams originate" which we can call "nature itself." This is because it is "a natural phenomenon" but still a "mysterious force which makes all existence; the best is to perhaps call it godhead." This force, as it manifests in dreams, reveals it has a "guiding cleverness" and "a superior intelligence in it."[25]

In nature, this force causes trees to grow; in humans it causes people to self-actualize; and in the paranormal dimensions this force causes synchronicities. This non-local intelligence (or hidden cosmic hand) is the flow of the universe itself. It wants the truth to be found and this is why it aids us in our highly strange research by giving us synchs, pointing us in the right direction.

Humans

I have already explored how the synchs may be coming from group intention *vis-à-vis* synchronistic egregores. Now we will look at how synchs may be coming from our individual selves. Keel "speculated on the possibility that 'We are the intelligence which controls the phenomena.'" This means it is "only when we have arrived at a fuller ... understanding of ourselves" that we will "begin to understand the latent forces"[26] involved in high strangeness.

This fuller understanding of ourselves can be seen in the Dynamic Ground, which "is the seat of the nonegoic pole of the psyche and the source of psychic energy." The "most basic function of the power of the Ground is to serve as the fuel ... the activator and enhancer – of psychic processes." This means it can cause synchs because it "is a force that is *gravitationally or magnetically attractive* [and] is a magnifier of all dimensions of psychic life."[27] RAW speculated the phenomenon may be facilitated by "unactivated parts of our own brains,"[12] which the Dynamic Ground could help us access. If the synchs are coming from a mysterious unknown human agency, this shows why our intention is important because it is ourselves fueling them.

Future Humans

RAW also speculated the source may be "the parapsychologists/computers of the 23rd Century beaming data backward in time."[12] The possibility that humans from the future are controlling the phenomenon is where Maat magick comes in. Maat magick is an outgrowth of Thelemic magick made more widely known in Nema's book, *Maat Magick*. The idea is that thousands of years in the future after "humanity makes the leap from *Homo Sapiens* to *Homo Veritas* (true human) and achieves real species unity" they then start to send energy backward in time to make sure humans in the present (past humans to them) achieve the necessary evolution so we can "reach *Homo Veritas* status." This means that Maat magick is about bringing the "Maat Gnosis into our current apocalyptic times to help humanity quickly evolve before destroying itself."[28]

The Secret Evil They

Sometimes people see the ample synchs in high strangeness as evidence of a conscious plot of secret evil forces. People are left to ask if they are "by [the] design" of human groups, the ultraterrestrial "Cosmic Coincidence Control"[18] or the invisible cosmic hand. It has been said that the "entire world has been deceived" and this "world-wide deception has been traced ... to a higher level than the Secret Society itself and originated in what can be termed a 'Mind of Mystic Power.'" The "very nature" of this vast cosmic meta-mind "is not entirely known" but it "encompasses religious mysteries of antiquity, as well as present day scientific marvels."[29]

The host of *The Higherside Chats*, Greg Carlwood, addressed this topic, saying that he thinks the work of synchromystics is "one of the most interesting topics out there" because it causes one to "really start to wonder ... how many things that enter our culture ... is organic?" And when the synchromystics apply their knowledge to making sense of what is happening in the world "it doesn't appear anything is organic. It seems like somebody is pulling the strings on culture." Carlwood says this reality causes one to start asking if the synchs the synchromystics point out are "natural" or are they "directed"? He says that in his opinion these synchs "seem too precise for human hands." I agree with Carlwood and believe in most cases they are too precise for human hands because the "embedding of symbolism is too well orchestrated, subtle and concise."[30] This indicates the "plotting and scheming of the human mind doesn't directly create the phenomena charted by synchromysticism."[31]

Carlwood says this fact causes us to question if there is "some entity on a higher level that is pulling strings and organizing culture like legos." He says he knows "it sounds crazy to talk about," but "when you see one of these breakdowns" by synchromystics such as Christopher Knowles and Michael Wann you naturally ask "how could it be so coincidental? It just defies logic."[30]

This points to the fact that in most cases the synchs are just a natural outgrowth of how reality is structured or higher order ultraterrestrial entities "rather than conscious tomfoolery on the part of a human agency such as conspiring Hollywood magickians."[4] However, I'm not so arrogant to propose I am 100% correct. Who knows, after all? And this is not to say that I think there definitely aren't hidden human hands attempting to shape culture. However, I do think the synchs and bizarre patterns you run across in high strangeness research come from a higher order of reality than the mind of humans.

To me, this is a very optimistic view of high strangeness synchs because perhaps real nefarious actors vying for ever more power and control over the world stage "strive for control, but the true natural phenomenon of synchronicity ... is the only thing they – whoever 'they' are – can't actually control, not in the ultimate sense of Rupert Sheldrake's conceptions about morphogenesis and synchronistic patterns."[31]

Downard echos the same idea saying that even groups "dedicated to a Grand Deception designed to pull the wool over ALL our eyes" have been "deceived" by the "Mind of Mystic Power."[29] Such human groups "can't control your private citadel of consciousness, and that means they can't control you, but they can control our synthetic crowd behavior." This is why it is important "to realize they are controlling us through synchronistic linguistics."[31]

Personal Experience

As I mentioned earlier, I have been a part of the OTO since 2001 and was the Treasurer of the Dove and Serpent Oasis in Atlanta for a couple years in the early teens. I can very much attest to the following: "One can only say if any world" wide secret plot that "seeks to utilize the organizing capabilities of esoteric societies then the world can rest safe in its bed; for most have considerable difficulty in organizing themselves, let alone cooperating with each other in some grand subversive design."[32] With that being said, it is silly when people think an OTO group or the local Freemason lodge in their county is plotting nefarious evil. What I am saying is that any public secret society, which you could easily join, such as the OTO or the local Freemason lodge, is not conspiring an evil plot. They are, most likely, only conspiring how to pay their rent.

For example, an ordinary citizen can't easily join the secret Yale group, the Skull and Bones Society. In 2004, we had an "all-secret-society presidential election" and both Bush and Kerry "refused to answer [the] 'Meet the Press' host ... when asked about the organization."[33] Is the 2004 Skull and Bones election merely a coincidence, or is it evidence to support that competent secret societies really do exist? Unfortunately, "in the light of history there is a dark side to" secret societies plotting world control as "the occult interests of Heinrich Himler and the S.S. suggest" an evil occult group "was intent upon world domination."[32]

Summary

The above section offers a glimmer of hope because it "can be beautiful and comforting to realize the universe might be conscious, as opposed to a lifeless mechanistic construct, at a time when the reductive materialist paradigm seems to be leading us into a dead end."[4] To me this gets at the positive effects high strangeness has on one's mental health. Indeed, it is hard to be depressed when one realizes the universe is strange beyond our wildest imagination.

And, finally, I think some researchers are too caught up in the idea of a *nefarious they* when it comes to synchs. It is as if their minds believe only a nefarious evil group could organize so many synchs. I hope this chapter helps show that this is not the case; and hopefully, being grounded in that fact will help in successfully navigating high strangeness initiations. Remember, evil is not as powerful as it would like us to think.

The Great Cosmic Punchline

As we continue looking at the theories regarding who or what controls these synchs, we are brought to the comic element of high strangeness. This Great Cosmic Punchline that may be in control of the phenomenon has also been called "The Cosmic Giggle Factor."[12] This factor is so present that RAW asked, "Are we being invaded by the galactic equivalent of the Marx Brothers?"[12] Keel says that "when you investigate a UFO flap area very carefully the whole phenomenon begins to seem like a robust practical joke perpetrated by some cosmic jokers."[34] Dealing with this cosmic joke factor is a significant component of high strangeness research.

Cosmic Jokers

Just who are these Cosmic Jokers? According to Keel, they were seen in ancient times as participants in a "great unseen conflict between God and the Devil." In modern times "the same conflict has been observed" and some have "explained it as a space war between the 'Guardians' (good guys from outer space), who are protecting our planet, and some evil extraterrestrial race." Keel says these are essentially the same scenarios, "only the frame of reference is different" because "the phenomenon carefully cultivated the religious frame of reference in early times, just as the modern manifestations have carefully supported the extraterrestrial frame of reference." As he tells it: "The quasi-angels of Biblical times have become magnificent spacemen" and "the Devil's emissaries of yesteryear have been replaced by the mysterious 'men in black.'" This game of switching frames of reference is what he terms "Operation Trojan Horse," which is "merely the same old game in a new, updated guise."[6] This scenario would not imply a cosmic joke being played on us *per se*, but a carefully orchestrated operation to fit with the prevailing norms of the time. Meaning, yes, "angels, elementals, and ufonauts" are all playing "amusing games"[6] but are doing so for a good reason.

The changing nature of the phenomenon is sometimes looked at in high strangeness literature through a negative lens. Some have claimed that the shapeshifting nature is an indication "that we are surrounded on all sides by nonhuman intelligences who habitually lie to us for no discernible reason other than to amuse themselves." The fact that these "entities are at least as old as human consciousness" is the reason for "the near-universality of the Trickster motif in legend and folklore."[26]

This changing nature is also explored as being nefarious by co-creator of *Twin Peaks*, Mark Frost, when he says these cosmic tricksters have "been with us since humankind came down out of the trees"; and if we were "able to look deeply at the whole of human history, we would see they have always been here." These ultraterrestrial cosmic jokers "have observed, helped, haunted and tormented and teased us since the beginning of time, for reasons entirely their own." We are unable to understand their reasons for teasing us because "their true nature is ... energetic, not physical, evolved in some ways light-years beyond our ability to understand" them.[35,A]

I believe the reason they change shape over time is not to trick us but to help us while at the same time not overwhelming the mind of humans at their particular stage of development. If there is any joke we are not getting, then it is because we are not smart enough to understand it. And as we shall see later in this chapter, the tricks may be to help us learn, meaning they are pedagogical tools.

Archetypes

Archetypes are "primary forms" of the mind, psychic "constellations," or symbols that resonate with the collective human experience;

A "The Superspectrum intelligentsia have an odd sense of celestial humor that only they would think in many cases was humorous ... they expect us to kowtow to their whims while they act as cosmic tricksters ... who enjoy showing off their ability to keep us off guard and jumping to their commandments." (*The Matrix Control System of Philip K. Dick and the Paranormal Synchronicities of Timothy Green Beckley*, 46%-48% of sample).

and as such they are "found in all societies," across all of human history. These ancient patterns of thought effect us as humans at a deep level because they "govern the psyche."[36] Famously, Joseph Campbell found evidence of archetypes when he saw that "variations on the same basic motifs [are] occurring universally throughout the myths" and literature "of all cultures."[37] This is because people from all cultures "are born with similar patterns of ... emotion, and reaction." Archetypes come from the collective unconscious not the personal unconscious, which is "acquired during the individual's lifetime." The collective unconscious "is a reservoir of psychic resources common to all humans (something along the lines of psychological instinct)" and is "passed down through the generations of a culture," meaning they are "inherited, not learned." As generations of humans "experienced similar phenomena, the archetypal images were formed" in the shared collective unconscious. Because of this, even though there are "cultural differences, the human experience has been similar in many ways throughout history." An example is seen in the fact that "all cultures have something in common in the way they react to 'hero' or to the concept of 'mother.'"[38]

The hero, who goes on a journey, facing obstacles, and obtains personal transformation in the process of completing his quest. And the mother figure embodies the role of providing unconditional love, support, and care. The universal nature of archetypes comes from our shared reservoir of human experiences, memories, and images stored in the collective unconscious.

However, archetypes aren't just abstract things existing in the human psyche, "their governance extends to nature, physical, biological reality, and through society, culture, language, art, work, [and] spirituality."[36] And an important thing to remember when it comes to high strangeness is that there "is a decidedly non-psychological aspect" of archetypes. "Specifically, there is a reality [to them] that exists apart from the mind of man." Jung himself "cryptically asserted that archetypes could sometimes appear in physical, objective reality."[5]

Jung maintained archetypes were psychoid, which is a "Jungian term that means a process that is able to bridge the gap between psychological reality and objective reality." Being in the psychoid domain, they as such belong "to the invisible, ultraviolet end of the psychic spectrum" and exist as "pure energy, remaining primarily invisible but occasionally manifest themselves"[5] in physical, objective reality. Especially pertinent to our study, I point out that "apparitions of the Virgin Mary, fairies, disc-shaped objects, circular patterns, and even angels and demons are included in the vast range of archetypal symbols."[5]

How Archetypes Facilitate Synchs

Author and psychic Alan Vaughan[B] provides an understanding of how archetypes facilitate increased synchs, pointing out that synchronicities cluster "around an archetypal situation."[39] This is because an "activated archetype's force field organizes the entire field to synchronistically rearrange itself so as to embody the archetype 'in form.'"[40] Vaughan says that a "clustering of meaningful coincidences" in one's life "suggests the operation of an archetype in" a person's "'blueprint' of life." Further, once an archetype "is initiated, it tends to repeat itself" in one's life path. Vaughan's personal encounter with "a maze of interconnecting coincidences" in his life opened him up to a reality that caused him to wonder "if there might be ... some transcendental plan of life that preexists and guides our individual destinies."[39]

The Trickster Archetype

In the above we looked at ultraterrestrial cosmic jokers. This section looks at the archetype of the cosmic joke: the trickster. According to Jung, the trickster archetype is an "archetypal symbol found in virtually all cultures" and is the "personification of the disruptive forces of nature – a mechanism to explain chaos."[5] Most importantly to our study, Jung said the trickster archetype "played a central role in all paranormal phenomena."[5]

The "trickster-like quality is also inherent in other natural systems, and so may be an even deeper characteristic of the natural world"[41] – indicating the structure of reality itself is in the form of a joke. Why would such an archetype exist? Is this a *Killing Joke* (a la the 1989 Alan Moore graphic novel about the Joker's origin story). Or is the punchline of the cosmic joke, enlightenment itself? To help us answer this question, the best stance to take when we see this archetype in action is to "understand this magical fellow is our ally, if we can but learn to deal with him correctly."[42] Dealing with her correctly involves embracing reality with laughter and a sense of humor. This approach will help us keep our psychological equilibrium as we go down the rabbit hole.

B Vaughan was integral to RAW's first *Cosmic Trigger* book and to D. Scott Apel's *Philip K. Dick: The Dream Connection*, Feb. 2015, two books important to my personal mythos.

Defying Rational Explanation: Why the Trickster Shows Up

High strangeness phenomena invoke the trickster archetype because it involves research into an almost unsolvable puzzle of reality. As it is speculated in the foreward to this book, "Perhaps the trickster shows up ... because of the limits of language. That is, the overabundance ... of meaning intrinsic to high strangeness" means that mere words can't "adequately capture, relegate, categorize, and tame the wily nature of these interconnections."[43]

Trickster and the Liminal

Another reason it shows up in this research is because the trickster governs liminal spaces; and as I have talked about previously, high strangeness is attracted to liminality. For example, Hermes, "the trickster"[44] of the Ancient Greek gods, is "a liminal god, present in the transitional space."[44] Jung said the trickster was "the combination of all opposites" and "the notion of opposites is very central to trickster theory." The "betwixt and between" is what's "called a liminal domain" and in this in between area is "where the binaries breakdown."[45] That paranormal phenomena manifest more easily when such conditions are present "suggests that the boundary-dissolving characteristics of paranormal experiences ... belie a deeper, weirder interconnectedness."[41]

Why the Tricks and Jokes

Why high strangeness is often accompanied by a plethora of jokes, tricks, and humor is a question that demands an explanation; but in short, it appears to be a pedagogical device. In myth we see that "trickster tales help us become conscious of aspects of life and culture that might otherwise be neglected" and then "by becoming aware of them, we can rearrange them or see why it is best to leave them as they are."[44]

In my collaboration with Bob Dobbs he would often say, "If you're laughin' you're learnin'." Of course, the idea behind the saying is that laughter can be a powerful tool for learning, as it can help to make information more memorable and enjoyable. The idea that humor can enhance the learning process has been embraced and explored by many educators.

There is even a "laughter yoga," which was "discovered by Dr. Madan Kataria, a physician from Mumbai," which uses breathing techniques with intentional laughter to promote psycho-spiritual health. It has been shown to help ease anxiety and also "helps with depression" because it provides "support, hope and coping skills," and helps facilitate staying "in the present moment."[46] There is also a certain amount of ego death when someone is laughing, which is one goal of many spiritual practices. Ego death can help with psycho-spiritual growth because it allows people to transcend ego-driven perspectives of themselves, thereby gaining insights into their true nature: which is more transcendent and eternal.

Shamans

Archaic cultures utilized shamanism as a spiritual practice. In these cultures, shamans serve as mediators between the human and spirit worlds, employing rituals or plants to enter into trance states and also providing ceremonies to facilitate the healing of their community. "Interacting purposefully with the trickster" was and is "the primary activity underlying the practice of shamanism." According to this spiritual tradition "the trickster was a spiritual entity that could impart deep knowledge or create chaos"; and the role of the shaman was and is "to carefully navigate between the two distinctively different possible outcomes when dealing with tricksters."[5]

As such, "the shaman has two faces. One face speaks the truth, and the other is a trickster ... the sharpe-witted hare – who never says anything in a straightforward manner." This technique of not speaking plainly is called "spiritual lying" and is "one of the primary tools of the trickster" shaman. Shamans use this technique on their audiences when they "cannot grasp the truth of a situation directly." Sometimes the recognition of truth "can only occur when one is tricked in stumbling" upon it. Another way of looking at this shamanic approach is that when the truth is so hard to understand a shaman must trick his audience "into achieving the proper state of consciousness to perceive the situation at hand with true clarity."[47]

This approach is seen in the Huichol, "the last tribe in North America to have maintained their pre-Columbian traditions."[48] Members of this tribe "engage in rapid, babbling conversations in which several people talk at the same time about almost anything. To the rational mind, this kind of behavior is maddening" and has the effect of making the visitor's mind become "totally scrambled." This causes the visitor's brain to simply "have to let go" and "in that moment, as" the person's "ego consciousness loosens, the Huichol suddenly change their conversational pattern, sensing that the visitor has now shifted to a non-rational perception – the domain where they live."[48] This demonstrates how a trickster – like approach can be a pedagogical tool, with the goal of opening up one's mind to the realities of high strangeness.

JESUS

The use of humor is most prominent in the shamanic spiritual tradition, however it is seen in other spiritual and religious traditions. For example, *The Humor of Christ* (1964) by Elton Trueblood shows that Christ "often laughed and often turned the provocative thrust of a rapier wit toward the proud, the pompous, the over-righteous." That is, Jesus used satire in his teachings to subvert the social norms and religious traditions of his time; his use of humor was meant to shock and challenge his listeners to think differently about their world and themselves. This "dimension in the ... teachings of Jesus," unfortunately, "has been almost universally neglected," however, understanding his use of humor is absolutely "necessary" to have an "adequate understanding of Jesus' meaning and method."[49]

STAND-UPS: THE NEW SHAMANS

Maurice Charney[C] claims that, "stand-up is surely the oldest, the most basic, and the universal form of comedy. Its roots are in the shaman, the fool, the jester and the clown." Modern-day stand-up comedians can be said to be fulfilling an aspect of the shaman's ancient role and comedy theorists have "linked the comedian to the archetype of the trickster." Stand-up comedians provide political satire but also cause us to "begin to question all of our assumptions," mocking "the foundations of 'reality' itself."

The role of the stand-up comedian is also seen in the fools and jesters who were employed in medieval and renaissance courts. "Their job was not simply to entertain" but was also to actively mock and ridicule their masters. They were also "granted a license not extended to the general populace to behave in odd and extreme ways and to voice ideas ... that would get others thrown in the stocks." Some people at that time even believed that fools[D] were men "touched by god" and took "their mad ravings as divinely inspired." Embracing the idea of the modern stand-up comedian as a modern day shaman helps us embrace the notion "that laughter itself is sacred" and is "a part of being human that transcends barriers of race, creed and colour" and is part of part of "our 'universal human vocabulary.'"[50]

C "Professor of English at Rutgers University and the author of several books on the history and theory of comedy, including *Comedy High and Low*." (bloomsbury.com/us/author/maurice-charney-129790/).

D In the Major Arcana of the Tarot, the Fool symbolizes new beginnings and a willingness to embark on a journey of self-discovery, embodying both the potential for psycho-spiritual growth and the inherent risks of the unknown.

Laughter and the Matrix

Mark Twain said that, "against the assault of laughter, nothing can stand."[E] For example, the laughter at a comedian's punchline can cause the matrix to lose control of one's mind, as a primary role of a joke is to bypass the cultural censor implanted in the audience's mind. When a person's internalized cultural censor is overridden, laughter often follows, indicating that they have gained new knowledge which the matrix did not want them to acquire. Through culturally-accepted entertainment (i.e., stand-up comedy), the comedian provides insights that the audience's internalized censor might have otherwise blocked.

Chaos magicians have pointed out that humor can be used as a weapon to "challenge the ideological essence of the ... socially-agreed upon Paramount Reality."[51] The godfather of chaos magick is Austin Spare, but the more widely known William S. Burroughs is "one of the intellectual forebears of chaos magick." Burroughs "saw the world as being a control mechanism," with "his goal" being: "to utterly break" and destroy "that control system." He believed he could use various occult techniques to "open a metaphysical doorway into the source code of reality and insert intentions" in order "to bend reality."[52]

The matrix's[F] "most effective weapon against this sort of 'reality engineering' is to simply keep people in the dark about how to use weapons they already possess (such as imagination ... and humor)."[51] This section is my attempt to help people view the proper place of humor in the great (actual or metaphoric) cosmic battle between light and dark.

Summary

With all of this being said, it makes sense as to why the high strangeness trickster is at play in our encounters with the phenomenon. This is because it is trying to get us to grok what is required to understand it, which is a radical reassessment of reality itself. To achieve this goal we need the shamanistic approach to knock us out of our old perceptions. The high strangeness researcher like the shaman of old, has to navigate the trickster, tip-toeing between chaos and knowledge.

As I have shown, "the phenomenon behaves like a dolphin: It plays with us" and is "a lot smarter than we are." Because it is way more intel-

E See, Holger Kersten, "Mark Twain's 'Assault of Laughter': Reflections on the Perplexing History of an Appealing Idea," in *The Mark Twain Annual*, Vol. 16, No. 1 (2018).

F When I use the term "the matrix," I'm using the more colloquial understanding of the term, which is: a perceived system or structure that controls and influences aspects of people's lives and suggests a complex web of societal norms, institutions, and technologies that shape individuals' perceptions and behaviors.

ligent than we are, "it uses humor at another level."[53] This "odd sense of celestial humor" that guides us through synchronicities "can easily throw us off-guard and leave us with a deep sense of paranoia." To help us tip-toe this balance between chaos and knowledge keep in mind that "the wise ones among us will duly realize that this 'mind shaggin' is not" intended to push us "toward insanity, but rather" towards "an invisible force ... Power X."[G,14] If we don't stretch our limited perceptions of reality we will miss the cosmic punchline, then the tricksters (be they ultraterrestrials or archetypes) will appear as "liars and put on artists."[6]

Highly Strange Trickster Animals

This section looks at trickster animals in general and the next section will look at the role of owls in high strangeness research in particular. Jung said the trickster "had the ability to change shapes, and often took the form of animals." This is because the trickster "was an archetypal figure that adapted its physical appearance to the beliefs, expectations, and mythology of different cultures in specific times and specific places throughout history."[5]

Working with power animals has been a critical component in my psycho-spiritual practice, so I have felt first hand their benefit. Power (or spirit) animals can aid our paranormal investigations, but there is also a psychological, tangible benefit to working with them. This is because there "is an archetypal power that resides behind ... and manifests through" animals. Each animal archetype has its own "characteristics which are reflected in the behaviors" of each individual animal. The shaman, through working with power animals, "works to reconnect conscious human life with nature and spirit." The animal archetype "helps the shaman to transcend the normal, waking consciousness so that [they can] more easily attune to the more ethereal realms." Every animal is "a symbol of a specific kind of energy" and when you become "awakened" to a power animal, it will release its "archetypal energies" into your life.

You connect with power animals in your imagination and while, "Most people equate the imagination with unrealtiy. Nothing could be further from the truth." This is because the "imagination is a power of the mind" and possesses an "ability which can open us to other realms, assist us in healing, help us to discover lost knowledge and to open to higher vision."

G Colin Wilson calls this "Faculty X," which refers to the innate, transcendent human ability, beyond ordinary consciousness, that allows individuals to access higher states of perception and understanding.

Also, "creative imagination" allows us to "begin to see the spiritual energies surrounding ... the physical world."

This may sound abstract, but working with power animals is simple. If you need to manifest more courage because you are going to give a power-point presentation at work, then working with the lion energy can help you orient your psyche to the concept of boldness so you can embody that energy in the presentation. By working with a power animal you "will be able to connect with specific archetypal forces ... through the animal and understand the patterns of your own life more effectively." As you begin to work with power animals you will "be able to develop a more unique view of yourself, along with a new look at reality,"[54] which is what high strangeness is all about.

The psychology "behind this is that you need to realize and respect something besides your present identity as your teacher" and accepting a power animal as your teacher can help you do that. I believe working with power animals is also a good stepping stone to working with spirit guides. This is because power animals are a "bridge between the worlds,"[55] ordinary reality and the paranormal reality. As such it is easy to see how working with a power animal can help a researcher in their personal life and also take their high strangeness practice to the next level.

Specific Trickster Animals

The Coyote: "is very definitely one of the known 'Tricksters' that plays a role in the shadow world of Carols Castaneda."[29] The coyote trickster is seen in the Wile E. Coyote cartoons, because "like many versions of the Coyote story, he is a trickster figure."[56]

The Rabbit: "One such trickster is Brer Rabbit, who was introduced to North America through the folktales of enslaved Africans" and "functioned as a resistance figure for the enslaved whose trickery was aimed at undermining and challenging the plantation regime."[57]

The Crow: "One odd phenomenon that surfaces repeatedly is that crows are commonly seen across cultures as tricksters."[58] Two crows came to my garden in Istanbul, when writing this section. I had never seen them in the garden before or since. As a result, I adapted the crow as my power animal to help in finishing this book.

The Owls Are Not What They Seem

The owl "can symbolize transformation,"[59] so it is no wonder it shows up in high strangeness, which is inherently transformative. The owl differs from the trickster animals discussed earlier as it does not specifically embody the trickster archetype. However, the owl clearly embodies the high strangeness archetype as a whole, seen in the fact that the owl is the animal totem of the quintessential high strangeness show, *Twin Peaks.*[H] In "the series there were so many references to the owls" and they always seemed "to appear when something is about to happen."[60] The show's main character, Agent Cooper, was told in a dream that "the owls are not what they seem," highlighting the owl's importance to the show's mythos. The owls represent the *sub rosa,* or the hidden knowledge of the series, which we can only comprehend from a visionary perspective.[I]

Mike Clelland's book, *The Messengers: Owls, Synchronicity, and the UFO Abductee* further cements the central role the owl plays in high strangeness, exploring the connections between sightings of owls, UFO experiences, and synchronicity. Clelland speculates owls may be a "screen memory" of abductees. The implication being that "some sort of illusory projection" of an owl is beamed into a person's mind "making" them "think that the thing he saw on the side of the road was an owl;" however "it might have been a small gray alien with big black eyes."[61] In addition his seminal high strangeness book demonstrates that "the owl connection encompasses more than the UFO experience," as it "also includes profound synchronicities, ancient archetypes, dreams, shamanistic experiences, personal transformation, and death." This illustrates that "owls are playing some vital role" from "the mythic legends of our ancient past to the first-hand accounts of the UFO abductee."[62]

Critique of Synchronicities

Due to the fact that some mainstream mental health professionals "cling to an exceptionally rigid scientific world view" when clients share "their preoccupations with meaningful coincidences," there is a tendency to "discount their views as mere psychotic delusions."[63] However, "The mental health field is gradually changing to allow more consideration of spiritual or mystical phenomena."[64]

This change is seen in the fact that a positive stance toward synchs was explored in the mainstream *Psychology Today* website by a mental health professional who wrote the book *Connecting with Coincidence.* The author, Bernard D. Beitman, M.D., says the majority of mental health profession-

H One of the best highly strange analyses of Lynch's show, in my opinion, is work of *The Temple of Babalon Choronzon.* Their old blog was about "Synchromysticism, Chaos Magick, [and] English Qaballa/ALW Cipher" and also explored the occult implications of *Twin Peaks.* Also see their book, *The Book of Numbers: Volume 1: Ufos, Aliens, and Ultraterrestrials*, February 13, 2022.

I Owls also show up in the Christian-centric high strangeness series, *Dark Holler* (Chapter 4: Cosmic Geography).

als do not "recognize the limitations of the *Diagnostic and Statistical Manual of Mental Disorders*." He urges professionals to start learning to differentiate the "meaningful spiritual, non-ordinary states of consciousness, from psychosis." He claims the answer to getting better at differentiating between the two is to "consider the concept of spiritual emergency developed by Stanislav and Christina Grof."[65] I will explore spiritual emergencies as they relate to chapel perilous in particular and high strangeness initiations in general, in volume two of this series, *My Cosmic Trigger: Perilous Chapels and High Strangeness Magick.*

Toward a Unifying Theory of High Strangeness

This section is called "toward a unifying theory of high strangeness," and I think it is fair to say the key word here is *toward,* meaning I am only hinting at this unifying theory. As Thomas Pynchon said, "the qualities and quantities will not come together to form a unified notion in my head."[66] So I will leave it to another writer to tie it all together. However, I think I've provided enough information to give you a good head start.

I believe high strangeness is the most revolutionary subject in the overall paranormal field. The paranormal field itself is revolutionary, because it is a "frontier science" which is "a kind of science that is in a unique, transformative, and even in a subversive position to rewrite the grander logics that ensnare the mainstream sciences in their everyday way of doing things." In this regard, transdisciplinary and parapsychological researcher, Jacob Glazier, Ph.D., says "to echo Derrida ... we must 'point beyond the field of the épistémè'!"[67] One way to do this is via high strangeness research and practice,[J] because it pushes us past the limiting grand narrative,[K] which has broken down and is no longer able to provide a coherent and meaningful framework for understanding our reality. To combat this limiting grand narrative, embracing highly strange approaches that allow for multiple ways of knowing and experiencing reality is called for.

We can find other academic attempts to push beyond the grand narrative and establish an interdisciplinary unified theory. This was spurred on

J The term "épistémè" is associated with the French philosopher Michel Foucault, who used it to explore the underlying structures of thought that shape the production of knowledge in different historical periods. It "refers to the orderly 'unconscious' structures underlying the production of scientific knowledge in a particular" era. That is, "it is the 'epistemological field' which forms the conditions of possibility for knowledge in a given time and place. It has often been compared to T. S. Kuhn's notion of paradigm." (Michel-foucault.com/key-concepts/).

K Jean-François Lyotard would characterize a grand narrative as an all-encompassing story that claims to provide a universal explanation for historical events, societal complexities, and human progress. He critiques grand narratives, asserting that their inherent totalizing nature oversimplifies complexity, suppresses diverse perspectives, and can lead to oppressive power structures.

with "a number of revolutions, first by Albert Einstein and then by Niels Bohr[L] in physics, and subsequently in biology, cosmology and, through the pioneering work of Pierre Teilhard de Chardin, in the transdisciplinary area that includes human mind and consciousness."

It is said that "another revolution is about to occur, bringing science to the threshold of a more comprehensive and integrated account of the observed phenomena" and this "currently emerging transdisciplinary unified theory is consistent with the goals and vision of both Albert Einstein and Teilhard de Chardin." This transdisciplinary unified theory "penetrates deeper into the domains of reality than the 20th century's mainstream physical, biological and psychological theories did" because it merges the mainstream general relativity of Einstein with Chardin's work which "laid the foundations of a unified theory where life and mind emerge consistently out of the physical world."[68]

High strangeness research is all about studying the consistent weirdness that happens when life and mind emerge into the physical world. As researchers of the phenomenon we are on the cutting edge of this unified theory, as we are the ones who are researching the effects of this unified reality. Accepting the fact that life and mind merge extends our ordinary accepted conceptions of reality and gives us a "coherent universe, where all things are intrinsically connected by a ... virtual-energy field at a fundamental level of physical reality."[68]

Personal Experiences

The entire next chapter is about my personal experiences with the type of synchronicity found in high strangeness. However, I will give a few short examples before we move to the next chapter.

Butterfly Valley

This synch occurred in Turkey's Butterfly Valley, a beach resort in the southern part of the country on the Mediterranean Sea. The resort at one time was a pirates' cove because the only way to easily reach it is through the sea as it is flanked by large cliffs on either side, making it a truly beautiful, geographic oddity. While at the resort we met a traveler from Georgia (the country) who was open to trying Dr. Greer's CE5 contact app. The app is designed to help humans initiate ET encounters, which he terms a close encounter of the fifth kind. I like to use the app at the

L Bohr's work laid the groundwork for later developments in quantum theory and was crucial in the early development of quantum mechanics.

Valley because of the unique geographic makeup of the area. The app reports using its contact protocol can sometime evoke experiences of high strangeness which it defines as "The inexplicable effects and synchronicity of events related to and occurring before, during and after field work."[69]

While introducing the app to our new friend, I nearly mentioned the potential for unusual synchronicities before or after engaging in the app's contact procedures, but held back to avoid influencing her experience too heavily with my own perspectives. That evening, my wife, our friend, and myself followed the protocol without observing anything unusual; however, the following day she unexpectedly encountered a friend from a European country with whom she had attended a yoga retreat years ago. While she was surprised by this coincidence, I wasn't, as I had anticipated such occurrences after using the app.

The Joker

Circa 2020 I was listening to an episode of *The Higher Side Chats* with guest Christopher Knowles.[70] In the show he was talking about high strangeness around the comic book character the Joker,[M] when I paused the show to go run an errand in Istanbul. I then walk fifty feet outside of my apartment and see a photo shoot happening on the iconic stairs in our neighborhood. I was shocked to see that there was a man dressed as the Joker and a photographer was taking pictures of him. When one gets involved in high strangeness research, little synchs like this occur frequently. I think the sheer number of these little synchs is what is most disorientating: a death by a thousand cuts type situation. The next chapter will detail the big synchs that have manifested in my life.

Conclusion

The trickster archetype and the mindset it facilitates is integral in grokking high strangeness. In an episode of *Gravity Falls,* (think, a cartoon version of *Twin Peaks* about a window area in Oregon), a character's whimsical mindset solves the mystery of the episode that the more serious-minded characters fail to figure out. As it is exclaimed at the conclusion of the episode, "Your silliness solved the code" that serious researchers "couldn't crack in a hundred years."[71]

It is also my hope that demonstrating the ubiquity of synchs in this research can help people not get destabilized by them. Primitive humans were perhaps overly amazed by the fact that the sun rose again each morn

M He is author of *Our Gods Wear Spandex: The Secret History of Comic Book Heroes.*

ing, due to their ignorance of how reality was structured. And so it goes with the abundance of synchs in our highly strange reality. They are as normal as the rising and setting of the sun. Author Mike Cleeland has suggested we *be not amazed* by them as a way to not be destabilized by their abundance.

Put differently, the synchronicities encountered while delving into this research arise as a natural outcome of a gnostic quantum reality, a concept science is only beginning to grasp. While I acknowledge that most synchronicities occur spontaneously, my research indicates that at times they are intentionally facilitated by ultraterrestrials and, perhaps in rare instances, by their human agents that have advanced technology and magical capabilities at their disposal. Nevertheless, my stance remains that synchronicity fundamentally embodies a positive universal force, making it doubtful that malevolent ultraterrestrials can effectively harness it, especially in comparison to those who align their actions with divine positive universal laws.

In regards to possible advanced technology being employed to facilitate synchs, we are apt to remember one of Arthur C. Clarke's three laws, the 3rd: "Any sufficiently advanced technology is indistinguishable from magic." And, for good measure, let us review the first and second, which are instructive for the *My Cosmic Trigger* project. The first: "When a distinguished … scientist states that something is possible, he is almost certainly right. When he states that something is impossible, he is very probably wrong"; and the second: "The only way of discovering the limits of the possible is to venture a little way past them into the impossible."[72] The *My Cosmic Trigger* project is all about venturing into the impossible, while staying sane and improving our lives in the process.

In this chapter we have seen the phenomenon uses humor and historically high strangeness researchers have used it as well. To me this makes a great case for the spiritual and intellectual value of humor. I'll not digress regarding the fact that nowadays the value of humor certainly seems to not be in line with the grand narrative. This use of humor is seen in the most famous high strangeness researcher, RAW and is even traced to the father of high strangeness, Charles Fort.

One of the main components of Fort's work was to "ridicule … the static, regulated, and humorless plight of science professionals who are locked in a prison-house of perceptions." Fort's highly strange data reveals the "folly of linear thought in a world of wild mystery and untamable chaos." The study of high strangeness "relentlessly storms the fortress of rigid belief and sends our 'certainties' reeling against the doors that open onto 'something other.'" This is a great way to end this chapter: storming the fortress of rigid belief.

Let us then be like Fort: in the face of this unplumbable reality be "anathema among all professional scientists" and those that are promoters of the Grand Narrative. Let us respond with "a celestial horse-laugh" to the rigid skeptics and while remaining in the reverie of our celestial laughter; let us stay "perched on the windowsill hurling all sorts of whimsical questions" and facts which do not fit "with their dead reckonings."[73]

References

1.Andreas Muller, "What Is Quantum Entanglement?: A Physicist Explains Einstein's 'Spooky Action at a Distance'," Astronomy.com, Oct. 7, 2022.

2. Peter Levenda, *Project Camelot Interviews,* Vol. 2, Scribd.com/ document/ 25510945/Project-Camelot-Interviews-Vol-2.

3. Nathan Isaac, *Penny Royal,* Season 2, episode 10: "Causeways," Time: 1:31.

4. Valis, "The Cryptic Cosmology of Synchromysticism," RealitySandwhich.com, April 24, 2008.

5. Andrew Collins and Gregory L. Little, *Origins of the Gods: Qesem Cave, Skinwalkers, and Contact with Transdimensional Intelligences,* E-book: pp. 69, 61, 61, 58, 57, 63, 63, 63.

6. John Keel, *Operation Trojan Horse,* pp. 178, 200, 200, 200, 200, 212, 281.

7. Jacques Vallée, *Messengers of Deception: UFO Contacts and Cults,* p. 210.

8. Allen Greenfield, *Secret Cipher of the UFOnauts,* pp. 21, 88, 90, 89, 82.

9. Gareth Knight, "About Dion Fortune," angelfire.com/az/garethknight/aboutdf.html.

10. A. Collins and Gregory Little, *Origins of the Gods: Transdimensional Beings, Skinwalkers, and the Emergence of Human Civilization,* Author of the Month: grahamhancock.com/collinslittle2/.

11. Jay Dyer, *Esoteric Hollywood: Sex, Cults and Symbols in Film,* E-book: pp. 305-06, 119.

12. Robert Anton Wilson, *Cosmic Trigger, Vol. 1: Final Secret of the Illuminati,* p. 32 of print book, preface to the 1986 edition, E-book: pp. 127, 164.

13. John C. Lilly, "E.C.C.O.," JohnCLilly.com/eccox.html.

14. *The Matrix Control System of Philip K. Dick and the Paranormal Synchronicities of Timothy Green Beckley,* Kindle Sample: 57%, 62%, 65%, 46% and 49%.

15. Allen Greenfield, "The Sirius Mystery and VALIS," oocities.org/dreamerbooks2003/the_sirius_mystery_and_valis.htm.

16. *The Exegesis Of Philip K. Dick*, November 8, 2011, pp. 117, p. 369-70, p. 370.

17. Phillip K. Dick, *VALIS*, p. 0.

18. Michael Hoffman, *Twilight Language*, pp. 103-04, 272.

19. Jim Brandon, *The Rebirth of Pan: Hidden Faces of the American Earth Spirit*, pp. 2, 185, 194.

20. Steve Mizrach, *UFOs Reconsidered as a Fortean Phenomenon*, Crash Collusion, Austin, TX.

21. Kenneth Grant, *Outer Gateways*, 1994, pp. 158-159.

22. Kenneth Grant, *Outside the Circles of Time*, 1980, p. 13.

23. Aleister Crowley, *Magick without Tears*, written in 1943, published in 1954.

24. Carl Rogers, *On Becoming a Person*, 1961.

25. "Marie-Louise von Franz: The Way of the Dream: Part 1," Youtube: Destructard, Time: 9:55-11:00.

26. "The Psychedelic Shaman Briefings, The Entities of The Imaginal Realm: Part 1," excerpt from: *Psychedelic Shamanism: The Cultivation, Preparation, and Shamanic Use of Psychotropic Plants*, by Jim DeKorne, bibliotecapleyades.net/bb/book_eight10.htm.

27. Michael Washburn, *The Ego and the Dynamic Ground: A Transpersonal Theory of Human Development*, pp. 121-22, 1988.

28. Denny Sargent, "Earthing the Aeon of Maat," lecture notes, dennySargentAuthor.com.

29. *Stalking the Great Whore: The Lost Writings of James Shelby Downard*, 2023

pp. 38, 38, 217.

30. *My Family Thinks I'm Crazy*, Episode 64: Greg Carlwood, August 10, 2021, time: 21:00.

31. Robert Guffey, "Synchronistic Linguistics in The Matrix, Or How Bob Dobbs Became the Tetrad Manager," *Paranoia Magazine*, Winter, 2000 ionbob.com/pdf/bob/synchronistic_linguistics_in_the_matrix.pdf

32. Gareth Knight's introduction to *Applied Magic by Dion Fortune.*

33. "'Bonesmen'for President," March 2004, NBCnews.com/id/wbna4500423.

34. John Keel, "UFOs, Mothman and Me," *High Times,* May 1980.

35. Mark Frost, *The Secret History of* Twin Peaks: A Novel, 2016.

36. Jean Huston, "Myths of the Future," *The Humanistic Psychologist*, Spring, 1992.

37. Stephen Gerringer, "Practical Campbell: The Mythology of Archetypes," Jospeph Campbell Foundation, JFC.org.

38. *Carl Jung: Analytic Psychology,* edited and adapted version of a creative commons licensed book titled: *Personality Theory in a Cultural Context* by Mark Kelland, 2015. pdx.pressbooks.pub/thebalanceofpersonality/chapter/chapter-5-carl-jung/

39. Allan Vaughan, *Patterns of Prophecy,* pp. 78, 86.

40. Paul Levy, *Undreaming Wetiko: Breaking the Spell of the Nightmare Mind-Virus,* E-book: p. 379.

41. Jack Hunter, "Parapsychology and the Varieties of High Strangeness Experience," *The Bulletin of the Parapsychological Association,* Volume 13, Issue 3, 2021.

42. Fred Alan Wolf, Ph.D., *Matter into Feeling: A New Alchemy of Science and Spirit.* p. 81, Chapter 4: the trickster in our memory.

43. Jacob Glazier, Ph.D., *A Grimoire of High Strangeness,* preface to this book.

44. George P. Hansen, *The Trickster and the Paranormal,* pp. 37, 47, 78.

45. George P. Hansen, "The Trickster, the UFO, and the Taboo," *The Higherside Chats,* Sept. 30, 2023, Time: 1:08 – 1:13.

46. Jen Glantz, "I Tried Laughing Yoga – and What I Learned about Myself Surprised Me," June 2019, nbcnews.com/better/lifestyle/i-tried-laughing-yoga-what-i-learned-about-myself-surprised-ncna1019436

47. James A. Swan, *Sacred Places: How The Living Earth Seeks Our Friendship,* p. 82, 82.

48. "The Huichol of the Sierra Madre," shamanism.com/huichol.

49. Elton Trueblood, *The Humor of Christ,* publisher's summary, January 1, 1975.

50. Scott Jeffery, "Stand-up Shamanism," nthmind.wordpress.com/2012/02/15/stand-up-shamanism/

51. Ludo, "Absolute Divergence from the Order of Consensus," in *Crimes of Perception: Individualism and Consensus Reality,* Enemy Combatant Publications, Flat, Alaska.

52. Samuel Austin, "William S. Burroughs' 7 Magic Techniques for Bending Reality," LiveLearnEvolve.com, May, 2019.

53. Chantel Tattoli, "Jacques Vallée Still Doesn't Know What UFOs Are," Wired.com, Feb. 2022.

54. Ted Andrews, *Animal-Speak: The Spiritual and Magical Powers of Creatures Great and Small,* 1993, p. 8 and 9.

55. Arnold Mindell, *The Shaman's Body: A New Shamanism for Transforming Health, Relationships, and the Community,* 1993, p. 95.

56. "The Dharma of Wile E Coyote," integral-options.blogspot.com/2007/12/dharma-of-wile-e-coyote.html, Dec. 2007.

57. Emily Zobel Marshall, *American Trickster: Trauma, Tradition and Brer Rabbit,* publisher's summary, Rowman.com, 2019.

58. Jackie Chappell, "Living with the Trickster: Crows, Ravens, and Human Culture," ncbi.nlm.nih.gov/pmc/articles/PMC1326277/

59. Sidian Morning Star Jones and Stanley Krippner, Ph.D., *The Voice of Rolling Thunder: A Medicine Man's Wisdom for Walking the Red Road,* 2012, p. 192.

60. Mya McBriar, "The Owls Are Not What They Seem," January 27, 2015, twinpeaksfanatic.blogspot.com/2015/01/the-owls-are-not-what-they-seem.html

61. Mike Clelland, "Owls and The UFO Abductee," Scribd.com/document/152000108/Owls-and-the-UFO-Abductee

62. Mike Clelland, *The Messengers: Owls, Synchronicity, and the UFO Abductee,* 2020, Publisher's summary.

63. M. Reiss, "Psychiatry and the Irrational: Does Our Scientific World View Interfere with the Adaptation of Psychotics?" *Psychiatric Journal of the University of Ottawa* 1990 Sep;15(3):137-43.

64. Chris Mackey, "Synchronistic Experience: Enlightenment or Psychosis?" SynchronicityUnwrapped.com, February 2023.

65. Bernard D. Beitman M.D., "When Is an Overload of Synchronicities Not Psychosis?" *Psychology Today,* May 2021.

66. Thomas Pynchon, introduction to *Slow Learner,* 1984.

67. Jacob W. Glazier, Ph.D., "Deconstructing the Paranormal: Toward a Critical Parapsychology," *The Bulletin of the Parapsychological Association,* Volume 13 Issue 3, 2021.

68. Ervin Laszlo, "The Spirit of Einstein and Teilhard in 21st Century Science: The Emergence of Transdisciplinary Unified Theory," Revista Portuguesa de Filosofia, 2005, Jstor.org/stable/40338169.

69. Dr. Steven Greer, *CE5 Contact,* iPhone App.

70. *Chris Knowles: Song to the Siren, Invoked Entities, & Rebuilding Babylon,* The Higher Side Chats, Oct. 20, 2017.

71. *Gravity Falls,* Season 1, episode 8: "National Treasurer."

72. Arthur C. Clarke, "Clarke's Three Laws," wikipedia.

73. Benjamin De Casseres, "Charles Fort: The Puck of Mysticism," *Crimes of Perception: Individualism and Consensus Reality,* Enemy Combatant Publications, Elat, Alaska, Self published Zine.

James Shelby Downard (1913-1998)

CHAPTER 10

MY LIFE IN THE COSMIC NET

Now made aware!
Catch a breath of this looking down.
Plain as night – blaring the bigmouth of the proselytizer.
Witness their faith: this is no laughing matter!
But, laugh likewise and crosswise, nonetheless

INTRODUCTION

Individuals engaged in high strangeness research encounter peculiar synchronicities in their lives related to the weird subjects they are studying. Previous chapters have presented theories on why and how this is possible. We've explored how these synchs manifested in the lives of RAW and Levenda, specifically in regards to the JFK mystery. However, these two authors are not the only examples of highly strange subjects showing up in weird ways in the personal lives of researchers; indeed, it occurs so often that it appears to be the norm, not the exception.

EXAMPLES

Synchromystic author Christopher Knowles reports that some of the topics in his novel, *He Will Live Up in the Sky*, are similar to real life incidents in his hometown.[1] Filmmaker, actor, author, and host, Sean Stone (son of Oliver Stone) reports this phenomenon showing up when he was making his movie, *Greystone Park* (2012).[2]

University professor and author, Richard Spence points out that Downard's ex-wife married another man who was also tied to the JFK mystery, claiming that Oswald was a visitor of his hotel and that he "repeatedly tried to tell what he knew" to the authorities which resulted in him being harassed by the FBI for more than 30 years.[3] Spence also reports that his mother grew up in the same Oklahoma town where Downard himself was born, pointing out that it was possible Downard and his mother might have met during childhood.[4]

James Day, author of *The Mad Bishops: The Hunt for Earl Anglin James and His Assassin Brethren,* says he was "jaw dropped, to say the least" when he "realized that David Ferrie ... and I both went to the same Jesuit high school" and even attended the same college and "even dormed in the same dorm."[5]

Day's book explores the life of Earl Anglin James, who was a "Bishop in the Old Catholic Christian underground, a network of churches independent from Rome, Constantinople, and Canterbury, but claim authority as Catholic prelates through the doctrine of apostolic succession." The book also explores the fact that James' life "links to many of the key players in the Dealey Plaza enigma," including the independent Catholic bishops David Ferrie, Jack Martin, and Guy Bannister.[6]

His Family Thinks He's Crazy

For a more detailed exploration of how this phenomenon unfolds and, most importantly, how it can impact an individual's life, we will look at Mystic Mark, the host of the *My Family Thinks I'm Crazy* podcast. Mark claims that at the same time he was getting into the history of Yale's Skull and Bones society, he had a "red pill suppository" moment. This was when he encountered the Ivy League secret society while studying on a neighboring campus in New Haven, Connecticut. Mark reports he "didn't really understand the full scope" of parapolitics in general and of Skull and Bones society in particular until he met someone who became his mentor, a Native American who had traveled from Arizona to New Haven, "on a spiritual pilgrimage to connect with Geronimo." Mark says he met his mentor at "really weird place: an ancient burying ground which is now a public park." He claims this mentor taught him not only about the theft and desecration of Geronimo's remains, but also about Native American spirituality.

This chance encounter is what started his "synchromystic journey," eventually leading to him podcasting in a "really serendipitous way." Mark equates the experience to a "claw machine" picking him up out of obscurity and dropping him into "this world,"[7] where he is a leading high strangeness podcaster. Based on my research, I am guessing Mark's mentor is the man who was featured in a *New Haven Register* 2012 article, where it was reported that he came to New Haven and now "regularly prays outside Skull and Bones, an exclusive secret society of Yale seniors and alums, because he believes Geronimo's skull is there."[8] According to CNN, in 2009 Geronimo's great-grandson brought a lawsuit that argued "a secretive society at Yale University holds the remains of his great-grandfather."[9]

In addition to randomly meeting his Native American mentor, Mark also speaks about the synchronistic experience he had around that same time, when he was delivering pastries in the former Yale home of Bush Sr., "the very same morning that he died." That is, Mark learned this former U.S. president and member of Skull and Bones had died while he was in the man's former college dorm, which was now the office of the Yale economics department. Mark adds, "These are the things that smacked me in the face" and caused him to say to himself "you should be talking to people about this." Finally pointing out that this synch was "one of the many coals in the fire under my ass that led" him to working for Sam Tripoli (standup comedian and host of the *Tin Foil Hat* podcast) and hosting his own podcast, *My Family Thinks I'm Crazy*.[7]

This highlights how the uncanny synchronicities experienced during high strangeness research can profoundly inspire individuals on a personal level. This suggests that the phenomenon may possess a journalistic inclination, actively facilitating the revelation of truth by bringing researchers face to face with the topics they are studying, so that the person will then be moved to share the experience with others.

This process is similar to how a dream aims to reveal deeper truths about oneself. This healing phenomenon of dreams seeks to uncover profound truths about the reality of an individual's hidden inner life, thus working on a personal level. The synchronistic encounters of an investigator of high strangeness motivate individuals on a collective level, as seen in Mystic Mark's case where he was spurred on to share his experiences publicly. Encountering remarkable synchronicities face to face prompts individuals to disclose them publicly, contributing to other people sharing their own experiences, and then others to do the same. On and on, until we all end up sucked through Chardin's Omega Point, which is a future state of ultimate convergence and unity – the culmination of human consciousness and evolution.

For the remainder of this chapter, I will examine the high strangeness subjects that synchronicity has brought into my life while giving a brief explanation of the theories behind those subjects. This will serve as a jumping off point for your rabbit hole into these subjects.

My First Psychology Class

During my senior year in high school, around 1995, I took my first psychology class. Interestingly, as I embarked on my first exposure to psychology as a discipline, which later became my career, our teacher shared with the class that he had been part of a mind control experiment during his time in the military. I will explain the details of what he taught us that day, but first I will give a brief survey of the history of mind control in the U.S. military and intelligence agencies.

History of Mind Control Research in the U.S.

In 1953 the Director of Central Intelligence officially approved the MK-Ultra project which then remained as a covert operation for more than a decade. The official story is that MK-Ultra was "originally intended to make sure the United States government kept up with presumed Soviet advances in mind-control technology" to stay competitive in the Cold War.[10] A less official story is that MK-Ultra was a continuation of work actually started in Nazi concentration camps under Hitler. This utterly absurd and terrifying idea is supported by the fact that the CIA hired the researchers from the "Nazi concentration camps to come and explain what they had found out so that we could build on their research."[11]

Another popularly known MK-Ultra experiment took place between 1955 and 1965 when "CIA agents used hookers to lure unsuspecting johns" to another location and "then dosed the men with LSD and observed the X-rated goings-on through a two-way mirror." The author of the book *The Search for the 'Manchurian Candidate': The CIA and Mind Control* says that "the CIA's obsession with mind control had its origins during World War II, when the agency's predecessor, the Office of Strategic Services, set up a 'truth drug' program whose purpose was to discover a substance that would make subjects reveal their secrets."[12] And during the Cold War, "the CIA secretly funded mind-control experiments on unwitting Canadians in a program code-named MK-ULTRA" and it is theorized the "experiments laid the groundwork for modern-day torture techniques."[13]

Project MK-Ultra has been officially admitted by the U.S. Government and documents about the project are available publicly on official governmental websites.[A] Also notice that the sources I give in this section are from mainstream news outlets: NPR, the Smithsonian Magazine, the San Francisco Chronicle, and the Canadian Broadcasting Corporation. As we see in the case with parapolitical research specifically and highly strange material in general, this information is often publicly available and reported on by mainstream news outlets. As Marshall McLuhan wrote,

---

A CIA Family Jewels Report: cia.gov/readingroom/collection/family-jewels, The Rockefeller Commission Report: fordlibrarymuseum.gov/library/document/0005/1561495.pdf, The Church Committee reports: intelligence.senate.gov/sites/default/files/hearings/95mkultra.pdf.

"Only puny secrets need protection. Big discoveries are protected by public incredulity."

Personal Experience

Back to my first psychology course and the fact that, reportedly, my teacher had been involved in a mind control experiment during his military service. Just to clarify, he didn't officially test us on his experience related to his own mind control (it wasn't "on the test"), but he did indeed present his experience as a fascinating case of psychology in action.

From what I recall, my teacher, a Vietnam veteran, mentioned that this incident occurred on a base related to that war, but I can't remember if it happened during or after basic training. Here are the details as best as I remember them: he recounted that a busload of he and his fellow soldiers was taken into town from the base. Before leaving the bus, a man acting in an official capacity uttered a command, prompting everyone to immediately disembark and enter an old-style nickel and dime store.

According to my teacher, either before or after this event (I can't recall), the soldiers underwent a course (or debriefing) led by a psychiatrist. The implication was that this psychiatrist was responsible for the experiment and their strange behavior. I can't recall if my teacher indicated this was a debriefing of the incident or the actual mind control programming. I am leaving the story vague to stay as close as possible to my actual recollection of what was told to us that day in class.

Upon entering the store, my teacher recounted that the group of soldiers headed straight to the magazine rack, systematically removing and tossing every magazine onto the floor. According to him, they engaged in this behavior seemingly without conscious control, compelled to discard the magazines without understanding why. Once the rack was emptied, the same man uttered another phrase, prompting the soldiers to swiftly exit the store and board the bus, which then drove away. He emphasized that they didn't purchase anything, browse normally, or exhibit typical shopping behavior. Instead, they simply threw all the magazines to the floor, seemingly under the influence of an unseen force, and then departed.

Again, this was presented as an example of psychology in action and, if I recall correctly, was presented as something like a case of mass hypnosis. I remember raised eyebrows (and exchanged side glances) from other students as he told the story: acknowledgment as to how weird a story it was.

Occam's Rabbit Hole

What am I supposed to think in regards to the reality of mind control research? Official sources report that it occurred, mainstream news sources report on it, and I was told by an authority figure in his State-sanctioned role as a high school teacher that it happened to him when he was in the military. Where does Occam's razor (the simplest explanation is more likely than the complex one) leave us with the question: is project MK-Ultra indeed true? In high strangeness research, Occam's razor often takes us through the rabbit hole.

As we continue in this chapter you can ask these same questions in regards to every topic brought up.

My Job at a High Strangeness Hotspot

My first job in the mental health field was situated on the outskirts of metro-Atlanta amidst 1,200 mostly wooded acres. This residential treatment center for children, specializing in their psychiatric care, resembled a summer camp environment. My job title was "counselor," but my job duties were what is often referred to as a "tech" in psychiatric hospitals, being responsible for managing the daily activities and needs of the patients.

The facility existed in an area marked by an unusual concentration of high strangeness phenomena. The *Penny Royal* podcast explores the Oakwood mental health facility in Somerset, Kentucky and how it relates to high strangeness. The experimental facility was built in 1973, but was closed shortly thereafter, due to a death of a patient and reports of pagan activities being practiced in the basement. The idea is that a psychiatric treatment center might be a high strangeness magnet because it would house clients, such as people suffering from schizophrenia, who might be "channeling the truth of the universe."[14] This theory of high strangeness window areas is similar to the theory of the graveyard being a magnet for the paranormal, meaning people experiencing intense emotions in the area are a magnet for paranormal phenomena.

My fellow staff members reported Bigfoot sightings (more below) as well as ghost sightings. One story I heard was of people seeing a headless Native American ghost and that cabins couldn't be built in one area because, overnight, the posts would mysteriously come out of the ground. It was generally thought these hauntings had to do with Native American activity in the past – and there is a substantial past history of Native Americans in this part of Georgia.

In addition to paranormal occurrences, I was also confronted with the parapolitical. One co-worker reported he was corresponding with founding Black Panther members and regaled me with stories of how his mail from them always arrived having been opened. Another African-American co-worker, who turned me onto Goodie Mob's song "Cell Therapy," was hip to the goings on at Mena, Arkansas and reported that his father worked at Area 51. Growing up, his family lived in Las Vegas and his career military father worked at the secret base because he could be paid more. He claimed his father was flown into the site on the days he worked. And, of course, I have already told the story about a co-worker's husband who may have been a witness of Operation Paperclip related activities and the cabal of Nazi leaders who survived the fall of Berlin and their loss during WW2.

Anneewakee

The next parapolitical item is of a very sinister nature and a great example of how dark aspects do tend to pop up in high strangeness research. The following all allegedly occurred when the facility was known as Anneewakee. Please note that the facility was under completely different management when I was working there and I never saw anything even remotely close to what is described below, while I was working there.

In 1990, the Associated Press reported that a "multimillion-dollar settlement has been reached ... arising from a sexual abuse ... scandal at the Annewakee Inc. psychiatric treatment center for adolescents." According to the AP news article, "five male former patients alleged they were sexually abused by [the] Anneewakee" founder and the "former co-director of therapeutic services." I have left out the names of these two individuals due to the controversial nature of their alleged crimes. I certainly don't have enough money to fight court battles with angry members of wealthy families. The total payout ended up being "$36.3 million, the highest ever in Georgia." At that time, the seventy-year-old founder of Annewakee was said to have been "serving an eight-year prison sentence after pleading guilty in April 1988 to sodomizing 12 male former patients" and the former co-director of therapeutic services, forty-two at the time, "was convicted in November 1988 of sodomizing two 16-year-old male former patients."[15]

Sadly enough, the above is just the beginning of this dark rabbit hole. Just search "Anneewakee founder" and go down it yourself.[B] I also encourage

B See, beta.reddit.com/r/troubledteens/wiki/index/anneewakee anyone interested in this dark subject to listen to the 14 episode podcast series, *Camp Hell: Anneewakee.* The creator of this series said he "found a rabbit hole of information" regarding Anneewakee that, in his words, "would continue to surprise me with the depths of its scandal and those involved."

However, I do want to give a trigger warning for the series, the ubiquitousness of trigger warnings these days, has perhaps led to people not taking them seriously anymore. I cannot stress enough how disturbing this series is; if you have had any sexual trauma, I would recommend you use extreme caution in listening to this series and only do so if you have a mental health professional with whom you can process the details of the show. Yes, it is that disturbing.

According to this podcast series, the Anneewakee operation was allegedly "able to expand continuously over two decades, all the while funneling millions of dollars to the upper management of the organization." The series maintains that this continuous expansion "can only be attributed to its many ties to people in power, some of which would extend all the way to the White House." The podcast also claims that the founder "was a political player" who facilitated political contacts that would "benefit him later." It is also pointed out that there were "a lot of ex-Georgia State politicians" on Anneewakee's board. Finally, it is said that because there were "a lot of powerful people" involved in Anneewakee, it is a "dark chapter in Georgia history." Invoking a dark chapter in United States history currently playing out, the series says that "Before Jeffrey Epstein there was [the founder of Anneewakee] and the network of people who allowed his exploitative actions."[16]

Anyone who has read Whitney Webb's work can get a sense of what may be at play here. A survivor of Anneewakee sums up the stakes in this issue, saying the founder of Anneewakee "hurt so many people, I felt like the balance between good and evil on this planet shifted."[17] Notice the idea of a battle between good and evil that we encounter again and again in high strangeness research.

As experienced parapolitical researchers may already be guessing, there is a lot to the story of Anneewakee that I could go into but I will not do so due to its explosive nature. However, here are some further resources if anybody is interested in learning more: the website, Anneewakee.me, and the book by Steve Salem Evans, *Anneewakee: One Boy's Journey.*

Finally, I again want to point out that when I worked at the treatment center that was once named Anneewake, I never observed or heard about anything even close to what is described above. By the time I started working at the facility in the early 2000s it was was run on the up and up and did good work for children with very severe psychiatric conditions. As I said before, it was run by a completely different group of people and called a different name when I worked there. I worked with some great people and gained a ton of valuable experience in the mental health field. The only thing that remained of Anneewakee when I was working at the facility were the rumors of what happened before: if you will, *the ghosts*. And, yes, what I was told by my co-workers from the Anneewakee days did confirm some of what is reported in the above mentioned podcast.

I even spoke with a very respected psychotherapist in the Atlanta area who had met the founder during the 1970s. When I told her about the podcast, she reported it was something of an open secret that the founder of Anneewakee was not to be trusted and that the discerning person could tell immediately (that he was shady) if you talked to him personally. She reported that at that time in America there was a runaway teen problem, which she and her colleagues were trying to help while he was trying to exploit it.

I have been recommended to leave out the Anneewakee saga in this book because some say that the mere mention of this topic will leave me branded "far right,"[C] which I am not. However, I feel I would be doing a grave disservice to the past victims of Anneewakee if I took that route. What kind of person would I be if I left this subject out, just so people wouldn't slander me? According to the above quoted podcast series, the facility was allegedly built via child labor, as this is what the patients who were at Anneewakee allege. The manual labor was allegedly spun as a therapeutic activity. This means that I literally worked in the structures they were forced to (allegedly) illegally build.

This is the mental health facility that got me my start in the field, and if it weren't for this facility I would not be where I am today in my career. I am reminded of the story addressing why the devil is always angry – all his work of evil leads to helping humanity; all the destruction he sows ends up benefiting the forces of good in the end.

Mound Builders[D]

As is the case in my study of the Carrollton Vortex high strangeness window area[E] (see below), there were also anomalous ancient ar-

C "Pizzagate, QAnon and the 'Epstein List': Why the Far Right Is Obsessed with Sex Trafficking," Politico.com, Jan. 2024.

D Also see, *The Ancient Giants Who Ruled America: The Missing Skeletons and the Great Smithsonian Coverup* where it is reported that a "Seven foot tall" skeleton was found in Caldwell county (where I'm originally from and live in the U.S.), p. 354.

E Not just including Carroll County Georgia but also the surrounding area, including: the "Troop Heard Corridor." See patch.com/georgia/douglasville/mysteries-troup-heard-corridor-0 and visitlagrange.com/quirky-stories-and-legends-of-lagrange/

tifacts found near Anneewakke. In 1901, for example, "a four feet tall stone stela was discovered face down on top of a hilltop shrine overlooking Sweetwater Creek." The art carved into the stone "did not look like any known Muskogean art normally found at mound sites in Georgia." The stela is now displayed at the Sweetwater Creek State Park in Douglas County; where it was observed by the American Petroglyphic Society in 2010, and they "quickly identified the art as being Taino Arawak" and was "a guardian deity worshiped in Puerto Rico."

It was also in Douglas County that the "oldest known platform mound and permanent agricultural village in Georgia" was discovered. It was "located on Sandtown Creek, across the river from Six Flags Over Georgia." Sadly, this mound was "destroyed without being studied during the construction of Six Flags," which is fourteen miles from where Anneewakee[F] was located. Also of note, is that there is a mound near the site of the old Annawakee treatment center, called the Annawakee Mound, near Anneewakee Creek and the Chattahoochee River.[18]

Muskogean town dwellers "carried with them advanced cultural traditions from Mexico" and consisted of what we now know as various Native American tribes, including the Creeks because "prior to arrival of Europeans, there were no Indian 'tribes.'" The "early Muskogeans eventually formed provinces that were governed by large towns" which "were usually located ... on major rivers such as the Chattahoochee." The founders of such towns "carried with them many Mesoamerican cultural traits" leading some to believe that "they may have been either Itza Mayas or the hybrid descendants of both Mayas and indigenous peoples." This theory is supported by the fact that the "language that most of the Creek Indians' ancestors spoke in Georgia was Itsate" and "The Itza Maya's[G] also called themselves, Itsati."

Bigfoot

I spent my last two years at this facility working the night shift, which becomes noteworthy as my interest in the possibility of Bigfoot in the area was initially sparked by a night security guard. One prevailing theory

F For more on the high strangeness of amusement parks see Walter Bosley's book, *Latitude 33: Key to the Kingdom: The Arcane Science and Hermetic Engineering of the Happiest Place On Earth* (WalterBosley.com). In this book "He explores the possibility of an interdimensional portal at the theme park and the influence it may have on visitors' psychic perception ... Bosley presents various theories ... including the existence of interdimensional beings and the manipulation of telluric currents." (The Confessionals 613: *Disneyland's Portal Device*).

G The Itza Maya were a subgroup of the Maya civilization, primarily associated with the ancient city of Chichen Itza in the Yucatan Peninsula. Known for their architectural and astronomical achievements, the Itza Maya played a significant role in the development of the broader Maya civilization.

suggests that the creature is a nocturnal, unidentified great ape. The night shift security guard recounted peculiar incidents he had observed: on one occasion he heard a considerable commotion in the woods, followed by a herd of deer darting out, seemingly chased by a predator; another night, he and another security guard reached a creek at a campsite's edge, where they heard persistent, loud growling, leading them to eventually leave.

I thought that this sounded like Bigfoot activity (the security guard was a normie, but thought these encounters were strange) so I searched the Bigfoot Field Research Organization Website, which includes a database of sightings in the United States, divided by state and county. I found the following encounter, reportedly taking place in 1974, which occurred a few miles from the facility. The report is a rare negative encounter with a Bigfoot, which is interesting when considering the dark history of Anneewakee.

An individual quoted in the report states that a creature "jumped out from the woods next to me and grabbed the saddle and back of the horse. As this happened … The horse bolted and ran … This thing was face to face with me. I remember the face and hands most of all. It had a HAND – not a paw. the hands were huge will [sic] hair on them and long nails. The saddle … had deep scratches … in it where the creature had grabbed and pulled at it. It had very human-like features but thicker and scary looking. The hair around his face and neck was very hairy … with piercing eyes."[19]

After conducting an exploration of Douglas county's neighboring counties, I discovered Bigfoot encounters within the regions where these counties intersect. This intersection was an extensive stretch of untamed land and seemed to indicate that this area might constitute a habitat suitable for the elusive creatures. Bolstered by this revelation and believing I was working in prime Bigfoot territory, I inquired among my colleagues to determine if anyone had encountered anything associated with the legendary creature.

One evening, a fellow staff member recounted an intriguing incident to me. According to their account, a great commotion arose among the camp's adolescent clients (aged 12-14) when they spotted an individual positioned just outside the designated campsite boundaries. This staff member personally witnessed the enigmatic figure, describing it as entirely white, prompting them to contact the sheriff's department due to the fact the individual would not leave the area.

In response, I shared my knowledge of Bigfoot and how some people have reported sightings of a white-furred variant. The staff member gazed at me attentively and declared, "That's exactly what it was!" With this physical sighting occurring on the campus, my resolve to embark on a hiking expedition in the area intensified. I came across a fellow colleague who possessed an open-minded perspective regarding the existence of Bigfoot and shared my excitement about the findings I had gathered.

One afternoon, we ventured off together into the woods of the campus in search of the elusive creature. During our expedition, I distinctly recall catching a whiff of an unmistakable skunk-like odor, albeit lasting only a brief moment. Additionally, while strolling along a creek, a small pebble unexpectedly landed in front of me. However, considering these occurrences as trivial, I neglected to mention them to my co-worker, assuming they held no significance. Later, I discovered that some individuals have reported a similar skunk-like smell associated with Bigfoot sightings, and the act of rock throwing has also been documented in encounters with the creature.

Of note is that we came across a large cache of rocks of varying sizes, ten yards long and five-yards wide. I'm not a geologist, so I am not sure if it was naturally occurring; but we did comment on it because it appeared out of place. We also found a crude lean-to structure made out of old tarp. It had a hole cut in the middle of it to allow smoke to rise through it and there were the remnants of a small fire. I thought nothing of this structure because I was then of the mainstream opinion that Bigfoot was simply an undiscovered nocturnal woodland ape. We speculated that perhaps some kids were using it for teenage shenanigans.

The large rock cache and crude lean-to structure would have been looked at differently if I had been aware of the theories that Bigfoot wear primitive clothes and build crude structures. That is, they are much more intelligent than a mountain gorilla. And I certainly wasn't thinking in terms of the high strangeness theory that Bigfoot are psychic, which I will explore below.

Psychic Bigfoot Shamans

A good starting point for exploring this aspect of Bigfoot is *Where the Footprints End: High Strangeness and the Bigfoot Phenomenon.*[H] The book "poses a danger to the foundations of cryptozoology" because it presents evidence that goes against mainstream Bigfoot investigators who "would have you believe that people around the world are merely encountering a lost ape." The research this book highlights is information dismissed by mainstream researchers: "countless Bigfoot reports involving glowing orbs, telepathic communication, and paranormal phenomena

H Also see *Bigfoot: Beyond the Footprints* by Mary A. Joyce and *Praise For the Hairy Man: The Secret Life of Bigfoot* by Andrew Colvin and Jeffery Pritchett.

that have more in common with tales of ancient gods and alien abductions than they do with primatology."[20]

The book *The Psychic Sasquatch and Their UFO Connection* by Jack Lapseritis is also about this aspect of Bigfoot and he reports that there is field research indicating that "the Bigfoot are psychic, multidimensional and able to slip into and out of an unseen dimension, hence [their] elusivity." To up the weird factor, Lapseritis reports there are many "first hand accounts that Bigfoot works in conjunction with extraterrestrials, as guards and scouts."[21]

Lapseritis's second book, *The Sasquatch People and Their Interdimensional Connection,*[I] is "the product of 55 years of accumulated knowledge based on [his] encounters with the Psychic Sasquatch" and 187 documented cases which "have clearly objectified the reality of Psi with this phenomenon."[22] I classify Lapseritis's books as high strangeness because they present research to back up the idea of a psychic Bigfoot.

The next book is similar to New Age texts, insofar as it is reported to have been channeled. As I have said earlier, high strangeness authors present research to back up their utterly absurd claims and New Age authors often report their information is from channeled sources, meaning they offer no research to back up their claims. I advocate combining and using both approaches. *The Sasquatch Message to Humanity: Conversations with Elder Kamooh,* by SunBow TrueBrother[J] is reported to have been channeled from a "Sasquatch shaman," an Elder Bigfoot named, Kamooh. The following consists of condensed, but nevertheless vital parts of Kamooh's messages.

Bigfoot (or Sasquatch) "were created by the Star Elders (ETs) before humans to care for Mother Earth and assist in spiritual evolution of [our planet's] collective consciousness." They are "helping us grow" and "raise our consciousness through spiritual evolution" and are able to do this because "they have advanced psychic abilities such as telepathy, mind reading, remote viewing, hypnosis, astral projection, dematerialization, teleportation, shape shifting, and permeating consciousness."

Kamooh, the Bigfoot shaman, addresses why evidence of their existence is not known, explaining that material proof "would threaten their safety" because said proof would then be "used by 'lower lords' (those in power who are leading the world in a dangerous direction)"

I "Sasquatch Working with Benevolent ETs to Uplift Humanity and Avoid Planetary Disaster," *ExoPolitics Today with Dr. Michael Salla,* (Aug. 2023), interview with Lapseritis. His website is sasquatchmessage.com.

J His website is scenicsasquatch.com

to inspire people to track or to hunt them. They also claim that Bigfoot and their ET "allies" are "unconcerned with science obtaining empirical proof since there will always be denial, no matter how much proof is provided."

Kamooh reports the planet is "under the control of the lower lords who want to take over our planet and separate us from our souls" and, as such, the "rehabilitation of our collective consciousness is the ONLY thing that matters and it is the reason" the Bigfoot are reaching out to us now. Their message is that "Humans must reconnect to 'spiritual consciousness' through Nature and within ourselves to restore our spiritual and psychic gifts."[23]

These channeled messages invoke the intersection of the parapolitical with the Bigfoot phenomenon. High strangeness researchers have speculated that the military "might want to understand the true nature of a dimension-hopping Bigfoot" because, if this were a reality, then "it could offer [a] potential high-payoff [for] military, intelligence and commercial applications." In addition, the accepted existence of a dimension-hopping Bigfoot would facilitate "a dramatic paradigm shift in science." This is because "Anomalies are the key to all paradigm shifts."[24] The fact that the existence of Bigfoot could cause a paradigm shift is what I call the *politics of Bigfoot* and why I think the knowledge of the existence of Bigfoot could change the world for the better.

Psi-Bigfoot & the Carrollton Vortex

You may be wondering how I found myself in a tale that involves psychic Bigfoot. To complicate matters: it involves an employee of a government agency investigating the paranormal, psi-Bigfoot dreams, the South's Skinwalker Ranch, and a vortex.

My Magical Artistic Practice

My spiritual practice infuses magick and art, as taught by Michael Bertiaux. My paintings are a way to deepen my magical practice; in that way, they are merely tools to further my spiritual consciousness. Bertiaux says "the genius of the artist is reflected in the ideal personification of his cosmic imagination."[25] In my paintings, I let my imagination run wild to develop my "cosmic imagination." As a result, I don't stop and ask "Is this true?" Instead, I trust the process, remembering that "art is the most efficient way of expressing how occult energies are manifest" and that "art is really its own Gnosis" because there exists an "alliance between art and esotericism."[26]

This approach to painting opens you up to mystical realities and provides a safe container to develop your "cosmic imagination." Bertiaux explains that an "artist is a magician when he allows the divine energy of ... cosmic illumination to enter into his multi-dimensional consciousness." This gnostic approach means the artist becomes "an instrument for divine and angelic activity in what he does." And relevant to the next section, I point out that this approach to painting is "highly mediumistic" because it allows "the ocean of creativity to rise within[the artist's] transcendental id."[25]

With all that being said, in 2008 I completed a painting entitled "The Sha-personic Dream Journey of the Outcast Wondering Yeti Shaman of the SouthEast United States." The painting was to reflect something I wrote in my magical journal at the time, which was that I felt I was contacted by a Bigfoot shaman in a dream. This was more phatic communication in the dream, meaning I did not receive any explicit messages.

In 2020, I was moved to gift this painting to a renowned folk artist in the South-East of the United States when I saw they were posting about the possibility of Bigfoot being seen on their property. This artist called my painting a "visionary piece," also claiming the Bigfoot "were tree knocking like crazy, a week before the shut down due to the virus. I think they were trying to get our attention."[27] At the time when I completed the painting in 2008, I thought of it as purely an artistic, mental exercise. Meaning, I didn't "believe" it to be true *per se;* at that time I had not even heard the theories about psychic Bigfoot. It was not until researching this book that I found all of the literature on psychic Bigfoot.

Whether or not one "believes" in the highly strange topics one encounters in this research is tricky, to say the very least. I argue that as we get further down the rabbit hole, the more we encounter topics that are beyond belief: they are so strange that a human simply can't believe them. I mean, how does one truly *believe* that reality is so strange that psychic Bigfoot shamans inhabit it?

The South's Skinwalker Ranch

Now we are brought to the 2020 book *The Meadow Project: Explorations into the South's Skinwalker Ranch,* which covers the extensive research into a location known as the "Meadow," which is "the location of many astounding events." The high strangeness is so prevalent at the Meadow that researchers "have even compared it to the Skinwalker Ranch itself with its own reports of UFOs, cryptid beasts, portals, missing time, crop circle-like formations, men/women in black, orbs, strange beams of light, mysterious beings and many other oddities."[28] Finding myself in the center of another Skinwalker Ranch was not on my endtimes bingo card, but such is the case in high strangeness.

Trey Hudson

Hudson has an intriguing background, reporting to me personally that he was taught remote viewing by an individual who was once associated with Lieutenant Colonel Jim Channon, the originator of the First Earth Battalion, which was the "idea of a new military of supersoldier to be organized along New Age lines."[29] Jim Channon and the First Earth Battalion was explored in the film and book *The Men Who Stare at Goats.*

In 1988 Hudson gained certification as an "All source Intelligence Officer" and was assigned to the "372nd Military Intelligence Detachment." In 1989 he entered "Federal Government service as a 'Security Specialist'" and retired in 2023. Hudson "has received training ... in various specialties to include intelligence analysis, security of WMD, anti-terrorism, counter-intelligence, emergency management, physical security, personal security, response to CBRNE[K] incidents, incident command, operations security, information security and many others."[30]

The University of West Georgia Psychology Department and the Carrollton Vortex

Hudson attended the University of West Georgia and majored in psychology. The University "is home to a world-renowned psychology department and one of the few universities offering degrees with a humanistic and transpersonal focus."[30] When I learned Hudson was from the University of West Georgia psychology department, I immediately guessed the Meadow was part of the larger Carrollton Vortex phenomenon. Please note that I have never been officially told by Hudson where the Meadow is located, as he keeps the exact location private.

The Carrollton Vortex was discovered by high strangeness researcher Andrew Stephens, also a graduate of the UWG psychology department. He has a lot of data indicating the area is a high strangeness window area, based on over twenty years of extensive research; however, most of this

K CBRNE incidents refer to events involving the release or use of chemical, biological, radiological, nuclear, or explosive materials.

research remains unpublished. He has shared some of it with me personally. I will fully explore the high strangeness associated with the UWG psychology department and the Carrollton vortex in volume three of this series, *My Cosmic Trigger: Gurus, Guides, Friends, and Ancestors in Highly Strange Places.*

The Monkey Bear Lady

Hudson reports all manner of high strangeness at the Meadow – portal boxes, teleportation, an artificial moon, slipping into other dimensions – but one of the weirdest things he reports is that a woman randomly came into their camp when they were doing their field research. His encounter with this woman is featured in his book and he talks about it in podcast interviews, referring to her as the "business woman of the forest." However, she is now more known as the "monkey bear lady." Hudson's encounter with the monkey bear lady is where his experiences at the Meadow, in his words, "really gets strange."

Hudson reports he was in the Meadow proper and had just witnessed an anomalous cube, when his team back at the base camp radioed him, saying a random visitor had arrived and wanted to meet him. When he returned to the base camp "there was a business woman waiting for me." Hudson calls her a business woman because she was wearing business casual attire which he said was "very much out of place" to encounter deep in the forest.

He was then blown away that this woman who had randomly found their high strangeness hotspot was also a graduate of the same highly strange psychology program. Hudson says he thought this person was trying to "trick" him by saying she also graduated from this department, so he tried to throw her off the track by asking "Who are some of your favorite professors?" He was convinced because she gave him the names of professors he knew. She is now known as the monkey bear lady because she wanted Hudson and his team to follow her to a separate location where she knew "monkey bears" were living, just down the road from where their base camp was. Monkey bears are her unique nickname for Bigfoot.

When I heard Trey describe his experience with this woman and that she also claimed to be a graduate of UWG's psychology department, I figured I probably knew her. The reason I figured this was because I trusted the high strangeness synchronicity principle so much. I reached out to Hudson and got her name, and, indeed, I knew the monkey bear lady fairly well, as she was one of my former classmates with whom I was still in contact.

I reached out to her about the incident and she told me her version of the events, which I then told Hudson, who then retold in his interview on *The Higherside Chats.* Hudson shares what I told him regarding "her recollection" which "was this … she drives around the forest to unwind" after work and this is why she randomly found herself at this location. Guessing Hudson and his team were hunting for Bigfoot, she wanted to tell them about her earlier encounters with monkey bears. She claims that she and her sister saw Bigfoot when they were younger and that "monkey bears" was their nickname for them.

The monkey bear lady told me several highly strange tales that increase the weirdness of this story, and I hope to go into those in detail in volume three of this book. But suffice it to say, based on her prominence in the Meadow project and based on the things she shared with me, I believe her to be a Sibyl of the Carrollton Vortex. I find it significant and funny that my friend's synchronous encounter with these paranormal researchers at the South's Skinwalker ranch is perhaps the strangest thing they encountered. It is hard to convey the humor in knowing the fact that one of my old classmates rolling up to a research expedition randomly caused so much consternation, even among ex-military. This could only happen with a graduate of the University of West Georgia psychology department.

Hudson says after the monkey bear lady left their camp, they were saying her arrival "was not making any sense" and, as a result, "everyone [was] trying to not get wigged out" because "it was one of those experiences that were so odd." In his book, Hudson reports that this synchronicity changed the perception of a mainstream Bigfoot researcher that was part of his team that night. Again, notice how an encounter with high strangeness changes one's consciousness.

Hudson's team found their synchronous encounter with my friend "so unnerving and weird" that a member of the team, a former Army Ranger, suggested they "circle the perimeter" of the campsite to make sure the encounter wasn't her "setting us up to be robbed." The synchronicity involving the monkey bear lady was so "outside our frame of reference" that, Hudson says, "we were all a bit on edge after encountering her." They even speculated that my friend was a Man in Black or "an otherworldly entity." Again, their reaction is a testament to the power of synchronicity in high strangeness research.

Here is what I theorize happened with my friend's synchronous encounter with Hudson and his team. Hudson claims that when my friend randomly arrived they "had just had that amazing experience with the cube or box and [they] were trying to do [their] debrief." I think this cube they encountered (which I speculated earlier may be some sort of portal technology) activated the synchronicity. It reminds me of how Dr. Greer says the CE-5 contact app can trigger high strangeness synchronicity, which I have witnessed first hand. Hudson also speculates that perhaps my friend was "being influenced and controlled" by influences outside of their understanding; and, if my theory that she is the Sybil of the Carrollton Vortex is correct, then this is possible. At any rate, Hudson said his encounter with me and the monkey bear lady showed him that "all this stuff seems to be linked."[31]

Critique of Trey

Before we finish this section, I must address what I am sure will be a criticism of my including Hudson's work in this book and having him give a blurb praising the book. He has spoken to this criticism, saying people often point out that "this guy's a government guy" and that "there seems to always be some sort of military or governmental intelligence nexus to a lot of these people that are talking about this sort of stuff, so can we trust him?"[31] In the comments section of his cited podcast interview, some listeners are so critical of anybody with any military or governmental involvement in high strangeness that they don't even believe Hudson's monkey bear lady story. I can confirm the monkey bear lady is real, and as a result I'm sure some may even suggest I'm covering for Hudson.

However, I would be lying if I said I wasn't a little paranoid when interacting with Hudson about these topics, given the fact that it is a matter of public record that the Department of Defense has spent millions studying Skinwalker Ranch. Is another governmental agency also studying the South's Skinwalker Ranch? Does Occam's razor take us through the rabbit hole with this question as well? I've asked Hudson directly if he is researching the Meadow as part of his Federal Government service and he says he isn't. But of course, if he were, I'm sure he wouldn't be allowed to tell me. One possibility is that he is publishing his research about the Meadow publicly as part of the Open Source Intelligence[L] gathering

L Former Assistant Director of Central Intelligence for Analysis Mark M. Lowenthal defines OSINT as "any and all information that can be derived from overt collection: all types of media, government reports and other documents, scientific research and reports, commercial vendors of information, the Internet, and so on. The main qualifiers to open-source information are that it

approach to learn about window areas. The other possibility is that he is simply doing this as a hobby. When we get into high strangeness, it is hard to say what is the *simplest* explanation.

Whatever the case may be, I encourage high strangeness researchers to remember the lesson from *The X-Files* TV show, where Agent Mulder collaborated with the independent parapolitical researchers who published *The Magic Bullet Newsletter*.[M] Meaning, just because a person has past or present connections with governmental and/or military agencies, doesn't mean we can't collaborate together to uncover the highly strange truth.

Bigfoot Dreams of the Carrollton Vortex

As I proposed earlier, my friend, the monkey bear lady, is a Sibyl of the Carrollton vortex, window area. Her encounter with Hudson at the Meadow points to this fact as does her visionary art work. For example, one of her recent paintings is about the role of the Divine Feminine in the transformation of mass consciousness. While writing this book she reported to me she had "a dream about a Sasquatch who spoke with a strange ethereal voice saying, 'I can heal you.'"[32]

A few months later another high strangeness researcher, who studies the Carrollton Vortex in particular and high strangeness in general, reported another Bigfoot dream to me. In the dream he said it was a Bigfoot "conference," meaning a large gathering of the creatures, which struck him as a "rare" and significant occurrence. To his logic, which I can't argue with, a group gathering of Bigfoot is rare because meeting *en masse* would increase the chance of detection. Meaning: if your main way of living is to avoid detection, then you would be a relatively solitary species. The implication is that when there is a group meeting it would be for special occasions. In the dream, he was told by a Bigfoot at this gathering that "we aren't what you think we are." He took this to be about the "spiritual nature of Bigfoot" and he knew it was a "very powerful" and "special dream."[33]

Interestingly, while writing this chapter I also had a group Bigfoot dream. However, it differed from the above two dreams in that there were no psychic messages directed my way. I was in the mountains and I saw "a group of Bigfoot in the daytime, about 300 yards down the hill. I go down and there is a governmental group."[34] Please note, I am not proposing my dream is as significant as the first two, as it could easily be explained that I

---

does not require any type of clandestine collection techniques to obtain it." (wiki/Open-source_intelligence)

M There was a short-lived spin off series about the group that published the newsletter, called *The Lone Gunmen* (wiki/The_Lone_Gunmen).

would have a Bigfoot dream while working on this chapter. But I did want to include it just for the sake of research.

Bigfoot and the Raising of Atlantis

Before moving on from the Carrollton Vortex, let's look at what psychic Bigfoot shamans have to say about Atlantis. I bring this up to shed some light on the channeled messages from the Carollton Vortex I received over twenty years ago. The channeling was from a representative of "the light command" and one of the messages was that "you and two Americans are going to raise Atantis [sic]."[35] The Bigfoot shaman quoted earlier claims that negative ultraterrestrials "have encapsulated our home-planet inside a control grid, keeping away the influence of the Star Elders protecting us." As a result, this moment in history is "the last opportunity your people can grasp to end" this control "and reestablish the Cosmic Order, before the lower lords apply the next phase of their control agenda."

This current predicament is relevant to the mythological lost civilization because it is the same "situation that your ancestors faced in the downfall of Atlantis." However, it is "being replayed today, but on a much deeper scale, that may cause unrepairable damages to your ... evolution and destiny." And if the current dire situation is "not stopped" it will end "with global destruction" and a "mass extinction level event, as it happened in the days of Atlantis."[36] Again, no pressure dear reader.

If this hairy shaman is correct, then raising Atlantis would be a good thing. Edgar Cayce's prophecies also concern a "rebirth" of and "rising of Atlantis."[37] In addition, Francis Bacon's *New Atlantis* (1624) presents a utopian vision for the New World. However, in 2024, I ask the question: is the United States of America closer to bringing global destruction, or facilitating Utopia on Earth? Yeah, my thoughts exactly – so seeking the help of Bigfoot makes as much sense as anything right now.

Gnomes

Our next subject is gnomes, or "little foot," if you will. The most commonly known gnome in the United States is the leprechaun, which is the name for these creatures in Ireland. In other parts of the world, there are myths of the *duende*, "a humanoid figure of folklore, with variations from Iberian ... and Filipino cultures, comparable to ... gnomes, or leprechauns."[38]

In North America there is also folkloric evidence regarding the existence of gnome-like creatures in Native American myths and explored in the 1915 book *Tales of the Little People: Eight Native American Legends of Elves, Dwarves and Fairies*. In Mexican folklore, the *chaneque* is said to be "a small creature, only about knee-high, with a playful twinkle in its eyes and an air of mischief."[39]

Of special interest to this section is the folklore around the *Yunwi Tsunsdi* which are "the small mystical beings that played a vital part in traditional Cherokee life and culture" and are talked about in their myths and legends.[40] These legends have also been explored in the academic literature. In an essay from almost eighty years ago, it is said the Native American myths of little people so "closely resemble European folk figures" that they "might be considered as a borrowing from European tradition." Notice the assumption is that the Native Americans merely stole their myths from Europe. However, the article does course correct, saying that the "Little People are so widespread in America ... and often so isolated from a suitable European tradition, that a foreign origin seems improbable as a general explanation for their existence."[41]

Scientific Evidence

If folklore of little people is so prevalent across all cultures of the world, then it would stand to reason their existence would be found in the archaeological record. The skeptic, who for some reason has read this far, breathes a sigh of relief, saying "definitely this isn't the case!" Sadly for them, in 2004 "researchers announced the discovery of *Homo floresiensis,* a small relative of modern humans that lived as recently as 18,000 years ago. The 'hobbit' is now considered the most important hominin fossil in a generation."[42] This species was "one of the last early human species to die out ... just before or at the time when Homo sapiens arrived in the region."[43]

One anthropologist, Gregory Forth, even speculates "that a relic population of elf-like ancient hominins might still roam the jungles of a remote Indonesian island." As Forth admits, "Twenty years previously, when I began ethnographic fieldwork on Flores, I heard tales of human-like creatures, some still reputedly alive although very rarely seen." He says he knows this information is shocking because it is "coming from a professional anthropologist" and he also knows that his "conclusions will probably surprise many." Finally, Forth says that the discovery of H. floresiensis (nicknamed "the hobbit") was "tantamount to the discovery of a space alien."[44]

Forth says that in writing his book, *Between Ape and Human: An Anthropologist on the Trail of a Hidden Hominoid,* he "hoped to convince his colleagues to place greater emphasis on the testimony of the indigenous people they encounter during their researches." This is because he maintains that "anthropologists who ignore information in the form of myths and anecdotes from ... non-literate and technologically simple communities risk missing important evidence."[44]

In the book *Cherokee Little People Were Real,* author Mary Joyce "features testimonies of men who discovered ancient little tunnels, small skeletons and even a child-size skull with all its wisdom teeth when they were working on early construction projects at Western Carolina University in Cullowhee, North Carolina." This book even provides a photograph of a coin that was reportedly found there and the image on the coin looks like a Leprechaun. Joyce claims this evidence points to the fact that an "ancient race of Little People once lived in the North Carolina Mountains."[45]

Gnomes in High Strangeness

Keel says "accounts of little humanoids with supernatural powers can be found in almost every culture."[46] And in the seminal book on high strangeness, *Origins of the Gods: Qesem Cave, Skinwalkers, and Contact with Transdimensional Intelligences,* there is an entire chapter called, "The Little People." This chapter features, "Lou White Eagle, an arrow priest of the Cheyenne and grandson of the famed Cheyenne high priest Edward Red Hat" and his experience with the little people.[47]

In high strangeness you often see a comparison of the UFO phenomenon to fairy encounters. Researchers claim there are "many connections between the UFOs and the 'fairy-faith' which survived in many parts of Europe into this century. Many UFO occupants are described as 'elflike' having smallish stature, pointed ears" and accounts of abductions are "very similar to the fairy 'kidnap.'"[48] One theory is that in the past, people mistook extraterrestrial encounters for being the fairy folk. Meaning, what we now know as aliens were once referred to as gnomes. And another theory, as I pointed out previously, is that the phenomenon changes shapes over time: in one historical moment appearing as the fae, then as angels, and now as extraterrestrials.

In *The Lost History of the Little People: Their Spiritually Advanced Civilizations around the World,* Susan B. Martinez, Ph.D., examines "the North American mound-culture sites, including the diminutive adult remains found there" explaining "that these stately mounds were not burial sites but the sanctuaries and homes of the Little People." She claims "the Golden Age of the Great Little People" ended when "this lost race was forced from their original home on the continent" now "known in myth as Mu or Lemuria ... during the Great Flood of global legend."[49]

New Age Gnomes

By invoking the New Age, I am specifically referring to channeling. The following material comes from two individuals (Carol and David Swing) in Western North Carolina that claim to be in psychic contact with gnomes. I base this on the fact that when I went to their workshop in Asheville, circa 2005, they were communicating with their gnome friends, telepathically (i.e. channeling). However, their story below appears to have occurred in the physical realm.[N]

The couple claim that in 1997, two gnomes "introduced themselves to us at our home in North Carolina" in order that we "could help to make the teachings of Avalon available once more." The gnomes claimed these teachings have "meaning for the survival of humanity and of all creation."[50]

The gnomes reported they were "the caretakers of the nature kingdom, and they lie in a realm close to the physical earth which places them on the front lines between humans and Mother Earth," and as a result, they "endure much emotional pain from the devastation of the Great Mother by humans." The Swings describe them as being "3 to 3 ½ feet tall" and "live to be thousands of years old." They claim "Gnome women wear their hair long, and they often braid it or interweave elements of nature such as shells, leaves, or feathers. Many of the Gnome men grow beards, especially the warriors."[51] This physical description will be relevant later in this section.

The Darkside of Gnomes

Author and journalist, Mary Joyce writes of visiting "private property where an ancient race of Little People still live in Eastern Tennessee." The gnomes living on this property claim that "all ET races come to Earth for some self-serving reason, so they believe there are bad guys and better guys, not bad buys and good guys." Joyce says that the gnomes "seem to be considering an alliance with the better guys known as the Pleiadians."

In keeping with the fact that in high strangeness dark elements seem to pop up, these Tennessee gnomes "also claim" there is a group opposing the Pleiadians: "bad guys they call The Dominators." Naturally, these gnomes

N See the book *Gnomes in the Garden. Celtic Faerie Teachings* by David M. Swing. The Swings' website is avalongrove.org.

"are afraid that Earth will end up being exploded by The Dominators," however, "humans have a certain amount of choice in the matter." I have decided to leave out what these gnomes claim The Dominators are doing with humans because it is one of the third rails of this research. It is similar to Amy's story in season two of *Hellier*. At any rate, the gnomes report "The Dominators call Earth ... 'The Farm'"[52] and have a sinister deal with certain humans in the military industrial complex in the United States and other countries.

Personal Experiences

This experience relates to a potential encounter with gnomes in the foothills of North Carolina during my 5th-grade year. The narrative becomes somewhat difficult to retell because in the early '90s, people referred to diminutive humans as the *m word,* now recognized as a pejorative. The appropriate term is now commonly known to be a "person of short stature" or "little people" but this was not widespread in the public consciousness at that time.

The complexity arises in telling this story due to the fact that the Cherokee refer to the mythical gnomes as the Little People and now the correct term for human little people is, "little people". I have verbally told this story in the past and run into confusion with people thinking I am referring to human little people when I am referring to the Cherokee Little People. To avoid this confusion, while being faithful to how elementary school children and adults spoke in the early 90s, and while avoiding any derogatory language, I will use the term "person of short stature" for when we were using the *m word.*

5th Grade Field Trip to a Garnet Mine

My elementary school principal was a rockhound, so we took rock-related field trips. One trip was to a mineral convention and the other to a garnet mine in a neighboring county. Looking back, I admire his killing two birds with one stone approach to being an elementary school principal.

I later learned there was an actual mine shaft on the property where we were searching for garnets, but for the general public it just consisted of digging in two dirt covered hillsides. This field trip consisted of two separate classes of fifth graders, approximately thirty students each. My class consisted of boys who were more prone to rule breaking. There was no toilet at the site, so we just had to go off into the woods to use the bathroom. My rowdy classmates and I (about five-to-eight boys) would say that we had to go use the bathroom and instead would explore further into the surrounding woods.

This is important to point out because it demonstrates we were off exploring further than our classmates and we were not where we were supposed to be. Keel says "for some reason, children seem to see the little people more often than adults."[46] I argue this is due to the simple fact that children have more time and energy to explore off the beaten path and be in places where they are not supposed to be.

To our surprise, we came across what we called a family of "people of short stature," which delighted our young minds to no end. We thought it was the funniest thing we had ever seen. I say this to point out that we found it so funny that it bordered on us being in a state of giggling frenzy. Throughout the day, we would sneak off to spy on this family of "people of short stature," and then would go back to our class digging in the main area, sharing what we thought was absolutely hilarious news.

The family of "people of short stature" was all the buzz on the field trip. I also recall talking with another classmate on the phone when we got home for the day to talk about the incident. I didn't talk on the phone that often when I was in the fifth grade, and point this out to convey just how much of a big deal this sighting was to a group of ten and eleven-year-old boys.

Each time we snuck back into the woods to spy on this family, we got a little closer. I myself got close enough to see that one was wearing a hat with a feather in it.[O] I also recall there were animals (birds) walking around among the family, who seemed to be working diligently on an unidentifiable task. There also appeared to be smaller ones, which we assumed were children.

One of my particularly rambunctious classmates snuck down very close and threw a rock at them. In his defense, it was more of a toss, meaning it was thrown in a tricksterish manner and not thrown with the intent to harm. I have no idea what happened after that, because I ran as soon as he tossed the rock. Whether they were gnomes or human little people, arguably a crime was committed on the field trip, as we harassed them all day and then a boy threw a rock at them.

I then retold this story of seeing the family of "people of short stature" at the dinner table that evening. Of note is that my mother was the teacher of the other class, meaning she was on this field trip. My father's explana-

O In the *The Elves of Lily Hill Farm: A Partnership with Nature* by Penny Kelly her illustration of a gnome features him wearing a hat with a feather in it.

tion was that it was merely a family of "people of short stature" living in the woods, possibly members of a circus.

This brings us back to Occam's razor taking us through the rabbit hole. Legendary comedian Dave Foley speaks to this idea when he talks about the skeptical dismissal of UFOs despite a mountain of evidence indicating their existence, saying skeptics think "it can't be happening so it isn't." He says this causes skeptics to put out "tortured debunking theories" which they expect us to consider as "more plausible and they'll call that Occam's razor, which is the exact opposite of Occam's razor." Foley says that actually the "simplest answer is they saw what they saw."[53] So what did I see that day on the field trip?

The high strangeness explanation would be that we came across the lost race of gnomes (the Cherokee Little People) that live in the caverns of the Blue Ridge mountains. My father's "rational" explanation[P] was that they were a "people of short stature" family of circus performers living in the woods. Keep in mind he said this with a straight face and this was accepted as the logical explanation in Vaughn family lore until recently.

First of all, there are no circuses in my home town area, and there are also no rumors that a family of human little people live in the forest. Come to think of it, I've never heard any rumors of people in my hometown area squatting in the woods. There are, however, rumors of the mythical Cherokee Little People living in this area. Also, the dwarfism trait is not 100 percent passed down to children, so there should have been a regular size child in the family if they were human little people.

If this were a family of human little people, I would imagine the parents of the family would have walked over to our teachers and informed them that their students had been harassing them all day. Also, if it were a group of human little people illegally squatting on the property, then I would imagine the owners would have had them removed, as squatters (of any size) aren't typically a good mix for children's field trips.

Back to Occam's rabbit hole: there is archaeological evidence of a lost race of gnomes, explained above and at least one mainstream anthropologist thinks this race could still exist. People report seeing these mythical gnomes in the Blue Ridge mountains and Native Americans from the region record their existence in their myths and legends.

So what is more likely? My father's *rational explanation* of a "people of short stature" circus family, squatting illegally on a garnet mine's property,

P See RAW's, *The New Inquisition: Irrational Rationalism and the Citadel of Science*. RAW said he "coined the term 'irrational-rationalism'" because of people who "claim to be rationalists" but are only "skeptical about new ideas that frighten them" (RAW 1988 interview).

or that little foot is real? Before you answer the question, consider the following.

The Witch Lady of Morganton

The story of the family of "people of short stature" seen on the field trip was so persistent that it was a running joke between my best friend and me even in high school. And while in high school, this friend and I ran across a self-produced video about the witch lady of Morganton at the local video store. The witch lady was famous enough that we immediately rented her video, even if it was on a lark and not a genuine desire to learn her teachings. I had known about the witch lady of Morganton since I was a kid, as every time we drove by her home (named "Grey Shadows"), my mom would point it out. Every time we were in the area, I would ask my mom to drive by the witch lady's house.

The witch lady of Morganton, Joann Denton, has historical import, seen in the fact that in 1976 she accurately predicted "the death of another woman, and would become the first person in modern American history to be arrested and publicly tried for witchcraft."[54] Doing more research on Denton, I was surprised to learn that she received a surprisingly large amount of press on the local and national level. Her fame appeared to peak in the mid-70s, but she has received local press as late as October 2022, when a local paper said that "Every year, Denton, known as 'The Morganton Witch,' holds a Halloween celebration at Gray Shadows, her home on Lenoir Street in Morganton."[55]

An article written about her in *Esquire* in 1976, "The Wicked Witch of North Carolina," mentions that she summoned "up the poor departed Scott Fitzgerald." Of note to this book is that Fitzgerald's wife died in Asheville, North Carolina, not far from Morganton.[56] Denton also received attention for staging her own funeral and running for mayor of Morganton,[Q] guided by her "guardian spirit," Elvis Presley. By the mid-90s, when I was in high school, Denton's star had fallen, but she was still a local celebrity, enough so that we jumped at the opportunity to watch her video, entitled *The Witch of Gray Shadows*. The list of topics covered were "Unidentified flying objects and descriptions of sightings around Hickory," "The curse of the Pharaohs: did the mummies carry AIDS?" ... "how

Q The 1904, *Master of the World*, is the last novel by Jules Verne and set in Morganton. In the novel "a series of unexplained events occur across the Eastern United States, caused by objects moving with such great speed" it prompts "John Strock, 'Head inspector in the federal police department' in Washington, DC" to travel "to the Blue Ridge Mountains of North Carolina to investigate."(wiki/Master_of_the_World_(novel).

to call dead relatives to visit" ... "Elvis ain't dead!"[R] "Poltergeist arson: do they leave gasoline cans behind?" and "Assaulted by a floating knife."[54] While watching the video, our attention was immediately grabbed because an early scene features Denton topless, riding a white horse with a fake unicorn horn.[54]

If it weren't for the gratuitous nudity, our high school attention may have not been kept long enough to see the segment which features her being interviewed. In this interview, Denton reports there are Native American legends of "magical little people living" in the mountains and foothills of North Carolina. My friend immediately paused the video and turned to me, exclaiming: "The family of '*people of short stature*'!" This was the first time I had heard about these legends and this discovery, provided by the witch lady of Morganton, stuck with me.

My story of possibly seeing the mythical Cherokee Little People on an elementary school field trip is one of my favorite stories, so naturally I told my now wife when we started dating. She had heard similar legends from Turkey, so we started researching gnome myths throughout the world, finding that there were indeed legends of them all over the planet. After discovering this information, we resolved to go back to the same garnet mine the next time we visited my hometown.

We did just that circa 2002. In the car, on the way there I called the number for the garnet mine that was listed in the phone book. The mine was owned by a family and named after said family. I am purposely leaving out the name of the mine to protect the family's (both human and gnome) privacy. A woman answered the phone and informed me that they no longer let anyone on the property because of "insurance reasons." I said, "This may be a strange question, but have you ever seen little people on the property?"

She replied, "Now that you mention it, yes I did. When my kids were little, we were looking for a place to swim on the creek after it had rained. And we came across a group of little people swimming in the creek. They were just whooping and laughing, having a good ol' time." I asked what they looked like, and she said "They had long beards and looked real old." I inquired regarding if she said anything to them. "No," she answered, "we

R Denton later claimed Elvis was alive and communicating to her via telepathy (endnote 54: 1:27). Also see *He Is Always on Our Minds: But a Mythic Hero Lives Forever* by C. Bancroft, who reports on a "self-published book, *The Truth about Elvis Aaron Presley: In His Own Words*" that the author Donald Hinton "says he helped Elvis Presley write." Hinton is a licensed physician. (*Tampa Bay Times*, Aug. 2002).

were scared, so we got out of there real quick." My wife overheard the conversation and will attest to the fact that these are its contents.

Back to Occam's rabbit hole. This is the South, if someone is on your property the natural response would be to at least say something or even threaten to call the police. In more extreme cases, a person might go back to the trespassers later with a firearm and make sure they left the property, my point being that running away scared because human little people are on your property and doing nothing about is not in keeping with the cultural norms of this area. Not to mention that forgetting about long-bearded, diminutive trespassers swimming in your creek, until someone randomly calls you, is not a normal approach to people illegally using your land.

Over the years, other people have told me their stories with the mythical little people. A friend in the OTO claimed to see one materialize in the New Mexico desert after doing some ritual work in the area while on a camping trip. They reported it was dressed in crude clothing and looked dirty; they thought their ritual work had piqued the being's curiosity as to what the humans were doing, so it materialized to get a closer look.

Naturally, every house I live in will feature a garden gnome. Shortly after I finished graduate school, a landlord saw my gnome statue and told me the following story. While visiting her Greek boyfriend, he told her that his island was shared with the magical little people, adding that "We don't bother them, and they don't bother us." A long-time Turkish friend reports seeing a "toddler" walking like an adult through her village in the Black Sea region, claiming it trotted through the village and up into the mountains. Her "rational" explanation is that it was just a toddler on a midnight stroll.

Another friend in the OTO reported accidentally grabbing a "goblin" while he was feeding his newborn. His explanation was that he was in a twilight state of sleepiness, feeding his child, and as a result the veil was thinner. He said he dropped the bottle and reached down to pick it up, accidentally picking up the now unhappy goblin.

Just after finishing the above paragraphs, someone reported to me that they had seen the *menehune* with a group of people while hiking in Hawaii. The menehune are said to be about three-feet tall and according to a Hawaii Public Radio writer, "They lived in the mountains and when they felt like it, they helped Hawaiians of old to build temples, roads, walls and fishponds."[57] This person said her group observed them in a creek working with a basket trap, catching fish. When her group told the Hawaiians what they had seen, they were calmly told it was the menehune.

Free Energy

Moving along, we return to a human topic of high strangeness: free energy technology, which refers to the idea of using renewable resources and advanced technology to generate power without fossil fuels. The belief is that the use of free energy would reduce pollution and solve the problem of climate change. It doesn't take a rocket scientist to understand how an energy that doesn't rely on traditional fossil fuels might raise the eyebrows of very powerful and wealthy people.

Cold Fusion

One free energy technology is cold fusion. Stanley Pons and Martin Fleischmann are renowned for their claim of discovering cold fusion, also known as low-energy nuclear reactions (LENR), in 1989. This announcement sparked significant scientific interest and controversy, as it suggested the possibility of a new, clean, and abundant energy source. Their story reached the mainstream news cycle and was featured on the cover of *Time* magazine in May 1989 with the title "Fusion or Illusion? How Two Obscure Chemists Stirred Excitement – and Outrage – in the Scientific World." Their work was also featured in articles by *The New York Times*, where it was said the two "had created nuclear fusion at room temperature in a test tube."[58]

If you are old enough to remember the cold fusion announcement, then you also remember just how quickly the mainstream news narrative turned on Pons and Fleischmann. One minute they were praised, and the next their discovery was considered false and they were crowned frauds. Remember: I said at the outset that high strangeness research involved *fringe science* and there is no place for a technology that would solve the energy and environmental crisis other than on the fringe.

The narrative that these two scientists were frauds continued in the mainstream press until around 2009, when *60 Minutes* did a segment on their discovery. The segment was called "Cold Fusion Is Hot Again" and starts off by saying "twenty years ago" it "appeared for a moment, that all of our energy problems could be solved ... But then, just as quickly as it was announced, it was discredited. So thoroughly, that cold fusion became a catch phrase for junk science. Well, a funny thing happened on the way to oblivion – for many scientists today, cold fusion is hot again."

The segment features researcher Michel McKubre who says that if "we can yield the power of nuclear physics on a tabletop. The potential is unlimited" because it "is the most powerful energy source known to man." *60 Minutes* reports that McKubre has witnessed this free energy technology "more than fifty times in cold fusion experiments he's doing at … a respected California lab that" also "does extensive work for the government." The segment claims "there's renewed buzz among scientists that cold fusion could lead to huge breakthroughs in energy production" and even reports they "found that the Pentagon is saying it too." They also point out that "The Defense Advanced Research Projects Agency, known as DARPA, did its own analysis and 60 Minutes obtained an internal memo that concludes there is 'no doubt that anomalous excess heat is produced in these experiments.'"[59]

So why did the narrative turn on Pons and Fleischmann? The mainstream explanation is because after their announcement "prestigious labs at MIT and Caltech rushed to reproduce the experiment, but didn't get the same results." After that the "careers of Fleischmann and Pons were destroyed as quickly as a nuclear flash – names once linked to a Nobel Prize were forgotten by nearly everyone."

Regarding the "prestigious labs" that failed to replicate Pons and Fleischmann's experiment, we turn to Dr. Eugene Mallova.[S] According to Dr. Mallova's view, the fraud was not on the part of Pons and Fleischmann but on the scientists that followed. Dr. Mallova's opinion (based on his review of the documented research) was that "MIT researchers had" in fact "found excess heat on July 10, 1989, successfully replicating important elements" of Pons and Fleischmann's experiment. However, he claimed that "three days later" the data "had been altered" in "the school's final report." This final report also "happened to have been funded by the Department of Energy." Dr. Mallova claimed this final report "had perpetrated 'scientific fraud as far as I'm concerned.'"[60]

What was the fate of an individual that championed the work of Pons and Fleischmann and was the Chief Science Writer for the MIT News Office from 1987-1991? Was this man given praise and accolades for trying to advocate technology that would solve the environmental crisis? Yes! That is exactly what happened!

And when I say that is exactly what happened, I mean the opposite: in May of 2004, Dr. Mallova was "beaten, stabbed, and left with 32 lacerations across his face." Even an article about his death in a mainstream news outlet raises suspicions about his murder, saying he "gave up everything to pursue the holy grail of nuclear energy" and asks if it "cost him his life."

S *Fire from Ice: Searching for the Truth Behind the Cold Fusion* by Dr. Eugene Mallova, 1999.

But why would a discovery that *The New York Times* called "the greatest discovery since fire" cause mainstream journalists to *even* speculate that someone would want to murder someone for promoting it? This same mainstream journalist goes on to say that if cold fusion were "replicated on a commercial scale, the unlimited, carbon-free energy source could release the planet from the yoke of fossil fuels."[60]

Cold Fusion Today

In 2015 it was reported that a "US Navy researcher... thinks Fleischmann and Pons may have been right" because "her team had gotten 'very significant' evidence" supporting the two scientists. This quote comes from Pamela Mosier-Boss, a researcher at the Navy's Space and Naval Warfare Systems Center in San Diego.[61]

Importance of Free Energy

Free energy would radically change the world, because once you "give the world enough electrical energy … you raise the world's standard of living"; and if you "raise the world's standard of living, and you raise the world economy."[62] Did a group of powerful people who desire to not raise the world's standard of living because it would take away from their profits have Dr. Mallova killed? Did a group of powerful people fund the suppression and then slander of Pons and Fleischmann because free energy technology would cause them to lose their fossil fuel profits? What does Occam's razor think is the simplest explanation – and does this take us through the looking glass?

Free energy technology would have a "paramount" effect on the nature of employment because it would "represent the inception of a basic new industry, which for the sheer size and scope might be properly compared with the steel, automobile and aircraft industries combined." In practice, "free energy will automatically introduce a new concept of employment" and change the "ancient edict that called for earning one's bread by the sweat of one's brow."[62]

This radical change in society is what Bob Dobbs has focused on in his analysis of Pons and Fleischman's discovery. Dobbs claims that "cold-fusion energy is a miracle – because it'll give us more energy than is put in" and, when implemented, "humanity will gradually be able to move out of the cities" because new social "situations will be set up where the usual energy production-consumption level was not possible before." For example: this would support living in off-grid communities deep in the forest. This utopian set up "perhaps ... occurred in Atlantis" and "perhaps we're going to retrieve" this way of structuring society. Dobbs claims that because we don't have access to this technology currently, we are "in hell." However, "there is hope" found in the fact "that cold fusion broke through, with Pons and Fleischmann."[63]

However, unlimited free energy is not all puppy dogs and rainbows. Meaning, it's not all positive. Free energy is frictionless energy and actually invokes friction in the social sphere. Stuart Gordon, the author of *Gordontown: a New Design for America by the Originator of the Peace Corps*, points out in his book: "there's a worse calamity looming on the horizon," that is even worse than "our dependency on others for oil." Gordon claims the calamity that widespread free energy use would cause is due to the fact that "most people don't know what to do with the spare time they have now." And if "living expenses would be lowered"[63.1] due to free energy, people would have almost unlimited free time. As the proverb says: idle time is the devil's workshop. Gordon's book is about structuring a community that could adjust to this new social environment of almost unlimited free time.

Personal Connection

My father's family was friends with the Pons family in Valdese, a small city located in Western North Carolina. Valdese is in Burke County, the same county where Morganton is located. Stanley was five years older than my father and one year older than my aunt, who reports that in high school she had a crush on Stanley. One of Stanley's brothers was in my parents' wedding in 1969. My father also played on the Valdese High School American football team with Stanley's brother. A yearbook photo shows my father tackling an opposing player, with the caption: "Senior lineman Greg Vaughn gains a 'hold' on the opposition as Church ... and Pons rush to his rescue." This particular brother of Stanley was also the quarterback that year and my father reports he was known for his scrambling ability.

I still remember sitting in the back seat of the car as a child while my parents were talking about the controversy surrounding their family friend. When I started my personal studies with Bob Dobbs, he was amazed I had this personal connection to Pons, as he had been talking about this discovery since the early 90s. On my behalf, my father reached out to Stanley's brother to pass on a message about Stanley possibly appearing on the podcast I have co-hosted with Bob Dobbs since 2010, *The*

BOB Show. We got no response, which I was not surprised by. I was not surprised because Stanley appears to have retreated from the public eye after being unfairly attacked by the mainstream press. There is an article cited on his Wikipedia pages which claims he has given up his American citizenship and now resides in another country.

Dr. Steven Greer

Dr. Steven Greer barely needs an introduction to fans of high strangeness. He is a former physician, founder of the Disclosure Project and the Center for the Study of Extraterrestrial Intelligence (CSETI). He gained mainstream attention in the late 1990s when, as part of his Disclosure Project, he organized a press conference held in Washington, D.C., where testimonies were given from individuals (some from within the Military-Industrial Complex) who claimed to have firsthand knowledge of government and military cover-ups related to extraterrestrial encounters and technology.

Greer's Contact App

Greer is a good example of a high strangeness approach to the UFO phenomenon because he often teaches about topics related to consciousness expansion and doesn't just focus on the nuts and bolts of extraterrestrial aircraft. Significant in this regard is his contact app called "CE-5," which refers to "Close Encounters of the Fifth Kind." A CE-5 is different from the fourth kind because the fifth kind involves human initiated contact with extraterrestrial beings. The CE-5 app uses spiritual approaches, such as meditation and remote viewing, to make the metaphorical phone call to our space friends.

Greer speaks to why the CE-5 contact protocol is important, saying that "if there is an intervention by this cosmic organization" of ultraterrestrials "they're going to need ... humans to interface" with. He doubts that it's going to be "1600 Pennsylvania Avenue or the Pentagon" that the ultraterrestrials reach out to first. Instead, he says, "It's going to be you ... and you need to own that responsibility." The ultraterrestrials will not want to interface with official channels because "they had betrayals"[64] from them in the 40s and 50s. Basically, Dr. Greer is implying they will be landing on the lawns of high strangeness researchers, *not* the White House lawn.[T] This is another aspect of my magick of high strangeness:

T "The Close Encounters of the Fifth Kind protocols, developed by Dr. Greer, have allowed direct contact with advanced extraterrestrial civilizations, making it the most subversive and dan-

turning your own lawn into a White House lawn that ultraterrestrials would want to land on.

Greer and Free Energy

Dr. Greer claims that the reason the existence of UFOs is suppressed by governments around the world is because of free energy. That is, the little green men obviously didn't get to Earth with gasoline and instead got here with some free energy technology. If this free energy technology were made public, it would sorely piss off a lot of very rich folks, not to mention completely disrupt society, a theory he explores on a recent and fairly mainstream podcast.

Greer says this free energy technology is being suppressed because of "money and power." He describes the people suppressing this technology as a "massive macro economic, geo-political power" that controls "hundreds of trillions of dollars in assets." In addition, the groups and people who control these assets "will do anything needed" to maintain this status "even if it means killing the planet."[U,65]

Greer says that unless we get off "these oil, gas, coal and public utility systems ... that not only is damaging the environment" but is the source of the "underlying world order that is so dysfunctional," we are headed for global disaster. How fossil fuels impact the environment is well-known known at this point, but what is less well-known is that "there has been conflict all over the world" because of nation "states jockeying for commodity and resource control." Ending this state of affairs is "not possible unless we bring out the underlying, covert, viciously sequestered, secret UFO technology."[64]

Personal Connection

Before Dr. Greer retired from his career in medicine, he was "chairman of the Department of Emergency Medicine at Caldwell Memorial Hospital in Lenoir, North Carolina".[66] Caldwell Memorial is the only hospital in my hometown of Lenoir. In the mid 90s, while I was in high school, Dr. Greer was starting to become known in the UFO community

gerous information released to the public ... Real disclosure comes from humans bypassing covert programs and making direct contact with extraterrestrial civilizations, showing that the majority of humans are enlightened, conscious, and peaceful." (*Contact Initiated: Close Encounters of the Fifth Kind: Dr. Steven Greer, Documentary*, eightify.app)

U This approach would be stopping us from advancing to a Type 1 civilization, as per the Kardashev scale. A Type 1 civilization would have the capability to efficiently utilize the planet's existing energy sources, and some theorize this could be achieved via advanced technologies, such as cold fusion. However, we need a global consciousness awakening before we can implement free energy.

and, naturally, I was aware of his work. My best friend's father was named Stephen Greer as well, and his family would often get calls looking for "the UFO guy." My friend's father recently confirmed this, claiming he would often say "you got the wrong guy" and hang up.

Greer's latest documentary, *The Lost Century – and How to Reclaim It,* focuses on examples of free energy technology, of both human and ultra-terrestrial origin. In the documentary, he reports on a case of free energy being used in 1902 by "a farmer and engineer named Stubblefield"[V] who was working with Nikola Tesla. Stubblefield had "something they called the earth battery or the Stubblefield battery, and it had rods going into the earth." The earth battery "was picking up this magnetic flux field of the planet and he was running his farm" with this technology. Greer points out that "Tesla was there with him," and shares an old photograph, showing Stubblefield on his farm with Tesla. Greer says this story is what he means by the "one hundred years, lost century,"[67] meaning free energy technology has been around since 1902 and has been suppressed since the time of Tesla. I believe the subject of high strangeness and its thorough analysis gets people in the necessary mindset to reclaim this lost century.

Interestingly enough, I have evidence of another farm being run via electricity generated on the property, from around the same time as Stubblefield. I found a case of this in an unlikely source, which is what high strangeness research is all about. My family owns property in Alleghany County, North Carolina, in the Blue Ridge Mountains. The local Chamber of Commerce published a series of "driving loop" brochures to promote the county and feature notable landmarks in the area. When I drove the Elk Creek Valley Loop over ten years ago I was intrigued to see the following description of the home of Joe T. Finney, a large 2-story home "built in 1903. It was quite modern in its time and featured running water, indoor bathroom, a telephone and electricity that was generated on the property."[68] When I first read this ten years ago, I thought it could be a misprint, or a case of high strangeness, so I kept it in the back of my mind. After watching Greer's latest documentary, I now wonder if Finney was somehow connected with Tesla and Stubblefield.

The Ones I Left Out

Believe it or not, I have left out many more instances of highly strange synchronistic connections. Some I have left out for space issues and others I have left out because they are too salacious to put in my first book.

V See: wiki/Nathan_Stubblefield

By "too salacious," I am essentially saying some are too unbelievable, as they are the third rail topics of high strangeness.

The experienced researcher can probably guess some of the topics I have left out. Yes, synchronicity has taken me into those orbits,[W] and it is indeed a small world, especially when the synchronicity principle is bringing all of these topics into your personal orbit. I will hopefully share these stories in further volumes of this book series, but it will mean I will lose more and more readers as we go further and further down the rabbit hole. Believe it or not, the content in this chapter are the more tame stories and topics.

I also want to be clear. There are two types of synchronicities that high strangeness researchers encounter. One is the degree of separation synch; my example here is the fact that Stanley Pons is an old family friend of my family. The other is when you meet someone who has experienced something highly strange and they simply tell you.

The skeptical argument against any highly strange theory is that people aren't good at keeping secrets; so if anything weird was going on, then the secret would be out. I have found the skeptics are correct in their assertion, people aren't good at keeping secrets. I have been told about highly strange happenings by people in the position to know. You would be surprised at what people are willing to tell you, if you just simply ask. When I meet someone who would be in a position to know something, I literally ask: Can you tell me anything secret?

Much to the chagrin of the skeptic, highly strange secrets are out. There are hundreds, if not thousands, of books written by whistleblowers divulging highly strange secrets. The only problem is that their accounts are so weird that they are beyond belief. The whistle has been blown for over one hundred years but has fallen on the deaf ears of an incredulous mainstream public.

Conclusion

Writing this chapter has shown me a curious fact, which is that the people who have witnessed and reported strange occurrences to me do not believe in anything weird, paranormal, or highly strange (for the most part). The stories I left out were straight out of an episode of *The X-Files*. My point is that experiencing or witnessing one strange thing

W Topics such as Cathy O'Brien, Jim Keith, DUMBS, *Confessions of an Economic Hitman*, exotic energy weapons, private islands, the uber-wealthy, and three that are so Downardian that I dare not mention them. As a psychotherapist, I may, or may not have heard things which support the most salacious topics of high strangeness, as opposed to disproving them.

is not enough to tip the scales and cause a shift in one's perception. It is too easy to shrug it off, ignore it, and go on about your life. If weird experiences are persistent enough, it can cause a shift in perception. To be clear, the most shocking stories I have gathered were all from normies: these were not high strangeness researchers. They were not believers in anything paranormal.

One instance of high strangeness you can ignore. However, what is one to do if synchronicity brings every major topic of this research into their personal orbit? My answer was to write this book. I have lived a normal life. I didn't go to private school or attend an Ivy League college. I'm an introvert and actually go out of my way to *not* meet new people. This is a testament to the power of the high strangeness-synchronistic egregore. The grand unified theory of high strangeness can be found in my personal story.

It appears synchronicity has brought all of these elements into my life so I can believe on a personal level. In the overall community, we talk a lot about how to convince normies of a larger reality. I believe this is a losing battle and, as a result, call for a shift to focus on high strangeness researchers better accepting and embodying the reality of the phenomenon on an individual level. Forget about convincing others: let's work on better convincing ourselves.

The theory I'm proposing in this chapter is that the synchs which occur with high strangeness researchers, i.e.: encountering these topics in their personal lives, is evidence the divine flow of the universe itself wants the truth to become manifest. That is, synchronicity is trying to help convince you of the truth. And it just so happens that this truth is highly strange. The synchronistic egregore is a journalist in a sense, because it is showing us the news, the truth.

Further, I maintain that it is not possible to accept the highly strange reality unless synchronicity brings you into its orbit – over and over – almost as if the universe is saying, "How many times do I have to bring you face to face with this stuff until you simply accept it as a reality?"

So what am I left to conclude? Mainstream news sources are reporting on the highly strange, whistleblowers are going public with the highly strange, and I am meeting people that report experiencing the highly strange firsthand ... am I supposed to just shrug and say, it's all just a big coincidence? That seems *crazier* than just accepting all this weird stuff is simply true. Again, this is where Occam's razor takes us through the rabbit hole.

I maintain that, in such a situation, to not believe would mean someone is caught in what has been called "the Scully Syndrome." This is a principle from screen writing and is a "self-applied case of Weirdness Censor by a character, particularly one ... who considers themselves rational or skeptical." A character that suffers from the Scully Syndrome will attempt to "offer a 'rational' explanation for a supernatural situation" and "they will usually end up offering an explanation that is itself so tortuous, convoluted and/or improbable that it also ceases to be rational."

The explanations that the Agent Scully character used in *The X-Files* drew "upon things that are seemingly more plausible and 'realistic' than the supernatural explanation." However, the way this character "puts these things together is" so "unlikely" and "full of holes" and "so ludicrous that the viewers want to bash the character's head against the wall, all while pointing out that accepting the supernatural explanation would, in fact, be simpler." This is indeed how I felt watching the series for the first time in 2021.

Yes, I know this is a TV show and the skeptical Agent Scully character was used as a plot device, but I have noticed the Agent Scully effect playing out in our highly strange times. Just like the Agent Scully character, today's normie skeptics have a "tendency to ignore any evidence of the supernatural that they might be presented with, no matter how conclusive, in favour of presenting ... more 'rational' explanations that are just as (if not more) lacking in supporting evidence." This is "a problem because it allows someone to use rationalism as an excuse to not consider any possibilities that challenge ... their current beliefs ... even when those alternative possibilities are actually valid and supported with evidence."

Yes, it makes sense that Agent Scully didn't automatically agree with her partner from the minute he told her about the X-Files, "but it's when Agent Scully starts constructing equally implausible 'rational' narratives, rather than accepting the evidence, that aliens, against all odds, actually did do it that it starts to become an issue."[X,69] This is a curious state of mind that I think we will start to see more and more of as consensus reality gets stranger and stranger. I imagine a scenario where someone is taken to a mental health hospital because they *don't* believe in psychic Bigfoot shamans.

For someone in Agent Scully's situation, the sanest reaction would be to simply accept Mulder's theories. After all, his highly strange theories match up with the highly strange reality that both agents experience on

X "The inverse of Occam's Razor ... can be summarized as 'When you hear hoofbeats, think zombie zebras from outer space, not horses'" Note: "The name is taken from Occam's Razor, combined with Arkham, which is a fictional Massachusetts town in the works of H. P. Lovecraft, and also the fictional insane asylum in Batman comic books. Thus, the term 'Arkham' is closely tied to the idea of madness or surprise." (TVtropes.org/pmwiki/pmwiki.php/Main/ArkhamsRazor).

a weekly basis. Mulder is grappling with the reality of the weird world, while Scully is living in a fantasy land of denial where there is a "logical" explanation for everything – even when she has witnessed otherwise with her own eyes. In this scenario Mulder is sane and Scully is insane.

It appears to me that reality is becoming so strange that it is the normies that are quickly becoming Agent Scully. And as the kids say today, "I'm here for it."[70]

Sources

1. Christopher Knowles, "*He Will Live Up in the Sky: The Tangled Web and the Woke Virus*," *The Higherside Chats*, Feb. 2020, Time: 42 mins.

2. Sean Stone, *Best Kept Secret*, (a six episode documentary series), September 3, 2021

3. Dr. Richard B. Spence, "The Limbo of Lost Memories: Searching for James Shelby Downard," in *Stalking the Great Whore: The Lost Writings of James Shelby Downard*, p. 471.

4. "Empire of the Wheel and the Mysterious Shelby Downard with Richard Spence," *The Walter Bosley Channel*, Time: 1:22:00.

5. "David Ferrie, Phony Bishops, and the Assassination of JFK, MLK, RFK: Interview with James Day," *TrineDay: The Journey Podcast*, Oct. 2023, Time: 3:18.

6. James Day, *The Mad Bishops: The Hunt for Earl Anglin James and His Assassin Brethren*, book review on Amazon.com by Noel Stenmark.

7. Mystic Mark, "Aeon Byte: American Saturn, Skull and Bones, Colonial Millenarism," *My Family Thinks I'm Crazy*, Dec. 28, 2022, time: 21:00-25:00, 35:00-36:00.

8. Alexandra Sanders, "Arizona Man Ventures to New Haven to Pray for Return of Geronimo's Skull," *New Haven Register*, July 26, 2012.

9. Deborah Feyerick and Brian Vitagliano, "Descendant Sues Skull and Bones over Geronimo's Bones," CNN.com.

10. Kat Eschner, "What We Know About the CIA's Mid-century Mind-Control Project," Smithsonianmag.com, April 13, 2017.

11. "Author Interviews: The CIA's Secret Quest for Mind Control: Torture, LSD and A 'Poisoner in Chief,'" *Fresh Air*, NPR.org, Interview with Stephen Kinzer, author of *Poisoner in Chief: Sidney Gottlieb and the CIA Search for Mind Control*, September 9, 2019.

12. Gary Kamiya, "When the CIA Ran a LSD Sex-house in San Francisco," *San Francisco Chronicle*, April 1, 2016.

13. Lisa Ellenwood and Chris Oke, "Brainwashed: The Echoes of MK-ULTRA," *Canadian Broadcasting Corporation,* Newsinteractives.cbc.ca/longform/brainwashed-mkultra, October 21, 2020.

14. Nathan Isaac, "The Game," *Penny Royal,* Season 1, Episode 7: time: 23:00.

15. "Settlement Ends Psychiatric Center Suits," *AP News,* March 21, 1990, web.archive.org/web/20190601000407

16. *Camp Hell: Anneewakee,* Episode one: "The Wake," time: 1-5:00.

17. *Camp Hell: Anneewakee,* Episode: "Plea," time: 1:00.

18. "Native American History of Douglas County, Georgia," Accessgenealogy.com/georgia/native-american-history-of-douglas-county-georgia.htm

19. "Unusual Incident: A Horseback Rider's Close Encounter," *Bigfoot Field Researchers Organization,* bfro.net/GDB/show_report.asp?id=447

20. Greg Newkirk, Review of *Where the Footprints End: High Strangeness and the Bigfoot Phenomenon, Volume I: Folklore,* by Joshua Cutchin and Timothy Renner, May 4, 2020.

21. Jack Lapseritis, *The Psychic Sasquatch and Their UFO Connection,* publisher's summary.

22. Jack Lapseritis, *The Sasquatch People and their Interdimensional Connection,* publisher's summary.

23. Jack "Kewaunee" Lapseritis, *Who are the Sasquatch and Why are They Here?,* This article presents a "condensed and highlighted" summary of the "vital parts of ... Kamooh's [the Sasquatch shaman] messages" channeled by SunBow TrueBrother, Dec. 2020, SasquatchMessage.com.

24. Nick Redfern, *Monster Files: A Look Inside Government Secrets and Classified Documents on Bizarre Creatures and Extraordinary Animals,* E-book: p. 145.

25. Michael Bertiaux, *Voudon Gnostic Workbook,* 1988, pp. 466, 266.

26. Bjarne Salling Pedersen, *Arts and the Occult: An Interview with Michael Bertiaux,* Avalonlibrary.net/ebooks/Three%20Interviews%20With%20Michael%20Bertiaux.pdf

27. Personal communication, unnamed painter, April 15, 2020.

28. Trey Hudson, *The Meadow Project: Explorations into the South's Skinwalker Ranch,* 2020, publisher's summary.

29. "First Earth Battalion," wiki/First_Earth_Battalion.

30. Trey Hudson's Amazon author page.

31. Trey Hudson, "The Meadow Project: Cryptid Humanoid Stalkers, Portal Boxes, and Monkey Bears." *The Higherside Chats,* September 2022, time: 49:00, 01:44.

32. Personal communication, Fall 2021.

33. Personal communication, Feb. 2023

34. "The Order of the Unfolding," *Dream Journal,* Jan. 12, 2024.

35. Tanranin Uhcheek Gozaknee, *The Red Planet Arrives: A Collection of Essays,* 2006, scribd.com/ document/ 205582634/ Tanranin-Uhcheek-Gozaknee-The-Red-Planet-Arrives

36. Sasquatch elder to Sunbow Truebrother, "Sasquatch Message for Humankind," *Fate Magazine,* Sep 21, 2022. fatemag.com/amp/sasquatch-message-for-humankind

37. Alan Vaughn, *Patterns of Prophecy,* 1973, pp. 158-67.

38. "Duende," wiki/duende

39. "Everything About Chaneque: Mexican Folklore Legendary Creatures," August 6, 2023, mythgyaan.com/chaneque

40. Lynn Lossiah, *Secrets and Mysteries of the Cherokee Little People,* January 1, 1998.

41. J. Witthoft and W. Hadlock, "Cherokee-Iroquois Little People," *The Journal of American Folklore,* 1946, American Folklore Society.

42. Ewen Callaway, "The Discovery of *Homo floresiensis*: Tales of the Hobbit," Nature.com, Oct. 2014.

43. "'Hobbits' on Flores, Indonesia," *Smithsonian,* National Museum of National History, humanorigins.si.edu, updated March 2016.

44. Dave Adalian, "'Hobbits' among Us? An Anthropologist Says Maybe," EarthSky.org May 2022.

45. Mary Joyce, *Cherokee Little People Were Real,* 2014.

46. John Keel, *Operation Trojan Horse,* 1970, (1976 Manor books edition) pp. 214-15.

47. Andrew Collins and Gregory L Little, *Origins of the Gods: Qesem Cave, Skinwalkers, and Contact with Transdimensional Intelligences,* chapter: "The Little People."

48. Steve Mizrach, "UFOs Reconsidered as a Fortean Phenomenon," *Crash Collusion,* Austin, Texas.

49. Susan B. Martinez, Ph.D., *The Lost History of the Little People: Their Spiritually Advanced Civilizations Around the World,* publisher's summary, 2013.

50. "Welcome," AvalonGrove.com/faeries/

51. "Fair Folk Descriptions," AvalonGrove.com/faeries/index.php/fair-folk-descriptions/

52. Mary Joyce, "Ancient Race of Little People Still Live in Tennessee" and "Little People Talk about God, Religion and ETs," 2016, skyshipsovercashiers.com/bigfootet2016.htm#live

53. Dave Foley, *UAP Studies Podcast*, June 8, 2023, time: 39:00.

54. "The Woman Who Was Arrested for Witchcraft in 1976," Youtube: *In Praise of Shadows*, Oct. 2022, 1:17-1:30.

55. Jason Koon, "Calling on Spirits: Local Mystic to Celebrate Halloween with Treats, 'Table Shaking,'" *Morganton News Herald*, Oct. 31, 2022.

56. James Seay, "The Wicked Witch of North Carolina," Oct. 11, 1976, classic.esquire.com/article/1976/10/1/the-wicked-witch-of-north-carolina

57. Noe Tanigawa, "*Menehune:* Clever, Burly Little People," *Hawai'i Public Radio,* Dec. 2018, HawaiiPublicRadio.org.

58. Robert P. Crease and N. P. Samios, "Cold Fusion Confusion," *New York Times*, Sept. 24, 1989, nytimes.com/1989/09/24/magazine/cold-fusion-confusion.html

59. "Cold Fusion Is Hot Again," *60 Minutes*, April 2009, cnet.com/science/60-minutes-video-cold-fusion-is-hot-again/

60. David Kushner, "The Coldest Case," ForeignPolicy.com, 2016.

61. "Navy Chemist May Have Rediscovered 'Cold Fusion,'" FoxNews.com, January 14, 2015.

62. Commander X, *Nikola Tesla: Free Energy and the White Dove*, pp. 103-4, 105.

63. Bob Dobbs, "Phatic Communion with Satellite's Machines," July 1996. ionbob.com/pdf/bob/phatic_communion_with_satellites_machines.pdf

63.1- Stuart Gordon, *Gordonstown: A New Design for America by the Originator of the Peace Corps*, 1980, p. 185.

64. Dr. Steven Greer, "Ukraine, Oil and the UFO Solution!," Youtube: *Dr. Steven Greer*, March 2022, time: 57:00.

65. Dr. Steven Greer, "Mystery Behind UFO/UAPs," Youtube: *The Shawn Ryan Show*, Jan. 27, 2022, time: 54:00.

66. "Steven M. Greer," commons.wikimedia.org/wiki/Steven_M._Greer

67. Steven Greer, "The Lost Century – and How to Reclaim It," 2023, time: 28:02

68. Alleghany County Chamber of Commerce, "Elk Creek Valley Loop: An 18-mile Driving Loop through Western Alleghany County," *Farm Valleys, Scenic Vistas, Historic Landmarks*, also see: highcountryhost.com/sparta-nc-country-backround-driving-routes

69. "Scully Syndrome," TVtropes.org/pmwiki/pmwiki.php/Main/Scully-Syndrome

70. Heather Paz, "Here for It: Can This Youthful Catchphrase Empower Us?" *Spirit Alchemy*, Apr 11, 2023, medium.com/spirit-alchemy/here-for-it-a3d1848f8316

Conclusion

High Strangeness is what You Can Get Away With:[A] The Great Cosmic Why and The Great Cosmic Wave

A great cosmic conversion: from mountains to dock!
Knowing your deed until the right time: Then!
Plagues are over, now: peace on a kindly repeat!
They can't impose on us, now: we're dripping with Archangels!
The ending is finished, take the meme of a thousand keys!

Stranger and Stranger

In the introductory chapter I quoted RAW, when he states: "if the McKenna scenario is right" then "we are pulling a cosmic trigger." This is from the first volume of his *Cosmic Trigger* book series in 1977; meaning, he was referring to McKenna's theories from that time. The following is from one of Terence McKenna's (1946-2000) last interviews, making it the most up to date "McKenna scenario." Predicting the future, McKenna claims that: "the level of contradiction is going to rise excruciatingly," so much so that "it's just going to get weirder and weirder, and weirder, and finally it's going to be so weird that people are going to have to talk about how weird it is," leaving them to ask, "What the hell is going on?" People will think "it's just too nuts, it's not enough to say it's nuts, you have to explain why it's so nuts."

McKenna gives examples of the weirdness: A.I., human cloning, potential encounters with extraterrestrials, human life extension; alongside distressing occurrences of brutality, genocide, racial tensions, and famine. This weird situation exists "because the systems which are in place to

A Inspired by the Andy Warhol quote, "art is what you can get away with," Some attribute McLuhan with first using the term, see: *Art Is Anything You Can Get Away With*, QuoteInvestigator.com, August 10, 2022. Also see: the song lyrics to "Jack" by the band Widespread Panic, indicating the wealthy are indifferent to the places frequented by those society has labeled, fools.

keep the world sane are utterly inadequate to the forces that have been unleashed." He predicts "changes so immense nobody could imagine them ever happening." Amid this chaos is "the good news," which is that "as primates we are incredibly adaptable to change. Put us in the desert, we survive, put us the jungle, we survive ... under Nixon we survive." McKenna reports the "mushroom said to" him that this weird situation is what "it's like when a species prepares to depart for the stars." This is because "you don't depart for the stars under calm and orderly conditions; it's a fire in a madhouse ... at the end of time. This is what it's like when a species prepares to move on to the next dimension."[1]

Writing this conclusion in February of 2024, it appears the McKenna scenario is correct. This means, according to RAW, we are pulling the cosmic trigger. This is supported astrologically as well: "Pluto will be in Aquarius from January 20, 2024 through September 1, 2024, briefly retrograde back into Capricorn ... and reenter Aquarius on November 19, 2024 ... where it will remain until March 8, 2043."[2] This is significant because, according to preeminent occultist and writer Carolyn Lovewell,[B] "the last time Pluto ventured into Aquarius, between 1777 and 1798, the world experienced the American and the French Revolutions" because "Pluto is Lord of the Underworld who often brings nuclear-explosion levels of alchemical change." Lovewell sums up the predictions of her favorite astrologers, pointing out that Pluto being in Aquarius will bring: "mind-blowing advances in AI... huge revelations regarding 'aliens,'" an increase of some of the darker sides of high strangeness, and "a massive flowering of a new, integral structure of human consciousness." She says that because Pluto has entered Aquarius, "major tectonic shifts will increasingly rock our very conception of" all aspects of reality, leaving us to ask: "what in the" heck "is even going on?!"[3]

Buckle up y'all, *it's only gonna get weirder*. Renowned writer and spiritual teacher, Paul Levy, maintains "we are living through the strangest time in all of human history." Which is saying a lot, considering he also says we are only at the foothills of the Himalayas when it comes to weirdness, meaning as we climb the mountain, the high strangeness will increase.[4]

Breaking Down And Breaking Through

A more traditional, academic look at our current weird situation is seen in the fact that the symbolic order is breaking down. Jacques Lacan's (1901-1981) concept of the "symbolic order" refers to the social

B Author of, *Existential Kink: Unmask Your Shadow and Embrace Your Power (A method for getting what you want by getting off on what you don't)*, 2020. Note, she wrote this book under the name Carolyn Elliott.

and linguistic framework through which individuals come to understand and navigate their reality. It encompasses the "social world of linguistic communication, intersubjective relations, [and] knowledge of ideological conventions."[5] Said another way, it is the symbolic meanings and structures imposed by language, culture, and society that in turn shapes how individuals perceive themselves and the world.

A highly strange explanation is provided by Clif High, an individual known for his work in the field of predictive linguistics and the Web Bot Project.[C] He suggest we are undergoing a "shift into hyper novelty" which is now "flowing all around us." And as a result, "the whole system is starting to crumble like the cookie held too long in the milk." This process is "now starting to become visible to everybody" which represents the "beginning in that big change."[5.1]

Non-academics are also picking up on the fact the symbolic order is breaking down. Comedian and actor Jamie Kennedy explains this breakdown process colloquially, saying: "I feel like every institution is being disrupted and completely leveled" and as a result "it's just weird times." He speculates this complete change was what "the pandemic did" and that "we will never go back to it being the way it was pre-pandemic." This is because on every level: "spiritual, mental," etc., reality has "just shifted."[6]

Reality Has Gone Bye-Bye: Ontological Shock

Author and podcast host, Kelly Chase, has focused on the psychological impact that high strangeness has on people, specifically exploring the effect of the information presented by UFO whistleblower David Grusch.[D] Chase explores "the process of metabolizing information like this," which is a process of "recognizing that we don't live in the world we thought we lived in." She says the information disclosed by Grusch is "but a shadow of what we'll be seeing throughout our society in the coming months and years."

Realizing that we live in a different reality than we previously thought existed causes "ontological shock." This is a "term used to describe a profound and disorienting psychological state that occurs when one's understanding of reality is dramatically altered. Usually due to an encounter or

C "Web Bot is an Internet bot computer program whose developers claim is able to predict future events by tracking keywords entered on the Internet. It was developed in 1997, originally to predict stock market trends ... The operators of Web Bot interpret the bot's results and make a report called the 'ALTA report,'" which "stands for 'asymmetric language trend analysis.'" (wiki/Web_Bot).

D She is referring to the hearing in the Summer of 2023. See, "UFO whistleblower doubles down on claims: 'This is a nightmare for me,'" Auren Irwin, TheHill.com, Dec. 13, 2023.

a revelation that conflicts with previously held beliefs about the nature of existence." Because ontological shock happens when one encounters high strangeness, "the process of dismantling the illusion of our consensus reality is a long one" and we "end up processing these things in stages."[7]

Advice

My advice to you: *start getting weirder.*[E] The symbolic order is breaking down, causing people to experience ontological shock, so it may come as a surprise that I suggest embracing more weirdness to provide more sanity. This is a hair of the dog that bit you type recommendation. Volume two of this book series will get more into the specifics of this advice, but, for now: talk to a psychic, dance naked on the full moon, become a Downard scholar and then become a Downard detractor, roam remote forests in search of ghosts, Bigfoot, and gnomes. As McKenna said, start "healing the inner elf through trance, dance and diet."[8] On the flip side, *start getting saner*. Begin journaling, recording your dreams, and reading every self-help book you can find. Enter psychotherapy to tackle your mundane personal issues. Jesus is coming and he is wondering if you have talked out your mommy issues, so to say.

The Why Of The Synchs: High Strangeness Initiation

In a recent episode of *The Higherside Chats,* host Greg Carlwood, asks noted author, George Hansen, why the weird phenomenon is happening. Hansen says that you have to first "understand what" before trying to "understanding why." This is because "a why question is usually not productive" because if you are thinking in that direction, it is more difficult to make progress.[9] While I understand the sentiment behind what Hansen is saying here, I think we need the why of high strangeness, now more than ever. This book has been an effort to help people understand the "what," so now I will present theories on the *why*. The phenomenon in general and the synchronicities surrounding it in particular, appear to be an initiation process for some. For example, "there is evidence to suggest the UFO puzzle is a learning program" to "try and evolve you" psycho-spiritually, as such, high strangeness phenomena are "a mechanism of education."[10]

E This advice recalls the scene from the film, *Animal House*, where Bluto (John Belushi) gives advice to an inconsolable, Flounder.

This highly strange initiation is a necessary educational process, as "people tend not to accept personal (i.e. subjective) revelations unless they are substantiated by 'science', but now that many such revelations have been substantiated by 'science' people are no more willing to accept them." This is because the human mind "is satisfied only by facts amenable to rational analysis." However, there is a part of the mind that allows one to understand the subjective revelations of high strangeness. This other "faculty of human consciousness" is "the intuitive ... faculty" and "one might also describe it as the fourth dimensional faculty."

This faculty is one that "appears sometimes in artists, the poet, the occultist, and in a certain kind of scientist," such as a Tesla. This strange faculty of the mind is not concerned with an "understanding of empirical things," but is concerned with insights "into the hidden side of things." However, this "faculty of understanding" is difficult to obtain "because it has its origin beyond the Abyss, where human laws of logic ... do not apply." Most importantly, remember that "initiation is necessary before" this uncanny faculty[F] can "be activated and utilized;" also, this type of initiation "can only be self-initiation."[11]

This initiatory aspect of high strangeness has been suggested by the seminal researchers of the phenomenon. For example, Whitley Streiber believes "they are here to help us make an evolutionary transformation" and "Jacques Vallée feels they function as sort of a control system, a 'barometer' regulating our relationships to the 'invisible' world."[12] This aspect has even been reported on in the mainstream news, when former Israeli space security chief said extraterrestrials exist but have not yet revealed themselves because, "They have been waiting ... for humanity to develop and reach a stage where we will understand" what they are.[13]

These ideas have also been explored in the New Age literature. It is pointed out that because ultraterrestrials have such "evolved spiritual consciousness ... they are bound by cosmic law not to ... override man's free will." As a result, contact with them "can only occur when man's consciousness has been raised to accept ... all the dramatic changes that will result on a planetary scale" when mass contact is made. On an individual level, humans "must be spiritually prepared to handle the higher vibrational frequencies that the space visitors bring with them by their very nature of their materialized forms." Before an intervention of the rule

F Colin Wilson referred to "Faculty X" as a latent kind of consciousness beyond ordinary consciousness, which is bogged down in trivialities and a tendency toward dullness. We are unconscious to its existence but it lies at the heart of all occult experience, as well as aiding us in gaining more purpose and meaning in life. Individuals can tap into it through self-initiation, heightened attention, and/or a meaningful engagement with life. See the Preface to Colin Wilson's, *The Occult*.

following ultraterrestrials can occur humankind must "expand its cosmic awareness," making "itself ready for some big changes."[14]

It appears the phenomenon in general and the synchronicities around it in particular, are evolving us psycho-spiritually, to ready ourselves for these big changes. High strangeness is the initiatory medium through which we are prepared, as encountering high strangeness changes consciousness. This is because the high strangeness "phenomenon, taken to its deepest dimensions, is *haunted*." The important thing to look at is not the "weird phenomena per se – but its effect on humanity." As a result, "how a phenomenon like Twilight Language processes humanity might be more productive" to contemplate and study.[15] Downard also considered the "possible whys and wherefores of" high strangeness synchronicities, which led him to speculate there was "a mental mechanism functioning below the threshold of conscious awareness … a type of psychic process" that could only be "sparked by a coincidental occurrence."[16]

As Eden Phillpotts said: "The universe is full of magical things patiently waiting for our wits to grow sharper."[G] One's encounter with high strangeness helps them grow stronger. In this regard, let us turn to the famous David Bowie song, *Starman,* for further edification of this process. Bowie sings that the extraterrestrial is waiting and would like to interact with humans; but does not do so because they don't want to overly astonish us. The high strangeness initiation (pulling one's individual cosmic trigger) makes it so our minds will not be overly blown when communion occurs. In the song we are reminded that if we can but sparkle, the Starman may land. To pull your cosmic trigger is to sparkle.

The Opposite to Landing on The White House Lawn

Noted writer on the alien abduction phenomenon and former head of the department of psychiatry at Harvard Medical School, John Mack, M.D., (1929-2004) said he was often confronted with the "reigning cliché:" if UFOs "are real" then "Why don't they land on the White House lawn?" According to Mack, the "most popular answer to this question" is that extraterrestrial beings refrain from revealing themselves overtly due to fears that government officials may react poorly about how to prevent widespread panic. However, he says he thinks he has a "better answer" and one that fits with my high strangeness initiation proposal.

G I first heard this quote on Paul Schatzkin's appearance on *The Higherside Chats*, T. Townsend Brown, Philo T. Farnsworth, Secret Science, and the Caroline Group, July 2023.

Mack maintains the "intelligence that appears to be at work here simply does not operate" in an overt manner. The phenomenon is "subtle, inviting … permeating our culture from the bottom up as well as the top down, perhaps opening our consciousness in a way that avoids a conclusion, different from the ways of knowing we traditionally require." Contrary to trying to provide ultimate proof it "provides enough evidence that something profoundly important is at work, but it does not offer the kinds of proof that would satisfy an exclusively … rationalistic way of knowing." Because it does not provide us with conclusive proof it requires humans "to embrace the reality of the phenomenon and to take a step toward appreciating that we live in a universe different from the one in which we have been taught to believe."[17,H]

Greg Carlwood, said he "always thought disclosure would be one single event" where for example, the President gives a "big speech" and from then on, "everybody just knows that there are aliens." He now sees this is a "little kid simplistic idea of" how the process of disclosure would occur. Carlwood points out that "in some ways we already got disclosure" and "only a certain fraction of people care."[18] This is what is called soft disclosure, meaning countless credible governmental whistleblowers have attested to the existence of extraterrestrials but only the initiated can wrap their heads around this reality. From this point of view – we are living in a post disclosure reality. Hard disclosure would be a landing on the White House lawn with aliens holding a press conference with the President of the United States. Also, notice the ethnocentrism in the skeptical view that the only way for aliens to be real is if they land at the capital of the United States. Here I need to remind my American readers that other countries do actually exist. I know, I found it shocking to learn as well.

The host of *Lightning the Void* podcast, Joe Rupe, says we are not going to get the answers we are looking for with UFO disclosure, "unless we do it" ourselves.[18] This means *we* are the UFO experts. This means *our* podcasts are the press conferences. This means *our* lawn is the White House lawn. When I think of this last idea, I am reminded that "the only hope left for human society is" for people to embrace the idea that "every person [is] a Monarch" and "every yard [is] a Kingdom."[19] This would make the lawn chair[I] *the* captain's chair on bridge of the *Star Trek* spaceship.

H "A more rapid approach would have made your species grow too quickly and split with inner weakness as a fruit tree splits that has been grown in soil with excessive fertility." End note 67, p. 114.

I See, *Lawn Chair Frontier* (2003), which was an "experimental and comedic" short film "written and directed by Kreg Thornley," who is Kerry Thornley's son, (imdb.com/title/tt0844320/).

The Practical Side of High Strangeness

Things are getting so weird in the world that high strangeness is no longer a frivolous pursuit but a deadly serious imperative. This is because we "are engulfed in war" and not one that is "simply ... fought with guns and bombs." In this "invisible war" the "skirmishes take place in ... one's own mind." The "less one is aware" of this fact "the more receptive one is to its ongoing process of demoralization." The unaware are "vulnerable, malleable, weak and ripe for control." When we become aware of this process we "can minimize unnecessary demoralization in those who wish to preserve their instinct for survival."[20] This process is summed up in a quote from the early 1990s comedic high strangeness show, *Eerie, Indiana*. The main character of the show, a middle school student, is summing up the paranormal phenomena he has encountered: "Bigfoot eats out of my trash ... A bizarre housewife cult in town has been sealing up their kids in giant rubber kitchenware" and "when I try to tell this to my family, they just think I'm weird. Better weird than dead."[21] Better weird than dead, indeed.

How High Strangeness Helps New Agers

High strangeness helps New Age practitioners because it focuses on the darker aspects of the paranormal and spirituality. Paul Levy, who is world renowned for his writings on the darker sides of spirituality, seen in his books: *Dispelling Wetiko: Breaking the Curse of Evil; Wetiko: Healing the Mind-Virus That Plagues Our World;* and *Undreaming Wetiko: Breaking the Spell of the Nightmare Mind-Virus*. Wetiko is a term originating from Native American cultures and is a psycho-spiritual disease associated with greed, selfishness, and destructive behaviors that harm individuals and societies. Wetiko is the archetype of evil itself. Levy reports that a New Age bookstore in the Portland area refused to carry his books because they were too dark.[22] This anecdotal report supports a tendency I have seen in the New Age and spiritual community for over twenty years.

Keeping one's head in sand, concerning darkness, is not a good approach. As McLuhan said: "There is absolutely no inevitability as long as there is a willingness to contemplate what is happening."[23] However, this implies we contemplate what is happening, and it turns out quite a bit of weird stuff is happening and a fair amount of it, is very, very dark. The reason merely contemplating what is happening changes the inevitable is because "as you start to piece together" what is going on, "rather than vaguely understanding" what is going on, it creates an internal realization.

And when "you have a realization it ripples into the field" and it facilitates positive results because "it doesn't take many to change the masses."[24]

However, in addition to this metaphysical benefit of contemplating the full truth, there is a tangible benefit as well. This is because, as the incomparably brave Whitney Webb says, "until we realize the extent of the problem we'll never be able to fix it ... because if you have a ... Disneyland version in your head of what the problem is ... the solutions you offer, are not going to be tailored to the actual problem," and as a result "nothing's going to get fixed."[24.1]

One of my critiques of the New Age community is the mistaken idea that looking into dark topics somehow makes them more likely to occur. While this idea does have some basis in sound magical theory, viz á viz giving energy to negative thought forms, it ignores the above advice. For these suggestions to work, we must contemplate what is going on. There is no way around this; it means we must gird our loins, look at darkness square in the face, and remain hopeful anyway. Remaining intelligently hopeful and responsive is the only way to nourish a positive future.

It is widely known in Jungian psychology that "the degree to which a person can grow" psycho-spiritually "is directly proportional to the amount of truth they can accept about themselves without running away."[25] This is known as confronting one's shadow. The Jungian concept of the shadow refers to the unconscious aspects of an individual's personality, encompassing both negative traits and untapped positive potentials that are not integrated into one's conscious awareness. Thus, the idea that true psycho-spiritual enlightenment can only occur by at looking at the dark aspects of ourselves is well accepted in theory, even though it is often ignored in practice. I think this fact can be seen in the negative behavior of spiritual leaders such as stealing followers' money and taking immoral sexual liberties with them. These excesses are so commonly known about spiritual leaders that they are almost thought of as cliches. I maintain this would not occur if these so-called spiritual leaders had the courage to look at the darkness within themselves.

I also maintain that true psycho-spiritual enlightenment can't occur unless we look at the darkness in our outer world as well. This notion is echoed by Jung, who was "of the opinion that if we have no imagination for evil, 'evil has us in its grip.'" According to Jung, "our lack of imagination for evil is the best way of making us ... 'an instrument of evil.'" Following the dark rabbit holes of high strangeness helps us develop our imagination for evil, which is of the utmost importance because when we lack this imagination, it "deprives us of the capacity to deal with evil."[26] I believe researching the dark aspects of the phenomenon, when seen as an alchemical process, can help us transmute the dark into light. Jung famously said that "one does not become enlightened by imaging figures of light, but by making the darkness conscious."[26.1]

How The New Age Helps High Strangeness Researchers

New Age channeled messages can provide another data point for their research. I often find an overlap from the data of high strangeness researchers and New Age channeled sources. I view this intersection as the most significant information. Also, aren't you simply curious what the ultraterrestrials *themselves* are supposedly saying? I get as many sources of information as I can and it seems silly to refuse to see what, for example, Pleiadeans from the future are saying about current events. Some refuse to look at this information, simply because some followers of New Age literature are, not to put too fine a point on it, lame. I believe such a stance is juvenile and, not to put too fine a point on it, also lame.

Barbara Marciniak is my favorite New Age channel and I have been following her for over twenty years. I had a mind-blowing synchronicity while in undergrad reading her book, *Bringers of the Dawn,* and have followed her ever since. There is a lot of bad New Age content out there and I can't vouch for any sources other than the ones I cite in this text. When I encourage high strangeness researchers to start looking into New Age sources, I am not referring to the stuff floating around TikTok and Instagram. Some of the New Age content I see there is horrifyingly bad. However, whatever faults the larger New Age community has, they at least give lip service to psycho-spiritual healing, even if a lot of times it is more of a spiritual bypass[J] than true healing. Many high strangeness researchers have a too-cool-for school attitude which makes them not open to the theory and practice of psycho-spiritual healing.

Becoming Highly Strange to Stay Sane

We aren't trying to convince the normals, that is a losing battle as history has shown. For example, in 1846 Ignaz Semmelweis proposed handwashing to prevent the spread of infections in hospitals but faced resistance and skepticism from his peers. This reaction highlights

J "The term was first coined during the early 1980s by a transpersonal psychotherapist named John Welwood in his book *Toward a Psychology of Awakening.* According to Welwood, spiritual bypassing can be defined as a 'tendency to use spiritual ideas and practices to sidestep or avoid facing unresolved emotional issues, psychological wounds, and unfinished developmental tasks.'" (*Spiritual Bypassing as a Defense Mechanism,* By Kendra Cherry, MSEd, VeryWellMind.com, March 17, 2023)

the challenges early proponents of groundbreaking ideas often encounter. However, "Semmelweis was not very tactful. He publicly berated people who disagreed with him" and "Over the years ... got angrier and eventually even strange." Finally, "in 1865, when he was only 47 years old [he] was committed to a mental asylum,"[27] where he eventually died.

The cautionary tale of Semmelweis demonstrates the danger of getting caught up in the mindset of needing to convince others of our weird world views. While, "offering receptive people accurate information is helpful, trying to convince them to believe as you do is not" because "proselytizing irritates and alienates." It better to remember that people "embrace universal truths at their own pace."[27.1] The compulsion to convince others of the strange truth can lead to intense anger and mental instability.

As a result, I suggest we not focus on trying to make regular folks weirder; but instead put that energy into making *ourselves* even stranger. This involves a deeper engagement with the high strangeness phenomenon, going beyond the mere aesthetic appreciation of weirdness. Over the years I have noticed that some people engage in this type of material for the shock factor. I believe this is an adolescent stance to take and thus, not helpful for oneself or others. I'm not interested in the game of shocking the normals; being weird isn't a game to me.

However, if you do go down the convincing rabbit hole, remember, if the truth is so strange, then its mere disclosure may cause the opposite reaction of the intended goal: facilitating emancipatory revelation. For example, "researchers acting through the 'Freedom of Information Act,'" who are attempting to "make manifest all that is hidden," may be doing so "in a way that" might actually be "helpful to" the cause of wetiko. This is what I believe is meant by the Downardian idea: revelation of the method. Meaning, when the truth is so strange, merely disclosing it, may put people in a state of mind where they are unable to believe the strange truth. This is especially the case if they are not prepared to hear something which may disrupt their previous view of reality. Having knowledge of the negative effects of disclosing truth will "supply you with the final information needed to create" a protective barrier from the "irresistible force" of wetiko. Revealing strange realities only can be beneficial when "presented in conjunction with knowledge of this mechanism."[27.2]

Also, if you want to engage this infinitely complex phenomenon properly, then you need to know the basics. This book is an attempt to present those basics, all in one place – to accelerate your journey. Meaning, I have done the tedious research, so you don't have to. Keep in mind that if you aren't familiar with the basics of high strangeness then there is a tendency to "misinterpret the information." Many have been "driven insane when their minds are unable to translate the signal properly," because people who can't translate the strange signal properly "fall prey to the negative aspects and their mental confusion attracts induced hallucinations ... and they can eventually suffer total deterioration of personality." The *My Cosmic Trigger* project in general and this book in particular, is designed to give you enough information to untangle any misinterpretations you might have in researching the phenomenon. This is important because, "once" a person can "untangle the misinterpretations" the negative effects of the phenomenon cease.[28]

Make no mistake, there are real psychological dangers in engaging with the highly strange. However, there are also very tangible psycho-spiritual benefits. This is because "the body wants to live at the edge of the unknown."[29] Also, hunting for the paranormal at least gets you out of the house. When someone is exploring abandoned buildings for ghosts, hiking remote forests in search for Bigfoot, or starring at the night sky looking for UFOs, it is hard to be depressed.[K]

The Magick Of High Strangeness

The practice of high strangeness magick involves four key components: confronting cosmic darkness, engaging in positive timeline magick, operating within established sacred spaces while also crafting new ones, and a retreat to the astral realm.

Confronting cosmic darkness: As I delve deeper into the mysteries of high strangeness and explore its darker aspects, I've noticed a transformative alchemical process at play – whereby unraveling the shadows has paradoxically heightened my sense of optimism as I transmute darkness into light. This is because, seeing the dark side of the coin, helps you more fully realize that "there's another side" to the coin. Whitley Strieber said without his encounter with a dark aspect of the phenomenon, he "could never be as knowledgeable or as richly endowed with spiritual presence as I have become."[29.1] The key here is looking at your research in this regard, as an alchemical process, which is in contrast to *doom scrolling*.[L]

K Greg and Dana Newkirk advocate this approach in their episode on area 51. (*We Recovered UFO Crash Debris from Area 51*, Episode 019, *Haunted Objects Podcast*, July 11, 2023, Youtube: Planet Weird).

L "the practice of obsessively checking online news for updates, especially on social media feeds, with the expectation that the news will be bad, such that the feeling of dread from this negative expectation fuels a compulsion to continue looking for updates in a self-perpetuating cycle" (Dictionary.com/browse/doomscrolling).

Utilizing sacred space and making new ones: Even the great Joseph Campbell talked about the power of sacred space, encouraging us to "move into a landscape, find the sanctity of that land and then there can be the matching of your own nature with this gorgeous nature of the land." This is a powerful magical act because it is "when you are in accord with nature" that she "will yield up its bounty." The gnosis necessary to utilize this approach is to see that, "every sacred place is the place where eternity shines through time."[30]

Positive timeline magick: The theory of "shifting timelines" suggests "that our focus and intention can act as a beacon, drawing us towards the timeline that resonates with our vibrational frequency." By "cultivating positive thoughts … we create a stronger resonance with timelines that reflect our desired reality."[31]Meaning, having positive thoughts can help us stay on a positive timeline where widespread global destruction does not occur and a more liberating future is realized. Negative thoughts are "haunting the future" or we can say, "imprinting the future," and as a result are making a more destructive outcome more likely. When we are stuck in these extreme negative thoughts, we have an "occluded vision that can't conceive of anything other than what we're told the future will be." We then "settle for" a negative future outcome because we "can't see how it can go any other way."[32] Practicing positive timeline magick mitigates this.

Retreat to the astral: In the first meeting of my group, Çhaplains öf Peril (Ç.Ö.P.), in January 2021, I pointed out that the group's genesis was based on my idea of a *retreat to the astral.*[M] Carylon Lovewell has further elucidated this idea, saying: "there's a battle for the future of humanity going on" and she urges people to remember "that the physical realm is not the only, nor even the most primary level of reality." This other level of reality is the astral realm, which is a "causative level of reality of which the physical world is merely an effect." She claims the battle for the future of humanity can now only "be won … at that astral level" because "the forces of disintegration have accumulated all the tools of physical domination." Due to the fact they have all of the tools on the physical plane they are "literally unbeatable at a physical level." However, we *can* beat these "forces of disintegration … on the non-physical level."[33]

A Real Bad Time to Bring Up the Truth

We currently find ourselves in a challenging situation regarding the truth: our world needs it now more than ever, but it appears this

M However, I am not suggesting giving up completely on taking democratic action, per se.

thing we call the truth, is beyond our wildest comprehension. After researching and writing this book, I have come to "the conclusion that the phenomenon is mainly concerned with undefined (and undefinable) cosmic patterns."[28] So, how do we grapple with a truth that is much needed yet inherently undefinable? I'm hoping you have some ideas.

Politics of Reality

The so-called, politics of reality, are at play "in the more alienated industrial societies" because in these societies "a certain type of consensual social reality tends to be singled out and invested with the authority of a paramount objective Reality." Then "all individual ... realities are appraised, devalued and found wanting" when compared to this paramount reality. Even though "this paramount Reality remains only a collective convention, it commands such universal allegiance that the pressures it exerts on us usually seem impossible to resist or circumvent."[34] Poking at the foundational structures of reality is a political act, because as the influential surrealist artist, Antonin Artaud[N] said, "the revolutionary forces of any movement are those capable of shifting the present foundation of things, of changing the *angle* of reality."[34] High strangeness not only changes the angle of reality – it turns the angle into an angel.

One way to look at the politics of reality is that we "are witnessing a battle for the human soul between two opposing ontologies." One view states the physical world "is the ultimate ... reality," determining consciousness and everything else. On the other side is the "transpersonal view," which asserts that "the physical world and all its laws represent only one of an indeterminable number of possible realities whose qualities we can only began to apprehend through the evolution of our consciousness." In this transpersonal view of reality, "consciousness pervades all realities and is the primary source ... of existence."[35]

History Of The Truth

The truth is rarely accepted at first blush. When dinosaur fossils were first discovered, the concept of large, extinct reptiles was initially met with disbelief. Some early finds were even considered hoaxes or misinterpretations. Also consider "the popular myth that the Wrights were se-

N "Both Artaud and the Surrealists attack rational, Western thought. In the first 'Manifesto of Surrealism,' Breton describes this aversion: 'the realistic attitude, inspired by positivism, from Saint Thomas Aquinas to Anatole France, clearly seems to me to be hostile to any intellectual or moral advancement.'" *Artaud and the surrealists*, by Laura Wetherington, (jacket2.org/ commentary/artaud-and-surrealists).

cretive, hiding their early aeronautical experiments from the eyes of the public." However, there is "a convincing argument that they were not" secretive, as evidence suggests "this was an excuse that American journalists adopted to cover their embarrassment for having completely overlooked the biggest story of the twentieth century. The truth of the matter was that the American media ... just couldn't bring themselves to believe that men had flown."[36] This means that the Wright brothers were open about their early experiments in flight, but the press simply did not believe them.

The Human Mind Is Not Set Up For The Truth

The inherent challenge of the human mind to fully embrace reality prompts the question: why is this the case? Anaïs Nin's[O] insight that, "we don't see things as they are, we see them as we are," sheds light on the issue, highlighting the complexities of perceiving even ordinary truths, let alone big truths (such as invisible germs causing sickness and flying machines). The phenomenon that the mind struggles to accept even ordinary truth is something I regularly observe in my role as a psychotherapist. This phenomenon also underscores the intricate nature of accepting a new and highly strange reality.

Keep in mind, the definition of Freud's defense mechanisms are: unconscious psychological strategies employed to protect the mind from uncomfortable thoughts or feelings by distorting or denying reality. This means that accepting the truth about oneself or the world can be so distressing that the human mind develops strategies to deny their reality. For example, take the Freudian defense mechanism of "repression," where distressing thoughts or memories are pushed into the unconscious. Another example is "projection," where individuals attribute their own undesirable thoughts, feelings, or characteristics to someone else, so they don't have to accept the reality that those negative aspects exist within themselves.

Defense mechanisms are implemented when someone experiences cognitive dissonance, which is the psychological discomfort that arises when there is a discrepancy between what the individual believes or values and

---

O Anaïs Nin (1903-1977) was a writer known for her intimate diaries exploring themes of love, self-discovery, and artistic expression. Freud's so-called, adopted son, "psychoanalyst Otto Rank gave his lover ... Nin a ring that he had received from ... Freud. Nin returned the favour with a ring that came from her father." (*The ring and the book*, Kathryn Hughes, the-tls.co.uk, September 1, 2017). "In New York" Nin "rejoined Otto Rank, who had previously moved there, and moved into his apartment. She actually began to act as a psychoanalyst herself, seeing patients in the room next to Rank's." And she also "appeared in the Kenneth Anger film *Inauguration of the Pleasure Dome* (1954) as Astarte" (/wiki/Anaïs_Nin).

their actual thoughts, actions, or experiences. This mental state then leads them to seek harmony by adjusting their perceptions or beliefs. For example, they may "make changes to justify the stressful behavior, either by adding new parts to the cognition causing the psychological dissonance (rationalization) or by avoiding … contradictory information likely to increase the magnitude of the cognitive dissonance (confirmation bias)."[36.1]

This means, it is not "the truth" that people inherently desire, "but an illusion they [can] bear to live with."[36.2]

I more deeply learned about the tricky nature of truth as a psychotherapist, when working with clients struggling with psychological trauma from intense sexual violence. The general school of thought is that you don't confront people with the details of their trauma until they have the coping skills necessary to handle the emotions that arise from talking about what happened to them. You must first provide people the psychological tools to deal with the emotional fall out of confronting and accepting their truth. Meaning, you don't jump into the details of their harsh truth on day one. I would even have to actively stop clients from going into the details of their trauma too early, because doing so can damage them and the others hearing them, if they are not ready.

The ex-CIA spy, Andrew Bustamante, speaks to the phenomenon of humans having a natural inclination to not accept reality, saying: "the brain is inherently very conservative of its energy, we often joke that the brain is lazy" and because the brain is lazy, it "just jumps to conclusions." When you "give it ways to jump to conclusions, it likes that," which is akin to "muscle memory." He says the "brain loves" this approach because it conserves energy by not making the brain go through the trouble of figuring something out.[37]

What Do I believe?

You may be asking: *OK, so what do you actually believe*? In the introductory chapter I did promise I would answer this question. However, first we need to define belief. Our AI overlords (Chat GPT) says: "Belief is a mental attitude or conviction that something is true, often without empirical evidence, shaping an individual's perceptions, decisions, and behaviors." The Cambridge dictionary says: it is "the feeling of being certain that something exists or is true." And a New Age source (a non-physical entity called Abraham) claims: "belief is only a thought I keep thinking" which then becomes "my habit of thought" or "a practiced thought." It is "only a thought I think a lot."[38]

This last definition implies a belief is something you have been thinking over a long period of time. Some of the information I presented in this book, I only recently learned about, so by this definition, I don't believe it. As RAW said, "I don't believe anything, but I have many suspicions." I also take Philip K. Dicks *what if* approach which he developed after his 2-3-74 theophany and is seen in the fact that "he constantly liquefies his revelations" gained from that experience. And because Dick "adhered to no single [religious] faith. The one tradition indubitably his," was the one "which exalts 'What IF?'"[39] After writing this book I have less fixed beliefs than when I started. In their place, I now have more suspicions and *what ifs*.

And, just like RAW, "I am so far gone in the stormy waters of gonzo ontology that I am willing to entertain" pretty much anything these days. However, as RAW also said, "don't understand me too quickly – I just said I was willing to entertain" all things highly strange, "I didn't say I believe it."[39.1] However, even as I say that, don't *misunderstand* me too quickly,[P] either.

Reality Tunnels

I don't use belief as my primary approach when engaged in high strangeness research and practice. I prefer to use reality tunnels as a guide, which I learned from RAW's writings. Reality tunnels are the individualized lenses through which people perceive and interpret reality, shaped by their beliefs and experiences. An understanding of reality tunnels helps with researching the phenomenon because it is by acknowledging and then expanding past these subjective filters, that we achieve a more open-minded perspective of reality. You're going to have a very unpleasant journey researching the highly strange, if you do not have a flexible perspective regarding the complexities of reality.

RAW said that since the late 60s he had "made it a point to read one or two periodicals every month put out by some political or religious group he despises, just to see what sort of signals are being screened out by his habitual reality-maps." He claimed this approach was "most educational" and "one of the best ways to discover how ... the self-metaprogrammer-works."[40] I have used this approach ever since first learning about it when I was an undergrad in the late 90s.

This technique is based on the idea that we are "all looking from the point of view of our own reality tunnels. And when we begin to realize

P For example, recall the points I made above, concerning endnote: 27.2.

that we're all looking from the point of view of our own reality tunnels, we find that it is much easier to understand where other people are coming from." And perhaps most importantly, "every reality tunnel might tell us something interesting about our world, if we're willing to listen."[41] Learning interesting things about the world, by considering as many reality tunnels as possible, sounds like a good thing to me; however, this approach is now seen as more taboo than it was when I first started using it in the 1990s. Considering multiple reality tunnels is also painful because we are already overwhelmed with more information than we know what to do with; choosing one reality tunnel keeps our immediate anxiety more manageable.

Andrew Bustamante, suggests a similar approach to discern the truth about what is going on in the world. This thinking strategy for decoding chaos, "means you listen to left leaning news but then you also listen to right leaning news" and "where they say the same thing, you have a high confidence that it's accurate." And "where they say everything else, doesn't necessarily mean either side is wrong, it's just starting to show you their biases." However, what you can "have confidence in is where they agree." He points out that "if you do that enough times, you start to have a foundation of truth" and can say "I have confidence that this is true. Because left leaning and right leaning news sources are saying this is happening."[37]

In addition to Bustamante's suggestion, I would add the importance of listening to what high strangeness and New Age channeled sources are saying about what is happening. The point here is that by looking at all sides of a debate we can triangulate the truth. Triangulating the truth involves drawing from multiple angles or viewpoints to arrive at a more well-rounded and objective assessment.[Q] Going back to the illusory left/right dichotomy in the United States, it seems which side of the aisle that finds this approach, most offensive, changes through time. Tracking the change in this regard, can perhaps help us see where more truth can be found, at any given time in history.

McLuhan's Approach: Beyond belief

Do I believe everything I have said in this book? No. If I were asked under oath whether I believed everything I have written here, I couldn't say yes. This is because I *believe* the phenomenon is beyond *belief*. Belief is something we use when we want to stop exploring, as I like to

---

Q Triangulation is an approach used in scientific research through using multiple theories, methods, etc., to improve the validity of the finding and mitigate biases.

say – it is impossible to believe this stuff, and I do not find belief particular useful.

As a result, I take McLuhan's "blithe attitude toward strict factual accuracy." "If a few details here and there are wacky" it "doesn't matter a hoot."[42] I also use his method of "exploring and investigating only," versus "trying to promote a [point of] view."[42.1] "I don't explain, I explore." Most importantly for this book, I adopt another notion of his: "I don't necessarily agree with everything I say." McLuhan also "said that he didn't see any point in making statements which weren't controversial,"[43] I agree.

So, with all that being said – the answer to the question of what I believe – should be clear as mud. However, let us hope that this explanation doesn't mean my name is mud.[R]

What *Is* Your Is-ness?

Like Alice was asked by the Caterpillar in Wonderland, the reader is wondering: *who are you*? Meaning, you are trying to figure out what my label is. As Nietzsche said: "Call me whatever you like; I am who I must be" and planting my tongue firmly in my check I say: "call me anything, so long as you don't call me late to dinner."[44]

E-prime

Before we look at what my label *is*, who I *am* to you, we will need to define the definition of *is*. When deciding on what someone's is-ness label is, "it depends on what the meaning of the word 'is' is,"[45] as Bill Clinton famously asked. Of course, such a question is politicking 101, but there is psychological and philosophical importance behind the question, seen in E-Prime, or English Prime. This is a linguistic form of English that excludes the use of the verb "to be" which would also include "is, are, were, was, am, be, been," and their contractions. E-Prime was developed to encourage clearer, more objective communication and reduce dogmatic thinking.

E-prime was a topic that RAW was passionate about, pointing out that in 1933, "Alfred Korzybski proposed that we should abolish the 'is of identity' from the English language." The abolishment of the "is of identify" is important because is, "takes the form X is a Y. e.g., 'Joe is a Communist,' 'Mary is a dumb file-clerk,' [or] 'The universe is a giant machine.'" Then,

R See, *My Name Is Mud – Meaning and Origin* (grammarist.com/idiom/ones-name-is-mud/) and "'My Name Is Mud'" which "is a song by American rock band Primus" (wiki/My_Name_Is_Mud).

in 1949 a "D. David Bourland Jr. proposed the abolition of all forms of the words 'is' or 'to be.'" This English "without 'isness,'' Bourland "called E-Prime, or English-Prime."

RAW explained English and E-prime by highlighting the differences between: "That is a fascist idea" versus "That seems like a fascist idea to me." The former sentence using regular English, "implies an indwelling essence of the medieval sort, does not describe an operation in spacetime, and mentions no instrument used in measuring the alleged 'fascism' in the idea." By contrast, the E-Prime sentence, "does not assume essences ... describes the operation as occurring in the brain of the speaker and, implicitly, identifies said brain as the instrument making the evaluation." RAW thought E-prime "draws us back into the modern quantum world where observer and observed form a seamless unity," whereas the normal use of English "assumes a sort of 'glass wall' between observer and observed."[46]

Take note of the conspicuous absence of E-prime in current political discussions. A candid assessment reveals that the essence of political discourse revolves around the concept of "isness." Also, observe its absence in the critiques of high strangeness below.[S]

I will also now address some questions that might appear irrelevant or even absurd to my readers. However, if you delve deeply into these topics, you will notice these labels being used frequently. I aim to cover all my bases, in case anyone ends up questioning these labels in relation to me.

Are You Dangerous?

No.

In an article in the UK's, *The Guardian,* it was claimed that Graham Hancock's Netflix show, *Ancient Apocalypse,* "is the most dangerous show on Netflix." Even though the article did say we shouldn't "dismiss Hancock's theory out of hand, of course. Because if he's right ... it would change everything we know about ourselves." However, it was asserted that we "certainly shouldn't treat his hodgepodge of mysteries and coincidences as fact" because doing so is "the danger of a show like this."[47] To be clear, I wouldn't encourage anyone to consider the mysteries and coincidences I present in this book as fact. For one, I'm not even sure of what is meant by the word *fact.* In fact, I say forget facts. Instead, I am encouraging people to re-introduce mystery into their lives.

S The astute observer will notice my critique of the critique is not using e-prime, a "fire with fire" approach.

We can do this by connecting with nature (and reality itself) on a deeper level. We can do this by heading to the forest in search of cryptids or by opening an angelic portal in our own back yards.[T] Of course, as always, supplement your engagement with more mystery with grounding activities to stay sane: copious amounts of psychotherapy, flossing your teeth, paying your taxes, taking showers, playing with your children, and calling your mother.

Creating more mystery is "a very necessary ingredient in our lives" because "Mystery[U] creates wonder, and wonder is the basis for man's desire to understand."[28] What I am encouraging doesn't sound dangerous to me. In fact, it seems to me that – anyone suggesting that inviting more mystery into one's life is dangerous – *is the dangerous one*. Also keep in mind that "President Richard Nixon claimed" Timothy Leary was "the most dangerous man in America."[48] I find it interesting that Nixon thought he was so dangerous, when Leary said "the whole point of" his work was that: "*Positive energy is as real as gravity*."[40] I happen to agree with Leary in this regard and sincerely hope I am not painted with the same *dangerous* label that Nixon painted Leary with.

Are You A Conspiracy Theorist?

No.

In our current times, "if we see things differently from consensus reality, we open up to being accused of either being a tinfoil-hat wearing conspiracy theorist, an idiot, evil ... or any number of unsavory things."[49] Yes, I see things differently than consensus reality, but I am not a conspiracy theorist. I learned from a college professor that conspiracy theories are "just a narcissistic fantasy." When this professor was teaching his classes on conspiracy theory, he taught the work of the Warwick University, professor of philosophy, Quassim Cassam, who points out that some people, "demand that conspiracy theories not be rejected without an appropriate evaluation of the evidence, but this demand makes no sense where no evidence is offered." Cassam also points out that conspiracy theories are "immune to counterevidence because it was never based on evidence in the first place."[49.1]

T See *How embracing the paranormal could produce a deeper meaning of life*, by Amanda LeClaire, February 10, 2023, (wdet.org/2023/02/10/how-embracing-the-paranormal-could-produce-a-deeper-meaning-of-life/).

U "The paranormal is not about ghosts or aliens or Bigfoot. It's about the mystery of existence itself. And that mystery is always shifting, always changing, always elusive." – John Keel, *The Eighth Tower*, (1975)

I would *never* advocate for believing in something when no evidence is given. Notice that the parapolitical topics explored in this text are backed up by mainstream news sources. When I first started researching highly strange subjects that poke holes in our fragile consensus reality back in the '90s, you were infinitely more likely to be called a left-wing hippie, than a right-wing conspiracy theorist, but again, we live in strange times.

Are You A Right Winger?

No.

Before answering this question in full, it is important to point out that parapolitical research was initially seen as a left-wing field of endeavor. One reason for this is that, arguably the first parapolitical topic, was the JFK murder. Being that he was a Democrat President, naturally more left leaning people were the ones questioning the official story surrounding his murder. One of the first researchers into the mysteries surrounding his death was Mae Brussell, who "wrote articles that were published in *The Realist*, a magazine published by Paul Krassner."[50] Paul Krassner (1932–2019) was an iconic American, author, comedian, and journalist widely known as being "a key figure in the counterculture of the 1960s."[51] Also, "among the icons of the 1960s counterculture, no one carried the torch in succeeding decades with more joy and vigor than"[52] he did.

The first reason Krassner was an icon of the 60s counterculture is due to the fact he "was a member of the Merry Pranksters,"[53] which "were followers of American author Ken Kesey[V] ... and are noted for the sociological significance of a lengthy road trip they took in the summer of 1964, traveling across the United States in a psychedelic painted school bus called Furthur." They are also known for "organizing parties, and giving out LSD" in what they called Acid Tests. Tom Wolfe "chronicled their early escapades in his 1968 book *The Electric Kool-Aid Acid Test*."[54] Reading *The Electric Kool-Aid Acid Test,*[W] checked out from my High School's library, is one of the books that peeked my interest in the subjects explored in this book. The exploits of the Merry Pranksters were culturally significant because when "the psychedelic movement was just about to explode onto the world stage ... it was" the Pranksters "who originated nearly every aspect of the new 'hippie' aesthetic: bizarre dress, communal lifestyle, psychedelic drugs ... and self-expressive rock and roll music."[55]

V *One Flew Over the Cuckoo's Nest* is a novel by Ken Kesey published in 1962.

W The Grateful Dead was the house band for the acid tests and their song, "The Other One," is about Merry Prankster, Neal Cassady – driver of the Furthur bus (dead.net/features/greatest-stories-ever-told/greatest-stories-ever-told-other-one).

The second reason Krassner is known as an icon of the 60s counterculture, is due to the fact he was a co-founder of the Yippies, (Youth International Party), a countercultural and anti-establishment movement during that time. He "was an unindicted coconspirator in the trial of the Chicago Eight, who were arrested in connection with anti-war protests outside the 1968 Democratic National Convention."[52] The trail of the Chicago Eight concerned a "series of riots" that "occurred during the convention, and eight protest leaders," including two co-founders of the Yippies, "Abbie Hoffman and Jerry Rubin."[56] In general, the Yippies were known for using humor and theatrical protests to critique societal norms and challenge political authority.

However, Krassner's "greatest legacy is *The Realist,*" which he started in 1958 and "kept going for 43 years, until 2001." The magazine published such notable figures as: "Norman Mailer, Dick Gregory, Jerry Garcia, Allen Ginsberg, Kurt Vonnegut, Groucho Marx … Ken Kesey, Richard Pryor, Marshall McLuhan, Woody Allen, Mort Sahl, George Carlin, Neil Postman … Joseph Heller, Timothy Leary, [and] Ram Dass."[52] The magazine was so influential that "*People* magazine labeled" Krassner the "father of the underground press."[57] Noted author and screen writer, Terry Southern[X] "called *The Realist* 'the most important publication in the United States.'"[52] The publication was seen as "an indispensable magazine for hippies and those who try to understand" them.[53]

I point out the above to illustrate that Krassner was the opposite of right-wing, being that he was literally a father of the 60s left-wing, counter-culture movement in the United States. Even though he was the embodiment of left wing, he was "the first to publish Mae Brussel's theory on the JFK assassination, and he was a go-to source for"[52] those interested in parapolitical topics.

Mae Brussel was one of the first[Y] modern day parapoltical researchers and her work so "impressed John Lennon" that he "donated money so Krassner could afford to print" it.[50] Also, of note in this regard, is that in "1972 John Lennon[Z] told publisher Paul Krassner, 'Listen, if anything happens to Yoko and me, it wasn't an accident.'"[58] Krassner described Brussell as a "house-wife-turned-crusader" who wrote "hundreds of articles detailing the unpleasant connections between what most people con-

X Writer of such notable films as, *Dr. Strangelove or: How I Learned to Stop Worrying and Love the Bomb* (Stanley Kubrick, 1964), and the 1969, *Easy Rider*, which was written with Peter Fonda and Dennis Hopper (wiki/Terry_Southern).

Y Another was Dr. Peter Beter, (peterdavidbeter.com).

Z See, *Uri Geller: On John Lennon's alien encounter, crashed UFOs and recruiting citizens for his micronation*, by Bethany Minelle, September 2022, news.sky.com.

sider" dark "chapters in American history," such as "the Kennedy murders and Watergate."[59]

In addition to being a leftist counter cultural icon of the 1960s, and championing Brussell's parapolitical research, Krassner also wrote the foreword to Peter Levenda's *Sinister Forces – The Manson Secret: A Grimoire of American Political Witchcraft (Book 3)*. And John Keel was "a friend and fan of" his, even putting "him into his superhero spoof, *The Fickle Finger of Fate*."[AA,60]

Parapolitical research in particular, and questioning the establishment in general, was still considered more of a left-wing endeavor when I started my research in the mid 90s and remained that way until only recently. Many in the community have commented on the curious fact that anything highly strange is now seen, by some, as pure right-wing.[AB] Serious parapolitical researchers are not partisan, pointing out their findings are so important that "we need people on the left and we need people on the right." Curiously enough, we have had a pole shift in regards to openness to parapolitical research; because in our present day "people on the left aren't embracing it as prolifically as people on the right." When it comes to anything even vaguely parapolitical "it certainly seems the left has thrown it right into [the] Qanon conspiracy crap rabbit hole ... box." However, when Krassner was publishing *The Realist*, it was the exact opposite. This highly strange fact has people in the parapolitical research community trying to "figure that out." Most in the community would agree with Nick Bryant, when he says: "I'm not on the left, I'm not on the right."[61] As a result, researchers such as Bryant are in an interesting position viz á viz the changing winds of the right and left's political philosophies. Do they change their findings based on this changing wind?

The presence of the right-wing in high strangeness has been discussed since the days of John Keel. The people today discussing right-wing groups interested in these topics are not breaking new ground in this regard. For example, in 1980, Keel reported that he saw a "big overlap ... of wild-eyed right-wingers, and many of the more bizarre beliefs of the John Birch Society and even the KKK were absorbed in the UFO lore."[62] Keel also said that "in the 1960s ufology swung in the other direction as members of the extreme right wing embraced the flying saucer cause."[63]

AA *The Fickle Finger of Fate: A Camp Classic For Adults Only*, John Keel (writer), Al Jaffee (Illustrator), (1966). Also see, JohnKeel.com/?p=2999

AB This is discussed in the *Tin Foil Hat* podcast, 720: *The New Order and the Biblical End Of Days* with Isaac Weishaupt & Jay Dyer, Oct. 31, 2023.

Not that it is any of your business, but I will share my political affiliations. I was a card-carrying member of the Libertarian Party at the age of 16, in 1994. On a trip to San Francisco, to see my aunt star in a Broadway musical, I saw a Libertarian Party bumper sticker with a 1-800 number. Being inspired by the milieu of the area (such as visiting Haight Ashbury) and being an inquisitive young person, I wrote the number down and called when I got back. I received the free literature in the mail and after agreeing with the philosophy, I moved forward to join the Party, two years before I could vote. This trip to San Francisco also sparked my interest in psychedelics; because my aunt had cable TV, I saw the famous Bill Hicks bit about how you never see positive news stories about LSD. This trip to San Francisco was very influential in my development and it is part of the reason I always identified with the spirit of the 60s leftist, counter-culture as detailed above.

Publicly,[AC] I will report that the only time I strayed from voting for the Libertarian presidential candidate was in 2008, when I cast my vote for Obama. After not seeing the change, that I felt was promised, I went back to voting third party. I even went to a Jill Stein (the Green Party candidate) rally in 2016. Given my lifelong affinity to third parties in the United States, I believe that "we shouldn't be hoodwinked into choosing sides in the phony dialectic process of Left/right" considering both sides are "responsible for the ascendance of the Money Power over humanity."[15] However, some seemingly imply that the only people into high strangeness are the far right, saying that it "was always inevitable that the UFO and far right scenes would end up in bed together."[64] If you would have told me back in the 90s, that in 2024, researching UFOs would be considered far right, I would have called you crazy. But again, here we are.

What I like so much about the phenomenon is that it is bringing both sides together. This is seen in "New legislation proposed by bipartisan lawmakers" which "aims to protect civilian pilots ... who report sightings of unidentified aerial phenomena (UAP)."[65] Democrat Rep. Raja Krishnamoorthi, "told reporters that lawmakers 'haven't gotten the answers that we need.'" And Republican Rep. Glenn Grothman, maintained "that lawmakers were looking 'to track down exactly what the military thinks of individual instances of these objects.'"[66]

AC Perhaps, like some politicians, I have a public and private position. "ABC correspondent and debate moderator ... asked" Hillary Clinton "about a statement she'd made in a speech saying 'you need both a public and a private position' on issues." ("Hillary Clinton answers for saying politicians need 'a public and a private position' on issues," Pamela Engel, Oct 10, 2016, *BusinessInsider*.com).

Are You a Satan Worshiper?

No.

I identify as a gnostic, mystical Christian and practice a psycho-spiritual shamanism; my magical practices are deeply rooted in these perspectives. A significant component of my magical rituals involve connecting with the angelic energies and I make it a daily practice to invoke angelic protection. My practice is not based on "belief." I practice and see the results and then my experience becomes knowledge, that can be reinterpreted at another time, in light of different experiences.

Additionally, you'll observe numerous references to Christian texts throughout the pages of this book. I have already pointed out how Crowley was not a "Satan worshiper" and if you turn to the cover of this book, you will see an angel guarding the planet. Yes, my approach to the teachings of the Christ, are on the esoteric side. For example, I like to contemplate such quotes as: "The time scale of my coming is subjective.… As I enter human events, the intensity of my bio-gravitational field will cause time to bubble and warp … islands of the future coming will arise. For a while, you will have the old and new existing side by side."[67]

Are You Racist?

No.

Some claim that suggesting a lost civilization is racist. The Society for American Archeology claimed that people like Graham Hancock, who are "proponents of this theory have suggested that white survivors of this advanced civilization were responsible for the cultural heritage of Indigenous peoples in the Americas and around the world."[68] Hancock responded to this accusation, saying: "When archaeologists label me as … a 'racist' … they directly disparage my personal reputation." He says that, calling him a racist for exploring the idea of a lost civilization "is a spurious attempt to smear by association. My own theory of a lost civilization of the Ice Age … is what I take responsibility for. It is nonsensical to blame me for the hypotheses of others, either now or in the past, or for how others have reacted to those hypotheses."[69]

I will also point out that there is a theory that a lost advanced civilization "were black Africans." This theory is based on the "notion that the Olmec were not indigenous Americans, but rather that they were black Africans who traversed the Atlantic Ocean millennia before Christopher Columbus … the general idea is that Africans established (or helped establish) one of the oldest major civilizations in the Americas." Some claim this theory "is just as colonialist as the Eurocentric model that Afrocentrists rail against."[70]

In this book I bring up highly strange theories around the mound builders. This theory is also labeled a far-right theory by some, because Andrew Jackson "used a lost prehistoric civilization claim to justify the Indian Removal Act, which ended in the Trail of Tears."[71] To be clear, I do not support Andrew Jackson's Indian Removal Act, nor would I have voted for Andrew Jackson if I were alive at that time.[AD] I have pointed out that there are legends of gnomes or a lost race of giants building the mounds, which some myths of Native Americans point to. For example, in one instance, early "explorers learned that the Dakota Indians called the place Mountain of the Little People, or Spirit Mound."[72] To me it is actually more racist to not believe the myths of indigenous people. As I already pointed out in this book: Forth says that in writing, *Between Ape and Human: An Anthropologist on the Trail of a Hidden Hominoid,* he "hoped to convince his colleagues to place greater emphasis on the testimony of the indigenous people they encounter during their researches." He says this is because "Anthropologists who ignore information in the form of myths and anecdotes from what he called traditionally non-literate and technologically simple communities risk missing important evidence."[73] In my opinion, it seems exceedingly racist for anthropologists to ignore the information of indigenous people, presented in the form of myths and anecdotal reports.

Another thing I think is racist, is to ignore the indigenous people's shamanistic world view. In this view of reality "shamans call together forces which are very real, causing things to happen which are contradictory to our normal reality, but which fit perfectly within their paradigm." For example, "if we ask shamans their views about the Earth," they would say: "the earth is alive." The fact that "shamans around the world share this view of a living Earth may be the final key in coming to understand sacred places."[74] Mainstream science denying the importance of this final key found in the shamanic worldview, is simply and arrogantly racist in my opinion.

Some also claim that the belief in the myth of Atlantis is racist, because the Nazi's embraced this myth, which I talked about at length in this book. The Nazi belief in this regard was related to the myth of "a pure Aryan race

AD I would have voted for Adams. It was "During Adams's presidency, the Democratic-Republican Party split into two major camps: the National Republican Party, which supported Adams, and Andrew Jackson's Democratic Party. The Democrats proved to be more effective political organizers than Adams and his National Republican supporters, and Jackson soundly defeated Adams in the 1828 presidential election." (wiki/John_Quincy_Adams).

with a glorious ancient past" which "was central to a transatlantic nineteenth-century occult scene (that featured a heavy German influence.)" It was "after Hitler assumed power" that "this belief was institutionalized in the form of ... an alt-archeology research outfit founded by Heinrich Himmler and the Atlantis theorist Herman Wirth."[64]

As I pointed out earlier, the myths around Atlantis were that it was an advanced civilization, consisting of good guys and bad guys. For example, "as the laws of nature were increasingly forced to bend to the will of the Atlanteans, they almost inevitably began to be used destructively." This then led to a "struggle of the Sons of Belial to gain complete dominance over the Children of the Law of One." This struggle between good and evil Atlanteans meant that the times of "Destruction were not far off." Eventually, the evil actions of "the Sons of Belial had become such an effrontery to nature that it was these forces, in the end, that destroyed them."[75] Put simply, the Nazi's that embraced the Atlantis mythos were trying to bring back the Sons of Belial controlled Atlantis. By contrast, New Age practitioners, are trying to bring back a golden age that existed when the Children of the Law of One, controlled Atlantis.

The New Age theory is that we are at the same point the mythical Atlantis civilization was at before it destroyed itself. As a result "we have been given the opportunity to develop our civilization to the point where the Atlanteans were in the process of making a very crucial decision: Power for the good of Earth and her people ... or power for exploitation and evil?" Just like the ancient Atlanteans, "we are truly being confronted by the two sides of technological advances. The one side promises knowledge to aid humankind," while the "other side leers seductively at the potential of destruction ... made possible by the same knowledge." The "final choice made by the Atlanteans ... is overwhelmingly made apparent by" the fact it was destroyed; "let us pray that the choice that we may one day be forced to make will not at some time in the future be known by the same cataclysmic changes."[75]

Billy Carson,[AE] the critically acclaimed Black American writer, speaks on this return to a past golden age; when the good guys of Atlantis, win round two. He says, "I have a lot of optimism in humanity, that we are going to come through this time," overcoming "the divide and conquer tactics ... we are going to see through all this illusion" and as a result we will "reform this global economic system into something that's positive." As we accomplish this, Carson believes "we're going to start heading back

AE "Billy Carson is the founder and CEO of 4BiddenKnowledge Inc" and "the Best Selling Author of *The Compendium Of The Emerald Tablets*" (4biddenknowledge.com/bio).

to the golden age again," which existed "in the past on this planet and I believe we are headed back to another one again."[76]

While researching this section, I came across more racist interpretations of Atlantis, learning that "Many writers on the subject ... spoke of the 'white' skin of the Atlanteans, who were a kind of master race tutoring benighted brown people in the divine art of piling rocks."[71] This is interesting because I had previously heard theories that the Atlantean race were not white. For example, the sources I came across pointed out that "the Atlantean skins were taking on a reddish hue."[77] And the other famous lost race civilization were also said to not be white, as it is claimed that: "the Lemurians were the major race at this time which had developed into the Uighers [and] the Naga-Mayas."[77]

The Uyghurs are a Turkic ethnic group now living in China. And "the Chinese government's campaign against" them is allegedly "multi-faceted and systematic," featuring "identity-based persecution, mass detention, surveillance, enforced sterilizations, forced labor, and forced assimilation."[78] Concerning the "Naga-Mayas," the *Hindustan Times* reported, "The Mayans of Guatemala – representative of the Maya civilization that flourished ... in Central America – believe their ancestors came to this part of the globe 20,000 years ago from the East." The "Kekichi Maya, has always had special attraction for India ... as their forefathers have told them that the 'Naga tribes of Nagaland'[AF] were one of the four original branches of the Maya civilization." Because of this oral history, these "people of Guatemala for long have been trying to establish contact with Indians and have a cultural dialogue."[79] The important point here is that none of these groups are "white" people. Unfortunately, there are individuals involved in all subjects that are racist. If you support your city's local football team you can bet a racist supports them too. I don't think that means all people who support those teams are racist. In my opinion, the same goes for having an interest in subjects such as Atlantis.

I would be remiss, if in the discussion of systemic racism in high strangeness, that I did not bring up the most destructive example of systemic racism: the United States drug war. The systemic racism present in the U.S. drug war was explored in the Netflix documentary, *13th*. This "2016 American documentary film ... explores the prison-industrial complex,

AF Nagas "are various ethnic groups native to northeastern India ... The groups have similar cultures and traditions, and form the majority of population in the Indian state of Nagaland" (wiki/Naga_people). Nagaland is "inhabited by 17 major tribes along with other sub-tribes. Each tribe is distinct in character from the other ... It is a land of folklore passed down the generations through word of mouth" (wiki/Nagaland).

and the 'intersection of race, justice, and mass incarceration in the United States'; it is titled after the Thirteenth Amendment to the United States Constitution, adopted in 1865, which abolished slavery throughout the United States and ended involuntary servitude except as a punishment for conviction of a crime." The Thirteenth Amendment "allowed for a constitutional loophole in which black Americans became criminalized and faced involuntary servitude in the form of penal labor."[80] The U.S.'s war on drugs "begun as a racially motivated crusade to criminalize Blacks and the anti-war left" according to the fact that "Richard Nixon's domestic policy advisor John Ehrlichman revealed" as much, "in a 1994 interview."[81]

I am discussing it here because I find it unwise to discuss racism in any context without at least briefly addressing the most prominent example of systemic racism. Despite the substantial impact the war on drugs has had on the Black community, it is perplexing that contemporary efforts in highlighting systemic racism, seem more concerned with tackling racism within Atlantis theories than actively raising awareness and advocating for an end to the U.S war on drugs. While it's commendable to highlight instances of systemic racism within high strangeness, it's crucial to recognize the relatively few people engaged in this subject overall. In addition, the proportion of people within our already very small community, who discuss racist Atlantis theories, is tiny – in the grand scheme of things. In my view, addressing racism in fields like Ufology without acknowledging the U.S. drug war, arguably the most racist institution, is one example of writing from a privileged position and reflects an inconsistency in addressing systemic issues.

One of the reasons I joined the Libertarian Party at the age of 16 was due to their stance on ending the racist U.S. drug war. In grad school I did advocacy work with The November Coalition, "a non-profit grassroots organization ... which fights against the War on Drugs and for the rights of the prisoners incarcerated as the effect of that war."[82] In 2016, I even ran to be a State House representative in Georgia. My campaign platform advocated for providing treatment options to addicts over prison time. I felt this approach was a small step to help end the drug war.[83] It is my sincere hope that writers focusing on systemic racism in the high strangeness field will expand their efforts to also include shinning a light on this disastrous public policy.

Are You Antisemitic?

No

The Southern Poverty Law center has pointed out that some antisemitic racists have suggested that "inter-dimensional alien(s) [are] in league with the Jews."[64] I do not believe this to be the case because I believe the phenomenon is way beyond human ethnic groups. I have not, nor ever will, suggest it has anything to do with Jewish people. My research simply doesn't indicate this racist view. In this book I have speculated that there might be people who stand to lose a lot of money if free energy technology comes out. And given the amount of money they would lose if this were the case, perhaps have reason to suppress free energy technology.[AG] In 2022, the profits of "Big Oil more than doubled ... to $219 billion, smashing previous records in a year of volatile energy prices."[84] I am in *no way* saying that Big Oil is run by Jewish people or the nation state of Israel. Given the latter's recent troubles, it does not appear they control the world in general or the global oil supply in particular.

The *only* conspiracy I believe in is when RAW said: "You should view the world as a conspiracy run by a very closely-knit group of nearly omnipotent people, and you should think of those people as yourself and your friends."

Are You A Nazi?

No.

I have heard rumors from paranormal researchers that Crowley worked with Hitler, however the evidence suggests the opposite is actually the case. Consider the fact that "the leader of the OTO after Crowley's death" was Karl Germer,[AH] who "was placed in a concentration camp" by the Nazis. This was because, "his official crime was that he knew and maintained relations with Aleister Crowley." In addition to this evidence, "Crowley claimed that he advocated the use of two magical signs which were to boost British morale and frequently used by Winston Churchill: the 'V' sign, which, in magical terms, is the counter of the Swastika; and the 'Thumbs Up,' ... which was published in a pamphlet of Crowley poetry during the most desperate days of 1940 and whose use spread throughout the nation."[85] There is compelling evidence to suggest Crowley worked with the allied forces (the good guys fighting the Nazis) laid

AG Perhaps the failure to implement free energy is due to "Hanlon's razor" which is the notion to "Never attribute to malice that which is adequately explained by stupidity" (/wiki/Hanlon's_razor).

AH After Crowley died in 1947, "Germer was ... the head of O.T.O." but refused to "initiate new members." In 1959 Grady McMurtry "tried to organize other O.T.O. members ... to lobby Germer to change his policy" but Germer "'ordered' McMurtry to cease his efforts." Germer died in 1962 "without naming a successor." In 1969 "McMurtry decided to restore the Order by invoking his emergency orders from Crowley which gave him authority" to "'take charge of the whole work of the Order in California to reform the Organization'" (wiki/Grady_Louis_McMurtry).

out in the book, *Secret Agent 666: Aleister Crowley, British Intelligence and the Occult,* by Richard Spence.

Some have seemingly suggested that even considering the existence of "secret Nazi super technologies [and] a belief in secret Nazi bases" and "escaped Nazi scientists working in secret technology and weapons labs"[64] is akin to supporting Nazi ideology. Perhaps the confusion in this regard, is due to the fact that that some people considering this legend are saying if it were true, then it would be a good thing. For example, the idea of a survival of a 4th Reich "took root during the mid-1970s, nurtured by the Canadian neo-Nazi Ernst Zundel, who argued that Nazis invented flying saucers and had taken their breakthrough technology to bases deep under the South Pole."[64.]

None of the authors I have cited in this book, that present evidence suggesting the existence of a secret Nazi 4th Reich, think it is a good thing. They clearly believe and state that if the Nazis survived WW2 and set up an extra-national organization to covertly influence world affairs – then that would be a very, very bad thing. To be crystal clear, if the 4th Reich survived and maintains a covert influence over world affairs with high tech weaponry, then it is an exceedingly very bad thing.

The idea of a covert Nazi influence on American politics was speculated by the leftist-hippie, counter-culture leader, Paul Krassner, saying that "when Hitler failed, his officers were brought to the US," some claim via Operation Paperclip,[AI] "to build that dream of the Fourth Reich." Claiming further, that "it is in this context that the Kennedys, Malcolm X, Martin Luther King, labor leaders ... and hippies are being slain."[59]Again, Krassner is saying this is a very bad thing.[AJ]

AI After "the Nazi empire collapsed," allegedly a "series of meetings was arranged at the Pentagon with Nazi Gehlen" and "Allen Dulles." Then "the Gehlen organization combined forces ... with the OSS." Gehlen's group were "Experts in ... illegal control of Germany" and allegedly "became the teachers of Allen Dulles" helping "form the new CIA in 1947." (*The Essential Mae Brussell,* p. 49). In "1961, following the Bay of Pigs incident ... Dulles and his entourage ... were forced to resign." JFK was murdered in Nov. of 1963. That same month President Johnson "appointed Dulles" to "the Warren Commission to investigate the assassination" which "was later criticized by some historians," noting "that Kennedy had fired him, and he was therefore unlikely to be impartial" (wiki/Allen_Dulles).

AJ "The Nazi Connection" aired on 60 Minutes in 1982 and centers around former U.S. Government prosecutor and Army intelligence officer named John Loftus, (youtube.com/watch?v=GX-FLYOHCGdw). Loftus authored, *The Secret War Against the Jews: How Western Espionage Betrayed The Jewish People* and *America's Nazi Secret: An Insider's History*. Also, "German scientists were responsible for putting the first American on the moon. Now, 15 years later, government investigators are asking whether some of them were also responsible for Nazi war crimes. Frontline examines their war records and the role of American officials who decided to bring them to the United States." (*The Nazi Connection*, PBS.org, Frontline: Season 1987, Ep. 5).

Are You A Flat Earther?

No. In considering this subject, I find it interesting that when I first started seriously researching high strangeness in the 1990s, it was not a thing. In fact, I never remember even coming across flat Earth theories at that time. Another interesting component of the flat Earth movement is that it has a tendency to be used to label anyone that is into high strangeness. Meaning if you bring up anything strange you are immediately asked if you are also a flat Earther. When I have told normals about the book I'm writing they have asked if I also think the Earth is flat. That's preposterous – nuff said. I also notice, this argument is used to dismiss Hancock's Netflix documentary series, when the skeptic says: "I once got trapped at a party with a Flat Earther. It was a very similar experience to watching this."[47]

Are You Into QAnon?

No. I actually haven't heard anyone in the serious high strangeness community supporting this theory. For example, there has never been a QAnoner on *The Higerside Chats*. Frequent guest on the show, synchromystic Chris Knowles, has even been dismissive of QAnon on the show.[86] Allen Greenfield has also come out against QAnon. While promoting his new book, *Secrets of the Real Black Lodge Revealed!* (Aug. 2023), he said that: "as times the world over – turned dark indeed ... the rarely discussed Black Lodge began to show itself in such phenomena as increased authoritarianism ... disinformation sources (Q-Anon comes to mind), I decided that it was urgent that the focus be more on The Black Lodge through all of history."[87] There are dozens of articles about the dangers of QAnon on Salon.com[AK] and thus, I can only conclude the supporters are promoting their theories on Internet spaces I do not frequent. I certainly have not seen it seriously considered in the highly strange spaces I have cited in this book.

You Quoted So-And-So, Are You A Supporter Of So-And-So?

No. I am not a Crowleyian, a Jungian, a Freudian, a Dickian, or a Wilsonian. If you'll allow me to be so bold, I will say I am a Vaughnian. As the great William Blake said, "I must create a system, or be enslaved by another man's. I will not reason and compare: my business is to create."[88] I do

AK Salon.com/topic/qanon

not support everything an author I have cited has ever said, nor do I advocate supporters of the cited authors. It would take me almost a lifetime to vet every single author I have quoted. If I have quoted an author, then it means I like that particular idea, and it doesn't mean I endorse everything they have ever said or ever will say. Someone else's interpretation, of someone else's reality, is not how I perceive reality[AL] and remember, the dark exists not too far from the light.

For example, while I deeply admire Ghandi's non-violent resistance ideology and efforts, I do not support some of Ghandi's alleged behavior. Meaning, I advocate non-violence, but I do not advocate that anyone take his alleged approach to "control male libido" by "using women – including some underage girls ... to test his sexual patience." Allegedly, this approach consisted of him sleeping "naked next to them in bed without touching them, making sure he didn't get aroused; these women were props to coax him into celibacy."[89] Also, while I agree with Kerry Thornley's "form of anarchy," which "was all about freeing oneself from government controls and affecting change in [a] subversive, yet positive manner." I disagree with his "envisioned Utopia ... a world free of sexual hangups," that also "included advocacy for pedophilia." Even his biographer, Adam Gorightly, said he "had assumed this stance was merely idealistic until" an old neighbor of Thornley reached out to him via email in 2003 and reported that Thornley allegedly tried to fondle her child of 7 or 8.[90]

The same can be said with Jim Brandon, the author of *The Rebirth of Pan*. This book was featured in the *Hellier* docuseries and the team was questioned for including it. Greg Newkirk addresses this, saying: "I'll say it again: the reason we don't actively promote 'Rebirth of Pan' is because there are rumors that the author – listed as Jim Brandon – is William Grimstad," who allegedly is a "Horrible, horrible guy."[91] Newkirk says this because the allegations are that he "was a straight up white supremacist and Holocaust denier, associated with David Duke."[AM,92]

Hellier, the *Penny Royal* podcast, the book *Origins of the Gods: Qesem Cave, Skinwalkers and Contact with Transdimensional Intelligences*, all talked about Brandon's *The Rebirth of Pan*. In the first *Cosmic Trigger* RAW talked about the "Grimstad-Downard theory" he learned about in their "Sirius Rising" tapes. He said the ideas presented in these tapes, were the "most absurd, the most incredible, the most ridiculous ... of them all. The only trouble is that, after the weird data we have already surveyed,

AL See, the Sun Ra song, "Somebody Else's World" (a.k.a. Somebody Else's Idea), (SunRamusic.bandcamp. com/track/somebody-elses-world-a-k-a-somebody-elses-idea).

AM *The Rise of David Duke*, by T. Bridgers, 1995.

the Grimstad-Downard theory may not sound totally unbelievable to us." RAW says that according to their claims, the Earth is being prepared, "in an occult manner, for extraterrestrial contact."[40] In the critique of citing the material in *The Rebirth of Pan,* we learn that what is "problematic" about citing this author "is when researchers aren't transparent about the provenance of the ideas they're sharing."[93] As you can see, I have been transparent in this regard.

Grimstad's alleged association with David Duke, is curious, given his association with his mentor, James Shelby Downard. It is curious because, "as Downard tells it," starting at a young age he faced a "mounting menace to himself and his father from the local Klan, which he dubs a 'quasi-Masonic criminal fraternity.'" This menace even "forced" the Downard family "to pull up stakes"[94] in Oklahoma and move to another state. In addition to claiming the KKK was physically threatening his family, Downard wrote extensively about the nefarious influence of the KKK, saying that only "some of the Ku Klux Klan's evil is known to the public."[16] But that is high strangeness for you – contradictions.

Furthermore, some people I quote in this book don't even support me! For example, Hoffman, another of Downard's mentees is against supporters of Crowley's philosophy of Do what thou wilt shall be the whole of the law, love is the law, love under will. Calling us: "High-minded Thelemic disciples of the enemy of the human race."[15] Hoffman has been described "by the Anti-Defamation League ... as a Holocaust denier and antisemite."[95] To be clear, I think some of Hoffman's theories are extremely insightful and help to provide a better understanding of high strangeness. However, I disagree with anyone that denies the Holocaust or claims that followers of Crowley's Thelemic philosophy are evil. Fans of Crowley can be annoying, but they are definitely not, "disciples of the enemy of the human race."

I like to use as many sources as possible. Notice in this conclusion I have quoted Anton LaVey (founder of the Church of Satan) which will turn off Christians. I quoted an ex-CIA spy, which will turn off JFK researchers. I have quoted from mainstream sources, which will turn off the alternative community. I have quoted from rare Zines,[AN] which will turn off the normal, mainstream community. Returning to the metaphorical lunchroom at Paranormal High School, I have used such a variety of

---

AN "A zine ... short for magazine ... is a small-circulation self-published work of original or appropriated texts and images, usually reproduced via a copy machine. Zines are the product of either a single person or of a very small group, and are popularly photocopied into physical prints for circulation" (wiki/Zine).

sources that I'm bound to have pissed off every table. This approach of using such diverse sources, aims to make a larger point: demonstrate how easily people's inherent biases are activated and that I am solely dedicated to the pursuit of the truth, not a seat at the lunchroom table. I'm on a diet anyway.

I also have a take what you need and leave the rest approach to the study of high strangeness. In studying the phenomenon, if you are looking for someone who believes 100% like you do, then you will find nobody's works to study. If we can't look at the ideas of people who have done bad things, then we would have no knowledge to study.

Are You Crazy?

No.

I ask, are *you* crazy? Not that it is a competition, but I will put my sanity up against anyone's. I would be open to taking a full battery of psychological tests and comparing them side by side with any skeptic. I am fully aware of what my tests would indicate, are you? In the proud tradition Jung and Reich, I am a psychotherapist also into weird stuff. Reich's body of work makes mine look like a Sunday school lesson by comparison. Also, let us not forget that McLuhan was once called crazy too. When Peter Drucker[AO] first met McLuhan, he reported being "warned that I would find a complete madman. Now he is asked to lecture at such places as ... General Electric, which either means the world is growing madder or that for the past 25 years McLuhan has been right."[96] Now that it is 2024, things are moving pretty fast out there in the weird wide world. So, before you renounce me as crazy, wait a month or two, and then decide.

What Is Crazy?

When I was working as a psychotherapist at a highly respected psychiatric and addiction treatment center in the Atlanta area, the hospital's medical director gave us an in-service, which were brief lectures given by staff members. He was an older gentleman, a man of few words, who "had seen it all," (sort of a mix of Kelso and Cox from *Scrubs*). The in-service in question concerned the cross-cultural components of what is considered "crazy." The doctor reported findings he had recently learned from the American Psychiatric Association, which were that: a belief in Voudon in Haiti would not be considered crazy but would be considered

AO Peter Drucker (1909-2005) was a highly influential management consultant, educator, and author. He is regarded as the father of modern management theory.

crazy in the United States. The point of his in-service was to explain that what is considered a crazy belief is contingent upon the dominant belief system of the culture.

I still recall the smile on his face as he gave us this culturally sensitive definition of crazy, while oblivious to the fact this explanation raises more questions than it solves. Meaning, what is deemed as crazy, is in no way based on whether something is objectively true. For example, if the religion of Voudon is proven scientifically to be true and the religion of Christianity is proven false, it doesn't change the definition of crazy. A belief is still defined as crazy, if it goes against the beliefs held by a majority of the culture. Crazy has nothing to do with being correct, per se.

Thomas Szasz (1920-2012) was a distinguished psychiatrist and author of the 1961 book, *The Myth of Mental Illness,* which deconstructed the label of calling someone "crazy" by asserting that mental illness is a social construct rather than an objective medical condition, thus challenging the traditional understanding of psychiatric diagnoses. Szasz says, "If you talk to God, you are praying; if God talks to you, you have schizophrenia. If the dead talk to you, you are a spiritualist; if God talks to you, you are a schizophrenic."[97]

Talking to the dead would not be considered crazy in China, as "ancestor worship has been widely acknowledged as one of the most significant cultural traditions in Chinese society."[98] In countries that practice "ancestor worship ... it is believed that the relationship between the living and the dead is one of inter-dependent synergy" and in this synergy "the dead and the living are believed to communicate and interact."[99] Someone in a country that practices ancestor worship is not considered crazy in communicating with their ancestors, but if they jump on a plane to move to America and start talking to their departed relatives, they now can be labeled crazy. The definition of crazy being culturally dependent presents unique challenges in our hyper connected world. What does it mean for someone that lives in two cultures? What are the implications, if in one culture they are considered crazy, and in the other they are seen as sane?

The idea that what is deemed as "crazy" is culturally dependent, implies that, "numbers sanctify." Meaning, "when more than a few people believe something it is not crazy anymore.... When the majority comes to believe it, it is officially beyond question, and you become 'crazy' only if you then dispute it."[100] Notice, that having the belief in Jesus rising from dead, is not seen as crazy even by atheists because millions of people have this belief. Atheists believe these people to be incorrect, but do not think them crazy, per se. However, they would most probably consider people that believe in Scientology mentally unwell, so maybe the line is also in how long ago these beliefs were codified.

RAW emphasized the sanctifying influence of numbers, and I would argue that time also holds a sanctifying power. Consider the Mormon belief in a magical tablet discovered by their religion's founder, Joseph Smith; which might be viewed as more crazy than the Jewish faith's belief in Moses and his tablets, containing the Ten Commandments. This perception arises from the fact that the belief in Moses has endured for thousands of years longer than that of Joseph Smith. Scientology believes in Xenu, a figure who brought billions of alien souls to Earth and banished them in volcanoes, which forms part of their cosmology regarding the origins of humanity. In a sense, this is no less plausible than any other religion. However, it is seen as most crazy, because it is most the recent and less people believe in it. No disrespect meant to any of these religions, and I should add that I do not believe anyone who believes in these religions to be crazy.

Yes, numbers sanctify but to some, numbers de-sanctify. The fact that the normals will only believe something if a large number of people also believe in it has an opposite. The other side of this coin is seen in the fact that some in the high strangeness community, will not believe in something if a large number of people also believe in it. Meaning, for these people anything that the majority believes in, is de fact wrong. Both sides of this coin represent a logical fallacy.

To me, the notion that something cannot be correct simply because it has gained widespread acceptance echoes the adolescent perspective that dismisses a once-favorite underground band as a sellout once it achieves mainstream success. A more mature outlook would involve celebrating the band's success, recognizing that broader acknowledgment now affirms the truth you knew all along: the band makes amazing music and the broader culture is benefiting by evolving their taste. I pose this question to the high strangeness community – do we aim for a broader acceptance of the truth, or do we prefer our weird perspective to remain in relative obscurity? Is it a search for truth or an identity?

Furthermore, "crazy" is often a derogatory label, and its use constitutes a form of ableism, a discrimination against individuals with particular struggles. Employing this term can be a means of dismissing others and of even self-punishment. Recognizing the later in my work as a psychotherapist, I advise clients against using the derogatory "c-word," when describing their mental health challenges. Labeling one's struggles as "crazy" is not conducive to effectively addressing and overcoming said struggles. I strongly believe "symptoms" are an attempt at solving underlying problems and the cure is often hidden in the illness. And yet I also sympathize with Charles Bukowski's words: "Some people never go crazy. What truly horrible lives they must lead." Not to minimize the awful effects of clinical mental illness, which I know is real, despite quoting Szasz.

The word crazy does not mean anything clinically speaking and it is not used by any serious mental health professionals when referring to the psychological struggles of their clients. However, let us look at what the word crazy is meant to refer to in the clinical setting. The use of "crazy" as a slur, most often corresponds to psychotic disorders, which "are defined by loss of reality testing, specifically by delusions, hallucinations, and disordered thinking." The thinking of someone struggling with a psychotic experience may be "disorganized or illogical" and the person may have "unrealistic beliefs and experiences." People suffering from these disorders will also have impaired executive functioning, manifesting as an "inability to function in daily tasks, and inadequate self-care." A client suffering from a psychotic disorder might insist "that he was having conversations with creatures from outer space and that only he knew their plans for poisoning the planet."[101]

However, for the sake of argument let's continue to use the term crazy. I've been crazy, and I have worked with crazy people. I know what it looks like, professionally, and personally. Having this unique vantage point allows me to be more open to strange material, than people who aren't mental health professionals. This is because I know what "crazy" is and isn't. For example, when I see a skeptic claim that someone's highly strange idea is merely explained by the fact that the person is crazy, I will then go look into the person. When I see the person making the utterly absurd claim is clearly, not crazy, it makes me more open to the weird things they are saying. I have found that the skeptical arguments against high strangeness subjects are often so poor that they have the opposite effect. Merely calling someone crazy is not the gotcha moment that the normals think it is.

In fact, "crazy" is more about the process than the content. If someone is talking about aliens while being aware it seems absurd to most people and they are able to reason out the ways that it may or may not be real, that indicates appropriate processing, while someone justifying cheating on their spouse, and being resistant to reasoning, may be less sane.

I have seen the skeptical critique of Elena Danaan – that she is merely crazy. This slur is casted her way because she claims to be in psychic communication with extraterrestrials.[AP] Danaan is "a field Archaeologist who spent many years working in Egypt and in France … she also studied Pagan spirituality, Magic and Alchemy" and is "trained and ordained as a Druidess." She reports being an "Extraterrestrial contactee since childhood," eventually becoming an "emissary for the Galactic Federation of Worlds." Her books: *A Gift From The Stars, We Will Never Let You Down,* and *The Seeders* have "inspired millions of people."[102] When skeptics call, Elana Danaan crazy, I know that is not true. This is because a person suffering from a mental disorder that would lead to them being called crazy, is not able to function normally, let alone put out podcasts, books, and conduct interviews and workshops. Whether or not someone is crazy or not often comes down to their level of functioning. That is what is meant by impaired executive functioning which I pointed out above. Somebody with impaired executive functioning is not able to have the amount of creative output that Danaan has. So, if she isn't crazy then what is she? It leaves us with two options: she is lying or she is telling the truth.

There is also a lot of confusion about the circumstances that cause someone to be "locked up" in a mental health facility. You can't be locked up for a weird belief per se, for one, insurance won't cover it as a medical necessity and the facility will not want you to come in, because they will not be paid for it by the person's insurance company. Also, facilities run at near capacity, so they aren't looking to lock someone up who is merely claiming to be in psychic communication with extraterrestrials. To be committed to a locked psychiatric facility you need to be functioning so poorly, you can't take care of yourself or be an immediate danger to yourself or others. A locked facility is considered an Inpatient unit. For example, in the state of Georgia, you can only be locked against your will for 72 hours in an inpatient unit. This number varies from state to state. Meaning, even if you are deemed a danger to yourself or others by a psychiatrist and are involuntary committed, you can only be kept against your will for 72 hours – even if you still maintain that you are in psychic communication with aliens.

All the stories of celebrities "escaping" from rehab, are not escapes per se. This is because rehab facilities are not inpatient units, meaning they are not locked facilities. If you need to detox from drugs or alcohol, you

AP I saw a similar critique of New Age channel, Tom Kenyon in the comments section for an episode of *The Higherside Chats, Song of the New Earth, Hathor Sound Codes, and Psychoacoustic Portal Tech*, (Feb. 3, 2024), saying his appearance was akin to the psychotic rants of someone on Meth. I've seen those firsthand in a clinical setting and can assure you they bear no resemblance. I have followed Kenyon's work for over ten years and think he is a great New Age source.

go to an inpatient unit until you have detoxed. Then you transition to a rehab facility after – if you consent to do so. As I used to tell the clients I worked with, there is no escaping from rehab, you can merely walk out the front door. On top of that, I would say: if you decide to leave, please stop by my office on the way out so I can give you a proper goodbye. However, it makes a much better headline to say, "celebrity escapes from rehab" as opposed to "celebrity leaves rehab at night to avoid the awkward goodbye and shame of leaving treatment early."

Not to alarm the reader, but everybody that lives in a modern society has a label in *The Diagnostic and Statistical Manual of Mental Disorders* (DSM). Everybody is in the book so to say. Or more accurately, everybody has a tendency toward a diagnosis in the book, the only question is if your label (or tendency) is working for you or against you. For example, research indicates "surgery was one of the professions with a high proportion of psychopaths." A study into this phenomenon bore the "subtitle: 'Are Surgeons Psychopaths? And, If So, Is That Such a Bad Thing?'" The reason it is not such a bad thing is because, "emotional detachment from the" surgery context, "in which they have to make life-and-death decisions can result in better choices being made."[102.1] Meaning, surgeons with a tendency toward being a psychopath are making it work for them.

On a recent podcast, Andrew Bustamante reports the "CIA recruits heavily for people that have anxiety."[AQ] This revelation blows the mind of the host, causing him to exclaim: "what?" Bustamante responds to this astonishment by asking the host, "what are some of the superpowers of having anxiety?" The host, who claims he struggles with anxiety, replies: "you're paranoid all the time." Bustamante gives a hand gesture, indicating this is exactly correct, because being paranoid is a "huge advantage" for a spy. Bustamante gives his wife as an example, saying that she has been "diagnosed" with "General Anxiety Disorder" and has been "deployed all over the world" as a spy. He reports she is able to make her anxiety work for her "because she learned the skills"[102.12] to manage it. Meaning, spies have a tendency toward paranoia and anxiety but are making it work for them by finding a profession where paranoia and anxiety are a job requirement. I mean, do you really want a trusting spy? That kind of defeats the whole purpose.

The following comes from published research findings conducted by Dr. Drew Pinsky, of *Loveline* and *Celebrity Rehab* fame. This psychological research is the "only research on celebrities" because "no one could get access to enough celebrities to do research"[102.13] on them. Pinsky was able

AQ I may or may not have heard something very similar in the clinical setting.

to get access to them because so many different celebrities were appearing on his radio program, *Loveline*. I was a fan of the show and remember him talking about giving each guest his questionnaire for this study. The results, which were published in an academic journal, "indicate that celebrities are significantly more narcissistic than ... the general population." And "Reality television personalities had the highest overall scores on the" Narcissistic Personality Inventory, "followed by comedians, actors, and musicians."[102.14] This means these individuals are making their narcissistic tendencies work for them, not against them. And remember, clinical labels are defined by the negative traits that led to their creation. These labels, like many others, aim to make sense of complex human behaviors, limited by our concepts. Their validity depends on their effectiveness in facilitating positive change and improving lives.

My tendency aligns most with the label schizotypal, which is "characterized by ... paranoia ... psychosis, and unconventional beliefs." Schizotypal individuals "frequently interpret situations as being strange or having unusual meanings for them." They often have "paranormal and superstitious beliefs"[102.2] and are "described as odd or eccentric."[102.3] Guilty as charged. The only question is if I am using the gift's of this tendency in society's and my favor, or if it is manifesting against me. It has manifested against me in the past, so I know what that looks like, if you give this book a five-star review then it is working for me. Albert "Einstein himself had schizotypal traits," that we can all agree he made work for himself and soceity, even though "he was frequently disheveled in appearance ... dreamy and distracted."[102.4] Again, guilty as charged. I am saying, maybe the sanest way to exist, is to turn your curse into your gift.

Being Wrong Doesn't Equal Crazy

Merely being wrong about something doesn't make you crazy. As RAW famously said: "Of course I'm crazy, but that doesn't mean I'm wrong." And conversely, just because you are sane doesn't mean you are correct. Notice how many things we are wrong about every single day as normal citizens, leading our mundane lives: I will never cheat on my spouse, my father loves me, my script will be sold, I won't be pulled over for driving drunk, my boss is competent and will never fire me. When a normal person, with zero non-conventional beliefs, is wrong about something, we don't say: "see, you were wrong, you are crazy, and everything you believe in is a lie!" People who research high strangeness are held to a higher standard in regards to being wrong. When one aspect of their research is proven wrong, they are unfairly labeled crazy.

Pulling Your Cosmic Trigger

I pulled my own cosmic trigger in writing this book and it is my sincere hope that you pulled your own while reading it. Everyone pulling their own trigger, leading to the collective cosmic trigger being pulled, is part of the overall *my cosmic trigger* hypersigil. The hypersigil is a term popularized by Grant Morrison and he explained it by saying it was a sigil that "extended through the fourth dimension." Also, his "comic book series *The Invisibles*" is an example of one. According to Morrison, the "hypersigil is an immensely powerful ... method for actually altering reality in accordance with intent. Results can be remarkable and shocking."[102.5] It is an evolving magical act that incorporates various forms of artistic expression, such as writing, art, music, or any other medium.

Unlike a traditional sigil, which is a symbol representing a specific intent or desire, a hypersigil is a dynamic magical working. The *My Cosmic Trigger* hypersigil is designed to create an egregore that is threefold, facilitating the following it its users: positive psycho-spiritual growth and healing; fun and abundance; and protection from mundane and transmundane danger.

The Danger

The dangers in this work may be many, for in addition to the inherent dangers of plumbing the very depths of the nature of reality; Frater Achad claimed, "we are dealing with a full-size world-mystery and a real fight between the Black and White Brotherhoods."[85] Some say this fight is occurring on "the greatest battlefield of all, the cosmic war between alien scale and human scale"[AR] or we could say "between the anti-Christ reign of number and the Holy Spirt realm of poetic serendipity."[15]

One Last Portal Before We Go

Coming back from hunting on my family's property this deer season, I discovered there was a purported portal near my NC home. For the record, I do consume the meat and view hunting through a shamanic and

AR Note, Bob Dobbs was advocating for a return to human scale in the 1990s. See: Dobbstown.com.

mystical lens.[AS] While listening to a podcast, I learned that some claim there is a Heavenly Portal in Moravian Falls, NC. Interestingly enough, ten minutes later, I drove past this town, which I had known about all of my life. It is forty-five minutes from my hometown, but I had never heard any of the highly strange legends concerning the area. Supernatural Christian sources[AT] claim it is "the second most angelic portal in the world with the Mount of Olives in Jerusalem being number one."[103]

Turning to New Age sources to learn more about the first "most angelic portal," we find that the "portal in the Middle East has been one of the main openings onto the planet."[104] One thing I look for in my highly strange research is when a variety of sources intersect; with the Moravian Falls portal, I notice similarities in New Age sources, occult sources, and Christian sources.

The Christian author, Anna Rountree,[AU] had a vision and encountered angels in this area thirty years ago, but claims the messages she received from them at that time are for 2024 specifically. In this regards she says that she is "hoping" God "will honor this 30-year anniversary" of when she first had the Heavenly visons. Rountree says she is "ready for a major leap forward" and that "even if the world is crumbling around us, if we are moving forward with our Lord, I don't know how much we will notice it."[105] Again, notice the resonance between this idea and one from a New Age channeled entity, Ion: "the sky may be falling but it doesn't have to fall on you."[AV]

The highly strange messages of the angels, Rountree reports receiving from the Moravian Falls portal thirty years ago, remind me of the messages John Dee received from the Enochian angels in the 1600s. By strange, I mean they are intricate and not vague messages of universal peace. For example, she was "shown a section of the protective wall the angels are building that eventually will encircle visitors and angels alike. It will protect the needed land as well as the Moravian Falls House of Prayer." She reports the Heavenly hierarchy informed her the "fortress" was "to be built here in order to protect this chosen area from the enemy," so that the faithful can "receive the fullness of the blessing," intended by the Ancient

AS See, *Hunting in the Human Way: The Shaman and Hunting Magic*, (Jan 2013, thewayofthings.org/philosophy/hunting-human-way-shaman-and-hunting-magic) Also see, *Heartsblood: Hunting, Spirituality, and Wildness in America*, by David Petersen.

AT See, *Christian Faith and the Supernatural* (Oswald T. Allis, christianitytoday.com, Nov. 6, 1964).

AU *Heaven Awaits the Bride: A Breathtaking Glimpse of Eternity; The Heavens Opened: Revealing a Fresh Vision of God's Love for You; The Priestly Bride; The Warrior King: A Battle With the World, the Flesh, and the Devil.*

AV IonandBob.com

of Days.[AW] Their glance will "bounce off its surface and cause ... the enemy ... to divert their gaze." This energy of the wall will cause "followers of the fallen cherub" to "look elsewhere."[106] Rountree reports an angel informed her that this fortress will "house a FIELD HOSPITAL and be a STRONGHOLD" and will therefore be "an ISLAND OF PEACE where the pilgrims rest." Here, "there will be healing for the wounded, protection in the times of trouble, and rest for the weary."[107]

I am not sure how a heavenly field hospital in a battle against the fallen cherub will affect property values. However, the New Age literature also speaks of similar geographic locations, calling them "Islands of Light." These are described as "communities of our coming New Age and where group ascension process can take place. They are one of our keys to breaking free from the Matrix program and duality."[108]

An Apocalypse of Hope, Not an Armageddon of Destruction

The word Apocalypse comes from a Greek word that means the revelation of a secret or lifting of the veil. Through a mainstream Christian lens we can say that "we are living in apocalyptic, revelatory times."[109] From a New Age lens we can say that "the veil between dimensions, *is* thinning rapidly, and the spiritual program has entered an entirely new octave."[110] Said more intellectually: just as "a Heidegger and a Derrida can enact the end of philosophy, just as Joyce" has "enacted the end of literature," in our current times we are now "confronted with the end of history upon our real and actual horizons." In addition, "this new situation is integrally related to a universal apocalyptic condition in our world."[111] My magick of High Strangeness is about the new mythology, the new rituals, the new research – we need to embrace in these times – which is at the end of history and the beginning of a new golden age. The praxis of this approach to magick embraces "an apocalypticism which also knows a new creation ... that can only be the consequence of the final ending of an old totality."[111]

As McLuhan said, "I have never been an optimist or a pessimist. I'm an apocalyptic only." And because, "Apocalypse is not gloom,"[112] the magick of high strangeness is one of pure cosmic hope. McLuhan's "sense that writing and teaching were about elevations of the soul never left him," shown in the fact that when "asked what his spiritual hope might be" he said: "our only hope is apocalypse," and "by this he surely meant reve-

AW "The Ancient of Days" is a symbolic title often used to represent the timeless and eternal nature of God in religious and mystical traditions.

lation and trust: new worlds will come."[113] Despite all of the dark subjects encountered in this research, I remain anchored in the trust that new worlds will manifest. This cosmic trust helps one stay hopeful, which enables you to stay on the most positive timeline – where doom is averted and instead a new golden age rises in its place.

Never forget, "hope can be a radical act" because "hope is political," so "don't lose your hope."[114] I argue that the goal of wetiko (the archetype of evil) is to remove hope by "the inculcation of apathy, amnesia and abulia in the target population."[15] We must shake the mind viruses of apathy and abulia, embracing hope; because "the flame must be revived at all costs. At all cost we must renew in ourselves the desire and the hope for the great Coming." It is because of the mind virus of amnesia that "we are constantly forgetting that the supernatural is a ferment, a soul, and not a completed and finished organism. Its role is to transform 'nature.'"[115] When we embrace the supernatural, we transform ourselves and nature.

Not an Armageddon of Destruction, an Apocalypse of Hope

As the events of 2024 unfold, we also see the mundane[AX] benefit of high strangeness. Meaning that since we are also living in the times of Armageddon, we see all the more clearly that this utterly absurd world view helps us understand the happenings of the now. As I have previously stated in this text, Apocalypse is a good thing and Armageddon is bad, being that it refers to a nuclear war between nation states of the Abrahamic religions. Some have said what is going on right now in the Middle East is "a holy war, not a geopolitical conflict." Understanding this particular character of the conflict "is necessary to understand it" because "it cannot be solved through military means."[116]

This holy war aspect of geopolitics has been explored in high strangeness literature since the early 1990s. An essay in Adam Parfrey's renowned counter cultural text, *Apocalypse Culture,* pointed out that "Christian fundamentalists ... are convinced that the Last Days prior to ... the final earth-shattering war that will precede the Second Coming of Christ – are here now." Fundamentalists, "impatient for heaven ... would speed up the process whereby their Savior will return for them in Glory. To this end, they are exerting ... their considerable influence in" Middle East politics, "in order that they bring about the conditions favorable to biblical fulfillment of Armageddon."[117] Strangely enough, a lot of this is centered

AX Mundane meaning, of the earthly world rather than the spiritual world. The retreat to the astral is on a trans-mundane plane, the spiritual world.

around searching for, what a 1998 article in *The New Yorker* called, "the apocalyptic red cow."[118] In 2024, "the red heifers from Texas will finally be of a ripe age to sacrifice." There are reports that red Texas cows are being sent to the region to fulfill Biblical prophecy. *The Middle East Monitor* even stated, "the red cow will blow up this region."[116] Only High strangeness provides us with a lens weird enough to understand a complex geopolitical situation involving Biblical prophecy, nuclear Armageddon, red cows, and Texas.

The following is where traditional Christians would differ from the view of mystical Christians who are inspired by New Age channeled messages, such as: Armageddon is "the Biblical name for the happenings that are being caused by the very same dark powers that influenced the development of the" concept of Armageddon in the first place. However, we are reminded to remember that it "is ONLY a *concept*" and as such, it is "composed of thought forms." The "strategies that would lead the concept's fruition ... is being" facilitated "by soul's that have come under the influence of" the same "dark forces" that originated the concept in the first place.

The strategy of these dark forces was to "condition 'believers' so they would invest "energy in ... negative thoughts and ... fear about 'the end times.'" This process draws to our "planet the doomsday 'prophecies' in Revelations." Put simply, the "dark forces" are "intent" on Armageddon happening "on Earth, which in their view would be total capitulation of light forces on the planet." However, we can cancel our subscription to Armageddon, because it "*does not have to happen*!" These "negative thought forms designed to lead to Armageddon can and will be transmuted into light to reverse the parade toward the planetary conquest the dark powers intend."[119]

Other New Age sources have also suggested that dire end time predictions are not inevitable. These sources claim that, "prophets such as Edgar Cayce, who predicted ... types of events we conceptualize as ... crashing the Earth's program," which would end life as we know it on this planet, do not have to occur. They don't have to occur, because "there is a higher order and this means that there is a higher possibility of altering this program of dramatic and massive shifts." Averting this doomsday program is achieved "through intervention by planetary healers like yourselves." In many instances, "planetary healers[AY] have been effective in preventing

AY A planetary healer "looks for the mechanisms and the feedback intervention that will allow the planet to evolve and integrate at a higher level" (Endnote 120). McKenna had a similar sentiment, suggesting that when we operate from the gnosis that everything is unfolding perfectly, then the mere act of witnessing positive elements, facilitates more and more manifestation of the positive, which then fosters the continued unfolding of favorable outcomes. (*Having Archaic and Eating it Too*: Workshop, Terence McKenna, 1990).

a total breakdown from happening on Earth," evidenced by the fact that "total disruption of all civilization has not occurred."[120]

We are now faced with "a question of life and death in the near future," concerning "whether we will give nuclear energy to serve our destructive image of the ... mother who symbolizes death or into the hands of a loving image" of the mother archetype that "could open a new version of utopia. Since both images are locked in our mind by a powerful unconscious, the outcome is in doubt."[121] I propose we expel the destructive image of the mother from the unconscious, while bringing to our conscious awareness – the "loving image" of the mother archetype – which can "open a new version of utopia."

Visionary entrepreneur and podcast host, Aubrey Marcus,[AZ] considers how we might expel this destructive image from the unconscious, by pointing out that "maybe we've co-created these upcoming existential crises." He claims he knows people who are "deeply into [the] prepper community" that believe civilization will collapse. And while, he is "participating to some degree in" that community, evidenced by the fact he is preparing himself; what he is "not participating in, is this sense of hope and glee about the upcoming potential disaster." Marcus says with some preppers, "you can really tell that they hope that it happens;" but for him "there is zero part of me that is looking forward to it" and would be "super happy to throw" out his food supplies.

Marcus speculates on why people seemingly desire the occurrence of TEOTWAWKI,[BA] suggesting that it may be linked to an unconscious need to feel a stronger sense of togetherness, which extreme challenges seem to foster. He believes that the desire for a collective experience of unity, similar to the way all New Yorkers came together after the 9/11 attacks, is an innate longing that humans have. Disasters have a tendency to open one's "heart to being in this tribal sense of we're all in this together." He points out this global catastrophe "may happen because we need it to happen and we're co-creating" a terrible "disaster so that we do come together but ideally it comes from the elevation of consciousness and recognition of our inherent state of interbeing."[121.0]

We need to rise above the unconscious or conscious wish for everything to collapse, whether it stems from the hope that people unite in the face of catastrophe or the desire to prove that you were correct to save all of that canned food. The total collapse of civilization would be a serious buzzkill. I caution readers who may have been seduced by the fantasy of a

AZ See, AubreyMarcus.com/pages/about

BA Acronym of *the end of the world as we know it.*

post collapse life, to think twice, before they continue to charge this negative thought form further. I myself used to be seduced by such a fantasy, so I am speaking from experience.

Surfing The Cosmic Wave

My humble book has reached its conclusion; but I ecstatically point out that: "the time of ends is upon us in one sense;" however "in another"[BB] sense, "it is the time of beginnings."[121.1] For this ending, I have adapted a Turkish saying:[BC] we ride the signs of the Apocalypse into the future. This means we surf the synchromystic signs of high strangeness into the Apocalypse to avoid Armageddon. This is what high strangeness research and magick is all about. We must ride the weird waves of reality into the Apocalypse, thereby lifting of the veil and facilitating revelatory knowledge, avoiding Armageddon: the global nuclear war between the nation states of the Abrahamic religions.

There are a lot of tasty waves to surf these days and it is because of this fact that the main message of this book is one of hope. So, come join me, where I'm floating – *off in the deep end* – the water's fine, and the surf is up. As we continue to surf into the golden age, learning the "secret language of the ancients," surely our friends shall say: "Look! he pretends to read this book. But it is unintelligible – it is nonsense."[122]

Pay no attention and paddle out to the next wave, secure in your knowledge that the "the importance of nonsense can hardly be overstated," because "the more clearly we experience something as 'nonsense', the more clearly we are experiencing the boundaries of our own self-imposed cognitive structures." Our kook[BD] friends and family, only see high strangeness as "nonsense," because it "does not fit into pre-arranged patterns" they "have superimposed on reality." If the waves don't crash on them first, they will learn that: "nonsense is nonsense only when we have not yet formed the point of view from which it makes sense."[122.0]

The kooks are struggling against the utterly absurd fact that "reality is becoming ... fungible" and as a result, "we are going to have a much different epistemology in a few years from now." This is "because" of the fact that, "causality as we understand it is just basically receding like the tide."

BB The author of this quote says, "I am AIWAZ ... who was revealed earlier and have now returned. From me came the LIBER AL, not from Crowley's subconscious fictionalizing" (Endnote, 121.1).

BC More roughly translated as, "We got on a sign, we are going to the apocalypse," the song Bindik Bir Alamete Gideyoz Kıyamete by Cem Karaca is about this saying.

BD See, "How to spot a kook in surfing" (surfertoday.com/surfing/how-to-spot-a-kook-in-surfing) and "The origin of the word 'kook'" (surfertoday.com/surfing/the-origin-of-the-word-kook).

As the causality tide recedes, the weird waters are rising, which means that the dabblers who are just, "knee deep in these waters," are "going to get wet." Sorry dabblers, this is "just the way things operate" in high strangeness. As Nietzsche said, "if you gaze long enough into an abyss, the abyss will gaze back into you." This means that if you only "poke around the outskirts of" the phenomenon, then "don't be surprised when you get pulled in the drama," sucked out to sea in a cosmic riptide.

Look y'all: there is no way to deny it now, "reality is changing, causality is becoming unmoored," so you are going to have to "learn to deal with it, because that is the real new normal."[86] You are no safer standing knee deep in the weird water because you can get sucked out to sea; and the kooks at the shore are in danger of the weird-wave crashing on their head.[BE] Your only hope is to grab a cosmic surfboard and paddle out to us weirdos. However, whether the kooks learn to surf or the high strangeness dabblers dive in fully, *don't make me no never mind* (as we say from my neck of the woods), because I choose the promise of the positive, that if we keep riding the waves of the millennial ecstatic's of the now: "we shall bring you to Absolute Truth, Absolute Light, Absolute Bliss."[122]

Pull Your Own Cosmic Trigger

Alan Moore, the author of the famous graphic novel, *V for Vendetta*, "said in 2014 in a promotion for the 'Cosmic Trigger' play,"[BF] that it is now "time to take the safety off and pull the Cosmic Trigger.'"[122.01] This means that the best time to pull your own cosmic trigger was yesterday and the next best time is to pull it NOW.

The godfather of high weirdness,[BG] Erik Davis, speaks of a "global weirding" and suggests that "grappling with weirdness may help us learn to work with disturbing ... transformations that overwhelm our ability to" even "comprehend" them. However, "getting to know" high strangeness at a deeper level: "provides a strange power ... not unlike the ability to be OK in the presence of corpses."[122.02] In our case, hopefully, these are only the metaphorical corpses of old systems and ways of being. In any

---

BE As the Merry Pranksters said in the 60s, "You're either on the bus or off the bus" (*The Metaphor of Being on the Bus*, wild-bohemian.com/onthebus.htm).

BF "RAW was excited when Ken Campbell did a stage play in Liverpool of 'Illuminatus!' in 1986. In 2014 Ken's daughter, Daisy Eris Campbell did a stage play of 'Cosmic Trigger,'" and "Moore supported the new play and provided the voice for an off stage character" (endnote: 122.01). Also see, *Time To Pull The Cosmic Trigger*, Liverpool, Feb. 23, 2014, Youtube: Complexity Ltd; *Cosmic Trigger: Ken Campbell's daughter captures Illuminatus! spirit in trippy epic*, TheGuardian.com, 2017; and CosmicTriggerPlay.com.

BG See, Erik Davis,' *High Weirdness: Drugs, Esoterica, and Visionary Experience in the Seventies*, 2019.

case, to access this strange power, which fuels our cosmic ray guns, we must have courage. This is because, "the only courage that is demanded of us" is "to have courage for the most strange … and the most inexplicable that we may encounter."[122.03] Developing our courage to encounter the strange can't be overstated because from here on out: everything is going to "get so much weirder so so much faster,"[122.04] and the cosmic clock now reads – "it is the eleventh hour."[BH,122.1]

Meaning, it is: "Apocalypse O'Clock" and the "epic extreme weirdness clock of aliens, AI, and nuclear tension is tick tick ticking." However, there are things we can do to "ensure this Apocalypse is a Revelation of Beauty instead of a Revelation of horror,"[122.04] which is nuclear Armageddon, or worse. We achieve this via[BI] pulling our individual cosmic triggers. Keep in mind that as we "approach the ascension" there is a "current … poised to play a major role in" the frequency "upshift of … humanity," that is also "part of the crystalline portion of the cosmic trigger."[123] This means that the high strangeness idea of pulling your cosmic trigger is intrinsically tied to the New Age ascension process.

In 2024, "the Atomic Age threat of global" Armageddon "is back, thanks to escalating nuclear tensions" and as a result "the figure of the rocket dangles precariously overhead, just as it does in the closing pages of" Thomas Pynchon's *Gravity's Rainbow*; and "as the Doomsday Clock ticks closer to midnight. By the time we hear the boom, it will be too late,"[124] but not if we pull the collective cosmic trigger and counter-blast the Atomic boom with the cosmic boom from our life saving guns. This is because "the Friction of a Cosmic" Trigger, "produces not suffering … but the Bliss of Eternity in Time and throughout Space."[125]

Sources

1. Terence McKenna, *Terence McKenna's Final Interview,* 1998, Youtube: Wisdom for Life. Full interview on *Sunflower Club with James McCrae.*

2. Aliza Kelly, *Pluto in Aquarius Is Bringing More Unprecedented Times,* TheCut.com, Jan. 18, 2024.

3. Carylon Lovewell, *How to take a stand in a crazy Pluto-in-Aquarius world?,* Mass e-mail list, Jan. 23, 2024.

BH The full passage reads, "Thou art not glad thou meddled with magick? There is no other way, dear fool, it is the eleventh hour." (*The Collected Writings of Jack Parsons, The Book of Babalon,* 1946, verse 61-62, sacred-texts.com/ oto/lib49.htm).

BI Carolyn Lovewell (carolynlovewell.com), says it is achieved through, "the life-saving magick of [Existential Kink]," which is "the crystallization of Wholeness as Battle Magick." (*Sleep Over with Carolyn and Laila,* Feb. 15, 2024, Listennotes.com/podcasts/sleep-over-with/existential-kink-and-battle-Mr7gm53NoeA/).

4. Paul Levy, Personal communication, Winter, 2023 and *"Invasion of the Body Snatchers" Comes to Life,* AwakenInTheDream.com.

5. *Symbolic Order,* cla.purdue.edu/ academic/english/theory/ psychoanalysis/ definitions/ symbolicorder.html

5.1. Clif High, *It's ALIVE! Explorers' Guide To Scifi World,* Feb. 19, 2024, Youtube: Clif_High, time: 59:00.

6. Jack Osbourne and Jamie Kennedy, *Exploring Satan's Grip on Tinseltown,* Youtube: Jack Osbourne, Nov. 2023, time: 11:00-12:12.

7. The UFO Rabbit Hole Podcast With Kelly Chase, *The Disclosure Field Guide [Pt 1]: Ontological Shock & Getting Reoriented,* June 16, 2023, time: 6:00-8:15.

8. *A Weekend with Terence McKenna,* Aug. 1993, organism.earth/library/ document/ a-weekend-with-terence-mckenna

9. George P. Hansen, The Higherside Chats, *The Trickster, The UFO, and the Taboo,* September 30, 2023, time: 50:17.

10. Jeremy Corbell, Duncan Trussell Family Hour, *episode 566,* May 2023, time: 1:22- 1:29.

11. Kenneth Grant, *Outer Gateways,* 1994, p. 40.

12. Steve Mizrach, *UFOs Reconsidered as a Fortean Phenomenon,* Crash Collusion, Austin Texas.

13. Adela Suliman and Paul Goldman, *Former Israeli space security chief says extraterrestrials exist, and Trump knows,* NBCNews.com, Dec. 8, 2020.

14. Timothy Green Beckley, *Psychic and UFO Revelations in the Last Days,* 1989, p. 76.

15. Michael Hoffman, *Twilight Language,* 2021, p. 159, 64, 37, 254, 165.

16. James Shelby Downard, *Stalking The Great Whore: The Lost Writings of James Shelby Downard,* 2023, p. 34, 260.

17. John E. Mack, M.D., *Abduction: Human Encounters with Aliens,* 1994, E-book: p. 634-635.

18. *U.F.Os, Censorship, Chat GPT, And Consciousness w/ Greg Carlwood,* Youtube: Lighting the Void, Aug. 6, 2023, time: 24:00, 28:00.

19. *Subvert From Within or Without – The Quick, Easy Way!,* SubGenuis.com/ pams/pam2p4.html

20. Anton Szandor LaVey, *The Invisible War,* in *Apocalypse Culture,* expanded and revised edition, edited by Adam Parfrey, 1987, p. 193, 195.

21. wikiquote.org/wiki/Eerie,_Indiana

22. Paul Levy, Personal communication, Winter 2023.

23. Marshall McLuhan, *The Medium is the Massage,* 1967.

24. Barbara Marciniak, *Mysteries of the Field, Part 4,* Pleiadians.com, Dec. 23, 2023, time: 55:00.

24.1. Whitney Webb, *PBD Podcast, Ep. 270,* Youtube: PBD Podcast, May 17, 2023, time: 2:02.

25. Leland Val Van de Wall, goodreads.com/quotes/ 4109265 -the-degree-to-which-a- person-can-grow-is-directly

26. Paul Levy, *Developing Jung's "Imagination for Evil" is the Doorway to Our Light,* awakeninthedream.com/articles/carl-jung-imagination-evil

26.1. Carl Jung, *The Philosophical Tree,* Collected Works 13: Alchemical Studies, Paragraph 335.

27. Rebecca Davis, *The Doctor Who Championed Hand-Washing And Briefly Saved Lives,* NPR.org, Jan. 2015.

27.1. Matthew, *Aspects of ascension and densities; awakening process; advancing in awareness; light vs dark battle,* February 2, 2024, MatthewBooks.com/february-2-2024/.

27.2. James Shelby Downard and Michael A. Hoffman II, *King Kill 33,* Rare Editions from Research Intelligence.

28. John Keel, *Operation Trojan Horse,* 1970, p. 283-4, … , 288.

29. Arnold Mindell, *The Shaman's Body: A New Shamanism for Transforming Health, Relationships, and the Community,* 1993, p. 153.

29.1. Whitley Strieber, *Really?!, with Tom and Dave,* episode 32, Feb. 15, 2024, Time: 21:37.

30. Joseph Campbell, *The Hero's Journey: Joseph Campbell on His Life and Work,* 2014, Audio book: Chapter 3, time: 11:00-15:05.

31. *How to Shift Timelines With Lucy Byrd Hope,* EarthAndWater.co/how-to-shift-timelines- with-lucy-byrd-hope/

32. Michael Hoffman, *Twilight Language,* 2021, p. 100.

33. Carylon Elliot, *my embarrassing naïveté and what became of it,* Jan. 26, 2024, mass email list.

34. *The Politics of "Reality,"* in Crimes of Perception, Individualism and Consensus Reality, mongoosedistrocom.files.wordpress.com/2022/11/crimes-of-perception-individualism-and-consensus-reality.pdf

35. John E. Mack, M.D., Foreword to: *Paths Beyond Ego: The Transpersonal Vision (New Consciousness Reader),* edited by Roger Walsh, Frances Vaughan, 1993, p. xi.

36. *They Wouldn't Believe the Wrights had Flown,* wright-brothers.org.

36.1. *Cognitive Dissonance,* wiki/Cognitive_dissonance

36.2. Nishant Mishra, *Anaïs Nin's Profound Quotes on Dreams, Love, Life, and Death,* medium.com/@thenishan, Aug 24, 2018.

37. Andrew Bustamante, *CIA Spy On WW3, Jeffrey Epstein, Israel-Hamas, AI & Social Media Brainwashing,* Jan. 2024, Youtube: Tom Bilyeu, time: 18:24, 24:00.

38. *A Belief is Just a Thought You Keep Thinking,* LawOfAttractionResourceGuide.com/ a-belief-is-just-a-thought-you-keep-thinking/

39. Erik Davis, *Philip K. Dick's Divine Interference,* April 15, 2005, TechGnosis.com/ philip-k-dicks-divine-interference/

39.1. Robert Anton Wilson, *Cosmic Trigger II: Down to Earth,* 1991, E-book: p. 93.

40. Robert Anton Wilson, *Cosmic Trigger I: The Final Secret of the Illuminati,* 1977, New Falcon 1999 edition, p. 62 & 61, 238, 168.

41. The Wisdom of Old Bob, PonderingWithKev.medium.com/ the-wisdom-of-old-bob-2645f655da7b

42. James C. Morrison Jr., *Marshall McLuhan: No Prophet without Honor,* Massachusetts Institute of Technology, mit.edu/~saleem/ivory/ch2.htm

42.1. Marshall McLuhan, *letter to Sheila Watson,* Aug. 31, 1964, from the personal archives of Bob Dobbs, posted on his Facebook page, Feb. 17, 2024.

43. Andrew McLuhan, *Our Cause is Effect: Practical McLuhan,* medium.com/@andrewmcluhan, Apr 26, 2021.

44. *Call me anything, so long as you don't call me late to dinner,* WordHistories.net/ 2020/07/22/dont-call-late-dinner/

45. Clinton's Grand Jury Testimony, Part 4, WashingtonPost.com/ wp-srv/politics/ special/clinton/stories/bctest092198_4.htm

46. Robert Anton Wilson, *Quantum Psychology,* rawilson.com/quantum-psychology/

47. Stuart Heritage, *Ancient Apocalypse is the most dangerous show on Netflix, The Guardian,* Nov. 2022.

48. Ari Shapiro, *Nixon's Manhunt For The High Priest Of LSD In 'The Most Dangerous Man In America',* Heard on All Things Considered, NPR.org, Jan. 2018.

49. Paul Levy, *Undreaming Wetiko: Breaking the spell of the Nightmare Mind Virus,* May 2023, E-book: p. 52.

49.1. Quassim Cassam, *Conspiracy Theories,* 2023, academia.edu/96463496/Conspiracy_Theories, creativecommons.org/licenses/by/4.0/.

50. Mae Brussell, wiki/Mae_Brussell

51. Paul Krassner, Soft Skull Press, SoftSkull.com/bookauthor/paul-krassner/

52. Danny Goldberg, *Goodbye to Free-Thought Icon and Merry Prankster Paul Krassner,* The Nation, July 2019.

53. Rock and Roles podcast with Danny Goldberg, *Ep. 2 – Paul Krassner and the Hippie Idea,* BeHereNowNetwork.com/danny-goldberg-ep-2-hippie-idea/

54. Merry Pranksters, wiki/Merry_Pranksters

55. Ken Kesey & The Merry Pranksters - Exhibitions, *The Psychedelic 60s,* University of Virginia Library, Explore.lib.Virginia.edu.

56. Chicago Seven, Britannica.com/event/Chicago-Seven-law-case

57. Paul Krassner, *Anarchist, Prankster and a Yippies founder dies at 87, New York Times,* July 2019.

58. Joan D'Arc, Al Hidell (editors), *From the Deaths of JFK and John Lennon to Government-Sponsored Alien Cover-Ups (1001 Pearls),* August 1, 2012, p. 36.

59. Paul Krassner, Introduction to, *The Essential Mae Brussell: Investigations of Fascism in America,* 2014.

60. Timothy Green Beckley, *The Matrix Control System of Philip K. Dick And The Paranormal Synchronicities of Timothy Green Beckley,* 2017, 52% of Amazon sample.

61. Nick Bryant, My Family Thinks I'm Crazy, episode 374: *Jeffery Epstein, The Franklin Scandal and Justice For Victims of Epstein,* Feb. 2024, time: 58:41- 1:00.

62. John Keel, *UFOs, Mothman, and Me: twenty years on the flying saucer beat,* Hightimes, May 1980.

63. John Keel, *Our Haunted Planet,* 1971, p. 98.

64. Alexander Zaitchik, *Close Encounters of the Racist Kind,* Southern Poverty Law Center, splcenter.org, January 02, 2018.

65. Steff Danielle Thomas, *Bipartisan lawmakers unveil legislation to close gap in UAP reporting,* TheHill.com, Jan. 11, 2024.

66. Stefan Becket, *Lawmakers investigating UAPs, or UFOs, remain frustrated after closed-door briefing with government watchdog,* CBSNews.com, Jan. 12, 2024.

67. Raphael, *The Starseed Transmissions: An Extraterrestrial Report,* 1982, p. 97.

68- Society for American Archaeology, *Letter to Netflix Concerning "Ancient Apocalypse" Series,* SAA.org, Nov. 30, 2022.

69. Graham Hancock, *Response to the open letter to Netflix dated 30th November 2022 from the Society for American Archaeology (SAA) concerning the eight-part docuseries Ancient Apocalypse,* GrahamHancock.com, Jan. 2023.

70. Kurly Tlapoyawa, *Hijacking History: the problem with the "Black Olmec" myth,* July 2020, Medium.com.

71. Jason Colavito, *The Strange and Dangerous Right-Wing Freakout Over Ancient Apocalypse,* NewRepublic.com, December 5, 2022.

72. Susan B. Martinez, *The Lost History of the Little People: Their Spiritually Advanced Civilizations around the World,* 2013, Excerpt at SimonAndSchuster.com.

73. Dave Adalian, *"Hobbits" among us? An anthropologist says maybe,* EarthSky.org, May 2022.

74. James A. Swan, *Sacred Places: How The Living Earth Seeks Our Friendship,* 2000, p. 209.

75. Brad Steiger, *Star Gods: Clone Masters of the Universe,* 1997, p. 65-66, 68.

76. Billy Carson, SRS #93: *Forbidden Knowledge,* Youtube: Shawn Ryan Show, Jan. 2024, time: 2:12:22.

77. Commander X, *Underground Alien Bases: Flying Saucers Come From Inside The Earth!,* 2012, p. 81.

78. Chinese Persecution of the Uyghurs, United States Holocaust Memorial Museum, ushmm.org.

79. Lalit K Jha, *Hindu-Maya Cultural Dialogue Takes Place in Guatemala City,* HindustanTimes.com, May 27, 2005.

80. 13th, wiki/13th_(film)

81. Nkechi Taifa, *Race, Mass Incarceration, and the Disastrous War on Drugs,* Brennan Center for Justice, Brennancenter.org, May 10, 2021.

82. November Coalition, wiki/November_Coalition

83. Anthony White, *The Fight to Find the Right Prescription for Treatment,* Marietta Daily Journal, Nov. 29, 2016.

84. Ron Bousso, *Big Oil doubles profits in blockbuster 2022,* Reuters, Feb. 8, 2023.

85. Allen Greenfield, *Secret Cipher of the UFOnauts,* 1994, p. 62, 57.

86. Chris Knowles, A Ritual Tour of 2020, Ghislaine Maxwell's Arrest, and the New Cult of State, *The Higherside Chats,* Aug. 18, 2020, time: 2:14-2:15.

87. Allen Greenfield's Fantastic page, facebook.com, Dec. 13, 2023.

88. William Blake 1757–1827, OxfordReference.com.

89. Mayukh Sen, *Gandhi Was a Racist Who Forced Young Girls to Sleep in Bed with Him,* Vice.com, Dec. 2015.

90. Adam Gorightly, *The Prankster and the Conspiracy: The Story of Kerry Thornley and How He Met Oswald and Inspired the Counterculture,* 2003, p. 93, 181.

91. Greg Newkirk, Twitter: @nuekerk, Jan. 1, 2021, twitter.com/nuekerk/status/1344882730232905729?lang=en

92. Twitter: @DailyGrail, Jan. 1, 2021, twitter.com/DailyGrail/status/1344862491810037762

93. Hayley Stevens, *The Fortean Pursuit of Truth and Neo Nazis,* Jan. 1, 2021, hayleyisaghost .co.uk/fortean-curiosity-nazis/

94. Richard Spence, Afterword to, *Stalking The Great Whore: The Lost Writings of James Shelby Downard,* 2023, p. 453.

95. Michael A. Hoffman, wikipedia.org/wiki/Michael_A._Hoffman_II

96. Peter Drucker, Twitter: @McLinstitute, Aug. 16, 2023, twitter.com/ McLinstitute/ status/1691799819432480949

97. Thomas Szasz, *The Second Sin,* Schizophrenia, 1973.

98. Anning Hu, *Ancestor Worship in Contemporary China: An Empirical Investigation,* China Review, Spring 2016, jstor.org/stable/43709965.

99. Choon Sup Bae; P J van der Merwe, *Ancestor worship – is it Biblical?,* University of Pretoria, HTS Teologiese Studies/Theological Studies, Jul./Sep. 2008.

100. Robert Anton Wilson, *Afterwards,* in D. Scott Apel's *Philip K. Dick: The Dream Connection,* 2015.

101. *Psychodynamic Diagnostic Manual,* 2006, p. 266.

102. Elena Danaan, elenadanaan.org/about

102.1. Joanna Bourke, *Some surgeons may be psychopaths – but that's no bad thing,* ProspectMagazine.co.uk, June 21, 2017.

102.12. Andrew Bustamante, *CIA Spy on Mind Games, World War 3, China, Russia and the New World Super Power,* Youtube: Tom Bilyeu, April, 2023, time: 1:35-1:36.

102.13. *Dr. Drew Did The First Research On Celebrity Narcissism,* Youtube: Dad Saves America, March 2023.

102.14. S. Mark Young, Drew Pinsky, *Narcissism and celebrity,* Journal of Research in Personality, Oct. 2006.

102.2. Schizotypal personality disorder, wiki/Schizotypal_personality_disorder

102.3. Schizotypal personality disorder, MayoClinic.org.

102.4. Nancy C. Andreasen M.D., Ph.D., *Einstein: His Life and Universe,* American Journal of Psychiatry, ajp.psychiatryonline.org, Dec. 2008.

102.5. Grant Morrison, *Pop Magic!* in *Book of Lies: The Disinformation Guide to Magick and the Occult,* Richard Metzger (Editor) 2003, p. 21.

103. Robert T. Bailey, PharmD, MD, *Spiritual History of Prayer Mountain in Moravian Falls, NC,* ProphetsReward.org/spiritual-history-of-prayer-mountain/

104. Barbara Marciniak, *Earth: Pleiadian Keys to the Living Library,* 1994, p. 190.

105. Anna Rountree, *Moving Forward in 2024*, annarountree.com/moving-forward-in-2024, January 1, 2024.

106. Anna Rountree, *The Lord's Anointing*, annarountree.com/june-2023-the-lords-anointing, May 31, 2023.

107. Anna Rountree, July 29, 2006 – *An Island Of Peace*, June 30, 2023, annarountree.com/ july-29-2006-an-island-of-peace.

108. *Meditation for Islands of Light Manifestation*, 2019, WeLoveMassMeditation.com/ 2019/06/meditation-for-islands-of-light.html

109. Wallace B. Henley, *We are living in apocalyptic, revelatory times*, ChristianPost.com, April 21, 2023.

110. Timothy Green Beckley, *Psychic and UFO Revelations in the Last Days*, p. 77.

111. Thomas J.J. Altizer, *Genesis and Apocalypse: A Theological Voyage Toward Authentic Christianity*, 1991, p.13, p 21-23.

112. Nick Ripatrazone, *The material and spiritual vision of Marshall McLuhan*, catholicherald.co.uk, March 1, 2022.

113. B. W. Powe, *When Marshall McLuhan met Northrop Frye: An Excerpt from B.W. Powe's Marshall McLuhan & Northrop Frye: Apocalypse & Alchemy*, Nov. 2014, mcluhangalaxy.wordpress.com/2014/11/05/when-marshall-mcluhan-met-northrop-frye-an-excerpt-from-b-w-powes-marshall-mcluhan-northrop-frye-apocalypse-alchemy/

114. Ted Hope, *Streaming's False Hopes, Is it too late to try again?*, tedhope.substack.com, Aug. 16, 2023.

115. Pierre Teilhard de Chardin, *The Divine Milieu*, 1957, p. 152.

116. Zachary Emmanuel, *A red heifer is the secret to understanding the War, Countere Magazine*, countere.com, Oct. 20, 2023.

117. Gregory Krupey, *The Christian Right and the Coming of the Penteholocaust*, in *Apocalypse Culture* (revised and expanded edition), Adam Parfrey (editor), 1990, p. 287.

118. Lawrence Wright, *Forcing the End, The New Yorker*, July 12, 1998.

119. Matthew through Suzanne Ward, *Revelations for a New era: keys to restoring paradise on earth,* (one of five books of the "Matthew Books" series written and channeled by Matthew's mother, Suzanne Ward), p. 317.

120.Juliano and the Acturians, Sanat Kumara and Archangel Metatron, through David K. Miller, *You are Planetary Healers*, Sedona: Journal of Emergence, July 2010.

121. Martin Grotjahn, M.D., *The Voice of the Symbol*, 1971, p. 94.

121.0. Aubrey Marcus Podcast, *Buddhism, AI, The Future, Deep Fakes & Aliens OH MY! w/ Duncan Trussell*, Aug 17, 2022, Youtube: Aubrey Marcus, time: 43:12-51:00

121.1. Michael Bertiaux, *Ontological Graffiti*, "Seance of May 11, 1969," 2016, p. 228.

122. Aleister Crowley, *Liber Porta Lucis / The Book of the Gate of Light*, (considered a Holy Book of Thelema), 1907.

122.0. Gary Zukav, *Dancing Wu Li Masters: An Overview of the New Physics*, 1979.

122.01. A.K. Wilks, *Pulling the Cosmic Trigger: The Contact Experiences of Philip K Dick & Robert Anton Wilson*, ParanoiaMagazine.com, 2017, ProjectPoseidon.blogspot.com/ 2015/06/pulling-cosmic-trigger-contact.html.

122.02. Erik Davis, *"AI EEEEEEE!!!": Something Weirdo this Way Comes*, April 11, 2023, BurningShore.com/p/ai-eeeeeee

122.03. Rainer Maria Rilke, *Letters to a Young Poet*, 1929.

122.04. Carylon Lovewell, *why it's more important than ever that we magick folk come together NOW*, mass email, Feb. 12, 2024.

122.1. The Collected Writings of Jack Parsons, *The Book of Babalon*, 1946, verse 61-62, sacred-texts.com/ oto/lib49.htm.

123. Archangel Metatron through James Tyberonn, *Universal Beginnings and the Crysto-Electric Cosmos, Sedona: Journal of Emergence*, Jan. 2010, p. 25.

124. John Semley, *We're All Living Under Gravity's Rainbow*, Wired.com, Feb. 16, 2023.

125. Charles Stansfeld Jones, *The Incoming of the Aeon of Maat: Correspondence of 1948 and 1949 Between Charles Stansfeld Jones, Gerald Yorke, & others*, collected, edited, and introduced by Michael Barham, Michael Staley, 2020, p. 195.

Afterword

The Paradigm Puzzle

By Anonymous, Ph.D.

The pieces of the puzzle don't fit together.... If we don't accept that fact, we will always be confused. Maybe that's because we've been handed a puzzle with invisible lines we've been told are "just the way things are." But what if they never fit in the first place?

This book is a bit like being handed a new puzzle. Instead of telling you how to think, it gives you more pieces to work with. Only Matt could've written this book and made more work seem potentially enjoyable. Over my time knowing him, I learned not to question too deeply the things he intuited. Eventually, I figure out they tend to be of the most profound kinds of truth, even if the details are a bit fuzzy.

So, I'm excited about the possibility that much of this might soon feel like common sense to us.

We often talk about paradigms and paradigm shifts. As the reader may already know, it was Thomas Samuel Kuhn who introduced the terms paradigm and paradigm shift to the literature around the philosophy of science. Good concepts make visible what seems invisible and hard to see, similar to how *high strangeness,* will do for many of us now. Kuhn talked about "paradigm" in two senses. The first sense is about the regular way science is done, all the norms and techniques and conventions, etc. The second sense of the term is an overarching set of principles that determines what can be studied as real. The two senses are intricately connected. When the current paradigm proves insufficient to deal with emerging phenomena, the adoption of a new paradigm is needed- a new way of approaching phenomena. New rules and a new way to understand, what is "real" and worthy of studying. What's "real" isn't about unanimous agreement; it's a mishmash of common sense, shaped by our limited experiences, interactions, and snippets of education.

In a similar vein, Matt challenges the ready-to-hand Western worldview, which tends to dismiss phenomena that don't fit within its assumptions. Phenomena that don't fit these preconceptions are often dismissed as errors or figments of a faulty mind. Yet, this misses the point. By separating phenomena from the meanings we ascribe to them, we might see them in a new light, opening up possibilities for understanding the world in more nuanced ways.

In other words, this book is saying, "The world is weirder than you think, and some people have been studying this stuff for ages, despite being called kooks and heretics. Pay close attention to what you consider nonsense. It may be just the key to something crucial..."

I am certain there's a lot of truth in that. Believing that all "anomalous" or "supernatural" experiences can be explained away as illusions or wishful thinking is equivalent to saying fire is just magic from the gods. We're in 2024; we should all be sophisticated enough to know that reality isn't confined to a single worldview.

Do we believe in a world imbued with "intention and meaning," or one made up of "just" atoms and molecules, or is it "a cosmic marionette show orchestrated by a divine puppeteer" or something far more intricate ... ? I found the ponderings of philosophers who see reality as a process, rather than a collection of things, as being helpful here. The current direction of science, including neuroscience, which emphasizes the fluid and interconnected nature of reality, increasingly resonates with this perspective. Many who have pursued this line of thought in the past couple of millennia say what can be seen as a thing or spoken of is already dead, and past in a sense. This is not a mystical statement. Ponder it and see its usefulness for yourself. What's alive is the process of doing, becoming, saying, happening ... What we can speak of and name is usually a frozen piece of something that's perpetually beyond our grasp.

In this view, the world is a tapestry of interactions, not final answers. Questions like "Are humans good or bad?" or "Do angels have wings?" become less important. It's a whole new way of seeing things. In this grasp, the universe can be truly strange, but we can still make planes fly and rockets reach space.

In essence, Matt generously shares his research and synthesis, suggesting that if we loosen our tight grip on our habitual worldviews, we may find a world with infinite possibilities, a sense of humor, and puzzles to be assembled in new, more fascinating ways.

So, here's to Matt, who shares his quest so bold,
In his words, a new universe unfolds.
A world of puzzles, humor, boundless skies,
Inviting us to open our minds, our eyes!!

Index

L

M

N